AF508291

Steven LaChance

BLESSED ARE THE WICKED
Special Edition

The Horrifying Sequel to *The Uninvited*
The True Story of the Union Screaming House

**Blessed Are the Wicked Special Edition:
The Terrifying Sequel to The Uninvited**
© 2024 by Steven A. LaChance.
All rights reserved.
No part of this book may be used or
reproduced in any manner whatsoever,
including Internet usage, without written
permission from Steven LaChance except in
the case of brief quotations embodied in critical
articles and reviews.
First Edition
First Printing, 2024
Cover design by Rick Brandt
Editing by Shannon Lusk, Rick Brandt
ISBN: 9798330212439

Dedication

This book is a testament to those who lost their lives and were forever changed, hurt, or destroyed in the aftermath of the Union Haunting madness. I cannot change the outcome, but I can pray they are watching from above and have found peace. This is dedicated to them and their memory.

Author's Note

April 8, 2023

Looking back at the guy who wrote this book so many years ago I understand just how much I have changed. I also have very different views on who I am as a person and how I differ now from the haunted person who wrote these original words many years ago. I must admit, there is still some fear about going back to revisit those dark years. No doubt I have changed. I have changed a lot. The dreams began coming less and less frequent after I wrote this book. This book was always about healing and healing was exactly what I have done. In way I felt like both Screaming House books were about healing. It was as if I couldn't let my past go until I theoretically burned it in a sort of effigy. A written effigy of sorts or the rhetorical version of setting it on fire and the letting the ashes scatter into the wind. I think the important thing about both books is the demonstrate exactly how a haunting can happen and all of the baggage which not only feeds the evil but also allows it to step in to control a life - in this case lives. One of the very early criticisms of this book, as well as The Uninvited, was the emphasis placed upon the personal aspects of my life. These comments have lessened through the years, and I hope it is because people finally are understanding that a lot of baggage, hurt, bad deeds and despair go into baking the haunting cake. It is a perfect storm of things which takes the haunting into an extreme level. Most of the time someone who is going through a haunting will be at one of the lowest emotional points of their life. To attempt understanding of these events, it is important to look at the full picture. This is why in the Special Edition of this book I am including the analysis and report from the Roman Catholic Church on the Union Screaming House haunting. The Church does a great job of explaining why aspects of the personal life are very important to these types of haunting cases. It is just not as simple as slamming doors and things moving around a room or home. The emotional side usually packs a stronger punch to the gut. It is direct and impactful, as the haunting uses those things which are hurting a person to drag them even further down a dark hole of fear and despair. I had a conversation with an Exorcist for the Vatican who told me the ultimate goal of these events is the complete destruction of the self- both mental and physical. He was right, and the report from the Church is very clear on this point. I hope you take the time to carefully read the Church's analysis. In my opinion, I think it is the most frightening part of this book. I know the report was a very hard read for me the first time I read it. It was not easy to see where I had made mistakes and I how I participated in my own haunting. For that reason, I feel the report is an important learning tool for people going through something and for those out there who are trying to help them.

Life is very different for me now and at times I do not recognize the haunted person I use to be. *Blessed are the Wicked* was a huge step in my healing. This book is about healing and letting go of hurt just as much as it is the haunting. You cannot have one without the recognition of the other. Keeping that in mind, let's travel back to 2012 when I learned how to handle the aftershocks of the haunting and learned in order to heal it all had to be forgiven. Forgiven or forsaken. The choice in the end was no one else's but my own.

I sat down on Good Friday of 2023 to go through the manuscript once again for this book. I had forgotten how many questions this book answers about the haunting. You know when you go public with your haunting you are going to have believers and non-believers alike ask you questions. I have never intentionally not answered someone's questions. However, from now on I think I will also direct them to this book because of the thorough job it does of answering someone's questions about the haunting – it's causes and its history. And now we have added the analysis of the Church at the end of the book as well. I have to admit there are some parts of this book I had pushed far away from my memory and that I think is a good thing - for the most part. One of the dangers has always been focusing too much on it only keeps it alive. I don't want to forget any of those years, but I also do not want to keep them in the present either. My life is in a very good place. I want that devil to stay gone. The vision my sister predicted for my life years ago seems to be exactly how it turned out and I now have a better understanding of my grandmother's words from the grave when she said, "It's in the bloodline, honey." I believe some hereditary plays its part in a haunting as well. It is in our DNA and part of who we are as people. We all carry the burdens of the past in who we are. There is nothing different or special about who I am. Everyone carries a bit of an ancestral burden with them. It is in your bloodline too, honey.

The overall book has not been changed. A few editions have been added, but overall, these are my thoughts and written words from the original manuscript. I hope you learn from my story, and I hope you learn from the report and analysis given by the Church. In the end, this was always the most important reasons for sharing this aspect of my life. I want to educate people about these things and how they work. I also wanted to be a voice for someone out there who may be going through something similar. We all have tragedies in our lives and a haunting is not different than any other type of disaster. I often refer to a haunting a spiritual type of earthquake because the big quake happens and then aftershocks are felt for years afterwards. This is the case for all of the tragedies which can visit a life. So hopefully you can see the healing in this book and apply it to your own life. All of us have our challenges and if it someone tells you they don't they are lying to you. I hope you find something of value for your own life in this book. I believe helping another is the most important thing you can lend your voice toward. My grandfather use to say, "By God you were not put on this earth just for yourself. You were put on this earth to help others." He was right, and I hope this helps someone else.

Today I live a very blessed life, but it was not always an easy road to travel.

Introduction

March 23, 2013, 3:36 a.m.

I see a big orange balloon bouncing in the distance. It is bouncing up and down from the ground to the air. I am running to try and catch it. I hear someone giggling, and I look over and there is my sister running next to me. We are very young. I might be three and my sister six. As I look behind me, my parents are standing next to a blue 1969 Ford. They are watching us run and play. They have this look of accomplishment on their faces, because we are playing for the first time in the back yard of our brand-new house. There is no grass. There is dirt and rocks beneath our feet as we run. Suddenly the orange balloon in front of us comes to its inevitable end, as it hits the sharp corner of a rock. My sister and I immediately come to a halt. The memory is over with the popping of the balloon.

This is one of my first memories. I relive it time and time again in my thoughts and in my dreams. There is some significance to this moment. I find myself searching for the answer. My life, from that moment on, has been a series of metaphorical bouncing, popping balloons. I close my eyes and I can still see the bouncing orange balloon, always just out of my reach, and always ready to pop. I find myself sitting here in the middle of the night, sad, and I wonder how it all could have been different, maybe if this one balloon would have stayed in the air, just for a moment longer? What would life have been like if my sister had not died? What would life have been like if my wife did not go off the proverbial deep end, leaving me with three children to raise? What would life have been like if there would have been no haunted house, or no haunting at all? Events in my life have represented a bouquet of balloons going in different directions, only to pop and shrivel to the ground. Then there is also the thought of the happiness we had felt, running in our own yard for the first time, a yard that we would grow up playing in. Swing sets, holidays, birthdays. Things I had always tried so hard to give my children. Those things we learn from our parents. My childhood was average and untainted by tragedy. There have been so many uninvited moments that have changed my adult life. Why couldn't my life have taken the path I thought it would? Why do these damn roadblocks always seem to get in the way? I find myself now like a child, upset because the balloon has popped and the Uninvited has stepped in. Tonight, I had a dream, and I was able to get a glimpse of how things could have been different. My sister was there, and we were joking and talking the way we always did. My ex-wife was there, and she was healthy, and we were happy with our grandchildren and the lives our adult children were leading. We were happy with each other. There was no haunting. It had never happened. Things were right and in place. The way they should have been. I did not ask for any of this, dammit. I didn't ask for much in this life. All I wanted was a normal life with a normal family. Why did it all have to go away? You sit here and you wonder because you know the life you are living is not the one you were meant to have, and you wonder because you know somewhere along the way something went terribly wrong.

What went wrong? Carl Sagan once

said, "You have to know the past to understand the present." What went wrong? I am sure that is a question many of us find ourselves asking. Are you happy with your life? Did it go completely the way you thought it would? Did the Uninvited come to visit you? Would you even be aware if it had? Are you still afraid of taking that shower because you never know what is lurking behind that curtain? Are the fears you have in this life real, valid, and substantiated? Or are you just bouncing along like a fragile balloon, without seeing that sharp rock ahead? I can't answer any of these questions for you. The answers are within you. The only thing I can do is to share my path with you, in the hope you might find something there that might resonate. Maybe somewhere in my journey you will find something you can relate to. Maybe I can save you before the Uninvited decides to step in - or are they already there? Do you hear them getting closer from behind you, breathing their rancid breath down the back of your neck, just waiting for you to notice them? I found my answers within the past, and just maybe you will find yours, but you are going to have to be brave.

It was May 2001. I needed desperately to find a place for myself and my three children to live. Our lease was up at the apartment where we had lived for two years. I was a single father, and I was about to find myself and my children homeless. Like many, I had answered just about every ad in the newspaper for rentals. One evening, I received a call from a man telling me about a house. He said it was a rather large old house that was in very good shape. He invited me to an open house, which was to be held that coming Sunday. As Sunday rolled around, you couldn't imagine our surprise when my daughter and I pulled up in front of this large, old, white house. It reminded me of my grandmother's house from when I was a child. We walked in. The smell of cookies baking hit us immediately upon entering through the front door. To our surprise, we were standing in a living room with cherubs surrounding the top of the walls, all the way around the room. All the original woodwork was intact, and a large wooden beam separated the living room from the family room. The house had two floors, three bedrooms, and a large family kitchen, with a mud room that lead to the back door. The upstairs bedrooms had a breezeway that could be accessed from either room. The basement had an old butcher's shower and a fruit cellar. It was more house than we ever imagined for the price, and we immediately made up our minds that we had to have it. Anyone who has lived in an apartment for two years with three children would understand our desperation. We had to have this house. We spoke with the landlord, and he gave us an application to fill out. There were many people there looking at the house, so we knew we would have to compete to be tenants. I handed my application to the landlord.

"You understand the responsibility that comes with living in an old house such as this?" he asked.

"Oh yes, I understand. It's beautiful," I quickly replied, not really understanding what I was agreeing to. "Well then, I will get back to you," he quickly responded, and was off to peddle the house to the other visiting house hunters.

He was a strange old man, and the way

he showed the house wasn't professional. He showed the house as if he were showing a museum. We felt like we were on one of those house tours often given to raise funds for charity.

A week went by. The phone rang one evening. It was the strange landlord, overly excited to tell me that he had selected my daughter, two sons, and me to live in the old house. I had to meet him that following day, at a restaurant not far from my work, to settle all of the paperwork and final payment. I thought this was a little strange, and I was a little disappointed because I couldn't wait to see the house that would now become our home. The papers were signed just as we planned on the following day. We were all set to move in at the end of that week. It seemed like years before Friday came that week, but it finally arrived. May 18, 2001, was moving day. The move was normal, and before we knew it all our belongings were stowed safely inside the old white house. I was removing the last few items from the moving truck when a car slowed down, almost stopping in front of our new home. The passenger said from the window of the car, "Hope you get along okay here," and then sped up and drove away.

That is how the nightmare began. Or is that the moment the nightmare finally escalated to a point where I would finally stop and take notice, because it no longer refused to be ignored? Looking back now, I have to wonder when the exact moment was that the Uninvited really stepped into my life. I would like to think I have a handle on that question, but the truth is I really am not sure when the nightmare began. It is all a series of events now, moments frozen in time that seem to have no beginning and no end. It all runs together. The haunting, you could say, was caused by the land the house was built on, not the house itself. The house was built in the same area where the slave quarters of a Civil War captain named Cromwell once stood. The things that happened on this land were about to become legendary, and the town of Union did everything it could to make sure the story would never be told. They did not do enough to keep it hidden. The truth is ready to be unleashed and it is far more disturbing than anyone had ever thought it could be.

Demonic infestation, oppression, and possession are the ugly things that stepped into my life, according to the Roman Catholic Church, in a 156-page report on the haunting. These are the elements that nightmares are made of, and this was my way of life until November 2011. This book is the second part of my story, from damnation to redemption and everything in between. The Uninvited stepping in was only the beginning.

Blessed are you when men hate you,
And when they exclude you, And revile you,
and cast out your name as evil,
For the Son of Man's sake.
—Luke 6:22

Chapter 1

May 2011

I can feel my body as it hits the door, and that door feels as if it is made out of concrete. Over and over, I throw my weight against the door trying to get into that room. I can hear my daughter screaming; the sound of her scream is sending me into a rage, like a wild animal - an animal with the need to protect its young. The house around me is shaking like an earthquake, filled with supernatural screaming, and I can't get to my children. I CAN'T REACH THEM BEHIND THAT DOOR!

There is something coming down the steps from upstairs. I can hear it heading to the other door in the bedroom, at the bottom of the stairs. I can hear the pound of each footstep on each stair, getting closer and closer. And there is a man's screaming voice, which is coming from the basement, filling the house with his agony. Whatever is causing his pain, I don't want it to get to my family. This is a pain I know I NEVER want them to feel. So, I keep throwing myself against the door. The next thing I hear is a low and guttural sound. At first, I am not sure what I am hearing. Then I understand, as my body hits the door with another thud. It is the sound of my own screams. I am screaming. And in that moment, I ask God to help me and the door slams open and I rush into the room. I yell at my boys to run out of the house. That is when I look at my daughter and I see that she is in shock. I grab her and begin to run out of the room. The unopened door behind me slams open. Something is chasing me as I run out of the house. I never turn around. I just run with my child in my arms.

I heard the chime of my grandfather clock and jumped off the couch with a huge gasp of air, ready to fight! It was just a dream. It was just a nightmare. A memory. I sat back down on the couch with my whole body shaking and my heart pounding in my chest. Thoughts were racing in my head. I began to reason with myself. I was not in the Screaming House. I was safe in my apartment. It was just a nightmare. It is 2011. Then I looked at my grandfather clock and noticed it was three in the morning. This was odd. My clock had a switch, which kept it from chiming in the middle of the night. My clock should not have chimed. I began to shake again. I sat awake the rest of the night, waiting for the chime. Four o'clock in the morning rolled around and there was no chime. Five in the morning rolled around and, again, there was no chime. Finally, six in the morning rolled around and the clock began to chime normally, on schedule, like it should have.

Bravery always comes with the rising of the sun. In the morning light, everything always seems manageable and okay. Maybe that is the reason I have never left Union. In Missouri, there is always a morning to follow the night. There is something to be said about where you put down your roots. I fought to make this my home, and I wasn't willing to give up the fight. To run now, it seems to me, would somehow lessen the victory. This is where I made my stand in life and, crazy as it might seem to some, it is very much a part of who I am now. Union is my home - nightmares, craziness, ghosts, and all.

Home Sweet Home

It is not easy to live your life as one of the haunted, you know? You can't exactly go on *Dr. Phil* for help, and at that time, Oprah wasn't calling. Where do you go and how do you begin to pick up the pieces, after the fallout? Everything within my life had been destroyed and I found myself now standing within the wake of my recovery, waiting for the next aftershock to hit. It was becoming very apparent to me this was going to be very different than any other type of recovery a person could go through. The paranormal storm was still looming on the horizon, and I could still feel its darkness pressing on my soul. It could be so easy to be seduced back into that darkness. All it would take was a single thought or the right action on my part, and I would find myself right back where I had fought so hard to battle my way home. It would be so easy to find myself lost once more. Lost is something I never wanted to feel again. Being lost is a situation no one wants to find themselves in. I had been on the edge of demonic possession and now I just wanted to stay stable, together, and calm. As a family, we had already been through enough. I needed to keep myself from slipping back into the grasp of the darkness, the abyss. How do I begin to explain the situation to someone who has never been there? How do I begin to tell you the fear I had of going backwards, and the strength I needed to move ahead?

Then there was Helen, the woman who lived in the house after I did. Helen, whose family I tried to help out of the same hell I was living in. Helen, who had found herself going from the mother of the neighborhood to a possessed monster who wanted to kill anyone and everyone in her wake. Helen was doing her best to put on an I-am-completely-healed face, but the truth is, we all knew she wasn't. They were never able to exorcise the demon completely from her, because her health issues made it impossible. The exorcism would have killed her. Instead, she was drugged to the point of submission. I looked into her eyes, and I knew somewhere, hiding beneath the drug-induced glaze, hid a monster, and it always sent a chill through my body and brought a tear to my eye, because I still felt responsible for not being able to talk her out of the house sooner. Would she ever be the same again? Sure, we put on a public show that everything was all right, but for those of us close to her, during those first years, we knew the truth. We were all living with the monster subdued. I feared at any moment the monster would come out, ready for battle, and try to hurt or even kill one of us once more. The possibility was always there.

It has taken me a long time to come to terms with those months, and even years, that followed the Screaming House haunting. Wouldn't you like to think it all ended once the door closed and we walked out of the house? To think that the nightmare ended as we started to piece our lives back together again. The truth is that sometimes the aftershocks can be more dangerous than the earthquake itself. This haunting has made an irrevocable change in my life. I will never be the same person I was in the beginning. People around me were used like pawns, all in a game of cat and mouse. And in the end, I was oblivious to the lengths to which evil will go to in order to destroy a soul.

Something Happened to Me

I had something happen to me recently, which upset me. I am talking really upsetting me. It brought back those memories from the Screaming House so clearly, I felt like I was back there living it all over again. I thought I was over it. I thought I had put it all behind me, but I was wrong. The voice of Lorraine Warren, the paranormal investigator, kept coming back to me with the warning that she gave Helen right after leaving the house in those early days: "It is far from over." I have to admit, in those early days I did not understand what she meant. None of us did. It was as if we thought we could magically go back to normal lives without a second thought as to what had happened or what we had lived through. I tried to forget it all. I tried to forget the screams, the shadows, Helen standing on my porch with black eyes and a gun behind her back. How do you forget someone trying to kill you? How do you forget all those things, which never made sense, and somehow live your life with people who would never really understand the total impact of what you had been through? I felt like my family and friends were in pieces and I was scrambling around trying to put everyone back together again. Surely this is how those who have lived through a war must feel. I felt like we had been through a war. Damaged goods left behind in piles of rubble with shrapnel in our backs, but our eyes were not blinded. Unfortunately, we could see. We could see clearer than we ever had in our lives. Over and over, with each passing year, Lorraine's words have proven to be true. This was the case recently, when once again I was reminded of Lorraine and her words of wisdom: "It's far from over."

I went to a conference to give a lecture on the Screaming House. It was being held at an old, deserted hospital in the Middle-of-Nowhere, Tennessee. The kind of place that in most cases would have been demolished, had it not been for someone getting the idea to preserve it for paranormal research. Don't get me wrong, there is a lot to be learned from a location like this, which is active beyond anyone's expectations. The deserted hospital is a gold mine of evidence, just waiting to be captured and studied. But there is always a part of me that wonders about the ethical implications of studying these lost souls. Where do you draw the line when dealing with the dead, and how would you feel if one of your loved ones was one of the many on display for research? I find it ironic that we will sign our bodies away to scientific research upon death. Is there any difference between the research and our study of lost souls? This is why I am very careful to try to support only those organizations that accept donations to preserve old buildings, and not those who operate only for profit. At this point, the hospital appeared to be doing everything it could just to keep its doors open. The historical preservation of the building was something I could support, and that is why I was there. Such places provide investigators with a place to go to learn their craft and to experiment with new ideas and research. Better to do it in a facility like this, than on a family that is living an unstoppable nightmare.

This particular building also had the added gem of an old psych ward on its upper level. Anyone doing paranormal research will tell you old psych wards or psychiatric hospitals are always especially interesting because of the types of activity they seem to either draw or maintain within their walls. This psych ward was no different.

Generally, when I go on these speaking engagements, I am the last person you will find participating in the investigation part of the event. It is not that I don't want to participate with the others; it is because I am more comfortable working my private cases with a smaller group. I feel that every time I investigate, I take a chance. Let's face it, the Screaming House marked me for attack at any opportune moment. So, if I am going to take a risk, I would rather it be to help someone than to run around a building simply for the hell of it. What do I need to prove to myself? I already know what is out there. I have lived through enough and have seen my share. Such was the case that weekend at the hospital investigation.

Everyone had separated into groups and they were investigating the building, each group breaking off onto a separate floor. I went inside the building because I needed to find someone. I asked a young guy, who had never been to a haunted location before, to come with me. He was standing outside because he was a little more than spooked by the investigative processes going on inside.

We searched everywhere for the person I was looking for, but we couldn't find him. The only place left was the top floor, where the old psych ward was located. I thought there would be a group up there and gave it no thought as we headed up the stairs. When we got onto the floor, I called out but got no reply in return. We walked around to the hallway and that's when I could feel the energy rushing toward me! I turned to face it just at the moment it hit me in the chest, throwing me against the wall!

My first thought was the novice kid I had

come up to the floor with. I knew if this thing knocked me to my knees it would go after him, too. "Run!" He didn't move. He just stood there looking at me in shock. "I said run!" Puzzled and shocked he yelled, "What?" I was trying to gain my footing. "We are in trouble. Move it! Run!" My words finally registered with him and we were on the move. We hit those stairs and did not stop until we were all the way down.

Thank God the kid was one of my son Matthew's friends, who had been traveling with us. I told him not to tell a soul. When Matthew found us, he took one look at me and knew something was wrong. He thought it was my heart, or that I was overheated. I did not tell him what had happened. I couldn't tell him. I couldn't find the words, and I didn't want to worry him even if I could. So, I kept what had just happened to myself. My chest hurt where it had hit me. It had hit me where it knew it would hurt. You see, I had recently had two stents put into my heart. My chest was hurting like hell, and I felt completely wiped out emotionally and physically. At that moment, all I wanted to do was go home. I wanted the safety of my home. I wanted to hide. When we got home the next day, I called Lydia, my daughter, to tell her we had made it home safely. When she asked me how the trip went, I completely broke down. It all came rushing out in a flood of emotions that shocked me as much as I am sure it shocked Lydia. I told her everything. I was angry I let it do that to me. I was angry I let it catch me with my defenses down. I was angry and the truth of the matter was that I was scared. There it was: I had said it. The words came rushing out before I could stop them. I was scared. After all of this time, and all of these years, it still had the means and the capability to frighten me. It knew where to get me. I was scared because it reminded me of those years during the Screaming House nightmare. I thought those feelings were long gone and buried. They all came rushing right back to the surface. I was scared because I never wanted the nightmare to come back to haunt me. Lorraine was right once again: it would never be over.

I sit here today, writing this in the same apartment where Tommy (one of Helen's misfits) was given a fatal overdose of heroin, just two blocks down the street from the Screaming House. You see, I never could get away, no matter how hard I tried. The closer I stayed to it, the more it would leave me alone. Sometimes I tell myself I am here to keep an eye on it, to make sure everything is okay, but I know I am just fooling myself. I have kept how close I am living to the house a secret from the paranormal investigator John Zaffis, because I know what he would say to me. Is it I who is addicted to this land, or is it this land that is addicted to me? Sounds crazy, doesn't it? I should know - I am a master at crazy. I wrote the book. My close friend, the psychic healer Terri Spiritdancer, put it all in perspective for me, which made sense. She asked, if I were in an accident, would I put up a tent and live where the horrible accident took place? Well, of course, the answer was no. Then she said asked me why I was living here. Even though her analogy made complete and absolute sense to me, here I am writing to you today. I feel as if I am damned no matter which way I go, so I might as well be here so that at least I can see it coming.

But I guess that is the story, isn't it?

Chapter 2

April 1988

My best friend, Zoe, sat across the table from me, shuffling the deck of tarot cards. Zoe was a pretty girl. She had beautiful blond hair and the most unique, sparkling green eyes you have ever seen. She placed the deck in front of me, tapping it three times with her finger. I had to laugh at the almost ritualistic way she was handling the cards in front of her.

"Cut the cards three times," she said with a mysterious tone to her voice. Zoe was notorious for being farcical in every aspect of her life. If you couldn't do something in a dramatic way, then why in the hell bother doing it at all? I cut the deck three times very carefully, as instructed. Zoe pulled one card slowly from the tarot deck.

"Okay, I will do just a simple one-card reading for you," she said, with an all-wise and knowing voice, as she lay the card down on the table in front of me.

It was a horrible-looking card. A lightning bolt was crashing into a tower, causing two people to fall headlong - I had to assume - to their deaths. Fire, rain, and jagged rocks were gruesomely depicted in this morbid scene.

"This is the Tower card," Zoe said, deep in thought.

"Well, it can't be something good," I replied, clearly worried at what I was seeing.

"The tower is a façade, Steven—a lie or a deception. It is you fooling yourself, as well as someone fooling you; there is duplicity involved. You have been telling yourself you have changed, that you have left your old self behind. The truth is that you have not. However, you have built this deception up so high in your mind that when the full realization reaches you, it is all going to come crashing down with a bolt of lightning. When it does, you are going to understand true grief and profound fear like you never have before. But all is not lost. Through this grief and fear, Steven, you are going to gain such clarity of vision that you will no longer be held prisoner to things like desire or ambition, and you will begin the process of rebuilding your soul. Steven, you have to do this to understand your destiny; some might even call it your life mission."

Zoe was really into what she was saying, and when she got rolling like this she could sometimes really creep you the fuck out. At this point, I was thinking she had been reading too much Tolkien, or I was going to hear that Darth Vader was my real father in her next visionary statement. I had to giggle at the thought.

"And I think you have been smoking too much pot again," I said, as I hit her in the arm lovingly.

"Seriously, man, this is what I am seeing here. This is some heavy shit. You got some bad juju coming your way, but it is all for the best," she said, still way too seriously. Now, the last time she used the words "bad" and "juju" in the same sentence was the night she tried to put a curse on her ex-husband and caused every cat in the neighborhood to start screeching simultaneously. Well, you might want to think it was coincidence, but I was there, and I saw what happened when she lit those black and red candles. I was poking fun at her that night, just like I was poking fun at her now. Maybe it would be in my best interest to get her off the subject, especially if bad juju was involved.

"Are you coming to my wedding?" I finally asked. I had to know. The wedding was only a week away, and my fiancée kept asking me why we had not heard back from Zoe yet.

"I really don't think in my right conscious mind I can do that. I mean, after what I have seen here today, you are headed for disaster if you go ahead with this black wedding. I just cannot give my blessing to something like that, man."

She was actually serious. She was going to avoid my wedding because a deck of tarot cards gave her visions of disaster ahead. Well, I had news for her: I was going to avoid the next big event in her life because a visionary game of Yahtzee was going to give me doomsday visions of titanic proportions concerning her life.

"You mean to tell me that after everything you and I have been through, you are not going to come to my wedding because you see bad juju in a freaking tarot card?" I really was astounded. Flabbergasted was more along the lines of what I was feeling at the moment.

"Exactly. I love you, dude, I do, but this is some heavy-duty shit. I'm telling you this is some shit you should not ignore. Let's put it this way, you go ahead with this wedding, and you better hope you get at least one crucifix for every fucking room for damn wedding presents, because it is going to be fucking game on." With that she took another big, long drag off the Kool she was smoking. We sat there for a moment, not saying a word.

"Well, suit yourself. You are going to miss a good time." I finally had to give in. With Zoe, that is what you eventually had to do. Once she had made up her mind, that was it. It was not like she was stubborn, but rather her resolve made it impossible for anyone to convince her otherwise.

"Yeah, well, I'm sure that a good time is what they thought they were gonna have before they went to Carrie's fucking prom, too," she started laughing as she took another drag from her smoke, "but we remember how that shit turned out for her."

"That's not funny. Besides, this is a wedding, not a prom," I said, laughing as well.

"No fucking difference—a dress, flowers, and fucking disaster." She was still laughing. "Except I'm worried you're the one who's going to be covered in blood before all is said and done," she said, getting a serious look in her eyes. "Figuratively speaking, of course. At least, I hope." She had a way of driving a point home, like driving a nail into your coffin while you were still living. This particular point hit me right between the shoulder blades, causing chills to race up and down my spine. Fucking creepy chick, but I loved her like a sister.

We talked for a little while longer that night and had a few more drinks. It was like old times. Even though we never spoke of it, you could feel that there was this tension between us. Something we both knew that was going unsaid. We knew this was the end of an era for both of us. The dynamic duo would live to see another day and many more adventures, but I could tell she could sense there was something coming, and I'm sure in her words she would tell you she could feel a bad energy beginning to form. At this point in my life, I neither believed in or paid attention to things of that nature, but Zoe did.

Finally, I got up to go home. I gave her a hug and was almost out the door when I could have sworn I heard her whisper very quietly, "Don't go." I stuck my head around the corner, "Did you say something?"

"I said I love you," she said, standing up to give me another hug. This time she walked me to the door.

"Tell Christmas I said hi," I heard Zoe giggle as she closed the door. I laughed too, because I knew she didn't like her. The truth is she had liked my former girlfriend, Eve, who'd replaced her, a whole lot more. My choice of Eve, Zoe could live with. My future ex-wife drove Zoe crazy. I started the car and headed down the street. I had to laugh on my way home that night, thinking about Zoe and her cards. What a ridiculous thought. Call off an entire wedding because of a tarot reading? Then I started worrying that Zoe might be making too many of her life's decisions based upon the draw of a deck of cards. I kept driving and thinking, with her voice ringing in my head.

"It is all going to come crashing down with a bolt of lightning. When it does, you are going to understand true grief and profound fear like you never have before."

Let's hope it was all just a game, just a game of cards. That is what I told myself at the time. It was just a game of cards. Funny, the things we will tell ourselves to get us through the night.

It's just a game of cards - the roll of the dice, the spin of the wheel – and, somehow, I think life is a little bit more complicated than that. Yet the draw of one card can mean a whole lot more. It has much more to it than just luck. The meaning of the Tower card in a tarot deck can foreshadow a whole array of things. I would find that the image from the Tower would come to mean many things to me on a

personal, and, in the end, a historical level. But
to tell you now would give away the story and
dilute your understanding.

Chapter 3

May 2011

Do you remember the moment in your life when you were forced to face death for the first time? Do you remember how you felt, and did it frighten you? I do. I remember having to face death at a very early age, and the effect it had on me, as I saw all of the adults, I cared for falling apart around me even though they were trying to hide it. I remember this event very well.

I had an uncle; he was the younger brother of my dad. He looked a whole lot like my dad. I remember that I would look at him and wonder how this person could look so much like my father. My cousin Renee gave me a picture of her father not too long ago. It was of us, my grandfather, and my uncle. We were sitting on a couch. I wanted so much to remember that moment when I looked at that photo. These were two people whom I loved very much, and they were now gone. In years to come, my cousin Renee would follow them in death and leave all of us behind. Her heart would give out, and she would be gone as well. The photo now remains; an otherwise forgotten moment with these two men, who looked like my father, imprinted on my mind. These two men who were now gone. I heard a song. A religious song about seeing the light, and it brought back a memory so clear that it took my breath away. It was of my uncle sitting in a chair in my boyhood home. He was skinny and frail, and, at the time, I did not understand he was dying. The cancer was already eating him away and diminishing the man I once knew. I remember looking at him. I could tell there was something wrong. I could tell he was sick, but I didn't have an understanding how sick a person could get. He was there with his family. Another one of my uncles was playing a guitar and he was singing. He was singing about seeing the light. "I saw the light," I could hear his voice as the song played on.

The moment sticks with me, and even now, as an adult, when I think about it, I have this overwhelming love and admiration for my uncle. He did not falter at this time of trial. He was resolved that he was soon going to see the light. I get it now. I guess it was one of those "aha moments," which Oprah talks about. I understand it completely. He knew he was dying and even though he might have been afraid, he was resolved and he wanted us to know it. "I saw the light."

He died shortly after that. It was a cancer that could not be stopped. I can remember my grandmother falling apart, and it was the first time I can remember my father crying. At that moment, I understood my uncle was gone. I came to the realization that he had passed, and that there would be a time when everyone I love would be leaving. I would be going as well. "I saw the light." I find comfort in those words today because of that moment. It was beautiful. That was how I learned about death, and because of my uncle, I will never be afraid.

"I'm ready to die.

The thought went through my mind as I lay on the hard table. The scalpel cut into my main artery, and I could feel the warmth of my own blood in contrast to the cold temperature of the room. The surgical team flocked around me.

"If this is it, I am ready to go."

The thought continued as the catheter began to make its journey to my heart. I knew I was in trouble. No other time in my life had I been in this type of trouble before, never this type of real physical trouble. My heart was only working at 5 percent capacity. It was amazing that I had made it this far without a heart attack, or without just simply falling over dead. At any moment, I could be put completely under, and my chest could be cracked open. There would be no time for anything if that were to happen. It would just be lights out.

"If it is my time, I am ready to die."

A sense of calm came over me as I let myself feel the resolve to give in to whatever fate lay ahead of me. If that fate was my death, then I was ready to give in to it. That declaration gave me a sense of peace. At that moment, I was not afraid of death. I knew what it meant if they had to do open-heart surgery. It would mean they would stop my heart. It would mean they would kill me. With that thought entered the realization that I was ready to die.

"Wait."

My granddaughter's face flashed in my mind. Her little hand holding my hand, her arms around my neck holding me tight, her little kiss upon my cheek, her big blue eyes looking at me with all the love a child can give. I heard her voice, "Papa? Papa? Papa?"

"Wait. What about her? What about Caroline?"

A single tear began to roll down my cheek. How could I have been such a fool? What would they tell her? What would they tell her happened to her papa? How would she ever understand why I was no longer there to be with her? What nerve I had, to give up so damned easily. What nerve I had, to give up so damned easily on her. I couldn't give up. I refused to give up on her and on that cold table, with tears in my eyes, I came to terms with the true meaning of this life, and to my surprise it had very little to do with me. It had everything to do with her and those who love me.

Bring those moments back—the happy ones, the painful ones, and even those moments of complete despair. I want them all. I want to keep them locked away where I can take them out whenever I choose to remember. I even want to call to mind those memories that involuntarily overwhelm me without my consent. I want to feel it all over again: the bad, the good, and the downright despicable. I want to experience it over again. I want to remember. These are the moments of a lifetime, and those memories left behind have very little to do with me, but they have everything to do with the ones I love.

I can still picture Lydia at 18, walking out the front door of my house, saying, "I'm leaving, Dad, and you can't stop me." God, I wanted to stop her. I wanted to tell her it was a horrible world out there. I wanted to tell her to wait a little while longer before growing up. I wanted to tell her to be Daddy's little girl just a little while longer. I wanted to tell her not to go, but before the words could come out of my mouth, the door slammed, and she was gone. My baby was gone. I remember feeling like I wanted to die that day. I had never felt such pain like that before in my life. It was huge and heavy. It ripped at my insides and tore at my soul. "I love you." It was too late. I was talking to a door already closed. My baby was gone, running down the street with her clothes in her hand, to the boy who was waiting for her in his car, around the corner. In a flash of a moment she was gone, and I would be forever changed. "I'm your princess, Daddy." I could see her standing in front of me dressed in a crown and those plastic shoes with sparkles on top. "You'll always be my princess, Lydia. Daddy's princess."

I remember Michael walking up to the high school the night of his graduation. "Is my costume straight?" I am still not sure why he called his cap and gown a costume. Was it just his way of trying to be antiestablishment? Michael was always a rebel with a big heart, standing up for those who were less fortunate than himself. Whatever the reason for his strange choice of words, it triggered something within me. It triggered a memory, a moment in time so real that for a split second, I was seeing him walking into school when he was in third grade, on Halloween, dressed in his Batman costume. "Is my costume straight, Daddy?" The innocence of it all took my breath away. He was standing there, looking up at me with those big, ice blue eyes peering through his Batman mask, his chubby cheeks making the whole thing look cuter than menacing. He was so proud of that costume. Months after Halloween, I would wake up on Saturday mornings to find him in front of the television watching cartoons with that mask and cape on, with Matthew at his side dressed as Robin. "Dad . . . Dad . . . Dad, what is wrong with you?" he asked, bringing me back to the present. I smiled at him, trying to hide the tear in my eye, not saying anything because of the lump in my throat. I straightened his cap and sent him on his way. The black robe fluttered in the wind as he walked away from me, and I had to laugh. "There goes my caped crusader."

Matthew, at 19, was waving goodbye to me from a car window on his way to live in South Carolina, for his first time without me. The moment playing the same way it played so many years before, when I put him on the school bus for the very first time on the first day of school. My mother standing next to me, ready to pounce, "If you take one step toward that bus, I will break your knees." Matthew waving goodbye to me with tears in his eyes as the bus slowly drove away. God, I wanted to stop that bus, and, for a moment, I did consider giving up my healthy knees to get him off and keep him safe at home. Now here I am, years later, still wanting to stop that car, but you need to let them go. You must give them the space to explore the world. As the car drove off into the distance, the only words that would come out were, "Be safe." Once again, I was left there, standing alone, and all I could do for weeks afterward was cry, because I felt like I had lost something. I felt like I had lost him, just like the others before. No one can prepare you for the day your children leave home.

There are two moments that are the most important of your life. The first is the day your children are born, and the second is the day your grandchildren are born. My granddaughter Caroline came into the world on a New Year's Day. Nothing could have prepared me for the emotional drain of my daughter Lydia going through labor. The thought of her enduring that unbearable pain, without being able to help her, was difficult. There was only a hallway between us, but it might as well have been miles, as far as I was concerned. The moment that I saw her with Caroline for the first time literally took my breath away. I could not speak. I could hardly move. I just stood there, and then I started to tremble. Words cannot describe what I felt at the moment I saw my child holding her child for the first time.

It was one of the most beautiful moments of my life.

Then Chelsea came along when Caroline was two. I held Caroline in my arms as we walked to see her baby sister for the very first time. She held me tight around the neck. "I love you, Papa," she whispered into my ear, and I could tell by the tiny shake in her voice that she was nervous. When we walked into the room, there was a white curtain pulled so we couldn't see anything at first, and then it was drawn back like a theater curtain at showtime. That is the moment when Caroline saw her baby sister for the first time. It took her breath away; an audible gasp left her body, the same way it always did for me at that moment. The same thing that happened to me when her mother was born and when she was born. And now we stood there, sharing that moment together, when Chelsea was born. It took our breath away. There's nothing like it.

These are the kind of moments that define who we are. It has nothing to do with us, in actuality. It has everything to do with those we love. How arrogant of me to think that this life was ever about me. In that moment, when I was ready to give myself over to death, I stopped myself because Caroline reminded me it was not my decision to make. Life is important and we need to fight for every second of it we can get. We need to fight for those who love us and those we love in return.

And when our breath is taken away, it needs to be for birth and not for death.

There was a time when I thought I was ready to give up the fight. When I thought I had no more fight within me, and all that was left was anger. How do you begin to start over when you have absolutely nothing left but anger? The same anger that got me in trouble was the same anger that saved my life. My rebirth was a slow one. My return to the living was often painful, if not misunderstood. I need to talk about those days, months, and years after the haunting. I need to get it out. I need to let it go. In some way, I feel maybe, if I share it with you, I will be able to put it behind me and begin to leave it back in the past, where it belongs.

I was walking in the park today when I heard a woman screaming. Anytime I hear someone screaming my automatic response is to prepare for the worst. Get ready for the demon. The scream felt like it was surrounding me. I realize now it was a trick of acoustics, due to the trees, as I was crossing the creek on the bridge, headed toward the playground. She was screaming, "Oh my God! No!" Four words. "Oh my God! No!" Most of you might have run to the source of the scream, but at first I just stood frozen. "Oh my God! No!" Then I slowly began to walk toward the sound of the commotion as I heard other voices. "Call 911." "Don't move him." "Get the children away." The last phrase was a good indicator I was in for something really ugly. "Get the children away." Away so they could not see the carnage that was about to lay before me. Away before their little minds were completely destroyed by a memory that would never be erased. But it was too late for me, because on the ground before me, in his mother's arms, lay a little boy gushing blood from his head. His mother was screaming as the boy was losing consciousness in her arms. "Oh my God, no. Please, baby, no." And for some reason, at that moment I remembered Rachel and the tragic end to her life. Rachel, who was the young mother on my paranormal team. I am not sure why. It could have been all of the blood and the shock of the scene, but the thoughts came to me just the way they always had in the dream. The shotgun against her forehead and then BOOM! The paramedics moved me out of the way to get to the child. Rachel was gone and still, at that moment, I stood there asking God if it were somehow my fault. I was asking God if all of the death and destruction were because of me and my unwillingness to see the truth. Were other people's lives paying the price for some kind of karmic bill, for a pendulum that had swung one way, which now had to swing the other way, before it could once again settle? Rachel's head exploded in my mind. I found my way to a bench, and I sat down as they put the little boy into an ambulance and drove away. The blood was still fresh on the pavement and glistening in front of me. I never should have taken those vulnerable people with me, and I should have protected those young people from the house during those dark days. In a way, I am the guilty one. I didn't know what I was doing. I didn't know the consequences of my actions. I didn't know it would try to eat us alive. Now I find myself waking up screaming. In some ways, it would have been easier to have been one of those who had died. Living the nightmare over and over is hell. BOOM! Rachel's head exploding in my mind once again. Boom.

Now I have a clear understanding of death. I have seen it over and over.

Chapter 4

November 2005

It was November 2005; we had all been through a lot. I guess that would be an understatement. We had all been through hell and back. Mr. Winters, the landlord of the Screaming House, had just rented the house to another family with small children. He had sent me a final e-mail stating that he could hear the children playing upstairs in the house: "I can hear their little angel screams. I hope their guardian angels are watching over them tonight." The family Mr. Winters was talking about in the e-mail lasted only four months in the house. Their small baby had begun to be terrorized by something within its walls. They would find unexplained scratches and such on the child. When they would try to take a picture of the baby, it would always be blocked by some sort of black shadow. It did not take them long to pack up and go.

I had to walk away from trying to keep people from renting the house. It became clear to me it was a losing battle. No matter how hard I tried, there was always going to be some unsuspecting family that was going to find their way into the grasp of Mr. Winters and into the door of the Screaming House. It was one battle I was going to have to let go. Besides, we all had our own wounds and scars from the haunting, which needed attention. Things were still very ugly and about to get uglier

"Steven, I can't find Kelly. No one will help me find her. Will you please help me find her?" Helen was frantic on the other end of the phone, asking me to help her find her daughter. She had just been out of the hospital for a few days, after her last episode, and was living with her older daughter, Patty. Her husband, Charlie, was living with some friends; at this point it appeared Helen and Charlie might be headed for a divorce.

"Charlie put Kelly up in some fleabag motel and now she isn't there, and no one knows where she is," stated Helen, out of her mind with worry. I was shocked at the thought a father would actually put his 16-year-old daughter in a low-class motel and then desert her without even checking on her, but then again, we were talking about Charlie.

"Steven, Juvenile Detention is looking for her and they want me to bring her to them." The situation was getting worse the more Helen talked. "Steven, can you please help me find her?" What else could I say but yes? It was a kid we were talking about. She did not ask for the hand she had been dealt. Things were not going well for anyone at this point, and I could not help thinking this girl was at the center of the fallout. Besides, the last thing Helen told me before hanging up the phone was that it was Kelly's birthday—one hell of a way to spend your sixteenth birthday.

Helen picked me up about a half hour later and the search began. We started at all of Kelly's friends' houses; each friend had a different story about when they had seen her last, and each friend sent us on a different path of dead ends until we reached the last house. Kelly's friend Markie was a young mother of 16, one of those girls you just knew would have at least two kids by the age of 18. She was a beautiful girl, with a striking appearance and a bad upbringing. She was living life the way her mother had before her, and most likely her mother's mother before her. It was hard not to feel sorry for Markie. "Kelly was here not too long ago, Mrs. March," she said to Helen with a painted smile on her face and a drug-glazed twinkle in her eye. "Where did she go?" Helen asked her frantically. "She went to town to see if she could find Scottie," Markie said, holding on to the door frame.

I looked at her, hoping she wasn't doing anything more than just pot. There was way too much meth going on in these parts, and Markie didn't look like she was doing too well today. Helen was cussing under her breath as we headed back to the car, because Scottie was the last boy Helen wanted Kelly to be hanging around with. Kelly's first love, Scottie was a good-looking boy with a bright smile and a bad side; he was the kind of bad boy that every mother feared her daughter would get mixed up with—good looks with bad habits.

Helen drove way too fast back into town. We drove up and down streets, looking into gas stations and stores. That is when we saw her. She was walking down the street with a group of kids. Helen practically ran over a couple of them as she swerved the car over to the curb and jumped out. I stayed in the car. This was between mother and daughter.

I am not sure what Helen said, but a few moments later Kelly was getting into the car with us, and we were headed to the Juvenile Office. There was a small waiting room in the front. I sat in an uncomfortable plastic chair in the waiting room as they immediately took Helen and Kelly into the back. It seemed I read every magazine in the place as I waited. As I waited, the receptionist occasionally looked up at me and smiled. It seemed like I waited for two hours or more without anyone coming in or out. I was hoping I would be home before my kids got home from school and, at this point, I began to wonder. The glass front door opened as three police officers entered. They immediately went into the back and a moment later they came out with Kelly in handcuffs and Helen following.

"What's going on?' I whispered to Helen. "She tested positive for pot, and they are going to lock her up in detention." I could not believe what I was hearing. Can you imagine if we locked up every 16-year-old who tested positive for pot? "You have to be kidding me!" I was completely shocked. We were allowed to walk with her to detention, which was just down the street. It must have appeared to be some strange sort of procession as we walked down the street— three cops, Kelly in cuffs, with us following close behind.

When we got to the detention center, we walked behind the building for intake, and two more police officers came out of the building. At this moment, Kelly decided to start fighting. Then Kelly decided to start screaming. "I want my mom! Don't take me away from my mom!" She was desperately trying to get to Helen. She was fighting five grown men. She was fighting, biting, hitting and scratching as they were trying to drag her physically into the building. Helen was screaming at them not to hurt her, as I was trying to hold her up. At the last moment, as they dragged her away, screaming, I saw Kelly's eyes had turned completely black, and I knew exactly what we were dealing with. They took Kelly away from us and put her in a cell with nothing in it, and no one but herself. They took her shoes and her belt away from her and immediately put her on suicide watch. I had never seen anything like it in my life. When I sit here thinking about it today, I can't help but relive those moments, as that child fought for the love of her mother to save her. Don't get me wrong - I hold nothing against anyone. Everyone thought they were doing what was best for the girl. I do believe that. But how do you explain this type of spiritual situation to a system that is not built to understand gray areas? Later that night, I got a phone call from Helen. She was sobbing. For some reason, the night watch had left Kelly alone for a short period of time. When they came back, they found Kelly in a critical state. She had ripped the flesh off her own arms with her own fingers.

Kelly was institutionalized for a period of time after that incident. During that time, we found out the reason that Kelly had been hurting herself. The voices, which had started in the house, were telling her to kill her mother and father. Kelly thought if she hurt herself, she could save herself and others from harm. How innocent we were to think that once we walked away from the house, all of a sudden it would all be over. This was its way of telling us that it was far from over. This was its way of letting us know that there was plenty more to come. I could feel my knees weaken as I held the phone to my ear. This was different. This was not one of the adults it had just attacked. This was one of our children.

The downside to putting someone into therapy is that sometimes all kinds of nasty, dirty things come to the surface. That is exactly what happened when Kelly decided she wanted to talk. Whatever was in the house had done its share of damage. Kelly talked about standing in her parents' bedroom with a butcher knife in her hand, trying to make the decision whether she should use it on them or not. Can you imagine? That is when she made the decision to start using knives on herself instead. That is when the cutting started, causing the weird series of scars on her arms, which she would later rip away with her own nails. Her reasoning for this was to try and subdue the voices by sacrificing her own flesh.

Then the sexual attacks began to happen. Kelly would wake up to find her bra had been removed from beneath her shirt. The first time she was confused; she thought she must have removed it in her sleep, but it began to happen over and over again. Then a picture was taken in her room, which showed what appeared to be a penis coming out of her wall. Everyone laughed and made jokes about the ghost penis and ghost porn. This just caused Kelly to become more anxious and extremely confused. What would you expect from a young, teenage girl? Then the rape happened. One boy, three girls. No one screamed, no one moved, no one could do anything as he raped all three girls in Kelly's bedroom. Not the type of boy you would have expected to do such a thing either. Not one of the three girls could fight or call for help, but all three remember the entire rape in detail. If drugs had been used, the girls would not have been able to remember anything at all, but all three remember every moment, but could do nothing to stop it from happening. The boy claims not to remember anything, and he was never convicted.

Yes, strange things come out when you put one of the haunted into therapy, and this was the case with Kelly. It became clear that while we were busy helping Helen, we lost Kelly in the storm. We needed to find a way to bring her back to us. It was obvious the damage was done and could never be fixed, but there had to be a way to make her whole again. We had to try.

Thanksgiving 2005

Thanksgiving came quickly that year and was a blessing. There was a tremendous amount to be thankful for and there was also a feeling we needed to be strong for whatever lay before us. There was a sense of closeness between me and the children, and it felt good. The oppression had been lifted and left me feeling clearer and almost as if I could give myself permission to be happy for a moment or two. We spent the day at my parents' house and there was the usual bantering of politics that went with the day of football and food. My mom and dad struggled getting the turkey in and out of the oven because, as usual, it was the size of an ostrich. Life seemed good and I was content, at least for the moment.

But later that evening, my brother Josh pulled me and our mother to the side with a worried look on his face. "I have some bad news," he said with a sense of seriousness. I could feel my contentment being sucked out of the room as I braced myself for whatever he had to say. I knew it was going to change things forever. I could feel it in my gut. "Your ex-wife is pregnant," he said without pausing. It hit me like a punch in the stomach. This was the woman who had left me years before because, she told me, she didn't want to be a mother. I could feel the room begin to spin. "Are you sure?" I asked, choking back the lump in my throat. "Yes, I am sure," he said, looking me directly in the eye. I didn't know how to feel or even how to react. I looked around the room and that is when I saw Lydia's face, with tears streaming down her cheeks. She had overheard the conversation. Before I could say anything, she raced for the back door, with me after her.

"How could she, Dad?" she said, screaming at me. "How could she? She didn't want us!" She was completely out of control. I tried to hold her, but she pushed me away. "I don't know, Lydia. You are asking me something that I can't answer," I said, trying to get my arms around her, but she wouldn't let me near her. At that moment, I felt my mother's hand on my back, and I heard her say, "Go back inside."

I was at a loss. Never before in my life had I not been able to say the right words to Lydia to make it all right. Never before had I not been able to hold her until the pain, caused by something her mother had done, subsided. At that moment, I went back inside, feeling defeated and kicking myself because I could not make the pain go away. Once again, feeling that anger toward my ex-wife rise in me. Then the thought hit me: We had never been officially divorced. I had been waiting until the children were older, to keep the courts out of it, but at that moment, all I could think was, "Oh my God." This news was going to change everything, and I knew it. I knew she would never want the children. That had always been perfectly clear since the day she left and threw Michael on the ground as he begged her not to leave. Besides, she was afraid of the child abuse charges I could bring down upon her head. But this woman was capable of anything. This is the woman who tried to kill me before she left.

Flashback, May 1996

The last married night of my life. Walking into the house, I noticed something lying on the floor. Looking closely, I saw that it was a snakeskin. I figured that Michael had picked it up from outside and brought it in. He was always bringing in weird things to show me. With everything that was going on, most likely he hadn't had the chance to do so. I went to turn on the TV and there was no power. The electricity had already been shut off. I called my mom and checked on the kids. They were doing fine. Every time I thought of them, I would choke up. It was one thing to do this to me, but to do this to them was beyond anything that I could imagine.

My now ex-wife arrived home shortly after dark. "They already shut the power off?" she asked, seemingly without guilt.

"That is generally what happens when you don't pay the fucking bill," I said, trying not to start a fight. She had not paid our bills for six months, and now she was taking the money from our account to start her new life. She had moved the funds, and I had no way of getting my hands on them.

"True," she said.

"I found a flashlight," I said, sitting down on the couch.

"Good," she said, sitting across from me in a chair. There was a moment of awkward silence; neither one of us knew what to say. "I'm borrowing a truck from a friend to help move," she said. "You can have everything. I have my children. That's all that matters to me," I said.
"Well, I will keep some stuff until you guys are ready for it," she said, and she lit another smoke. It seemed strange to me that the woman sitting in front of me, whom I called my wife, was acting like someone I had never met before. She even smoked differently. This person in front of me seemed like a stranger.

That is when I felt a thump on my back. At first I just ignored it. "I don't know how long it

will be," I said, playing with the flashlight in my hands. I felt the thump on my back again.
"I understand, but you guys will be okay at your parents'," she said smugly.

"Why don't you live with your parents and see how you like it?" I asked, getting pissed off. That is when I felt the thump on my back a third time. This time it was hard enough for me to take notice.

"What the hell is that?" I asked, getting up.

"What is what?" she said, not moving.

I turned the couch over, and, to my shock, I saw a huge snake in the lining of the couch. It uncoiled, the light from the flashlight catching its eye, which was the size of a cat's. "Aw fuck, no! I'm outta here! Forget it! I'm gone before the locusts set in!" I said, heading toward the front door.

"What am I supposed to do with it?" she was pleading at the door.

"You were the one that wanted to be on your own. Well, sweetheart, you are on your own. I am outta here," I said, heading to the car.

I drove away, feeling a sense of relief that it was finally over. I couldn't handle it anymore. Then the questions began to form in my mind. How did a snake that size get up the stairs and into the house? Why didn't it go for the cat? The cat was fi ne; I saw it in the bedroom when I went in to change clothes. I was going to sleep on the couch that night. And that was when a chill went down my spine. That was where I would have been sleeping. It was obviously a python of some sort, to be that large. I mean, not the sort of thing you find in your couch every day. What are the odds of something like that? It could have wrapped itself around my neck while I was sleeping. And there it was. You know that gut feeling you get when you know you are on to something? She was going to leave the kids at the grocery store, and that sinking feeling in my gut told me she had other plans for me . . .

Thanksgiving 2005, Continued

After a while, my mother came back inside with Lydia, who seemed quite a bit calmer. I immediately went over to her and put my arms around her. "I love you, and we will get through this like we have gotten through everything else she has ever thrown at us. Okay?" Lydia looked up at me, nodding her head, and then hugged me even tighter. I never knew what my mother said to her that night. That was and is between them, and it should stay that way. Sometimes it takes a grandmother's love when there is no mother.

A few days later, I heard Lydia yelling into the phone from the other room. When I went into the room, I saw her slamming the phone down. "What was that all about?" I asked. "I got it off of my chest, Dad," she said as she marched defiantly back into her room. Later I would find out she had called her mother. Again, I never knew what she had said, but I know my daughter, and from the look on her face, I would not have wanted to have been on the other end of that phone line. Sometimes it is better to let a child have their say. Let them get it off their chest. They need to be able to say what they need to say, and that is what Lydia did on that day. She got it off her chest.

Chapter 5

December 2005

I am standing at the end of a long, dark hall. I don't want to move because I know whatever is on the other side is something I should fear. I can feel my heart beating faster and faster within my chest. A voice rings down the hall, wanting me to come closer. "Come here and see what gift I bring." I take the first step slowly, almost involuntarily, but I know even if I wanted to stop, my legs have already betrayed me. With each step closer I can feel my pulse race faster. I know the voice waiting for me is not a friend. "Come here and see what gift I bring." I feel like a caged animal with nowhere to run and nowhere to hide, like cattle being led to the slaughter. I reach the end of the hall.

Sitting in a chair is someone all too familiar to me. I have seen this face before. This face, as it climbed through my bedroom window. This face, as it held me down. I know this face, the sharp white teeth and the white of those eyes. He sits in a high, winged-back chair. He sits there, holding a huge snake in his hands as it hisses, its eyes glowing with fire, entwining itself down his body, wrapping itself around his leg. I want to run, but instead of running, my body once more betrays me, and I sit in a chair directly across from him.

He pets the snake as he begins to speak to me. "And the serpent said unto the woman, 'Ye shall not surely die: For God doth know that in the day ye eat thereof, then your eyes shall be opened, and ye shall be as gods, knowing good and evil.'" He continues petting the snake, as his white eyes stare directly into

mine. "And the great dragon was cast out, that old serpent, called the Devil, and Satan, which deceiveth the whole world." He stopped for a moment and then he leaned forward for effect. "Do you understand what I am saying to you?"
"I am not sure," I replied.

"Women will always follow the bigger serpent, and in this case mine is bigger than yours." Then he started to laugh uncontrollably. The room begins to spin with the sound of his laughter.

The next thing I know I am falling and falling . . .

My body hit hard as it fell on the floor from the bed. I lay there for a moment, not sure where I was or what I was doing. It took a good full moment to realize that I was looking under my bed. Lydia came walking into the room. "What are you doing on the floor, Dad?" I grumbled a few words and then got up to get the boys ready for school.

December used to be my favorite month of the year. How did I go from being a Clark W. Griswold prototype from the Christmas Vacation movie to what my children affectionately called "The Grinch"? It's not like I didn't try to get into that kind of mood everyone was talking about. I did try. I tried, with every ounce of my heart. I tried for my kids, but everywhere I turned there was something to remind me of loss, something that was gone, that I longed for, and someone that I missed.

I could relate to Scrooge every year when I would watch A Christmas Carol, wishing I could be visited by the Ghost of Christmas Past just once. Just one visit, so I could once more see loved ones who had passed, but of course my ghosts were demons and that would never happen for me. I would not be like Jimmy Stewart's character in It's a Wonderful Life, and there would be no visits from angels, whom I could help get their wings. The idea of Christmas had been depleted from my spirit at this time in my life. It was a time of sadness and regret. I did what I had to do in the best way I knew how for my children, and that is how I made it through. December was not a happy month for me. December was a dark month—the darkest month.

The first week of the month that year, I heard from Father Paul, who was the priest who had lifted the demonic oppression from me just two months prior and was still in the process of helping Helen through her problems. Father Paul invited us to his church because he wanted us to meet Father Michel, the exorcist from the Vatican, whom Father Paul had turned to for advice on our cases. This is the priest who recommended the blessing that lifted my oppression.

Of course, I was excited to go to see him and hear him speak. It was also good news, because Kelly had been given leave for a long weekend to come home, and she would be able to go with us, as well. The evening came quickly, and we arrived at the church a few minutes before the Mass was to begin. I came with Marie, one of the investigators who worked on the Union case. She was very excited to get to meet an actual exorcist from the Vatican. Marie was still carrying around her many scars from the haunting and could not let them go. I was hoping that Father Michel would say something tonight that might help her, as well. I was not prepared for when Helen and Kelly arrived. Helen was looking fine for the evening, which was a huge relief, because at this time the pendulum could still swing to either side of the fence. One moment she could be right as rain and the next, well, we will save "the next" for a little later. It was Kelly who shocked me that night. She was wearing a black sweatshirt with a hood pulled up around her face as she slid next to me in the pew.

Helen slid in the pew behind her, putting Kelly in the middle between us. I tried saying a few words to Kelly, but I got no response in return.

Shortly after their arrival, Father Paul entered and Mass began. The instant he began Mass, Kelly began to shake next to me in the pew. I mean the girl really began to shake. Her behavior continued as she held on to the pew in front of her. She began digging her nails into it and her breathing became uneven. She began to complain about the rise in temperature. She was shaking, digging, and her breathing started coming out in bursts. I looked at Father Paul, who saw what was going on and had an eye glued on the situation. This continued through the entire Mass, and I was grateful it was a short one.

When Mass was completed, Father Paul stepped out for a moment and then came back and introduced a man whom he called his friend, Father Michel. I was instantly taken with the priest. Once Father Michel began to speak, Father Paul walked back to where we were sitting and took Kelly by the hand. He told us he would bring her back. And with this they were both gone, exiting out of the back of the church.

I began to focus on Father Michel, and he was fascinating. He explained the steps of possession: the invitation, the oppression, and the possession. He explained the goal of the demonic force was pure and utter destruction of the possessed and of those around the afflicted. Then Father Michel said something that struck a chord with Helen, and I saw her start to cry. He said that the goal of the demon was not to possess a soul that was already damned, but a soul that was pure and good—a soul that was, in essence, up for the taking. I knew in that instant what was going through Helen's mind, and why the tears came so readily, because the same thought hit me in the same way. We were not bad people at all. This did not happen to us because we were bad. This happened to us because we were good of heart. Good of heart were the words the priest used, and those words meant more to the two of us, sitting there in that little country church, than anything anyone in this world could have ever said to us. It was the right thing to say to us at that moment. We needed to know this happened to us because we were good of heart.

During Father Michel's sermon, he looked straight at us when he wanted to make a point that he wanted to stick. There might as well have been no one else in the church that night. He was obviously speaking to us, and some of the other people there started to pick up on it. They would occasionally look our way, to see who he could be talking to or looking at. Then it was time for the question-and-answer period to start. Now, there was this one woman there who seemed to make a point to notice Kelly's reaction to the sermon. She also noticed when Father Paul took Kelly away. She also seemed a little shocked to see a black girl in her church when she arrived. You know the type. You can read them like a book. They don't even try to hide their disdain through their righteousness. Well, she had question after question. I could tell Marie was getting a little fed up with her by the fifth question by the way she shifted in the pew. Marie is a kind and gentle soul, but it is sometimes very hard for her to hide her feelings. She can wear them on her sleeve, and in this case, there was a flashing sign on her forehead indicating that she wanted this woman to give it a rest and let someone else ask a question.

Finally, the talk was over, and people got up, ready to leave. We walked to the back of the church where Father Paul was waiting with Kelly. To my surprise, her jacket hood was down, and Kelly stood there, happy and smiling. People were putting money into a collection plate, and there were blessed medals there you could take, if you wanted one. To all of our surprise, Kelly took five dollars out of her pocket and asked Helen if she could give it to the church. I looked at Father Paul with a shocked look on my face, and he just smiled. Kelly walked to the collection plate, dropped her money in, picked up a blessed medal, and put it into her pocket.

The woman who obviously had a problem with a black girl being in her church in the first place saw this, and in a loud voice said, "Did you see what that black girl just did? She took money out of the collection plate. I saw her do it. She took money out of the collection plate and put it into her pocket."

Father Paul saw everything that had happened, because he had been watching proudly with me. He turned to the woman and said, "That is not what happened. She put money into the plate, and you should be ashamed of yourself for standing in false judgment of another." The woman hurried out of the door with a shocked look on her face and was gone.

But the damage had been done. Kelly stood there, shocked and embarrassed, and she put the blessed medal back and told Helen she would wait for her in the car. No words needed to be said, but it was clear to me and to the priest that we had just witnessed the demonic at work one more time. Whatever blessing the priest had done for Kelly was tainted by the demon at work within that disdainful woman.

We stopped, and we talked with Father Michel for a few minutes. He asked questions about how we were doing. He told me to keep watch on everyone and to be aware that things were far from over. Again, those words of advice, that the demon was still afoot. Father Paul walked with me out of the church, and he asked me how the investigation team was doing.

"Oh Father, I left that behind me."

"Maybe you should reconsider that. Maybe you have been given this second chance to help others. God doesn't give third chances, Steven!"

That is the night I decided to go back into investigation in order to help others. I called Bill, who had promised to keep Missouri Paranormal Research, the group I started in 2004, safe for me until I was ready, and I told him, "I'm ready to come back right after the New Year."

When you live with three guys and one girl, the job of decorating the Christmas tree usually gets forfeited to the girl. In years later, we would find out this was for a good reason. So, the business of putting up the tree always went to Lydia. This meant we always had to have an artificial tree, because Lydia was deathly allergic to anything resembling a real Christmas tree. A real Christmas tree would cause horrible hives and put her straight into the ER with an asthma attack. So, I always supplied her with an array of artificial

Christmas finery The centerpiece was an eight-foot, artificial pine, which was way too large for any living room we ever had.

The reason the tree was so big was because I picked up the wrong size during the purchase process, and, to our surprise, once it was put together, it would have been fit for the White House lawn. But it was our tree. It fit. It had a story behind it, and no matter how large it was and how hard it was to make it fit into the house every year, it fit because it was our story and once you lit it up, it could be seen from space - and you have to love that. Really, I had no clue how Lydia managed to put it together every year, but somehow, she managed, and she would get really mad at us if we got in her way. Some years, it would just miraculously appear. But I would always make a point of telling her how it was the most beautiful tree we ever had, and for some reason every year it seemed that way. Well, it seemed that way to me. You need to take notice, when your child does something like that for you out of love. It was important to her, so it was important to me.

Once the tree was up, the cat wars would start. Now, this could either be your favorite part of Christmas, or your worst nightmare. The point of trying to keep two young cats out of the tree is beyond me, because it is a hopeless cause. That year, though, Lydia got smart and let the cats find a branch for themselves in the tree. And you know, for some reason I would find those cats sleeping in that tree, and there was no war and no one screaming and no one getting sprayed with squirt bottles. Lydia seemed to have this tree harmony thing going on, and for once it looked like the whole tree thing was going to work. To my surprise, it did for the most part.

There were a few deviations from the whole harmony system, mind you, but for the most part, everyone seemed happy with the new Christmas integration thing General Lydia had going on.

Everything seemed to be going fairly well, for a Christmas season. I actually felt like I was making it through without too many incidents, and for once I would find myself listening to the Christmas station on the radio and even having fun going Christmas shopping. Things began to change the night of Lydia's Christmas dance at school.

Around here, the Christmas dance is a big deal. It is something the girls plan for a whole month ahead of time. Of course, there is the question of what to wear to the Christmas dance, which is important when you are a teenage girl. Lydia's grandmother would always step in on those occasions and save the day. On this particular night, Lydia's date had to go to work right after the dance, and she needed me to pick her up, which of course I had no problem doing at all. Actually, I was relieved the young man had to go to work. As a joke, the boys and I had given this young man a questionnaire to fill out on how fast he could run from gunfire. Lydia did not find it amusing, and we all were in trouble for that one for a good week or so afterward. He actually wasn't a bad kid, but it was our place, as the men of the house, to tease her just a little. At least we thought so, until we found out it was not such a good idea, and we never did it again. That is why my son-in-law never had to sign and date the contract the boys had for him. I stopped them before he got it. It was ten times worse than the gunfire questionnaire. His quiz covered all types of bodily harm.

That evening, Matthew was the only one

home with me. Michael was staying all night at some friends. We were playing video games on the PlayStation when Lydia called and told me to come and get her. I looked at the clock, and was pleased at the time, but a little disappointed that she hadn't stayed out a little longer on a night she had planned for so long. I told Matthew to get his coat and come on. We walked outside and got into the van, and as I put the van into reverse Matthew screamed for me to stop. I slammed on the brakes, thinking I had just hit something. I was hoping it wasn't the goofy kid next door.

"I need to get a snack before we go," he said.

"What? You need a snack just to go across town and pick up your sister?"

"I'm hungry," he said.

I am sure Matthew was hungry, because he always was. I had a hard time keeping food in the house because his growth spurts had become enormous and, as a matter of fact, he had become enormous. He wasn't fat; he was already standing at six feet, five inches tall, at 14. I told him to hurry up. While I waited, I listened to a Christmas song playing on the radio. Then I heard him scream and saw him running out of the front door.

"Dad, it's in there!" he said frantically.

"What's in there?" I asked.

"The black shadow thing, it came after me."

"Matthew, that has all been taken care of. It can't be in this house," I said, trying to reassure him.

When I went inside to look around, I got that all-too-familiar feeling, and a shiver went through my body. I walked into the kitchen. There stood open a cabinet door and a Pop-Tart, still in its package, lay on the floor. I bent over to pick it up and the light bulb blew in the fixture above me. I stood up quickly and walked out the front door. Matthew was waiting for me in the van.

"Did you see it?" he asked.

"No. I didn't see anything. By the way, here is your Pop-Tart. Try not to get crumbs all over the freaking place." My thought was to keep things as normal as possible, without overreaction.

I climbed back into the van and put it in gear. As we began driving, Matthew, shoving the Pop-Tart in his mouth, blurted out, "It scared me to death, Dad. It came rushing at me and I just ran outta there!"

"Keep it to yourself for now. We'll talk about it later." I stared forward, trying to concentrate on the road ahead of me. Suddenly, something strange caught my eye. "Hey, do you see that light in the sky?"

There was a strange light in the sky, which I assumed was a helicopter, or something along those lines. I pointed it out to him to get his mind off what had just happened. I knew the more he focused on it and built his fear, the more likelihood of something taking hold, and I could be dealing with a haunting all over again. I would get out the holy water and the blessed candle and bless the house after everyone was in bed. This was not the first time I had done it, and it wasn't going to be the last.

"That is a really strange looking light, Dad."

"Yeah, most likely a helicopter out looking for something," I replied. We were headed down a dark stretch of a two-lane highway at this point.

"Stop the van, Dad! Stop the van now!"

I slammed on my brakes, thinking

someone must have been on the side of the road hurt, or he was hurt, or something horrible was happening.

"What's wrong? Where in the hell are you going?" I asked.

Matthew had climbed out of the van and was standing at the back, looking at the farmer's field across from us, slightly elevated from our view.

"There," he said, pointing his finger toward the field and the sky.

"Wha—" I never got the word fully out of my mouth. There, hovering above the field, were three lights. They were just there, stationary.

Is that the light I told you to watch?" I asked him.

"Yeah," he whispered back quietly. Come to think of it, we were standing on the highway in the middle of the night, so I was not sure what all of the whispering was about in the first place.

Now, this is where your rational mind kicks in. I told the kid to follow this light to get his mind off the fact that we are haunted, and this thing follows us and now we are standing beside the road in the middle of bumfuck nowhere, looking at the sky. This strange light was hovering in what appeared to be a triangular shape, from what I could tell by the placement of its lights. Then, all of a sudden, from the center of this thing, a bright white light shoots straight to the ground. At this point, I was done, over, cooked and baked.

"Okay, back in the van. We are going," I said to Matthew, firmly grabbing his arm to get the motion started to get the hell out of there.

"What do you mean? This is cool," he said, still looking at the sky.

"I said, back into the damn van. This is

someone else's life, not ours. We have just stepped off-track or something here, Matthew. Now back in the damn van, and we are never going to talk about this thing again." By this point, the spotlight went out on this thing. We were back in the van and I was hurrying down the road—speeding down the road was more like it. I found myself looking into the rearview mirror making sure we were not being followed, and, feeling extremely silly for doing so.

"What do you think that was, Dad?"

"That was a helicopter. That was a helicopter, and it was searching for something. That is all it was," I said firmly.

"When did they start making helicopters triangular?" he asked.

I turned up the Christmas music, focused on the road in front of me, and avoided the question. As soon as Lydia got into the van, Matthew told her what we had seen and she quickly told him he was crazy, which brought a smile to my face.

What was it? The truth is I don't know, but when you are out on a dark country road in the middle of the night, things can look pretty damn mysterious. I would like to think it was a helicopter, and they were looking for something in the fi eld that night. I would like to think that. A few days later, Matthew came home from Grandma's house with an article from the newspaper. Looks like we were not the only ones who saw strange lights in the sky that night; they had reports from three separate towns reporting the same type of thing. But hey, I am the ghost and demon guy. I am going to leave the lights in the sky to the Travis Walton types. At least for now.

I think there should be some rule that you can have only one type of paranormal experience. At least, that is the way I viewed the world at that time. The bummer of it was that this was something Michael would have really gotten into, and he wasn't even with us. Michael got into things like that. Then, on second thought, Michael would have been running into the fi eld to get a closer look, and I would end up doing a whole different type of book and show. I guess I could call the book *Christmas Lights in the Sky: The True Story Of* … You can fill in the blank.

For me, Christmas begins with a tree and it ends with a tree. The one thing I do every year, without fail, is take a small Christmas tree to my sister's grave. I don't make a big production out of it. It is done very quietly and there are only a few people who know I do it. I have never missed a Christmas, and as long as I am living, there will always be a tree on her grave for Christmas. This is the only time of the year you will find me visiting her grave. It is very hard on me. There are some years that are easier than others. Then, for some reason, there are those years that knock me to my knees, and I find myself not being able to breathe. I can't talk to her there. "There" is not for conversation. "There" is a painful place. "There" is a cold and lonely place, and believe me when I tell you, she is long gone from "there." I think maybe she knows I will be there every year. Maybe she knows it is a place where she can come and get a glimpse of me, if she can't do it in any other way. But deep in my heart, I know that place is only a memorial. The real conversation happens in my dreams and in my heart. Damn, I miss her, and I don't know why, still to this day, she is gone. I understand the acceptance part of things now, and I am no longer mad or angry at God for taking her. I know there is free will and that things happen for a reason, but I really cannot find a reason for this. I search so hard in my heart for it, but I keep coming up with nothing. When I needed her the most is when she left. I still find myself sometimes forgetting that she is gone, even after all this time.

How do you forget something like that? How do you forget, after all these years, that someone is gone? Then there are times I catch myself sitting here and wondering if I can even remember what she sounds like anymore. You may think you have that sound burned into your memory, but it begins to fade as you age. I want to hold on to it. I am having trouble remembering it now. What did she look like? The vision of her in my mind's eye is starting to blur. Please don't let me lose that memory. It is all I have left of her and once it is gone, it's gone. These feelings come out in a rush, when I least expect them. The anger is gone. Now all I am left with is the loss and the sadness that comes with that loss. I don't blame you for it anymore, God. I am so sorry that I did. I just couldn't accept the idea of "it is" back then. Back then, it had to be someone's fault. Please forgive me.

Christmas begins with a tree and ends with a tree, and this year was no different.

That night, I sat with Lydia after the boys went to bed, and we drank hot chocolate from Christmas mugs, and we laughed and talked. We liked to turn off the room lights and turn on the tree lights on Christmas Eve. I would sit on the couch with my quilt, and Lydia would sit in the chair with hers. We would talk for hours about this and that. During a quiet moment, I noticed the shadows from the tree lights on the walls. Then my eyes carefully scanned all of the holes in the walls that surrounded us.

Why would they put holes in the walls?

"You know, I still don't understand why the boys punched all of these holes in the walls the way they did. Were they fighting or were they just goofing around?" I asked Lydia, quietly.

"They didn't," she replied.

"Then who did?" I asked, hoping she was not going to say it was her.

"It was you. It was you before you saw the priest."

I didn't know what to say. I had no words because I did not remember doing any of it. All that time, I thought the boys had done it. I couldn't understand why, and I had been furious with them over it, but it was me? How do I handle that?

"I don't remember . . ."

"It was Bad Dad," Lydia said, cutting me off. Then the full impact of what she was telling me hit me. It wasn't me. It was Bad Dad. I wasn't just fully oppressed. I was borderline possessed. I had been going through phases of blackouts. I had been Bad Dad, and I started to cry.

The lights from the concert illuminated the August night sky with blues, greens, and reds. I knew exactly where I was. This was the yearly ritual that called an end to summer. The yearly summer fair. In a few short weeks, kids would be going back to school, and those old enough would be off to college or out into the real world for the very fi rst time. This was the end of my eighteenth summer, the summer of 1983.

The crowd around me surged forward. I was standing front row–center. I was standing at the feet of the one and only Charlie Daniels, who was now looking down at me from his hat pulled down way too low, fiddle in his hand, singing a song about a boy who had sold his soul to the devil. The crowd went crazy as the lights changed from blue to red and the band turned into demons that backed up Charlie's devil fiddle.

That's when I saw her. I had not seen her since we had graduated just a few months back, but even within those few short months something seemed to have changed in her. The red light played upon her long flowing red hair as she danced almost in a trance, her own little tribal moves, not seeming to notice or care that there was anyone else around her. Her eyes were closed. She was moving to the music as if possessed, without a care in the world. She was a free spirit. Why had I never noticed that about her before? Why couldn't I be free like that?

The crowd went wild as the band came to a screeching halt, bringing me back from my daze. To my surprise, she was staring back at me. For a moment, we caught each other's eyes, and the sound from the world around us seemed to silence, just for a moment. She had caught me looking at her, and she began to laugh. Obviously caught, I began to laugh as well.

"Good night, Washington, Missouri, and God bless!" Charlie Daniels shouted to the crowd, bringing the magic of the moment and that night to an end.

I woke up from the dream, stunned. It was more of a memory that had just replayed than anything else. It was something I had forgotten long ago and had not remembered until just now. It was the moment that the woman I would marry had caught my eye. With all of the bad things she had done to us, to me, to the kids, I thought I had buried moments like these so far down they could never come back to haunt me. Sometimes your memories are the worst demons out there. Sometimes your memories can haunt you more than any old house can. The haunting of the mind – now that is the place where the big boys play. Finding reasons for things that have no explanation – that is something that can drive you crazy. Institutions are full of people searching for answers where none exist, at least it would seem to me.

    I wiped the tears from my eyes as I sat on the side of the bed for a moment. With a deep sigh and an "I hate Christmas" grumble, I started this holiday day.

Chapter 6

December 26, 2005

The world went into slow motion. I could feel the cold of the windshield against the side of my face as I looked at the horror in my daughter's eyes as the glass began to spider out from the impact beneath her head. I was reaching and reaching for her, but I couldn't grab her in time. And in a whoosh, we were pulled back with a violent jerk, and I could hear Matthew scream from behind me.

It was the day after Christmas 2005 at 1:36 in the afternoon. We were on our way to my parents' house for dinner. Michael was thankfully not with us. He had spent the night with my younger brother, and we were to meet him at my parents. Matthew was playing around in the back seat and did not have his seat belt on. I was looking in the rearview mirror, yelling at him to get it on, as I came to a stoplight. In front of me was an older pickup truck that was hauling some junk to the dump. The truck had a cement bumper. The driver had his right turn signal on. He went to make a right turn and immediately slammed on his brakes, changing his mind and deciding to make a left. CRASH!

Lydia and I both had our seat belts on, but they did not hold. The airbags did not deploy. Matthew was thrown around the back of the van. Both Lydia and I had busted the windshield with our heads. When the movement stopped, all I could hear was a ringing in my ears, but I knew I had to help my children.

I stumbled out of the van. The driver of the truck came up to me and I pushed him out of my way. The world around me was spinning. I could hear nothing but ringing and everything seemed so damn bright. I made my way to Lydia's door. Matthew was already out of the van, and I grabbed him and asked him if he was all right. He nodded his head yes, and I told him to sit on the curb. I got to Lydia, and she was crying. I grabbed her, and I could make out she was telling me that her head was hurting. I felt the side of her head and there was a huge lump already forming. I sat her down on the edge of the curb as the police arrived.

I looked at the front of my van and saw it was completely totaled. I reached for my cell phone and called my parents. My dad answered. I was trying to gather my words; I kept feeling like at any moment I was going to pass out, but I had to keep going for the kids. I had to keep going. I finally got the words out that we had been in an accident, and he told me he was on his way. I was feeling kind of drugged. I was talking to the officer, trying to explain to him what had happened, and I couldn't believe they were telling me it was my fault. I mean, the guy had slammed on his brakes and changed his freaking mind at the last second. I was in control of my vehicle. No one could have made a stop like that. I looked over at Lydia, and she was doing better. She was playing with Matthew, trying to keep him occupied.

My dad arrived. I walked over to his truck and, about halfway there, I felt my legs give a little. This did not go without my dad noticing; he always seems to be aware of everything dealing with his kids and grandkids.

"Are you okay? Where are the kids? Are they okay? Tell me, are they okay?" he asked, grabbing my arm with a look of concern and fear on his face.

"The kids are fine. I'm fine. I just hit my head. Lydia has a pretty good bump that I am going to have to have checked out. Matthew is fine."

I turned down an ambulance because I did not want to scare Lydia any more than she already was. I took her to the ER myself. They ran a CAT scan on her, and it turned out to be nothing more than a mild concussion. They told me what signs to watch for, so I kept an eye on her, and secretly I kept a watch on myself as well. After a few days, we both seemed to be doing much better. There was no way I could have known that the deterioration process was already taking place, nor about the amount of damage that had been done to me. I had not been checked when I should have been. There is no way for me to know now if they would have been able to stop what was to come. Sometimes, in an attempt to care for our children, we end up causing greater harm to ourselves. If I could have that day back again, there are so many things I would do differently, but you cannot turn back time. The damage was done. Over time, the damage makes itself evident in the part of the brain that controls speech and motor skill function and, in my case, it also caused what they call a post-traumatic narcolepsy. It is not reversible, and it can be a degenerative disorder that I live with on a daily basis. Medication helps to control and mask its effects, but it is getting worse as the years pass. There have been some indications lately that it is starting to affect my short-term memory as well.

Some people in my situation might look at this and say the demon caused it or it was the result of the haunting. I am not going to give any undue power or credit over to it like that. This was my doing. This was what I did to myself. I thought I was doing the right thing. I thought I was keeping it together for my kids, when what I should have done was to step out of that crash and let myself fall to the ground. Sometimes there is more dignity and heroism in letting go, instead of hanging on. Sometimes I have had to learn these lessons the hard way. Now, there are days when I will myself to speak and the words come out wrong, in a stutter, and all I want to do is cry. Or there are times when I have been afraid to hold my grandchild, because on that certain day my arms or hands have been uncontrollable, or, I have been falling down a lot because my legs won't move. I have kept this hidden, and I don't talk about it with anyone. It is my little dark secret that I keep to myself. When I go to a convention, I pray they have me speaking later in the day so my medication has taken hold, so I can speak without a stutter. If I am scheduled for the morning, I get up extra early to take my medication, so I can make sure it is working in time. It is unbelievably frustrating when you can think clearly but the words won't come out when you try to say them. On the one hand, I am whole and on the other hand, I am broken. Sometimes I think I just keep piecing myself back together again, over and over, but in the end, I am still here, and I am writing this to you.

This is not something I should have to hide. It has nothing to do with the person I am or the thinking processes I go through. I have spent years ashamed of it or afraid to share it with someone because I thought they might think less of me. It has become part of who I am, and I am not the kind of person who can hide things just because it might make someone more comfortable with me. I am not looking for pity, either. There are times I wish I could turn back the clock and do things differently than what I did on that day. What would have happened if I had left a few minutes earlier or later? Would I have been able to avoid the outcome? The truth is, you cannot go back and do something over. The truth is, you are given the hand you are dealt and sometimes you just have to play it out. I would rather play my hand and think of my life that way, rather than walking around, thinking of myself as defective. I am who I am, and there is nothing defective about that. We all have our challenges in life. My life is no different than yours in that way. We do the best we can with what we have. My mother always taught me that and still today reminds me of it, when I am feeling down, or a day is particularly bad. I am just simply playing my hand, the same way as you.

Chapter 7

New Year's Eve 2005

I like the idea of new beginnings. I like the idea of a fresh start. I like the idea of New Year's Eve. I like the idea that everything left behind is behind and now you can move onward to something better, with new possibilities. It is the wish for something new, the wish for the removal of darkness, to finally let in the light. How could I have been so fucking naive to think that the possibility existed for me? To think that somehow, with the passing of days, the clock, a number, that instantly all would be well, and we could move on, and "happily ever after" would finally become a reality for us. I am a true romantic at heart. Why did the "happily ever after" always seem to pass us by?

This was the first year we went our separate ways on New Year's Eve. Lydia and Michael both went to friends' houses for the night, leaving Matthew and me at home to fend for ourselves, which turned into a night of movies, pizza, soda, and snacks - all of these being Matthew's favorite things. I can remember feeling a little bit out of place without the other two kids at home with us. We had always been together for every single holiday up to this point. This was the first without them. And I can remember trying, for Matthew's sake, to keep my spirits high.

Midnight rolled around as midnights always do, but as usual, this midnight had that extra special, magical touch of an expectation of something new. I held my breath and waited for the phone to ring … nothing. I waited a moment longer … nothing. Then the room burst with its ringing, to my relief. It was Lydia.

"Happy New Year, Daddy. I love you!" she said, sounding like she was having a very good time.

This made me happy because she really needed it. "Happy New Year to you, too, princess," I said, holding back the lump in my throat.

She got off the phone quickly to go back to her slumber party with her friends. No sooner had I hung up the phone than it rang again.

"Happy New Year, Pops." It was Michael. He was not one to let a moment pass too far away without remembering.

"Happy New Year to you, too, son." I resisted the "be careful" speech because there is the right moment and there is the wrong moment and this was the wrong moment for that kind of thing.

I hung up the phone and I looked over at Matthew, who looked at me and said, "Hey, let's make another pizza. I'm hungry. Aren't you hungry, Dad?"

Now, we had already made three large pizzas and there was no possible way I was hungry, but I looked at him and smiled and said, "Another pizza sounds great, buddy."

Before me was a long dark hallway. I stood for a moment not understanding what I needed to do. I looked behind me - blackness.

Over the loudspeaker a female voice, "Move forward, please."

I needed to move forward. I slowly began to step forward. Slowly I began to move. I could hear sounds. At first, they seemed almost inhuman, but as I began to work my way down this corridor, I understood they were coming from behind doorways, locked, hospital-type doorways. I could see some of their faces. Distorted faces. What I was hearing was the sounds of the insane. I continued moving forward, not understanding where I was headed, the orchestra of the insane moving me onward. I came to an open doorway. I stopped. I knew deep in my soul that I was supposed to walk into that room.Over the loudspeaker the sound of the female voice again, "Please step into the open doorway."

I had a feeling whatever was in that room was something important, and I really had to find out what it was. I took a step toward the open door, my heart pounding. I took another step. Please, Jesus, give me the strength to endure what I need to endure. I took another step and another. I was standing at the doorway. I could see a chair. One of those tall chairs, almost Gothic in style, with a high back, the type of chair where you can't tell if anyone is in it or not. I took a step into the room.

The female voice again. "Please step closer to the chair."

I took another step closer to the chair. I stopped in my tracks when the chair slowly began to turn around on its own. I wanted to scream as it began to reveal itself to me. I wanted to run, but I couldn't move! What I saw was worse than anything imaginable, and it sat before me in that chair!

It was my ex-wife! Bound in a straitjacket! Drool coming out of her mouth! Her eyes as white as snow!

"Evil has many faces," she said with an evil giggle. I looked at her in complete and absolute horror.

"Don't you understand?" she giggled at me again. I ran from the room as she began to

I ran down the hall and just as I reached the blackness, the Man came out of it and grabbed me by the throat!
"Don't you understand?" he said to me as he licked his pointed teeth. Then he began to laugh as I began to scream.

Matthew was shaking me. It was still New Year's Eve. I had fallen asleep watching one of Matthew's crash-'em-up movies. "Dad, Dad, wake up. Listen." I sat up, still trying to clear the nightmare from my mind and trying to focus on what he was trying to tell me. "Dad, you have to listen," he said. By the sound of his voice, I could tell he was frightened.

That is when I heard it: someone running their hand down the outside of the house. Occasionally, there would be a pause and then it would sound like they would take a fist and bang on the side of the house as hard as they could, causing the pictures to rattle on the walls. I looked at Matthew and put my finger to my lips to tell him to be quiet. I was not quite sure who was out there, but I knew I had to be ready for anything. The next thing we heard was someone walking up to the porch steps. I have to tell you, at this point my heart began to pound within my chest and I was ready to go to battle with whoever was messing with my house. The doorknob began to move on the door. Back and forth slowly, but the door was locked. I knew it was time to let them know someone was home.

"I don't know who the fuck you think you are, but I have just called the police and you had better get moving!" I said in the loudest voice possible.

Now, I expected whoever it was to either

head down the porch at this point or come through the door. I was ready for both possibilities. I was not expecting what happened next. In an instant, whoever was on the porch jumped from the porch to the roof of the house. This was a distance of over 14 feet! They ran down the distance of the house one way and back up on the roof and then they were gone. What they did was impossible. Matthew and I sat there with our mouths open. We knew what we had just witnessed was not humanly possible. The other option was one we did not want to consider. Matthew quietly walked over to the blessed candle, which had been given to us by Father Paul, and set it in front of me.

"Light it," he said, handing me a lighter. I lit the candle and we let it burn until morning.

The phone call announcing that my ex-wife had given birth to a baby girl came shortly after the New Year. At first, I wasn't sure what reaction she expected out of me, or what reaction I should have to the whole thing. This was the woman who left us high and dry because she didn't want to have children. This was the woman who had clearly stated she wanted to divorce her children. This was the woman who had nothing to do with her children, and for the past couple of years knew very little about them. What possible reaction could she be looking for from me? Was I simply to forget everything and put it aside? This was one big, huge clusterfuck, and once again I was the one who was going to have to pick up the pieces and put my kids together again from the damage she was about to cause. I knew the cannons were loaded and aimed directly at my daughter this time, because damn, this baby was a girl.

How did I feel about the baby? I was

scared for the child. I knew there were all kinds of possibilities ahead for that baby of hers, and I knew the guy she was living with had no clue as to what she was capable of. He had no idea of the monster who was hiding just beneath the surface of her fake, manipulating facade. Yes, I was frightened for the child. My ex-wife was mentally ill. I had tried to get her help. I had tried to do everything I could to get her counseling, but she only went to four sessions and then she abruptly stopped. The problem is that I should have had her committed when I could have, but I was in denial. How do you do that to the person you love?

Did I love her?

Yes, at one time I did love her. Nothing before or after has ever measured up to the love that I felt for her, but she destroyed it all, leaving me empty and alone. Now, where that love used to be housed, all I could feel was emptiness and the feeling of being betrayed, not only for myself, but for my children as well. There was a time when the doctor told us we could never have children. I thought our children were and are the most wonderful blessings in the world. How could she feel as if they weren't? How could she now claim that she had never wanted them? There was a time when a child was all that we wanted. I guess for you to completely understand that driving desire, you have to be told you can't have any. How can your feelings change on a dime the way hers had? What happened? And the elephant in the room, which was now hovering above all of us, was: why was it okay for her to be a mother to this new child and not the three she already had?

I had no idea about the collision course she was on. I had no idea she would turn to drugs and alcohol the way she did. I had no idea she would turn to prostitution the way she did. I couldn't see into the future. Things went from bad to worse. Where she was concerned, things went from worse to a complete disaster. All I could do was watch from the sidelines and wonder where the woman I had married went, and why she was gone. It was almost like a completely different person had stepped in and she had stepped out. There were no signs of her left. She even acted differently - mannerisms changed and the whole nine yards. Friends of ours talked about how they could not trust her alone in their houses because things would come up missing, and how they didn't even know her anymore. I sat back and watched the complete, total destruction of a person and there was nothing I could do. Of course, I carried guilt. But sometimes, after someone does so much to you, that guilt turns into anger.

I was angry. I was angry for not having her committed. I was angry because I knew I had to keep her away from us because she would try to hurt us if it crossed her mind at any given point. I was angry she was eaten up with a mental illness. I was angry that the person I originally fell in love with no longer existed. But most of all, I was angry because now I had to tell my children that the woman who did not want to be their mother had just had another baby, whom she wanted to be a mother to. You cannot imagine all of the feelings associated with her and all of the things I had to now try to hide from my children. Prostitution, drug addiction, and alcoholism were just some of the things I had to add to the list of things I was now hiding from them. Now there was this baby—a betrayal of massive proportions I could not hide. What reaction did the woman want from me?

"I have some papers here at the hospital you need to sign, stating you are not the baby's father, since we are really still legally married," she said into the phone, with a sickeningly sweet voice I had heard many times before when she wanted to get something out of me. I thought it over for a moment and then I answered.

"Listen, I am not signing anything. You got yourself into this mess because you obviously could not keep your legs together. Now you can damn well figure how to get yourself out of this mess on your own. I am not signing any papers for you without a divorce and an attorney present." And I slammed down the receiver, hanging up on her abruptly. I knew instantly I was forcing her to file for a divorce. It was time. The children were old enough. I also knew I had enough on her to ensure custody would not be a problem. I took a deep breath and got ready for the oncoming battle.

Chapter 8

February 2006

The pounding at the door was so hard, I thought the door would come off its hinges. There was a voice screaming from behind it, "Open this door, you stinking, motherfucking cunt!" I knew this scene. I had lived it before, the pounding on the door and the vileness of the voice from behind it. It seemed as if I was back to that Halloween day when Helen came to kill me.

Slowly standing up from the couch, I moved to the window and carefully pulled back the curtains. There stood Helen, who could sense me watching her from the window, her head snapping to look my way immediately. Her eyes were completely engulfed in blackness, beady as shark eyes. Instead of holding the gun behind her back where I couldn't see it, she now held it in plain view, almost beckoning me with it. "Open the door, you chickenshit, fucking ass bastard!" She placed the barrel of the gun onto the center of her forehead playfully and started to giggle. It was clear to me at this point we were off the real-life script and were now headed into new territory. I quickly closed the curtains and backed away from the window.

"I'll kill you on a Monday. They'll bury you on a Thursday. They will forget you on a Friday." I looked toward the front door and to my horror it began to breathe in and out, in a rhythmic succession of death deep breaths and rattling sounds. "Let me in! One moment and it will all be over. One moment and it will all be done." Helen continued to giggle as she begged for entrance from the other side of the

closed breathing door. My two cats began to hiss at the door. They had their backs arched, adding to the strange sounds filling the room. "One bullet right in the middle of your forehead is all it will fucking take. Open the door!" I tried backing away from the door farther. "Open the door, you fucking pussy!" I put my hand on the couch for leverage because it felt like the room was spinning. "OPEN THE GODDAMN DOOR!" I tried to scream "NO," but the sound wouldn't come from my throat. Then a guttural, evil laugh came from the other side of the door, low at first and then building in momentum. An evil laugh that turned into a throaty whisper, "Have you checked your children lately?"

A scream engulfed the house, and in an instant it dragged me from my nightmare and sent me on a dead run from my bed through the house. It was Lydia! She was not in her room! I fell to my knees, trying to get down the hall as I heard her scream again! I heard something running across the roof above me and I knew I had to get to her! I made it into the living room, and I saw her sitting up on the couch, screaming! "What's wrong? I'm here. I'm here," I said, trying to calm her down.

"I was sleeping, and I woke up. There was this black shadow of a man standing over top of me, looking at me," she said, shaking, with tears in her eyes. I immediately went on a rampage, checking all of the doors and windows. Everything was still locked down and nothing had been disturbed. The logical part of me would say that we both had a nightmare at the same moment, but logical explanations with my family went out the door a long time ago. We did not have the luxury of logical. The last time I questioned the logistics of a situation, I got bitch-slapped in the face for it.

A parent knows when there is something wrong with their child. I don't care how old that child might be. A parent knows when something is wrong. I could sense, when Lydia began to evolve, that things were not kosher. We had already been through the adolescent rebellion stage. This was different. She was behaving differently. She was showing all of the signs of depression. She wasn't sleeping. She wasn't eating. It was a literal emotional roller coaster around our house. There were times I could just simply look at her, and she would start crying. I would ask her, and sometimes beg her, to tell me what was wrong and she wouldn't. I was standing on the sidelines, watching the life being sucked out of my child, and I had no idea why. Her brothers had no idea what was going on either. It seemed with each passing day, things were getting worse and worse. I thought at one point it might be a boy problem, which got a laugh and a door shut in my face when I tried to talk to her about it.

Then one evening, we were sitting at the dinner table with my parents. My mother was sitting next to Lydia. I had not noticed that Lydia had been wearing these green, cherry-patterned sweat bands on her wrists. Nothing ever passed my mother's watchful eyes. My mother asked Lydia why she was wearing them. Lydia wouldn't answer her. My mother asked her again and again Lydia wouldn't reply. So my mother simply reached over and removed one, and to my shock there were cuts all over Lydia's wrists. She had been cutting herself. My heart broke instantly, because I knew right away what it was all about. I think instinctively I knew where this was headed. I had fooled myself for a long time that I had been able to piece this girl back together after her mother had deserted us, and now it was coming back to haunt us. I had only been able to prolong the damage, and now it was time to face the music.

The next morning, I was sitting on the couch, looking through the yellow pages to try and find a counselor, when Lydia came out of her bedroom. "You are not going to school today," I said to her, not really knowing what else to say.

"Oh, yes, I am," she snapped back at me immediately.

"We are going to find you someone to talk to about everything," I said calmly. At this point Lydia went off the deep end, screaming and yelling that she was going to school, and I couldn't stop her. She went for the door, but I made it there before she could, and I literally blocked the door with my body. She was fighting me and hitting me. Crying and screaming, she was completely out of control. I took the hits and then I just held on to her. I felt as if I was completely losing her. I held on to her as long as I could, and then she got away and went back into her room. I then called the emergency room to ask them if they knew where I could get help for her. They told me to bring her in there for evaluation, and they would help me. Well, Lydia was listening to this conversation and started screaming she wasn't going. The nurse asked me to give her the phone. The nurse told her to either come with me, or they were going to send someone to get her. At this point, Lydia got her purse and we were on our way.

They tested her for everything. Finally, a counselor came in to speak to her, and I was asked to step out of the room for what seemed like an eternity. When I was asked back into the room, Lydia looked a whole lot better. That is when the counselor began to explain to me what was going on.

Lydia had been having flashbacks from her childhood of the physical abuse her mother had put her and her brothers through. That is when Lydia started telling me what my ex-wife did to my children. Lydia remembers being hit in the face so hard that her mother's hand had blood on it when it came away from her face. She remembers her mother lifting Matthew above her head and throwing him down a flight of stairs, of her locking Michael and Matthew in the basement all day and not letting them upstairs to use the bathroom, so they would have to use the drain in the floor. Lydia remembers sitting in school, terrified about what was happening to her brothers at home at the hands of their abusive mother. The stories went on and on, each one more horrible than the last. I sat there and listened as my world came crashing down around me once again. The shock was almost unbearable, as was the helplessness of not being able to fix this for my child and the guilt that I did not know it had been going on. Why did I not see this was happening? How did I overlook the abusive behavior the mother of my children was exhibiting?

I knew my ex-wife did not bond with our children like a mother should. Lydia told me, after her mother left, that there were two versions of my ex-wife. She had two types of personalities, a Jekyll and a Hyde, so to speak. Lydia described her mother as "restrained and patient" around family and completely and utterly macabre and spiteful when she was alone with the children. She was "Little Suzy Homemaker" when I was home and "Mommie Dearest" when I was at work. When we asked Lydia why she did not tell us, she said it was because she did not know it was supposed to be any other way. That knocked me right between the eyes. They lived with it because they did not know anything else. They thought her behavior was that of a true mother. Thank God she did not severely hurt or kill one of them.

The worst of the abuse seemed to be focused on Matthew. I just thought he was a clumsy kid. He had two concussions in the last two years their mother was living with us. She would always give me some story about how he must have fallen, and I had no reason not to believe her. Boys can be daredevils, rough and tumble, right? I now know where he got them. How could I have been so damn blind and stupid? I did everything in my power to keep them safe, but the monster was living with us all along. How do you even begin to deal with that? How will I ever begin to forgive myself for not acknowledging the obvious?

Because Lydia kept all of this bottled up inside her for so long, she finally had to let loose in some way and when she did, it came rushing out. You can't run away from your past. Sooner or later, it will catch up with you.

My ex-wife has admitted to the abuse. There are no secrets and no guessing games needed to be played anymore. Because of the nature of this section, I have to admit it was one of the most difficult chapters I have ever written. If I write my exact feelings about the emotions inside my heart, I just might frighten you. I just have to hope in my heart that what goes around, does come around in many folds. My ex-wife needs to pay for what she did to my children. That is what I feel inside, and I can't make that go away. I understand that there is mental illness, and she is a sick individual. I have been absolutely sympathetic to her condition. I was compassionate when she told me she was an abused child, even though it may have been a manipulation, because that is also a characteristic of her disorder. But above all, I cannot and will not forgive what she did to my babies. I just can't let that go. I was there and I saw Lydia fall apart. But Lydia is strong; she put herself back together and as a family we went on with our lives and we dealt with the difficult things. But after hearing the truth, any love or sympathy I had felt for my former wife was completely gone. It had been obliterated.

Chapter 9

March 2006

We were contacted by New Dominion for the show, *A Haunting*, at first by e-mail to see if we were interested. It seemed so strange to the kids and me that someone wanted to tell our story, since it was so fresh and raw. It had only been a matter of months and we were already being contacted to do a show about it. The series was going to be filming for its third season, and from what we could tell, it seemed that they were doing a great job with the stories. Helen sat down with her family to discuss it, and I sat down with mine to do the same.

How do you make the decision to come forward with an experience you know a certain part of society is not going to believe, on one hand, and is still so fresh on the other? There were so many factors to consider, and one of those big things to consider was the fact that the kids were still in school, and this was a national television show that many of their peers would see. How would employers react to the show? Was there the possibility of being labeled as that *crazy* family? Although, there was the advantage of being able to tell our story to help those who were afflicted with a haunting or were experiencing paranormal activity. The idea of helping others scored big points for me, and I am proud to say for my children as well. In the end, we decided to do the show for that reason alone. Hopefully, others who were experiencing the same affliction would understand that they were not alone. And for those who were considering renting the goddamned Screaming House, they would realize it would be a good idea to look someplace else. That is why we agreed to do *A Haunting*. There would be no money involved. We did it for principle. We did it for free.

We gave the producer the names of a lot of people to talk to for the show, including Lorraine Warren, John Zaffis, Father Paul, and many more, but in the end, they decided to use just the families, the original psychic, and Dr. Cheste, the psychiatrist from St. John's Mercy. I always wondered why they chose to overlook John Zaffis for the show, and I never really quite understood it. John had helped me so much through those darker days and had been of great guidance. It seemed to me he was a missing piece of the story. I know it also puzzled John why he had never even been contacted to participate in the episode, and when we talked about it later, I had no answer for him, other than I was just has confused as he was. I think he would have added a valuable perspective to the episode. I think they missed the boat by not including John.

Less than one week before filming was to take place, I stepped out onto my front porch to leave my house after a little snow had just fallen and fell down the stairs, cracking my tailbone. Now, I don't know if any of you have ever cracked your tailbone before, but it is one of the most painful things you can do. My feet hit a patch of ice at the top of the stairs and the next thing I knew I was airborne, landing directly on my tailbone. I passed out upon impact. When I finally came around, I thought I had broken my back. I couldn't stand. Hell, for a moment or two, I couldn't move at all. I finally began to crawl back into the house and was able to grab the phone, to call my parents for help. They took me to the doctor.

"Cracked tailbone," the doctor said with

a wince and a smile. "Can't put a cast on that," he said, laughing. My doctor, Dr. Baker, is one of those good, happy-go-lucky types of guys. He's the type of fellow you normally want to have as your doctor, with just the right type of bedside manner, but on this day all I wanted him to do was to stop the pain. "Stay as comfortable as you can. A heating pad might help. Take these for pain," he said, as he handed me a prescription for Vicodin. I lay on the couch for the remainder of the week in my drug-induced, heating-padded stupor, praying I would feel better by the time filming day came around. Guess what? I didn't. Come to find out, it takes a long time for you to recover from a cracked tailbone. As a matter of fact, the damn thing still, on occasion, causes me distress, even to this day.

Filming day had arrived. We were going to be filming at a bed and breakfast, a rustic cabin-type place, in Marthasville, Missouri. It was obviously chosen for the atmosphere. They wanted us to dress casually and comfortably. I imagined they wanted us to match the relaxed atmosphere of the location. So, after numerous clothing changes, we all finally decided on the right look for the right effect and headed out the door. I was in pain. I mean, I was really in pain. When we got to the location, we met the director and the crew and talked about how the day was going to go. My interview was going to be first. I popped three Vicodin and some Advil and got ready for the long haul. The set decorations took a good hour. Then the interview started. The questions were asked, and I answered. This went on for eight hours. If you watch the episode, by the end of the interview, there is a part where it looks like I have tears in my eyes. They are real. They were caused by the pain in my ass.

It took about 16 hours to interview us that day. That was just for my family alone. Helen's family was filmed on a different day. Can you imagine, all of that interviewing done for a one-hour show?

Although it was an interesting experience for us all, we had to put it out of our minds for a while, because the show would not premiere until October. We would have to wait eight long months, and the wait is always the hardest part. Eventually, you forget you did it and you move on with everyday life.

The phone rang. Bill was talking excitedly on the other end. He had been excited when I told him I was ready to start investigating with the team again. Of course, Bill wasted no time going out to find locations so that we could start flexing our research muscles. Missouri Paranormal Research had been gaining a certain amount of renown when I had stepped away from it that past autumn, and it seemed a shame to shut it down when things were going so well. As I look back on the situation, I should have let the team go and worked on private cases. I should have given myself more time to heal. The truth of the matter is I did not realize how vulnerable I was at the time, and I didn't take into consideration that maybe haunted survivors had no business dealing with other haunted locations. Despite my afterthoughts, I still agreed to help, and Bill was excited.

"I just did a preliminary investigation on a location for us, Steven," Bill said. He could hardly catch his breath. "You would not believe the evidence we caught at this place." The location was a secret house, which had been deserted for years. Its whereabouts were not too far from the infamous Zombie Road. "We caught a full-bodied apparition on film," Bill exclaimed. He was so excited that he choked on the word apparition. The hook had been baited and I was quickly being pulled in. Bill had already been hooked himself, and if you ever saw this photo, you would say the same thing. The photo was unbelievable. It was an image of what appeared to be a man walking out of a fog, rounding the corner of some steps. This photo would be considered the beginning of unbelievable evidence. Oh, I was hooked. I couldn't wait to get to this location to see what all of the fuss was about. Bill and I couldn't wait to get the entire team there so that we could get to the bottom of what was going on at this old, deserted farmhouse. Never once did either of us ever consider there might be something else at play there. Why would there be?

We picked a night. We gathered a team. We met at the undisclosed location. I remember walking into this house for the first time. It was old, something out of an old horror movie. The house was reminiscent of something from the movie Salem's Lot, or at one time may have housed Norman Bates's mother. I remember the old staircase had that ominous feeling to it. As I approached it, I could feel chills running up and down my spine. I began to wonder what the hell I was doing there. Once I was on the upper level, something happened that took me by complete surprise. I felt a rush pass by me and heard the sound of a child's laughter. As I looked into the room where I heard the laughter, I saw a young girl, frightened and shivering in a corner. I glanced at her again, but she disappeared quickly. She was there and then she was gone. Shocked by what I had just seen, I stormed down the stairs and ran out of the house.

"Dammit, Bill, you didn't tell me there was a little girl in there!" I screamed, obviously angry, pointing at the house.
"Wait a second, what are you talking about?" Bill asked, seeming very surprised.

I stepped back from him, surprised at my own reaction and looking at the shock on his face. I couldn't believe he had no idea. "There is a ghost of a little girl in there, Bill," I whispered. I was starting to understand that he had no idea what I was talking about, and in my emotional upheaval, I stood there not quite knowing what to do. "I believe you. This is just the first time I've heard about her, is all," Bill said reassuringly. There are usually two options presented when dealing with a child spirit. Option one is the sad truth: a child has not moved on for one reason or another. Some believe, after studying near-death experiences (NDEs), that there is a period of darkness before the light, and children, being children, are afraid of the dark and sometimes they will not move on because of this fear. Others believe it is the sudden loss of the connection to the parent, and they become lost looking for Mommy or Daddy. In my opinion, both of these scenarios are very sad, and if you were to dwell on them for too long, they not only appear sad but become heartbreaking. At least it seems that way to me.

There is a second option, which is one you pray you are not dealing with. That option is the spirit is not a child at all, but something sinister or negative in nature, masquerading as a child. Once the sinister being that presents itself as a child has gained your trust and grasped on to your emotions, it can attach to you and cause living hell within your life. Who actually knows which option is correct? All I know is, when you are alone in the dark and you hear a baby crying, but you can't see it, your intellect is willing to grasp on to anything so that it will make sense. The theories become a way for you to cope, rather than an actual understanding of the supernatural event at hand.

We went back into the house, where I found Carol setting up a video camera in the same room where I saw the young girl. Carol, who had lived through the Screaming House investigation with us, immediately sensed something out of place, and could tell by my face something was going on. "Okay, Steven, tell me what is happening," she said, with a look of concern over the top of her tripod and camera. Marie, who was not far behind, heard Carol and immediately piped in, "What is going on?" Both of them knew me too well and both of them knew the ins and outs of the game. I did not want to cause them great anxiety by telling them I had come across a child's spirit. This is because of their past experiences with the Screaming House and its deceptive nature. To reflect, for the sake of understanding, Marie, Carol, and I had dealt with a similar experience in Union. The apparition of a little boy in the Screaming House turned out to be an option three—a "hook" to take us deeper into the evil lurking within. I knew as soon as I told them that I had seen a child, the horrible memories were going to come rushing back, and their guards were going to go up - way up.

"I saw a child spirit. She ran into this room and then vanished." I tried to give a sense of calm as I said it, so that no one would overreact to the situation, but both of them instantly reacted in the way I knew they would.

"Aw, hell no," Carol instantly responded, and for a moment I thought she was going to pack up her camera and go home. There was

never a question about the validity of what I
had seen. The three of us were way past the
point of questioning each other. We just
instinctively knew and trusted each other.
Together, we had been through a lot. We had
been in the foxhole together too many times.

"Well, what are we going to do about it?"
Marie asked, with her hands on her hips and a
heavy exhale. We considered Marie the eternal
mother. Tears began to trickle down her face
as Carol and I made eye contact. She
immediately asked what all of us were thinking,
"Could this be something other than a child?"
Sometimes I think Marie took it to heart
because she was the mother of six children,
and she felt so deeply about the well-being of
any child. It is not that she didn't have her
guard up. Her guard went up immediately. It
was the fact that she knew in her heart we had
to do something to cross over that little girl.

At that exact moment, from somewhere
in the room came a child's giggle and the
sound of running feet across the floor, which
stopped right in front of us. The three of us
stood there with shocked looks on our faces,
without saying a word. It was almost as if we
couldn't breathe. Then I felt cold little arms
wrap around my leg, as if to hold on just like
the way my children used to do when they
were little. Tears began to roll down my face, to
the shock of the other two. "She is holding on
to my leg," I whispered to them softly. "She is a
child." Tears began flowing down the cheeks of
the other two, and there was an exchange of
whispers.

"Oh, my God," Marie whispered.

"What do we do?" Carol asked, looking
me sternly in the eye.

I felt the arms release my leg and we
heard the patter of feet once again run across

the floor, and then she was gone. "We are going to try to send her on," I said, with much resolve. "Let me go get Lady Light."

Lady Light has very powerful gifts when it comes to dealing with issues from the other side of the veil. I remember the first time I met her, I was immediately taken with her. She has an aura about her that cannot be denied or ignored. Some people say she is a natural witch who is able to walk comfortably in the dark and in the light. When I first met Lady Light, I could tell that she was a troubled soul. I have chosen not to discuss it here because it is only her story to tell. However, I saw great gifts and beauty within her, so I introduced her to Madame Star, my closest friend and Wiccan sister, who set her on the right path of healing, inner growth, and learning. To look into Lady Light's eyes is to look into what seems to be lifetimes of struggle and knowledge. It is very hard to explain how a person can have such a powerful, natural vibe about them. Lady Light is a gifted witch. I am not referring to the green hag witches on Halloween, with the big noses and warts. Witches live among us in everyday life, and they are the most gentle of all humanity. A true witch understands the connectivity of everything in life, from nature to people. So, before you turn up your nose at witches or Wiccans, I would suggest you take the time to get to know a few. Chances are you have a few living in your neighborhood, or even next door. In the case of Lady Light, she is a powerful witch for both the living and the dead. That is why I turned to her for help.

I found Lady Light standing outside the house and I quietly walked up to her, not wanting to cause a scene or draw too much attention to the situation. "I need you to come inside with me," I whispered into her ear. She looked up at me with those eyes, and I knew she was surveying me for any signs of what was happening. Whatever she saw in me, she immediately responded, "Okay, let's go." On the way into the house, I brought her up to date on what had been happening and what I felt needed to be done.

"Steven, moving a child on is very tricky work. It doesn't always work," she said, stopping me on the first landing of the steps. She was looking me in the eyes, and she was serious. "There are so many things that can go wrong, and there are so many things about the child we simply do not know, and if anyone tries to tell you they do, they are lying. You know this." She knew I knew she was right. The truth of the matter is, you never really have the full story on anything or anyone.

"The best I can do is try. I hope you brought a candle with you." I knew she would be asking me for one. I had pulled out a candle from my bag before I grabbed her.

"Wouldn't come to this party without one," I said, pulling the candle out of my jacket pocket to show her. She looked up at me, smiling with approval. "Well, then let's go see what we can get done," she said with a sense of resolve, almost like a surgeon getting ready to go into a difficult procedure— except in this case our patient was already dead.

Carol and Marie were waiting for us when we entered the room. Lady Light gathered us into a circle; we sat on the floor and she lit the candle. Bill stuck his head into the doorway to say something, and immediately took in the scene and was gone. This was something Bill just could not handle. The Screaming House had been enough for him. His beliefs were shaken to the core when he was thrown across his bedroom by a black mass one night after a Screaming House investigation. His beliefs had already taken a huge blow from that case, but for an agnostic to take part in a cross over was asking way too much. I laughed at his reaction. I couldn't help it and it helped to relieve some of the tension, but soon we returned to the task at hand.

The room seemed to spin as Lady Light had us hold hands and concentrate on the candle flame in the center of the circle. The flame itself seemed to grow as the outside world seemed to close in around us. In a very short time, we found ourselves in existence with nothing but our circle, the flame of the candle, and the sound of Lady Light's voice. No particular words. Nothing I could write would let you know exactly what was said. The one thing I can tell you is, I know the child was with us because she was standing right outside our circle. I could see her. She was wearing a simple white dress, but what struck me about her more than anything, and what I will carry with me for the rest of my life, is that she had the most beautiful blond hair I have ever seen on a child. It seemed to be a gentle and beautiful moment, but, all of a sudden, something went wrong.

Lady Light began to become agitated. Outside the circle, it started to grow dark. You could feel fear enter the room. Something had changed and we all knew it. Lady Light clutched my hand tighter and tighter. And then she spoke quietly; the only word I remember her speaking during the whole experience was "Run." She wasn't screaming or yelling. It was whispered and stern. "Run." She was looking straight ahead and she was speaking to where I had seen the image of the child, and I knew she must be communicating with the child now. "Run." Then the candle in front of us went out.

Marie immediately turned on a flashlight, which she had sitting in her lap. We all sat there looking at each other for a moment. Not really saying anything. Not really knowing what to say. Finally, Carol spoke, "Did it work?" Lady Light raised her head and looked at Carol, "I really don't know. There is a male presence here that I think is keeping her captive. I know that sounds crazy, but I think it could be something to do with her life on this side. Like maybe he is still trying to hide a secret, maybe sexual abuse? I really don't know."

When you think about the situations and the things that can hold us in place in the afterlife, it is really disturbing. I know I have written about this before, but it always seems to come back to haunt me, time and time again. The evil of humanity is a constant theme that is found in the evidence of most of these situations. Sometimes I feel like standing on the rooftops and shouting this lesson I have learned. You need to be careful what you do to others in this lifetime, because it can and will affect you in the afterlife, and not only will it affect you, but the people you damage as well. It really is that simple. Again, a lesson on the connectivity of everything and everyone involved, and how it all works in unison in the grand design. We have a world where you can see hate, violence, and degradation consuming every moment and around every turn. Why do you suppose that is? Why is the innocence of a child always the first thing to be damaged in the wake of almost everything? This was another damaged soul, trapped within a labyrinth of horror because of the evil of someone who could not control their inhumane urges. This was an attempt to hide their sin against this innocent child, and to try to keep her under their influence for eternity. I could only pray we were able to set this innocent child free. Sadly, later that night our question was answered. One thing we always did as a team was set up our equipment and then leave the location, locking the doors for a period of time. This way, there was nothing but the equipment inside to record any activity, without any human interaction. Shortly after the attempted cross-over, we did one of these lockdowns. I am now going to share something with you that has never been shared with anyone, including the team, until now. There was certain evidence Carol never shared with the team because she felt it should not be shared publicly. (There are also pieces of Screaming House evidence that are still under lock and key that have never been shown because we agreed not to share it, for personal reasons.) Part of this secured evidence is a video clip that Carol had caught during the lockdown of the little girl laughing and playing through newspapers on the floor in the upstairs level of the house. We were unsuccessful crossing her over.

Part of me feels like I failed this child much in the same way I failed a baby's spirit, hanging in the tree at the Screaming House. How could I not feel this way? Even though I try to tell myself I did everything in my power, I still feel like I failed. She is still there. Whatever evil specter is keeping her there still has its hold on her. I don't want to imagine what that hell is like for her. She will be there long after I am gone. I failed a child, and it is a burden I carry with me. This is one memory I can't bury, and sometimes I wish I had never stepped foot into that house. I can't erase the past. It happened. I did my part to try to change things, and I continue to do my part today. It doesn't change the fact that a little girl ghost roams the halls of a house in an undisclosed location somewhere in Missouri. I can still feel her cold little arms as they wrapped around my legs to hold on to me like she would her daddy.

I know I took this so hard because of the baby hanging in the tree at the Screaming House, who I never was able to help. That is true and is true every time I feel like I fail a child. It just seemed to me that every time I turned around, I was faced with another ghost of a child, and all I seemed to be able to do was fail where they were concerned. This was way before I shot the film, Children of the Grave, and it is still a fear of mine today.

Chapter 10

Flashback, 1988

I stood before the mirror, looking at myself. I didn't look half bad, dressed head to toe in the latest Christian Dior. I should have been nervous. My older brother was pacing back and forth. "You know you don't have to do this," he whispered to me, right before it was time to go out.

"I know," I replied, with a smile on my face.

"A plane ticket and spending cash anywhere you want to go. Let's go right now. Just tell me where you want to go."

Unfortunately, he was serious. He was actually making me an offer, just like in the show, *Let's Make a Deal*. Actually, I should have waited around to see if I was going to be offered Door Number 3. But I took Door Number 1. "I am right here where I want to be and this is the person that I am going to marry." I was serious, and he knew I was no longer joking around.

"Okay, then let's get this done," he said, and we headed into the chapel.

The church was full, with nearly 400 people. This was no small affair. The aisles were lined with candles, and everywhere you looked there were white roses and lilies. The soloist was singing a song from *Ice Castles* as we entered. Could you get more eighties than that? The soloist was a former Miss Missouri, whom I had dated years before. As a matter of fact, there were more than just a few ex-girlfriends in the church that evening. I often wonder if they had showed up just to see if I would actually go through with it. They had to be surprised at the fact that someone had actually gotten me this far, and even more surprised in the simplicity of my selection of a mate; they obviously lacked the insight to see the elegance and the wisdom of my choice. They didn't understand that my bride was the complete opposite of them and represented something "real" to me, something pure and untouched in its beauty—something they would never be able to understand.

The organ pounded out the processional as the crowd stood. The doors at the back of the church opened, and for the first time in my life, the sight of someone took my breath away. I felt my knees buckle. My brother steadied me by grabbing my arm. She was a vision. The light hit the crystals on her gown, sending shards of light throughout the chapel, which seemed to make her glow as she made her way down the aisle toward me. The train of her gown was following her halfway up the aisle. Her choice was beyond words or description. The gown was old-fashioned and simple but fit her completely. The crowd let out an audible gasp at first glance. She was magnificent. This was her moment, and she took full advantage of it. Those in the church that night, who might have been there to criticize, were silenced. The beauty queens never could have pulled off such natural beauty. She reached me at the altar, and I took her hand. She looked at me with those beautiful blue eyes that seemed to sparkle in the moment, and whispered to me, "I love you." I could not reply. I was breathless. I was speechless. I was head over heels, completely and absolutely in love.

March 2006

The damn divorce papers came. I knew

at some point I would have to deal with them, but nothing prepares you for the coldness of it all. I was expecting a simple divorce, but what I got when I opened the papers was the shock of my life. The woman who wanted to divorce her children was asking for joint custody. It seemed to me this was an obvious financial ploy. She had no genuine interest in the children, but she must have convinced herself that by gaining joint custody the child support would be reduced or even eliminated.

This meant the kids were now dragged into the middle of this mess. My ex-wife couldn't be civil enough to leave the divorce between us. I needed to hire a good attorney. I needed an awesome attorney. No, I needed a barracuda of an attorney, who would not let go until we got what we needed to make everyone (me, the kids, my mom and dad, aunts and uncles, and anyone else involved with the kids) happy with the end result. And since no one knows who the anti-Christ is, or if they are practicing family law, I had to settle for the next best thing, Cheryl Mark Roberts. She was the champion of family law and family rights, and a straight barracuda when it came to deadbeat parents of either sex. Finally, after I had the attorney problem solved and an appointment was made, I decided it was time to speak with the children.

I have never been the type of parent who tells my children which parent to choose. I have never really had to ask the children which parent they would want to choose, either. My ex-wife always made those choices for us. But I was pretty sure with her "Mommie Dearest" track record, this was not going to go well for her, and the score card was going to go heavily in my favor against joint custody. Sure enough, I spoke to each child individually and proposed the idea of joint custody. Their mother was quickly voted down. As a matter of fact, Lydia wanted to come with me to see my attorney to voice her opinion and concerns in person, which I agreed she should be able to. Also, I had a signed separation agreement that stated that my ex-wife sign her parental rights away to me when she left. Come to find out, her attorney had no clue it existed. Well, when Lydia arrived at my attorney's office, she let loose and gave numerous reasons why her mother was not a fit mother. She also informed us there was no way on God's green earth her mother was ever coming near her or her brothers anytime soon.

Now here is where it gets interesting. My attorney sent my ex-wife's attorney a counteroffer stating the children's disapproval and reminding them of the separation agreement. She also stated that it was highly unlikely joint custody would be granted. Eventually, I discovered that the reasoning behind the motion for joint custody was, in fact, my ex-wife's scheme to get out of paying child support. At this point, my attorney called "bullshit" and stated that my ex-wife was going to pay child support, as well as provide the children's health care. It turns out that my ex-wife made a huge mistake early on when filing the disclosure papers. She listed that she had smoked pot within the last six months when she completed the forms. Can you imagine? And how her attorney did not catch that mistake, we will never know. Because of this blunder, my attorney suggested I request that my ex-wife be drug tested. Guess what? Within 48 hours, my ex-wife was no longer asking for custody and she agreed to be responsible for all of the financial stipulations of the divorce. You've got to love Cheryl Mark Johnson.

Flashback, October 1988

There were nights that I would find my wife up, sitting in the dark. Alone. Quiet."

"What are you doing?" I would ask.

"Couldn't sleep," she would say.

"Are you okay?"

"Fine. Just sitting here," she would answer.

There were nights when I would catch her in a restless sleep. Murmuring. Mumbling. Nightmares, I would suppose, but she would never mention them. I wonder now if she ever remembered them. I would always calm her and she would go deeper into sleep.

"Steven, it is just not right." It was Zoe, on the phone with me. "She is not acting like a mother should. Listen to me, dear heart. This is her first baby. She should be all over it, but instead she is acting like Lydia hardly even exists. Come on, isn't there something wrong with this picture? Did you talk to the doctor about postpartum depression?"

"Yes, and he said that he thought she was just fine," I said.

"Well, I think I would be finding another fucking doctor, if I were you. Look, she is not doing anything for this baby that she should be. A mother does not act like that. I am telling you, there is something wrong here. You don't think she is suicidal or anything like that, do you?"

"Oh come on, Zoe, of course I don't." Was I reassuring her or was I reassuring myself? At the moment, thinking about it gave me a chill because I was not sure what I was doing.

"You hear about this kind of thing all of the time. I just do not want to see you on the ten o'clock news, crying your guts out because the bitch decided to flip her 'Sybil' switch."

"Oh come on, Zoe!" I said, sounding aggravated.

"Well, if I were you, I would keep one eye on Miss Christmas and one very close eye on your daughter, 'cause something is not fucking right." She always had this way of driving a point home with a big old mallet and a spike.

Even though I hated to admit it, this time Zoe was right. Something was not right. How should a new mother behave? Hell, I had no clue. I had never been through this before. Granted, we were not under the best of circumstances. Maybe it would just take some time? Maybe once things got a little better, so would she? Just maybe? Shortly after that is when the crying spells started. It seemed that for the slightest reason, she would begin to cry. She would not tell me why. There would be no reason for it. She would just start crying.

One night I found her sitting in the dark, crying.

"What is wrong with you?" I demanded.

"Nothing. Just leave me alone," she replied through her tears.

"No, I am not going to leave you alone. You are going to tell me what the hell is going on!" I was clearly pushing now.

"I said NOTHING!" she screamed in return.

"You need to tell me what is happening with you."

"I'm just sad, okay? I am sad with everything. I am defective. I am not a good mother. I can't do anything right. Everything I try to do I mess up. Everything."

"What are you talking about?" I lowered my voice.

"You are just better at everything than I

am. You are a much better parent than I am. You take much better care of Lydia than I could ever do," she said.

"This is not a competition. This is something that we are supposed to do together," I said, trying to understand where she was coming from.

"Then why do you have to be so damn good at it? I mean, Jesus Christ, can't you fuck up something once in a while?" she asked.

"I am trying to do what is right by both you and Lydia." "I get jealous of the time that you two spend together," she said.

"Jealous?" I was more than a little shocked.

"Yeah, jealous. Everything revolves around her. Everything."

I could not believe what I was hearing. "This is getting fucking weird," I said as I started to head down the hall toward the bedroom, with her on my heels.

"Well, you asked me. You wanted to know what I was feeling. Well, sometimes I am jealous. I'm jealous of the time that you spend with her and not me!"

"Are you listening to yourself? Are you really listening to yourself and what you are saying? You are the one that comes home and I can hardly get two fucking words out of you. Hell, maybe I'm the one who is jealous! Did you ever think of that? Did you ever think that I might need to talk to you every once in a while? Did you ever consider the fact that I might be lonely?" I was getting angrier by the second.

"I can't talk to you!" she said, storming out of the bedroom, with me running after her.

"Don't you turn your back on me! You wanted to talk! Then let's fucking talk, sister!"

"I am not going to talk to you when you

are like this!" she said, throwing herself onto the couch.

"Why are you so self-centered all of the time?! Why does everything have to revolve around you?! Well, you are a mother now and it CAN'T!" The veins were clearly popping out of my neck now.

She let out a scream, "STOP IT! STOP IT! STOP IT!" She was pulling out her own hair and beating herself in the head. I stood there, watching. I stood there watching the scene in horror, not knowing what to do. "STOP IT! Stop it! Stop it … stop it . . ." She broke down crying. I went down the hall into Lydia's room and got her ready to leave. I headed for the door with her in my arms. We were leaving. I did not know what else to do. "Where are you going?

Where are you going?" She came running, screaming and crying.

"I am not sure I can handle this anymore. I love you, but all of this is just too much," I said, fighting back tears.

"What are you doing? What . . . are . . . you . . . doing?" She was sobbing now.

The moment of truth. Do I walk out that door to a life of sanity? Or do I try to pick up the pieces here and make this work? I looked at her. Tears were running down her face. She looked awful. Was she in there somewhere? Was she hiding from me? "Where is the woman I married?" I asked.

"I'm here. I am just a little confused right now, but I am here," she said.

I walked over to her and I put my arm around her. There we stood in the light of the hallway, a family trying to stay together. We were holding on for dear life - me, my wife, and my baby.

I guess that is when I really started to

ignore her mental illness. There were times when she could not handle things, when she would beat herself in the head, and I would see her literally pull out her own hair. Looking back now, I knew she was slipping away, but I had no idea how to handle it. Sometimes I would tell myself it was just her overacting to get a reaction. I do feel guilty for that now, because I do know now, she was not acting. However, she hid this illness from me from the beginning, so the blame does not lie entirely in my corner.

In the years that followed, I would get phone calls at work with her crying and sobbing for me to come home. What do you do with that? I was doing everything I knew how, just to keep our heads above water, trying to keep us all together. There were times when she would turn off the alarm and I would wake up late for work, with her begging me not to go. All of it comes back to me now. And I see it for what it was. I was trying to do my best in the eye of a storm I could not control. I did not know my wife was losing her mind. I did not know she had begun planning to hurt us. I simply did not know.

Chapter 11

April 2006

Tommy lay face down in the grass in the morning dew. His breathing was shallow. He was naked down to the waist, with his shirt tucked into his belt, the way it always was. His left hand was relaxed, as if he was sleeping, but his right hand was clutching the blades of grass, holding on as if he could fall from the side of this planet and go floating off into space.

The morning dew sparkled on his blue-gray skin, almost as if he were covered in glitter - glitter from a rave that would never happen, a party that would pass him by. Tommy was dying. He already was suffering from exposure and hypothermia. The coma had taken him in the early hours of the morning, right about three. Tommy lay face down in the backyard of a stranger's house, dying. He was dying of a heroin overdose, and he was only two yards away from the Screaming House.

Tommy was not a stranger to the Screaming House, and we can only imagine that in his stupor he was headed to the front porch to sleep. The current residents would have been surprised to step out on the front porch to find him, but they were never given the chance. During those dark years, Tommy would always sleep on the porch of the Screaming House when he had nowhere to go. He was one of Helen's misfits, whom she loved and mothered. She was always able to see past the wrong in a kid and see the goodness within them. Tommy was no different, where she was concerned. There were many nights and many mornings when we would step out onto the porch to find him there, curled up on one of the chairs or stretched out upon the swing. He was almost a fixture there, like any other of us. There was Tommy, sleeping on the porch again. None of us thought anything of it. We never judged him or questioned him. I think deep down we all knew this was, for that moment in time, his only place to go. With all of the craziness during the haunting, this scared kid found solace on that porch when he needed it.

You have to wonder just how bad his life really must have been. I always liked him. But I always knew never to feel sorry for him, either. The last thing you want, when you are in a horrible position, is someone to come along and feel sorry for you. I knew that because I had lived it. I understood he was like all of us— just struggling to get through it all. Helen understood this, too. Helen understood Tommy.

Did I know he had once spent time in jail? Yes, of course I did. But I also knew he was an extremely talented artist. We all make mistakes in our lives, and this 21-year-old kid was not any different from any of us. I wasn't going to make judgments on his past. He didn't spend time in jail for murder, if that is what you are thinking. I knew his crime was very minimal. I once knew what it was, but I don't want to say now, because the details have slipped over the passing of time.

However, I do remember it was small in comparison to most crimes.

The point is, the boy paid his price for it. Once you are marked at such a young age, it is very hard to find a way to start over. It is even harder to start over in a small town like Union with a record. Dreams? Sure, the kid had his share of dreams, like anyone else, but he also had a close, watchful eye on him wherever he went. It is hard to see how your dreams are going to come true, when you live in a small town, convicted of a felony, with barely a place to live. I could see the pain in the boy's eyes, because I saw the same pain in my eyes every day when I looked into the mirror. Pain is pain, no matter what causes it or whatever way you want to cut it. We were very different in so many ways, but in some ways, we were very much alike. We both knew the pain life could throw at you. We both understood struggle. Tommy had a record, and I had baggage.

The Screaming House had its influence on Tommy, the same way it affected everyone else who was exposed to it for any length of time. The day Helen was planning on killing Charlie, Tommy helped Helen look for the clip for the rifle. When she could not find it, he was the one who suggested a serrated knife would do more damage on flesh than a regular household butcher knife. What I have always found most disturbing is he asked Helen if he could go with her to watch her kill Charlie. That was very unlike Tommy. Not only was it unlike him, but it was strange because he had always liked Charlie, and Charlie had always liked him. I remember Helen talking about that day, talking about how everyone in the house was so calm, and how no one tried to talk her out of doing it. She would tell me it was like everyone was under some type of spell. No one was acting the way they normally would. Tommy was one of those acting out of character that day. He was the most helpful, even to the point of wanting to go along. He was her right-hand man. He was behaving as her accessory, helping her premeditate how to commit the murder.

Thank God Charlie got away from Helen that day before Helen could cut off his manhood, because that is where she was holding the knife on him. Tommy was the one who helped her plan it. A houseful of teenagers, and no one tried to stop her. Every single one of them was acting out of character. I remember going to get Helen out of the house, and how the kids were acting on that day. They looked at me as if they wanted to kill me. The scariest part was that all of them had black eyes. Black eyes, just like I had seen with Helen. I have no doubt the house had its influence upon Tommy, the way it had on everyone else, and that bothers me even more now. The kids were all acting as if they were under a spell. Not one of them was acting right by that time, during the haunting. Not one of them has lived a good life afterward, either. Very few of them are still living today. Taken out of this world in horrible ways. Their deaths have been tragic, at the very least, and downright horrific at the most. Tommy was no different.

"Steven! Tommy is in the hospital. He's in a coma." Helen was on the other end of the phone line, delivering the news. She was crying as she was telling me what was happening. I couldn't believe what she was telling me, but at the same time there was a part of me that half expected the news to come, and I felt guilty for it. I wanted to see good things happen for Tommy. I wanted to see a happy ending for him, but at the moment he was in ICU, the result of bad heroin, and they were not sure he was going to make it. If he did, he was going to be brain-damaged for the rest of his life.

I hung up the phone, and I had to sit down and take it all in. A life wasted. Then the sheer loneliness of his last lucid moments hit me, and I had to wonder just how aware he was, lying there face down in the grass in the middle of the night, with no one to help him. Was he aware of his circumstance? Was he aware he was in trouble? Did he try to call out? Did he try to scream? The tears began to roll down my face as I considered the possibilities. Tommy was left alone with his final thoughts, found face down in the dirt. We all deserve better than that. He deserved better than that. The questions about the heroin found their way into my thoughts. Don't get me wrong, I can understand the need for escape. Hell, our society is built upon escapism. We spend millions of dollars each year just for the sole purpose for the need of escape. What I don't get is the death dance. What I mean by the death dance is the tempting of that purpose, the self-destructive version of Russian roulette. One bad round into a vein and that's it.

Tommy had every reason, and if you ask me, every right for the need of a little escapism. Let's face it, life up to this point had not exactly been a night at the opera. Hard to keep a positive fucking attitude with the way things had been going for him. I have to wonder if he was feeling more than a little self-destructive. But why would Tommy let someone stick a needle into his arm and fill his veins with an unknown substance, not sure exactly what it was going to do to him? Sure, you might be told it's safe, but the truth of the matter is you really never know, and who can you really trust? Obviously on this night, Tommy trusted the wrong person.

Five days later Tommy died. They pulled the plug and the tubes because there was no brain activity and no hope for him. Whatever talent he had for art went with him, and no one but a few people close to him will ever know how talented this young boy was and what we all have lost. No one will ever know of his sense of humor, his huge heart, and his ability to give to others. The indignation of a young one's death is the way it steals from us all of the untold gifts of a possible future unrealized and untold.

I knew Tommy and I knew of these untold gifts and the person that he was, but you never will. Up to this point, those of you who may have heard of him, know him as the young man found face down on the grass, who died of a bad heroin injection. No one wants to, or needs to be, remembered like that. He was much more than that. We live. We make mistakes. We have our triumphs, sadness, talents, and those we have touched in this life. We teach others about life more than we learn. Tommy, I learned from you. I felt as if I had lost a friend. Helen and Charlie felt as if they had lost a son.

There was an investigation into Tommy's death. At times, it felt as if not enough was being done, because who was concerned with a misfit felon of a young man, who died of a drug overdose? A few years passed, and more young people began ending up in the hospital and the county morgue from a type of bad heroin being passed around. Finally, an arrest was made and justice was served, but not in Tommy's name.

To this day, there are reports of people driving by the Screaming House and seeing Tommy sitting on the front porch, emotionless, staring off into space. I have personally seen him a few times. I have to wonder if he returned there to the porch because that is where he was headed on the night of his death. If that is the case, he finally made it home. My other thoughts are more sinister and disturbing in nature, and I don't like talking about them. In those thoughts, I wonder if the Screaming House captured his soul and now he is caught there, without the ability to move on. I would like to think it is the first case and not the second. But then again, with that fucking place, you can never be sure.

Chapter 12

Early May 2006

"Steven, you have to get over here, now!" It was early in the morning when I got the phone call from Charlie. He was frantic on the other end of the line. The only thing he would tell me was that Helen was not acting like herself and I needed to get over to their apartment now to help him. I had a pretty good idea what I was in for, even before I hung up the phone. I could hear the fear in Charlie's voice. I knew the sound of that fear. I had heard it before. The sound of his voice told me I might not be dealing with Helen at all this morning, it told me the monster might be loose.

I hurried and got dressed. On the way out the door, I grabbed my wallet, making sure I had a few blessed medals from Father Paul placed firmly inside one of the inside pockets. I reached the front door and turned around to go back inside. I reached into one of the kitchen cabinets to pull out a jar of holy water to bless myself. After now convincing myself I was ready, I once again headed for the door and the car. I drove to the apartment carefully, paying very close attention to everything around me. I knew if my fears were correct, It was capable of trying to stop me from reaching Helen and Charlie. I had been down that road before, and today I wasn't going to take any chances.

A chill went through my body as I remembered some of the incidents that tried to stop me before. Just then, a large trash truck seemingly came out of nowhere. I slammed on my brakes and put my fist to my horn. I was right to be very careful. The driver flipped me his middle finger and I was stunned, because he was the one who almost hit me. You have to understand the unreasonableness of it all, and that the actions of all those around you may be influenced at any given time. Was it possible the driver of the truck was being overtaken by some mysterious evil force, controlling his actions and his mood? Was I put on the road to potential disaster without me knowing it, even before I stepped from my house or into my car? Then, of course, there is always the everyday possibility that the guy was just an asshole, and there was nothing more to it than that. Even in my post-haunting world, I still had the ability to see an asshole as just being an asshole.

I pulled into the parking lot, ran up the steps to Helen's apartment, and knocked on the door. Charlie answered it with a frightened look on his face. At that moment, I knew Helen had tried to kill him again. I was not even through the front door, and I could see Helen sitting on the couch with her head down where I couldn't see her face. The first thing I heard was her voice. The voice I knew all too well. A voice that wasn't Helen's at all. The monster was out, and it was ready to play.

"What the fuck is he doing here?" she asked as she lifted her head. I got a clear look at her black eyes. The shark eyes I was all too familiar with. I started to back out of the door again without even thinking. It was complete reflex, and I had to stop myself from running.

"Charlie called me. He called me to help," I said, not really knowing what else to say at the moment. I knew I was stalling for time, trying to figure out my next move, knowing she was already three steps ahead of me.

"The bastard took her medicine away

from her," she grinned, with that low, smoke-filled laugh. I knew Charlie, and I had no doubt what It was telling me was true. The one thing I couldn't understand – why didn't Charlie get that the only thing keeping him alive was Helen's medication? As long as It could be subdued with medication, there would be no problems. However, once the medication was taken away, the monster would become unleashed and allowed to roam. It was easy to understand. But Charlie resented the money it took for the medicine. He hated it. He would rather spend his money on booze and women than on keeping his wife healthy and this thing under control enough for it to be safely and properly handled.

"Charlie, get the doctor on the phone," I said to him. He jumped to it, ready to do anything at this point because he knew he had fucked with the system. I turned my attention once again toward Helen, and I could see a moment of clarity coming over her. Whatever this was had always been transient with her. The longer it went untreated, the longer it would stay around. However, she had been under treatment for quite a few months at this point, so it was having trouble staying with her consistently.

"Steven, I thought I was dreaming. I woke up, standing over Charlie with scissors in my hand. They were telling me to kill him, and I was going to do it just so they would stop showing me such horrible things and leave me alone." She started crying at this point. It was a good thing Charlie woke up just when those scissors were getting ready to come down into his chest, because she would have killed him without a second thought. That was the last coherent word I heard from Helen that day. The rest of the day, she was slipping back and forth from delirium to the monster. The drive to the hospital made me extremely nervous because I never knew if It was going to decide to fight us on the highway, and I was more than relieved once we got her there.

The routine was the same. She spent three days in the hospital and was stabilized. After returning home, it was an immediate visit to the priest. Medical, psychological, and then spiritual, I still follow these rules when dealing with my cases today. It was always successful with Helen, and it has always been successful with all of my cases. I know there are many questions going through your mind. To answer everything right now would be to give everything away. There is more to come.

Shortly after this incident, Helen found out only by accident that Charlie had moved his girlfriend into the same apartment complex they were living in. Not the same building, but the building next to it. Of course, Charlie denied it and said he was not seeing her, and then it turned into he used to see her. Of course, Helen would catch him secretly talking to her and all hell would break loose. However, even then, Charlie would insist they were just friends, and nothing was going on. It was always just Helen's imagination. Now, you have to stop and consider just how bright of a man Charlie March really was. His wife, at this point, had tried to kill him twice. The first time, she tried to cut off his penis with a knife. The Catholic Church had determined that she was possessed by a demon. The psychiatric community could not explain what was going on with her and believed it was the result of her living through a haunting. The medical community had seen things happen to her they could not explain. She was currently taking medication to keep what they believed was a demonic entity subdued—or something along those lines. Now, would you do something deliberately to piss this woman off? In my opinion, Charlie March, at this point, deserved the stupid husband award. Not only that, Charlie kept trying to take away the only thing keeping him alive, her medicine. Seems to me like this man had a death wish.

Late May 2006

Kelly was pregnant. Kelly was pregnant with Tommy's baby and Tommy was dead. How does a teenager even begin to comprehend or deal with those feelings? Kelly was carrying his legacy and if you were to ask her, she would tell you, "I am going to have Tommy's son." It made you want to cry, the way she would cradle her arms around her stomach when she would say it. This was her way of holding on to Tommy and trying desperately not to let him go. She was trying to be brave, but you could tell she was scared. Tommy had left her all alone in a cruel, judgmental world. Kelly was in a world that shunned pregnant teenage girls and was especially forbidding of pregnant black teenage girls who were already on probation. You just had a feeling that things were going to end up wicked for this girl. Absolutely wicked.

The bleeding started early one morning and Kelly knew she was not only losing the baby, she was losing the only part of Tommy she had left. I was there to take her to the hospital with Helen, and I never saw a girl grow up so fast in one day. I saw her age before my eyes. I saw her lose her baby in the back seat of a car on the way to the hospital, along with her innocence and the remainder of her connection to her dead first love. How do you deal with that? There are no words that can comfort a mother who loses a child. There is no sound more sorrowful than the sound of a mother when she hears her baby is gone, and, in this case, it was combined with another loss as well.

I heard her cries, and I knew at that moment she wanted to die as well. She said it without words. She said with her every breath and the look in her eyes. The look in her eyes was the look of sheer terror. She must have felt that she let Tommy down in some way. She must have felt as if she failed to keep him alive, with the miscarriage of the baby. She must have felt that she had let him go, and she couldn't stop it. The depression that followed was massive. Kelly became extremely self-destructive, and there was a time when we all thought we were going to lose her.

I could not help but think that this plethora of bad luck was caused by some unworldly force. The wheels of catastrophe that were once set in motion by the agony of my family still turn and are present in the lives of people who have been involved with the Screaming House, in some shape or form. People were dying now. The stakes were rising and if this is what the demon had in mind, it was getting more horrific than any of us could have imagined. The game was still being played and we were still the pawns on the board. Tommy and the baby were added to the casualty list, and the game of our lives went on.

Chapter 13

June 2006

The old woman sitting in front of me was a town historian, of sorts. She was giving me the history of the Captain Cromwell addition of the town. I had never stopped trying to piece together the history of the haunting. I still hoped, if I could make sense of the haunting, I could stop the proverbial freight train we had all found ourselves on. The old woman rocked in her chair as she spoke to me. What she was telling me sounded more like a story from a romance novel than a historical account. She was in her late eighties, and she seemed to have a sense of satisfaction on her face as she told me the story:

"The troubles and problems with the Cromwell addition in this town go all the way back to the 1800s. Minerva Cromwell was a lady of stature and society. She had been born into wealth, to a prominent Kentucky family that moved to Missouri for better days and better times. She was beautiful, and it was often said she moved with the grace of angels' wings. However dramatic that statement may have been, her beauty helped her to marry a well-established captain from a well-established family. They built a life together in Union, Missouri, that everyone admired and envied. The captain loved his bride with the deepest of loves. He worshiped her deeply, and she adored him just the same.

"They built their homestead in the grandest of fashions. The town of Union had never seen such a grand display of wealth and elegance. The home had the fi nest of all things within it, and it shone bright white with black trim. The land had horses and stables upon it. Barns and outbuildings were built and servants' quarters were erected. The property was a constant bustle of activity, just to keep the place going and happy. Just for Minerva and her captain.

"At first, things were perfect, and times were good. However, the captain would be sent away to fight battles and do things that captains must do. Minerva would get lonely when he was gone. The captain, seeing her loneliness, gave her a large woman named Ivy to care for her while he was away. It was said that Ivy had a way with the black arts—a talent she would use to her benefit and that she did not mind sharing. Now Minerva and Ivy became very close. At least, that is what Minerva thought. Ivy was not stupid. She knew that to get the favor of the captain, his wife was the easiest way to make her life tranquil, and she set about doing just that.

"During one of his long absences, Minerva became taken with one of the young, teenage servant boys. Ivy knew that it was easy to get Minerva to play during the captain's absence. Some say Ivy conjured up a spell to help move things along, and one night Minerva brought the teenage boy to her bed. Shortly after that, the captain returned and before long, Minerva became pregnant." The old woman paused for a moment, looking at my face for a reaction. I gave her none but continued to listen. "Well, I think you are a smart enough man to figure out where this is headed for yourself. I think you can figure out why no one talks about the good old captain and his wife. They are an embarrassment to this community. You see, son, when the captain figured out that baby was not his, there was hell to pay, and I am talking hell on earth. The kind of hell this town had never seen before and has never seen since. It has stuck with it, and it has been passed down through generations. Not the kind of thing they can just get over. You see, the good old captain loved Minerva so much that he loved her to death, and that is all I am going to say about it. There are just some things that are better left alone, and my advice to you is to leave this alone."

With that, she became quiet and would not tell me anything more. I wanted to know why I should leave this alone, and she just changed the subject on me. I knew the problem had never been the Screaming House itself. I knew the land was bad, but I could never really get anyone to tell me why.

Now I knew I was on the right track, and I had someone sitting in front of me who had the whole story, but she would not tell me anymore than that. I almost felt like she was threatening me somehow, and I had to wonder if she had been put up to deliver the message to me to leave it alone. You know - give me enough information to keep me happy, and then tell me to leave it the fuck alone. You have to laugh when you think about it. That night, I lay in bed trying to go to sleep with these thoughts rolling through my mind.

"She moved with the grace of angels' wings." There was something creepy about that statement, and I kept thinking about it, over and over. Then, I remembered the last e-mail I got from the landlord of the Screaming House, in November 2005, and the statement he made: "I can hear their little angel screams." Angel again. Then I remembered the angels that surrounded the living room in the Screaming House. Maybe it was nothing, but I have to tell you, in the middle of the night it sure did creep me the hell out. Why angels? What if I was dealing with some sort of strange sect of people who worshiped fallen angels? The Book of Enoch talks about them. And it is clear in Revelations that when Lucifer was cast out of heaven, he had an army of angels who were cast out with him.

"And there was war in heaven: Michael and his angels fought against the dragon; and the dragon fought and his angels and prevailed not; neither was their place found any more in heaven. And the great dragon was cast out, that old serpent called the Devil, and Satan, which deceiveth the whole world: he was cast out into the earth, and his angels were cast out with him." —Revelation 12:7–10

Was it possible that I had stumbled upon some type of strange sect of people who believed in and worshiped fallen angels, in a literal sense? When you start to kick around the idea in your mind and you actually take the leap, it begins to make sense and fits the situation. It also explains the hold that this haunting was having upon everyone involved. I don't know how many times I had talked to priests, demonologists, and others who deal with this sort of thing, and they all have agreed that this particular haunting behaved very differently than those before it. It fit all of the characteristics of a severe demonic haunting. It came with everything a haunting like this had to offer, but it also had many new things as well.

The strange thing is, I remember the landlord once claiming to me that he belonged to a sect of spiritualism and religion I had never heard of before. It is one thing to deal with simple demons, but we were climbing way up the hierarchy here, way up the hierarchy. When I was growing up, there had always been strange rumors of cultlike activity coming from this town. You didn't hear about it coming from anywhere else in the county - just this town. What if I had managed to stumble upon this strange cult of people and I was digging into something I shouldn't be digging into?

You know, the Voodoo religions believe in fallen angels. Maybe I was dealing with some sort of Voodoo-driven cult, which was a thought that gave me chills. Follow my thinking here. What if it all started with Ivy? What if that was the warning I had been given?

The religion of the slaves was based upon African beliefs and practices, such as ceremonial spirit possession, spiritual healing, sorcery, and drumming and dance. These were also used as a form of worship. An ancestor cult called Kumina and the belief in obeah (sorcery) are living survivals of the African heritage. They believed strongly in supernatural influences. African religions believed there was a supreme and distant Creator who was generally uninvolved in human life, but that a group of angels actually protected and guided us. It is also believed that certain people or sorcerers could use ghosts or evil spirits for malicious purposes. Christians seek power and inspiration from the Holy Ghost, but the sorcerer would seek power and inspiration from Satan, demons or the "fallen angels."

Catholic teachings believe that the fallen are demons, but somehow I would think it is a case of semantics in the course of beliefs. Seems to me the fallen would rank right below Lucifer and would be a hard opponent to deal with. Many religions place the fallen as a separate entity, which in this case I believe is what we were dealing with. These people practiced Voodoo mixed with Catholicism, and the main source of their beliefs was based upon the exaltation of the fallen angels. Sounds crazy, doesn't it? Instead of praying to God, these people would pray to the fallen, much in the same way as the African sorcerers would in the Voodoo religions. Would they also offer the fallen sacrifices in exchange for power or whatever they needed? The thought sent a chill through my body because I knew I was on to something. Why was the house always rented to families with children? Who was feeding what to whom for power? Not crazy at all now is it? The perfect sacrifice would be children. Let's face it, biblically this would not be the first time children were sacrificed in some form or another. Remember Abraham almost sacrificed his own son to God. Remember the unholy always attempts to be a mirror reflection of the holy. Even if it is sometimes in a bastardized form. Sometimes this bastardized form is even more powerful because of its pure mockery of God and the scripture.

I kept going over and over the conversation in my head. It became clear to me, at that moment, that everything that had been said to me was said for a purpose, and that purpose was twofold: to give me information and to scare me enough to get me to stop. I have to be honest with you—in the middle of the night, it was doing a damn good job of scaring me. So good, that I began to pray my protection prayers, and I am glad I did because nothing could prepare me for the case that was going to land in my lap the next day. Another case of possession in Union, Missouri. I fell asleep thinking of angels and the nightmare began.

The sound of wings was over my head, as I was running up a very steep hill. I could hear them, but they were just out of sight. I was running as fast as I could and I was falling. And as I fell, I could feel something swoop down at me like a large bird attacking. I scrambled to my feet and began to run again. The sound of the wings was all around me as I ran. There was a strange, low voice, which was filling my head as I tried to escape the flapping of the wings.

A low, guttural female voice cackled, "Run, boy, run."

I was hurting. My legs were hurting. I was on the verge of total exhaustion and total physical collapse, but I knew if I stopped, they would converge on me and tear me apart.

"Run, boy, run."

The hill became even steeper in front of me. The sound of the wings became louder and more massive. They were gaining in numbers!

"Run, boy, run."

I fell and began to claw my way up the hill as the deafening sound dove in closer. I heard a screeching above me. That was when the voice inside my head began to laugh. I was completely and totally exhausted when the sounds and darkness began to consume me.

That was when I felt the sharp pain of something pierce through my heart and I heard the laughing voice growl, "It is finished."

"GOD!" I came awake with my hands reaching straight up into the air as if reaching toward heaven. I fell into a heap upon the bed and began to weep. I knew instantly what I had just experienced. There was no thought process needed to calculate, no need to reason it all out. I had just been attacked by the fallen.

"God, save me from this evil." I sat there praying because I did the only thing I knew how to do at that moment. It came easy and when you think about it, what else was there left for me to do? I was defenseless in the eye of the storm, but this wasn't something new. Like I said many times before, I had been there all along. It was like being in the eye of a hurricane. You know that false sense of security you might feel in the eye of the hurricane, and then all of a sudden the shit hits the fan all over again? I had been living in a false sense of security for far too long. Hell, I had even told the world how strong and how resilient I was. I was just deceiving myself within the eye of the storm. I had no idea - resilient my ass. Say a few prayers over him, give him Communion, and his life is forever changed. Was I living in some sort of fairy tale? Wasn't it me who told you that fairy tales didn't exist? That what seemed like perfect lives and solutions, would always turn out tarnished in some way? Well, this wasn't just tarnished, this was damn well broken.

I got out of the bed and I stormed down the hallway to get a drink of water. I was standing at the sink, drinking my water, when I heard a noise coming from the living room. I hurried to see what was going on just in time to see a shadow figure fleeing out of the open front door. I raced to the door and looked out into the night. There was nothing and no one there. It was what I call a calling card. It meant a case was coming. It meant a bad case was coming. I sat down on the front steps in the night and smoked a cigarette as I watched the sun rise.

I sat there considering everything I knew already about angels and religion, and as I watched the sun coming up, I saw the morning star. "Lucifer," I whispered to myself. A cold chill ran through my body, because I knew the meaning of his name. Lucifer means "light bearer" (from the Latin words, lucem ferre). It was the name given to the morning star.

"What a contradiction of terms," I continued to think as I lit another cigarette. I was raised a Christian and I knew what Christianity taught. I knew Christianity taught that the fallen angels were the original demons. I knew that somewhere in my own beliefs I held this to be true. But the question of the fallen seemed to keep coming up, whenever my life was concerned now. Angels in general kept coming up where this house and land was concerned.

From the first day I moved into the house, I had dealt with the fallen. I tried to hang a picture of angels on the living room wall. It kept falling onto the floor, hitting me in the back of the legs. Was it just a coincidence the one picture I had trouble getting to hang on the wall just happened to be picture of angels in God's good favor? The angels that bordered the ceiling were part of the cherubim. This choir of angels was one of the fallen choirs. Makes sense once you think about it. The picture of angels in God's favor would not stay on the wall, but the cherubim who bordered the ceiling in the living room could, because they were part of exactly what the problem of the land was.

Then there was the warning, the carving on the front porch post when Helen lived in the house. Neither of us had ever seen anything like it before. It was an up-and-down arrow shape, with things coming on and off of the arrow. I sent a copy of it to my good friend, Madame Star, who lived in California. She was a Wiccan, who was born to a Santeria high priestess. Her grandmother was also a high priestess in the art of Voodoo. I had a hunch it might be related to something along those lines, and I knew she would know. And sure enough, it was. She explained to me that it was a curse someone had tried to put on the house. She explained that you read this symbolism from top to bottom. She read it to me and this was the meaning: "Like Adam and Eve were cast out of the Garden of Eden, and Lucifer and his angels were cast out of heaven into the fiery pits of hell, so should those who cross this threshold."

She told us to get rid of it and we did. We really did not even consider there to be anything to worry about. We actually thought that most likely some teenager found a book and was trying something they thought was cool at the town's haunted house, but even now I have to wonder. I think it was much more than just a kid playing around. Once again, it was the falling of the angels. My thoughts had to go back to the Tower card Zoe pulled so many years ago. The fall from grace also came to mind again.

"Daddy, what are you doing sitting out here on the porch?" Lydia seemed clearly puzzled as she saw me sitting there, and I am sure it might have looked strange to her. "Watching the sunrise," I replied with a forced smile. "You are so weird sometimes," she said, as she went back inside. She had no idea just how weird our lives were and how weird they could get. I couldn't shake this feeling of danger ahead.

You know that feeling you get deep inside that you just can't seem to shake? That feeling that tells you all hell is about to break loose, and you had better get ready for it? You know it is coming, but you are powerless to stop it. I looked over to my right, and I saw, just sticking above the grass, a can with something sticking out of it. I must have stared at it for a good couple of minutes, wondering what it could be. It was strange, because I had not noticed it there before. I got up, walked over to it, and picked it up. Inside the can was a dildo wrapped in a note. The note said, "Fuck you, Steven. I am coming for you, and I am coming for your children."

I was in total shock at what I was reading. I thought it had to be some kind of sick joke someone was playing on the crazy, haunted guy. But for one moment in time, I could not move. Then I had to react. I hurried up and I buried it beneath a bunch of garbage in the trash can, closed the lid on the can tightly, and went inside to wash my hands.

Bill called me in the early evening. We had a case in Union, and from what he was telling me it sounded like a bad one, something about a child wanting to kill her infant sister. How in the hell do you deal with that? My first instinct was to say no and tell him to tell them to seek psychiatric care. I mean, that would be anyone's first reaction.

Then I remembered the calling card from the night before, which had sent me to the front porch until morning. I remembered my own children going through the nightmare they did. After what seemed like an eternity, I told Bill I would go check the case out. I could hear Zaffis in my head, telling me to be careful in everything I did. "Steven, it is very hard to work on cases, being in a case yourself," he would often say to me.

I knew that much of the emotional

baggage I carried would go with me to this case, and I had to make sure that didn't happen. Sometimes that is easier said than done when a small child is involved. Every time I look at a child who is going through hell, I see the faces of my children. It is a good thing and a bad thing, at the same time. It is emotional hell for me, but it is good for the child I am helping because I will go to great lengths to find a resolution. I have to deal with my own demons once again, after the case is over, and once again after everyone has gone home. Sometimes those are the worst of times. The memories and the guilt can be too much to handle.

Bill called me back to let me know he had set up the consultation for the next night, He gave me the phone number and directions to what turned out to be a house in the middle of town. I told him I was going to take Preacher with me. We actually had a member of our team who was very close to becoming a Methodist minister, but he never finished fully. He was a tall, skinny man with piercing eyes and a good sense of humor. I always loved working with Preacher because he usually would get right down to business and to the point. He had a way about him that people seemed to respond to without question or argument, and if this was a case involving children, I was not going to have any patience with bullshit. The sooner we could get to the bottom of the cause of the happening, paranormal or nonparanormal, the better for the children's sake.

One thing I could always count on Bill for was detail. Detail is very important when you are going into a private case. You never want to go into a private case with your ass hanging in the wind. When Bill got a private case ready, I knew he had taken the clients through an extensive questionnaire that he went over with them, and which he would then go over with me. He would label any red flags he assessed during that interview so that I knew to be aware of these things. If at any point he felt there were too many red flags or there were danger signs involving the case, he would throw it out. He is an awesome case manager, and it is an art very few people understand or can even do properly. I knew that when I walked into that house with Preacher, we were going to be ready for whatever came our way.

The next night went precisely as planned. Bill's directions took Preacher and me right to the front door of the house. The house smelled like someone was cooking dinner. All of these smells were mixing together, along with what I could swear was some pot mixed in, along with a strong odor of incense and Lysol. I knocked on the door. The husband opened the door, an average looking guy— white collar, I guessed by the way he was dressed. He seemed nervous as he asked us into the house.

He offered us a seat on one of two couches in the living room, and he sat across from us on the other. Preacher immediately got down to business and started to question him. Now, things can go one of two ways with husbands from my experience. First off, there is the husband that believes that his wife and anyone else who tries to help are complete nut jobs. This is the guy I always feel sorry for because he doesn't have a clue. However, we come across these guys quite often. Then, there are the husbands who have seen, heard, and witnessed something. These guys are the ones more than ready to talk. They will tell you anything as long as you can get the shit out of their house so their freaking life can get back to normal.

This guy was a witness guy who wanted us the shit out of his house. He had seen some shit, lots of shit. And this guy wanted to talk and talk and talk some more. The magic moment came when he asked Preacher what he could do to get his normal life back. I had to drop my head because we did not call him "Preacher" for nothing. And what Preacher had in store for this family was going to rock this guy's world.

"Well, what you need to ask yourself is, is my house in order? Would I be happy for Jesus to walk into my house today, or is there anything here that I would be ashamed of him seeing?" Preacher said firmly, looking him straight in the eye.

At this point, the poor guy jumped up and stuff began to fly. He started filling Preacher's arms with all sorts of things. Porn, alcohol, more porn, a bong, a pipe, more porn, another bong, more porn, more porn, a fifth of Jack, more porn, another pipe, and more porn. The guy looked around the room, exhausted. Preacher and I were in total shock. The guy looked around one more time and then suddenly dove for my feet. "Excuse me," he said as he came up with more porn for Preacher's already full arms. "There, that's it," he said, out of breath as he looked at Preacher proudly. "My house is now ready for Jesus. Is that it? Will the shit stop now?" Preacher, after asking for a bag and placing the non-Jesus items in it, began to explain to the guy it was going to be a little bit more complicated than that. The guy's face turned white and he almost began to cry.

"Listen, man, my wife isn't acting right.

Shit is walking around here. I had something attack me in my bed. And my daughter says her doll told her to kill her four-month-old sister. We need help here." The guy was clearly crying at this point. Preacher set down the bag of items, went over to him, and put his arm around him. "Would you like to pray with me?" he asked. The man nodded yes and they began to pray together. When the prayer was over, the man lifted his head, and it seemed as if it had helped him. He appeared more composed and calm. Immediately, I felt a shift of energy within the room, which quickly drew my attention away from the husband. It was an almost instant coldness.

The wife had entered the room.

Preacher sat back down by me as she placed herself next to her husband. Instantly, I began to assess her. She looked horrible. She had sunken eyes, gaunt cheeks, and pale skin. There was no color to her skin other than gray shadows. I recognized her behavior the moment I saw it.

She was cool, calm, and collected. She even admitted smoking pot without blinking an eye. "I need it to relax sometimes." I was getting nowhere fast and I knew it. In the meantime, Preacher was setting up a time to go to church with the husband, who was more than ready to throw himself on the altar at this point. We left the couple with the promise to return for further evaluation with equipment.

I identified what the problem was. I knew the wife was possibly attached, and there was part of me that feared she might even be already under a possession, but I had no proof. If she was, the demon was playing a clever cat and mouse game with me. Part of me was also very worried because this house also was on the Cromwell addition of town. So, we could very well be dealing with the same type of thing we had dealt with at the Screaming House. I had the feeling she knew me, like she was looking through me. I was scared, because I was close to it and I also knew what it was capable of. I realized I was playing with fi re. But in order to get the ball rolling, we needed evidence. We needed something to act upon. I decided to send Preacher back in a few days with a recorder to interview the wife without the husband being present. My thought was to shake up the game a little and to see what confirmation we could come up with. So, that is what we did. A few days later, Preacher and another male team member went to the house in the middle of the day to interview the wife alone. Preacher came back with the tape and we sat down to listen.

Recording Transcript

Preacher: Can you tell me about your daughter?

Wife: My daughter is four years old. I can't keep up with her anymore. She is out of control.

Preacher: Did your daughter say she wanted to hurt her sister?

Wife: She did more than say it. I found her in the crib with her pillow over her sister's face, trying to smother her. She said her doll told her to do it.

Unknown Whisper: Do it.

Preacher: How did you handle it?

Wife: I panicked. I spanked her. I don't think I am a very good mother.

Preacher: Why do you say that?

Wife: I don't think I love my children.

Unknown Whisper: Kill her.

Preacher: You said, before we sat down

here in the kitchen, that you don't like it in here.
Why don't you it in here?

Unknown Whispers: Bitch. Kill her.
Bitch.

Wife: I don't like the refrigerator.
Preacher: Why the refrigerator?
Unknown Whispers: I did it. I did it.
Bitch.

Wife: I find the door standing wide open
all of the time, even after I just closed it.

Unknown Low Voice: I opened the
refrigerator.

At that moment, I stopped the tape.
Preacher was looking at me with his mouth
wide open. "I told you, Preacher. I told you it
was hiding from me," I said, clearly excited. But
who was I going to get to help solve the
problem? I was not going to be able to turn to
the Catholic Church for this one, for reasons
that I am going to leave unsaid here. Some
things should remain private.

I had to think and I had to think fast.
Then I remembered a friend of mine from
Louisiana, named Reverend Martin Thompson.
Reverend Thompson was a Southern
Evangelist and an exorcist. I immediately got
him on the phone and told him what was going
on. I let him listen to part of the tape on the
phone. He wanted me to send a copy of the
tape to him through file sharing, which I did.
Not even an hour later the phone rang, and he
was on the other end of the line.

"I am on my way, Steven. It is going to
take me a day to get to you, but I am coming.
Do not tell her I'm coming to perform an
exorcism, but someone better have a serious
talk with that husband of hers, because when I
get there, it is going to hit the fan, the Lord's

fan, if you know what I mean."

We set the plans in motion, and I hung up. Preacher looked at me, as if to ask if everything was okay. "Everything is all right, Preacher. He is on the way. He will get into town tomorrow night, and we will go over there the next morning. You need to get ahold of that husband and school him on the ways of the Lord, because help is coming in the form of thunderous Holy Ghost power." Preacher looked at me even more puzzled. "Just wait until you meet Reverend Martin Thompson. "

Reverend Thompson hit town the next night, right on schedule. He checked into the local hotel and rested up to gain his strength for the next day. We were going to meet at Preacher's house first, to say our hellos and to partake of Holy Communion before going to the apartment. To my surprise, Reverend Thompson called to ask me for directions to the Screaming House so he could get a look at it before meeting with us. I gave him the directions. I waited at Preacher's and sure enough, right on time, Reverend Thompson pulled up and jumped out of his car.

"That darn house you lived in, Steven, is about the spookiest place I have seen in a while. I pulled up to it and the darn front door opens. Now, I am not sure if it was letting something out or if it was inviting me in, but I tell ya, I would like to take a crack at that one, if I ever get the chance." There was no doubt in my mind that I was sure he would. There was also no question that it would be a fair fight. You could just feel the energy coming off of this man, and instantly I knew I had made the right choice.

After we visited for a few moments, we got down to business. We discussed what we were going to do and how things were going to be handled. Then, the last thing we did was gather around the kitchen table, where the reverend administered Holy Communion. I have taken Communion many times before in my life, but this moment, in this small kitchen, it meant something. There was power in it. It was the raising of our armor before battle. At that point, it was the closest feeling to what it would be like to go off to war - just maybe a small inkling of how that might feel. At that moment, we were being fortified.

When we got to the house, everything was seemingly quiet - actually serene. The husband had been instructed to tell his wife we were bringing in an investigator from out of town who was a specialist with this type of haunting. She seemed to be buying that idea. We were also instructed to refer to the reverend as Martin. The first thing Martin did when we arrived was turn off all of the power within the house at the power box. He then placed different gauges in different rooms. In the girls' bedroom, he placed a temperature gauge, which we could read from the living room. While someone was talking outside with the wife, Martin came up to me and said, "Watch that temperature gauge and I will show you something real cool." He was holding a crucifix in his hand as he headed into the girls' bedroom. I was watching him on a monitor as he placed the crucifix on the "evil doll," with a huge smile on his face. To my surprise, the temperature in the room started to rapidly drop. It dropped over twenty degrees in under a minute and then held steady.

"See, looks like something ain't right with that doll. We need to get it outta here. Either I get rid of it, or you send it to Zaffis for his museum." He went into the bedroom and grabbed the doll. As soon as he left the room with the doll, the temperature immediately went back to normal. I sat there in amazement.

The wife immediately saw what was in his hands. "What are you doing with that? Put that down." Then the screaming and crying started. This went on for about an hour. The husband finally intervened. He removed the doll himself and put it in Martin's car.

We were now sitting in the living room, Martin beside me on the couch and the wife glaring at us from across the coffee table. She was pissed at both of us. "Will you hold this for me?" Martin calmly handed her a Bible, which she took out of reaction. She didn't even take the time to observe what she had been handed. She looked at the Bible in her hands and then looked at Martin, and it was clear at this point that the war had started. She drew her arm back with the Bible in her hand, and she slammed the book on the floor. "Now why would you throw a perfectly good book like that on the floor?" he asked her calmly, picking up the Bible.

"I don't like religion. I don't appreciate it. And I don't think I like you," she said to him in total disgust, with eyes glaring.

"That's okay, but would you mind holding my crucifix?" The first thing that went through my mind was why in the hell would he give her a sharp object to hold?

"Keep it!" she said to him, immediately.

It was about eight in the evening when the exorcism began. The ritual was very emotional at times. There was one critical moment when I knew the tables were turning. She began to cry and when she began to cry the whole room began to cry with her. I myself cried uncontrollably, and I am not sure even where it came from. Some will tell you it is when the Holy Spirit has entered the room, and that is when I noticed some sort of an energy shift had taken place. You could feel evil exit and God arrive.

Call me crazy and say what you will, but I am just telling you what happened. At this point, the woman collapsed, and we laid her down on one of the couches. Everyone left the room except for Martin and me. Martin looked at me with the tears rolling down my face, and I looked at him with the tears rolling down his face, and he said, "Cool, isn't it?" Then, all of a sudden, the woman jumped up from the couch, pushed past everyone, and rushed for the front door. Martin yelled, "Catch her, Steven!"

When I eventually caught her, she was doubled over outside on the front stoop. She was going to be sick, and she was having trouble standing. I leaned down and I put my arms around her waist, and I held her up as she began to vomit. She began to vomit up a black substance, continuously. I have never seen someone vomit so much in my life and I have never seen anyone vomit up this blackness that was pouring from her body. While she was doing this, I could feel the bones in her body begin to move. Her vertebrae, her ribs, everything was readjusting itself. She was cracking and popping beneath my arms and chest. I was completely blown away by the whole thing.

When it was over, she collapsed like a rag doll in my arms.

I carried her back into the house, and I laid her back down on the couch. She appeared to be sleeping. My face must have been white because Martin looked at me with a smile on his face and said, "You felt it, didn't you? You felt the demon leave her body? Didn't you?" I looked at him and all I could do was nod my head in agreement. "Something you will never forget, kid. Never forget that for sure," he said as he leaned over to check her.

After an hour, she stirred, sat up, and started to talk. The first words out of her mouth were, "I want my babies." I looked at her face. She looked like a different person. No more sunken eyes. No more sunken cheeks, in fact they were rosy. The husband went next door and got the children, and when he gave her the baby she started to cry. And I have to admit there was a second there when I was a little jealous of them. I reflected for a moment, wishing I could have had my wife suddenly wake up and want her babies. I patted Martin on the back and said, "Good job." I was proud of what we had accomplished there. The last time I saw Martin, he was getting into his car, and with a nod of his head he was gone. Even though I would miss him, I would cherish the things he had taught me and the experience we had shared together.

The whole experience did leave me with more questions. Why Union, Missouri, again? More specifically, why did another case of possession happen within the boundaries of the Cromwell addition of town? The odds of two possessions happening so close together are very slim, at best. It just did not make sense. What was wrong with Union, Missouri, and what was the secret this town was hiding? My theory about the fallen angels and cult activity might not be too far off of the mark. Something bizarre was going on in this small town and I was going to find out what it was.

Chapter 14

Flashback, 1992

I loved working in the theater more than anything else in existence. You never knew what to expect from one moment to the next. It was this constant, ever-changing world. I found it exciting and exhilarating. There was only one time in my life when I really felt like I belonged, and that is when I was in the theater. Whether I was working or I was on stage. I have never felt at home anywhere else but the theater. The rest of my life, I have been nothing but a fish out of water. It's kind of sad, walking around feeling like you don't belong because you are not where you should be. The truth is, we all make concessions for our life and for those within our lives. I was so happy in the theater, and I would spend hours there. Maybe it was an easy place for me to hide, because I knew at home I had a wife who was falling apart. It was my place to escape and when your place to escape becomes your job, it's all over. You become a major workaholic. I was unbelievable. I would get there early in the morning, and I would not leave until very late at night. On Tuesdays, we would usually have a party for whatever show we had in town, and that usually meant we would go out with the cast afterward to show them around. Those nights could and would often last until dawn.

It was my job. I had to do what was required by my job, and I relished it. I would hit those doors and anything that was going on in real life was gone in a second. As soon as I crossed that threshold, I was on a whole different planet, where those outside problems didn't exist, where wives who cried all of the time and pulled their hair out in the middle of the night were not there. I could tell my receptionist to hold my calls when my wife would call on those days she thought she could not handle life anymore. When she tried calling, over and over, I would just have her turned off. It was that easy. My life was Evita, Tommy, Les Misérables, The Phantom of the Opera, and numerous concerts and stars who would come and go in a constant flood of chaos. Why would I want to go home? I would dress in the best suits and best ties, and I loved it. All of the time, things were getting worse at home, and I didn't know, or I didn't care, to pay attention, because I was living the life I had always wanted to live. Right or wrong, it was how I kept my sanity and my marriage together. Without it, we were all going to fall apart, and I didn't know if I was going to be strong enough to pick up the pieces. There are two sides to every story. This is my side of it. This is what I did wrong. I know it. Sometimes it is easier to hide from the problems rather than face them.

We were living in the city. Our house was one of those "yuppie rehabs," the kind you see in magazines with track lighting and those huge pocket doors. We had the latest in security, just in case someone decided to step over the line into our little yuppie bubble. Heaven forbid if they did, because the police responded quicker for us than they would for, let's say, houses two or three streets over—the streets we avoided. It is kind of sickening, now that I think about it. We were everything I now find pitiful. Maybe that is the word to explain the life we were living. Pitiful.

I remember it was a fall evening and the drive home was perfect. The leaves were in full change. The reds, oranges, and yellows contrasted nicely with the brick of our brownstone as I pulled up. Fall in St. Louis is one of the prettiest times of the year. I walked up the walkway, admiring the trees and just the whole atmosphere of the neighborhood. It would be Halloween soon. The kids loved Halloween, and I had to admit that I loved it, too. I had to admit that I loved everything about my neighborhood. I loved everything about my city. I stepped up the stairway and I could hear little footsteps running around inside. I had already been spotted. They knew that I was home.

The front door opened with a flurry of excitement. Lydia, of course, was leading the pack. "The pictures were flying off the wall and were hitting Mommy in the head," she said, flushed with excitement.

"In the head," Michael added, punctuating what she had just said.

"What are you three up to?" I asked, ready to get in on the game I thought they were obviously playing.

"Daddy, you must listen to what I have to tell you." Lydia said, with the verbal skills of a 20-year-old, not a five-year-old. "The pictures were flying off of the wall, and they were hitting Mommy in the head." Matthew was standing to the side, giggling about the whole ordeal.

"Where is your mother now?" I asked.

"She is laying down," Lydia excitedly told me.

"Laying down," Michael said, again punctuating what was just said.

"Lying down," I corrected them as I set my things down. I went down the long hallway to the bedroom. It is no wonder that these were called shotgun houses. You shoot into the front of them, and the bullet would hit every room before going out the back. And if you were lucky, you got to live on two floors with a beautiful staircase dividing the two. Our bedroom was in the back, on the first floor.

"You kids stay in here and watch some TV," I said on my way, causing Matthew to giggle with delight.

The bedroom was dark as I entered. I started to turn on the light. "Please keep the light off," my wife's voice asked, coming from the bed. I walked over to the bed and sat carefully on the side of it next to her.

"You want to tell me what happened?" I asked.

"It was awful. You are not going to believe me, even if I tell you," she said quietly, not moving on the bed.

"Of course I will. Why wouldn't I?" I asked.

"The kids were just horrible today. I couldn't get them to listen. No matter what I did, I could not get them to do what I wanted them to do. They wouldn't pick up their toys or stop running in the house," she said. I was a little confused, because this was the typical "the kids would not listen to me" routine. As usual, I was not hearing anything out of the ordinary from her. I did not understand why she was in bed with the light off as the kids were having the run of the house.

"Okay?" I said, trying to be supportive. However, the fact of the matter was, I never could understand having to be supportive over normal childhood behavior.

"Well, I lost my cool and I told them I was going to spank them if they didn't listen to me, and a picture came off the wall and hit me in the head. They still were not listening, so I tried to grab one of them and another picture came off the wall and hit me. Every time I would try to stop them, Steven, I would get hit in the head with a picture or something.

Something in this house was trying to hurt me or stop me from trying to get my children to behave." She started to cry.

"What pictures are you talking about?" I asked. I have to admit the whole scenario seemed too wild and far out to believe, but I was playing along because I had been down this road before, and I knew things would go much easier if I just gave in to it.

"Just look around. You'll see," she said.

That is when I looked around and there were indeed pictures off the walls, lying on the floor. "Sure thing, honey, there are pictures lying on the floor," I said, trying to make sense of it all and trying to calm her at the same time.

"See, I told you so!" she said through her tears.

"Tell you what, I will pick up this mess. Why don't you sleep and I will take care of dinner," I said. I knew from past episodes that it wouldn't do any good to try to talk sense into her when she was like this. The best thing I could do was close the door and let her sleep. And that is what I did. I went around, putting the pictures back on the walls.

"Is Mommy okay, Daddy?' I turned around to see Lydia standing there, watching me pick up the pictures and hang them back on the wall.

"Mommy will be fine, she just needs to rest. What do you suppose happened to the pictures?"

"I don't know, Daddy. The madder Mommy got, the more they hit her," Lydia said.

"Hit her?" I asked.

"Zoomed off the wall and hit her," said Lydia with both hands to add effect to the statement. "I see," I said, hanging the last picture on the wall and making sure it was good and straight. Then I turned to her. "Tell you what, how about Happy Meals tonight for dinner?'" I proposed. With a screech of delight, Lydia was on her way to get her brothers ready to go, while I stood there puzzling over the whole ordeal. It didn't make much sense to me. After all, I had not been there, so how could I know?

July 2006

I needed to do what I needed to do—and what I needed to do was raise my children. I did do a community production of Guys and Dolls when the kids were in their early teens. I wanted them to see me at least do one thing. It had nothing to do with ego. I wanted them to see that part of me. They were so young; I knew they would not remember what life was like then. But it was important for me to get them into the theater and work. They helped work on the sets and they got to learn how to hang lights. When it came time for the production to actually open, they got to see people stand on their feet for their dad. It was a side of me they had only heard war stories about, up until that moment. War stories are fine and all, but to actually see it, well, you can't replace that kind of memory. Now I know that just maybe my grandchildren will hear about that part of my life. I would hope so. You want your children to know you as a person, not just as a figurehead. I wanted them to know me, and to know me you have to see me in my element. The theater is my home. They got to see me at home and not just from sitting in an audience. They got to get their hands dirty in it. I wish I could have told the judge all about it on the day of my divorce. I wish she could have known about my hands-on approach to raising my kids. Lydia wanted to come to court with me. I wouldn't allow it. There is no reason to expose your children to the ugliness of a divorce hearing. They don't need to witness the undoing of their family institution. In this case, it was dreadful.

The judge asked my ex-wife questions about the children, and she had trouble answering all of them. She sat there with a smile on her face the whole time. She did not know Matthew was a football player, or that all of my kids were required to play instruments in the band. She had no idea that Michael wanted to be a geologist, or that he was considered a gifted child. She did not know Lydia was a straight-A student who loved music more than life itself. She was clueless about these things, and she covered up her shortcomings with that Cheshire grin when she could not say anything of real substance.

When it was time to speak on my behalf, the judge asked me about the children. I told her all of these things and more. I expressed to her how proud I was to be the father of these wonderful human beings and how I was doing everything I could to raise them. The judge told me I was doing a great job. Then she granted the divorce, but before she granted it, she looked at my ex-wife and asked, "You understand you are giving up your parental rights?" She replied, "Yes," with a smirk on her face. The divorce was granted. Afterward the judge said that in all her years working within a family court she had never seen anything like that from a mother.

I was unsure about my feelings. What I had just witnessed had made me sick to my stomach. I was thankful I had the wisdom not to let Lydia come with me. I felt shell-shocked. My ex-wife was acting like it was a moment to celebrate with the people she had come with.

She had just given up her parental rights, and she was going to celebrate it. There is no other way to say it. We all know the marriage did not mean anything to her, because she had someone else's baby while she was still married to me. However, this was a strike against the children. It was so obvious during the proceeding that even the judge picked up on it.

I walked away from the courthouse knowing that I was going to get hit with an onslaught of questions from the children when I got home. I realized I was going to have to answer some tough questions and deliver some tough answers they were not yet prepared to hear. My children were going to have their hearts broken, once again. It was a difficult decision to make, but I concluded that it was the children's choice whether or not to have a relationship with their mother. I had never kept her away from them. All I asked was that it be supervised. They now had the choice of how they were going to deal with her. I was out of the picture. They were now old enough to make those decisions for themselves. I knew she could not physically hurt them anymore, but emotionally, I wasn't so sure. That relationship had to be theirs and theirs alone.

I could no longer protect them from her, even though in my heart I wanted to try. But sometimes, in order to protect them, you end up hurting them even more. So, I took a deep breath and, to my surprise, none of the kids really seemed to care when I presented them with this idea. I think that their mother had put them through enough heartache already. The damage was done. Maybe some of that hurt would heal, but they would have to do it without me. I could no longer put myself in the line of fire. My wife had died years ago. The moment I walked into my house on the night she told me she was leaving; she was already gone. The person who remained was someone I did not know, and a person whom I did not marry. My wife was dead, and who was left was now a stranger.

I went to bed that night with a sense of relief that the divorce was finally over. I could start to heal now, but I was not exactly sure what I was healing from anymore. I mourned the loss of those early years, those good moments, but the bad so far outweighed the good that now all I could feel was relief. She no longer had any legal hold on me or even my name, anymore. That is really what I found myself grieving. I was mourning the fact that I no longer could feel anything good about her. That is a horrible thing, to have someone do so many awful things to you that you can't mourn the loss of the good times you once shared. But nothing could outweigh the emotional terror and distress she caused my family.

Reflecting, I tried to see her as the angel she once was when we were young, but then I remembered she was Jekyll and Hyde. She stole my youth and my time to love away from me. I don't know if I will ever be able to love again. Trust is gone. Where my trust in another should be, there is a very thick, dark, emotional wall. At times, I feel disappointed in myself because I know that I should let it go. If I am still the one harboring the pain, then she is still in control of my life. I feel as if I can never forgive myself for being deceived and dragged down a dirt road. The deepest part of me needs me to forgive myself so that I can move on emotionally. But we all know that forgiving ourselves is the one thing that is hard to do.

Chapter 15

August 2006

The security alarm went off with a crash on the front porch!

I was back in my home in the city. I walked slowly down the long hall to the front door. The walk seemed like it was taking forever. With each step I took, the pounding of my heart became louder in my ears. The screaming of the security alarm intensified, building anxiety. From the other side of the door I could hear a voice yelling. Through the glass in the door I could see some sort of low movement. Something was moving around on my front porch. I cautiously opened the door to reveal the porch and whatever it was.

"Thas okay, I jus don know where the fuck I'm at," the voice was slurred and obviously drunk. I walked slowly onto the front porch to see a homeless man, drunk as could be, lying there.

"Thas okay, I jus don know where the fuck I'm goin!" the man was shouting, in a drunken stupor. I could hear the police sirens in the distance.

"The police are on the way, sir. You have set off my security system. If I were you, I would get going," I said sternly, trying to get him off my porch where he had already spilled the contents of his bottle. It had obviously broken when he fell. I did not see any blood, so I knew he was not hurt.

The man's head was down and I could not see his face. "Did you hear me, sir?" I asked. The man's head slowly rolled back to reveal his eyes. All white with no iris or pupils, nothing but white. So familiar, I had seen those eyes before.

"You think it's that fucking easy?" he giggled. I backed away from the door into my hallway as the man rose to his feet.

"Get away from here!" I said in a panic.

"You are not going to get me to go away that fucking easy," he giggled.

"You don't belong here. You need to go!" I said, my voice trembling.

"Fuck you. I am home," he said, laughing.

The police cars pulled up, and he collapsed once again onto the porch. "Thas okay, I jus don know where the fuck I'm at." He was once again the drunk. The neighborhood was filled with red and blue lights. The police officers came to take him away.

I woke up with Michael looking at me with a puzzled look on his face. I had fallen asleep on the couch, and he was playing a video game of some sort. I looked at the screen and I saw zombies with white eyes. "You okay, Dad?" he asked, looking at me with his hands still moving the controller.

"Yeah, I am fine," I said. The dream had shaken me up some. It was almost a replay of a night when a homeless man had fallen on my porch and hit my door, setting off the alarm. I let the police take him away that night without question. I didn't bother asking anything. I gave my report, and the trouble was gone.

The "trouble" was a human being - someone I had not taken the time to learn anything about. He had crossed the line into my world, and in my world, folks did not take a moment to find out about people like him. Out of sight and out of mind. Just as long as we did not have to deal with them, it was just fine that way. I thought about it and I felt the guilt creep into my gut. If there were one person in this world who had the right to haunt my dreams, it would be him, because when he needed someone, I didn't give a damn. I let him get taken away.

The funny thing is, three years after that incident, I found myself homeless with three children. Thank God I had somewhere to go, but still we had no home of our own. We were homeless. I guess you could call that "the karmic fuck of it all." What if everyone had turned their backs on us? I could have been just like him. Any of us could. That is something really scary, when you stop and think about it. I could have been just like him and someone could have done the same thing to me. A feeling that could only be described as guilt ripped into my gut as I thought about it.

"Where's your sister?" I asked Michael, who answered without looking. "She is still on her date with her boyfriend." I immediately looked at the clock. It was not quite midnight. She had about ten minutes before she was busted. I hated curfews and making the kids abide by them, because, the fact of the matter was, I hated them when I was their age. But there was this little voice that reminded me of all the trouble I would have gotten into if it had not been for my curfew, or the times I got in trouble when I broke it to do those things that I did not want my kids doing.

A great way for parents to ensure that their children will not come home drunk or stoned ever again is to trap them in conversation when they get home. You talk to them for a very long time when they come in. Now, understand they want nothing more than to run to their rooms, but because they want to totally convince you they have been angels, they will talk to you for however long you want.

So, my suggestion to you is to have fun. Find many topics of interesting conversation. The whole point of this is they have to endure it. Now, if they are standing, which is my favorite, they will try not to sway or lean heavily or hit the wall with their bodies. This can be a very difficult thing to pull off when you are discussing with them how you make sandwiches. Have them make you a sandwich, or a frozen pizza - that will take even longer - leaving more time for discussion.

The whole point here is that they will think twice before ever coming home in that condition again, and you have avoided having to have the regular, boring parental convo - and you get fed. Beautiful, isn't it? Works every time. You will only have to do this once or, if the kid is named Matthew, you might be doing this once a month for a while, but you do get fed unless he decides to cut open the pack of hot dogs with a samurai sword. Then there will be blood, and you will be in the ER for a long time.

So there I was, waiting to bust Lydia for curfew. Hoping she would not pick this night, of all nights, to test the curfew waters. I knew it was coming and she was going to do it sooner or later, but tonight I wanted things to go smoothly. Headlights in the driveway, and then I waited for it and waited for it. No car door, which means now I had to be an asshole and turn on the porch light and walk out onto the porch, showing the young man in the car and my daughter my displeasure with the long wait for her to come in. So I do. And as I do, I see a can off to the side of the porch. A can like I had seen before. And like before, there was something sticking out of it. I knew if I went for it now, I would be caught, and I did not want the kids to see it. So, I did my routine and went back inside. I flipped the light on and off a few times and thank God I got car-door closure. I heard the sound of the car pulling out of the driveway and leaving as my beautiful daughter stomped up the porch steps and slammed open the front door to indicate she was finally home from her date and was truly pissed off at me.

"Did you have to do that? I was coming." She stomped into her bedroom and slammed her door, music on. Home safe, my mission was accomplished. All three children were now inside and secure. My job as their parental figure was complete for the night. Now all I had to deal with was that can, as soon as I could get outside without a fuss. All three of them had to sleep at some point. At least I prayed.

I sat on the couch and turned the TV on. The news was its usual depressing self. My mind was on the can outside and wondering what kind of note I was going to find in it this time. "British Houses of Parliament temporarily shut down due to anthrax alert." I heard this coming over the TV and sighed because it was five years after 9/11 and we were living in a whole, new, frightening world. Sometimes, it was easier to tune out the chatter from the outside world than to deal with the onslaught of what seemed continual fearmongering, which kept filling our airwaves on a daily basis. Was today a "red" terror day or a "yellow" terror day? It was so easy to get caught up in it all if you allowed yourself to, but something always told me that is exactly what we were supposed to do. Get caught up in it all. When the right-hand dictates fear, you are not necessarily paying attention to what the left hand is doing.

I was lucky all three of the kids were sleeping pretty heavily in no time flat. I took a deep breath as I quietly got up from the couch and headed for the front door. I turned the knob slowly in order to try to open this door with as little sound as possible. I was successful, as the door swung open with little or no noise. I stepped out onto the porch and walked down the stairs toward the can waiting for me. There in the can, like before, was another dildo. Please forgive me, there is no other name for it, and I am almost embarrassed to say the name of it today. But there it was, and around it was wrapped another note. I slowly unrolled the note to see what it had to say.

"I am coming for you, and I am coming for your kids."

I stood there for a moment, in the light of the moon, just staring at the note in my hands. What was I going to do? My first instinct was to call the police. Seemed logical to me; the police are there and they are supposed to protect you in these types of situations. So, I snuck back in the house, grabbed my phone, went back out onto the porch, and I dialed the police station directly. I thought this would be better because at the moment, it did not seem like a ground-breaking emergency that would require a 911 call. I asked to speak to an officer, and after a moment an officer came on the line. I explained to him what was going on and he just listened. Then he said, "You're the guy that lived in that haunted house?" I told him I was, but this, as far as I knew, had nothing to do with that. I again stressed that we were being threatened in a very strange way. The officer's tone changed with me.

"Well, it is most likely nothing. Just somebody trying to get under your skin and really there is nothing we can do until they make some type of physical move toward you or your children, but I feel that is highly unlikely." I could not believe what I was hearing. He was not going to help me. "I will make a report that you called . . ." I cut him off before he could finish, and asked, "Would you like the note and things for evidence, to go with the report?" He told me that it would not be necessary.

I hung up the phone. That is when it really hit me hard that there was not going to be any help coming. I was not going to have anyone who would care. I was going to have to begin to think how I was going to take care of this on my own. Then I settled into it. I was used to that. Now I knew the rules of the game, and I understood how I needed to play it. I opened the trash bin, and I slammed the can and its contents into the trash. I would kill somebody, if I had to, in order to protect my family.

From inside the house, there was loud banging, and I could hear Michael screaming. As I ran into the house, I noticed the banging was coming from the walls, and just as I went to comfort Michael, it stopped. Michael was clearly freaked out. I told him it was nothing, just a tree limb and some wind. He must have believed me, because he rolled over and went back to sleep. Once you explained something to Michael, he was all right. That is just the way he has always been. He was always the quickest child to fall apart, but always the easiest to put back together.

There was no real explanation for the banging and pounding. The noise had stopped right above Michael's head. I went around the house, making sure all of the windows and doors were secure and locked. I could take no chances at that point. I hate feeling helpless, and I hate not knowing where something is coming from. Give it to me and let me deal with it, and I can handle anything you have to dish out. However, not knowing who or what I was dealing with was going to drive me crazy. Not knowing a motive or reason for it made it all the more terrifying. I guess I am a lot like Michael, in that respect. We can handle anything once we have the explanation. We are both easy to put back together that way. I sat back down on the couch and I flipped the TV back on. I fell asleep as they were saying something about Serbia.

Matthew woke me up the next morning. I had slept the whole night on the couch. "Pops, you have to wake up, she is driving me nuts," he said, as he made a funny face. Lydia was obviously up to something, because she was in full force "General Patton" mode to get the house cleaned for me. She came into the room, hands on her hips.

"Leave Dad alone and get busy. I told you we are going to get this done and THEN you can do anything you want, but not until this is done." I wanted to hide my head just a little longer, but I knew the vacuum cleaner was coming and she was going to make a special emphasis on the area of carpet around where I was sleeping. Sure enough, I could hear Jaws power up. My sister and I both had named our vacuum cleaners "Jaws" for the kids. It was just something that stuck, and the cats were terrified of it, so the name seemed fitting. The roar of Jaws came into the room and, just like I predicted, the area around the couch was getting special attention. I rolled over and looked up at her with one eye open. "Oh, Daddy, I didn't mean to wake you," she said, as my sweet, loving daughter. I mumbled something at her as I got up from the couch and headed into the bathroom for a quiet shower.

It is amazing how the simplest things in life can take away just about every thought or problem you have. A hot shower is one of those things. Bathroom door locked, no one can disturb you. God, it can be pure heaven on earth. No kids fighting or asking for something for ten minutes. Then, there was sound of something being inserted into the bathroom door lock, something turned, clicked, and Matthew was in my kingdom. "What are you doing in here?" I asked.

"I had to go, Dad, I couldn't wait. Besides, she is being a real witch to me today. She wants me to do everything." He was talking a mile a minute and my solitude was completely gone.

"Sorry, Dad. I told you I couldn't wait. That would be my brand," he said as he went laughing out the door. I could hear her screaming at him from down the hall. I quickly got out and dried off because I could not breathe. I was thinking maybe I should take him to a doctor or something because that smell was not normal.

That is when I heard Lydia yell from down the hall, "Take out that trash!" My heart dropped to my feet when I heard those words.

"Oh my God, he is going to find the can." I had not pushed the last can down into the trash last night. I quickly threw on my clothes and went running. I pushed past Lydia in the hall, who had a shocked look on her face. I opened the front door, stepped out onto the porch, and saw Matthew and Michael standing there. Michael was holding the note. He was reading it while Matthew had the can and its remaining contents in his hands.

Michael looked up at me with a puzzled look. "What is this?"

I did not know where to start. Lydia

came charging out the door to yell at all of us and stopped immediately because she could sense she walked in on something. Besides, Matthew did have a dildo in a can in his hands.

"Put all of that back into the trash and let's go inside. I will tell you."

Lydia immediately became uneasy. "You are going to tell us what?" She looked at me as Michael handed her the note. "Oh my God, Daddy," she said with tears in her eyes as she read it.

All I ever wanted to do was live a good, full, and happy life with the three of them. I wanted nothing but happiness and normalcy, because of all of the crazy things we had to deal with my ex-wife before she left. I wanted to put my children back together and I wanted to keep them safe. And then from there, it was supposed to be happily ever after. But the outside world kept getting in and fucking things up. It seemed no matter how hard I tried and how hard I fought, I would still have to break some type of horrible news to my children and see that look in my daughter's eyes. I remembered, once again, Lydia with her tears streaming and crying, "Oh my God, Daddy." It breaks my heart still. I cannot go there without it tearing me apart. I looked at other families and I tried my best to give them that sort of life, and what we got in return was nothing but a complete and absolute nightmare. Now I stood there on that day, and I once again had to see that fear in her eyes. The sound of her voice, which will give me bad dreams until the end of my time on this earth. "Oh my God, Daddy."

"Sit down," I said, as we went into the living room. "This was the second message like this I have gotten from whoever is sending them." Michael immediately jumped up, grabbed the phone, and handed it to me.

"Call the police now, Dad," he said, boldly, which at the moment made me want to smile, but I knew that what I had to say next was not going to go over well.

"Sit down, Michael," I said, calmly. "The police told me last night, they cannot do anything unless this person makes some sort of physical move against us." The room got deathly silent.

It seemed like hours before anyone spoke. "You mean we are all alone in this?" Michael finally spoke up. "Yes," I said, looking at him directly to emphasize to him the seriousness of what I was telling him.

"That is why we need to start doing things a little differently. We need to start checking in with each other more, keeping things locked at all times. Not taking the same routes to wherever we go. I have thought a lot about this. It seems to me, if we never set a pattern of behavior, it would be very hard for someone to follow us." The boys were both nodding their heads in agreement.

"I don't know if I can take this, Daddy. This is just too much," Lydia said with tears still in her eyes.

I went over and I knelt down in front of her. "It is going to be okay. I am not going to let anything happen to you. I have always kept you safe. That is not going to change now. I promise." My promise is something my children know stands true. They understand that once it is given, it is kept. The words "I promise," once spoken to my children, hold a lot of weight. I forced her to look me in the eyes and I whispered sternly, "I promise."

Life became different from that moment on. Our already damaged, false sense of security had been broken once more, and this time it was clear we were not going to get it back. All of us were living in the past, even though we did not want to admit it. I think that day, I broke some kind of trust between Lydia and me, which would take years to heal. It was almost as if she felt I was hiding something from her that I shouldn't have been. And I guess I was keeping it away from them, but there were a few reasons why I was. One of those reasons was the graphic nature of the attack. Who would want to share that sort of thing with their children, especially their daughter? The other reason was I wanted to keep their lives as normal as I could. I hoped I could handle it on my own, without them ever having to know about it. Maybe it was a dumb move - and now I know it was, because it was going to become impossible to hide it from them. I hope it has not caused too much damage, because all we ever had in this world was each other.

Chapter 16

September 2006

The phone rang. It was early in the evening, and I was sitting on the couch contemplating what I was going to make for dinner. The thought of going to grab some burgers for the night seemed a likely choice, and the boys were in agreement with me. I picked up the phone, half expecting it to be my mother, but it wasn't.

"Mr. LaChance?" The voice on the other end was male. I had never heard this voice before, and my first thought was it must be some kind of telemarketer. "Yes, this is Mr. LaChance," I said with a firm voice in order to take control of the call, just in case the sales pitch was coming.

"This is the Steven LaChance who lived in the haunted house in Union, Missouri?" Usually when a phone call started out like this, it was someone either wanting to know where the house was or a paranormal team wanting to know if they could investigate it. I never gave in to these calls or e-mails. My thought was to keep the location of the house as quiet as possible because the new family living there had enough to deal with without the intrusion.

I took a deep breath, "Yes, this is him." I was waiting for the usual routine to begin, but it quickly became obvious that this call was going to be of a different sort.

"Mr. LaChance, you do not know me, but I know everything there is to know about you." The statement caught me off-guard, and I had no idea where this was going. My first thought was that this could be the person who had been leaving me the little notes.

"Yes?" I asked. It has been my experience that you are going to find out a whole lot more by just being quiet and listening. Most of the time, people do not stop to listen and miss something important that was said. The one-word question is always the best way to go.

Then you just sit back and listen.

"I am not going to tell you my name, because that is something you do not need to know. What I will tell you is that I know a whole lot about you and what is going on in your life. Things you have no clue about are at work around you, and you need to hear what I am saying and take it to heart. Because if you don't, your family is going to get hurt." Two words struck a chord within me, and I was fighting the urge to lose my cool with this caller, but instead I just answered, "I am listening."

His voice was serious, and he sounded concerned as he continued with the call. "Mr. LaChance, I am dying. It does not matter to me if you listen or not. I have cancer and it is slowly eating away at me, but before I go, I want to right at least one of the wrongs I have participated in." When he said he had cancer, that is when I noticed his breathing was labored and his voice was weak. "You are on a path of destruction, and you have no clue. Right now, all of your phone calls are being taped." That got my attention because I had noticed a strange clicking recently whenever I had been on the phone. "This call is being listened to as well. I can guarantee you that. They know where you are going, and they know exactly when you will be back or are coming home." This was starting to sound a little too much like the "men in black" for me.

"Who is watching me?' I asked, with a little bit of disbelief in my voice.

"The point I am making to you is that who is watching you is not of consequence, but it is what they want from you that is." He began to cough heavily into the phone. I could hear a wheeze as he continued. "They want you to stop what you are doing. They want you to forget about the house and your experiences there and move on with your life, keeping your mouth shut. You are being followed and watched constantly, and with malice. You have no idea what you have stepped into here. These are not the type of people you want to make angry. They have enough resources to wipe you off the map without a second thought." I noticed my hand holding the receiver had begun to shake.

"If you expect me to believe you, then you are going to need to tell me who they are." There was a deep pause and then a breath before he continued.

"If I tell you who, then you are already dead. You might be dead already and this is not going to help you at all. But you need to listen. They have tried to stop you, and you keep on going. When they tried to hide information from you, you would just take another avenue to try to find it. They have tried to stop you, and you just will not stop. There are some things in this life that are better left alone, and this is one of them." He coughed again, and it was clear he was getting worked up.

"Let me tell you a story of a captain who sold his soul. He did this because he was heartbroken over the death of his wife. The wife he had killed - along with a baby. Some would say Voodoo was involved. Some will tell you it was black magic. I am going to tell you the truth. It was far worse than anything you could imagine. The angels fell from heaven,

Mr. LaChance, and some people have found it to their benefit to worship the fallen, instead of God. You might want to call it a cult. Many have died through the years by threatening their way of living. Money and power is a great motivator in the dirty actions of men who have it and do not want to lose it. You, Mr. LaChance, are in the way. When someone or something gets in the way, they are either moved or they are eliminated. You, Mr. LaChance, are in danger of elimination because you will not let it go. I have no care for myself. I am already dying. If they come for me, it might be a blessing to end my life now. But you have everything to live for and you are pissing them off."

I took a deep breath and sighed. Something in my gut told me he was telling me the truth, but my stubbornness was getting in the way.

"Tell me something to convince me they are watching me?" I asked.

"What were you doing, sitting on the porch recently in the middle of the night, into the morning hours?"

I shot back instantly without thought. "Anyone could have seen me. Even you could have. You are going to have to do better than that," I said defiantly. He was clearly getting agitated with me.

"The police refused to help you with your little problem. You are pretty much on your own with that one, aren't you? Little presents getting in the way?"

I grabbed the phone tighter. My knuckles were white. "Are those from you?" I asked.

"Don't be a fool. Of course, they are not from me. I am a dying man and have no energy to stalk you or your family, but someone out there does, and I think you are not going to like him very much. You need to stop now." His voice went from stern to relaxed, in a matter of moments. "I have said all I have to say to you. I have nothing else. You are either going to listen to me, or you are going to regret it."

I had to ask, "The person leaving me presents. He is one of them?" The voice began to chuckle.

"No, he is not one of them. He is just some rogue, messing with you on his own. They already know who he is, and believe me when I say this, he is not part of them. They will not play childish games with you like that. When they come for blood, you will not even see them coming. You, my friend, have some serious problems on your hands. You need to listen to what I am telling you, or those problems can and will blow up in your face, and they will take out innocent people in the explosion. Could be someone you know has already met up with them and it was too late. Could it have been on purpose, or were there supernatural forces at work? Doesn't matter really; the end result was still the same. Blue in the dirt is a horrible way to go. That was a calling card, and you did not get it. The supernatural is real. You know this more than most people walking around. You know what the supernatural can do, but still, you ignore it. I don't want to see you end up a suicide, Mr. LaChance. Do you understand?"

He had made his point. He had given me the proof because no one knew where Tommy got the lethal dose of heroin. The police didn't seem to care. Even if they did consider him some type of derelict young man, it did seem odd that they didn't try harder to find the person or persons who gave him the deadly injection, which would kill him in the end. They just did not seem to care.

"Yes, I understand," I said, and the caller hung up. I quickly looked at the caller ID to see if I could get a number, but it said UNKNOWN. Then, in the silence of the room, once again in my life, I began to rationalize the irrational. In the end, I would decide he was lying, or he was the person leaving me the notes. He had read about Tommy in the newspaper. It would be later when I would fully understand he was telling me the truth.

Chapter 17

October 2006

Storm clouds surrounded me. In the distance I could hear the boom of thunder. The clouds in front of me were rolling and illuminated by the occasional flash of lightning. The air was heavy and cold as the wind began to blow around me. A storm was coming.

I was kneeling in a meadow. I was crying. The grass around me was whipping faster and faster with the blitzkrieg of the wind. The clouds were now overhead as the lightning began to hit the ground. Their strobes made the surrounding grass flicker even more in the cold, increasing wind as the booming of thunder hid my whimpering in the grass.

Ahead of me was a hooded figure in white. Shrouded in white from head to toe, the figure had its back turned to me and was screaming at the sky. Hands outstretched toward the oncoming clouds and heaven, with the lightning now coming down just ahead, smashing to the ground. In my mind, there was a feeling of recognition inside me, which told me to get to my feet and head toward the figure in white. Was this Armageddon? Did Jesus stand before me, facing the oncoming storm? The oncoming clouds were in front of me now. I began to struggle to my feet.

The wind was fierce now and I began to run toward the figure in white, while the lightning crashed to the ground around. Closer and closer I got to the figure in white. It was screaming something to the sky I could not understand. "ייס הר יל ריבהלLieesישפיפמ לש לאה" the figure kept screaming to the skies over and over again. Could it be Arabic or Hebrew I was *hearing?* "ייס הר יל ריבהלLiees'ישפיפמ לש לאה" *the figure continued screaming over and over again.*

My mind was telling me that I needed to get to Jesus. I had to touch him and talk to him. I ran faster and faster until I stopped directly behind the hooded, shouting figure. "Jesus?" I shouted through the deafening sound of the storm. The ground was now rumbling beneath my feet.

"Jesus, is that you?" I asked.

The figure slowly lowered its hands and spoke in a language I could understand, with a deep chuckle, "No, I am not your Jesus." The voice seemed low and almost morbid.

"Then who are you?" The figure slowly turned around as I spoke.

"I am one of the forsaken, just like you," the figure faced me and began to pull away his hood.

"Jesus did not die for my sins." He began to drop the robe from around his body to reveal black bleeding stumps where wings once were. "Your Jesus left you alone a long time ago, you fucking fool."

I woke up with my heart beating out of my chest. I lay there for quite some time, and I tried to calm myself down. The damn nightmares had begun to come more often and become more bizarre. The sun was shining through the windows, and I needed to get up to start the day. Today was the day of the A Haunting premiere.

I stepped into the shower with the hot water beating on my back. It was awfully quiet in the house. I must have slept while the kids left for school. I was a little irritated that they didn't wake me up before they left. It was kind of an unspoken rule, between all of us, that we never left without saying goodbye to each other. I turned and let the hot water run over the top of my head. The water felt great as it ran off my head and down my back. I was thinking about the evening that was ahead. It almost seemed like a lifetime since we had filmed for the show A Haunting, and tonight we were going to get to see the end result.

I was feeling a bit of anxiety about the whole thing, because my life was getting ready to go out to millions of people. I was trying to weigh the possibilities of how people were going to react. The show was hugely popular at that time, so there was no chance that people would overlook it. They were going to see it. People in the town of Union were going to see it. I think that what worried me most was the local reaction. You know, the people you see in the grocery store, the gas station, and church. Those are the people who mattered. I was getting ready to tell the town of Union that it was haunted, in a very public way.

I heard commotion near the bathroom door, and then the sound of it opening. My first thought was that Matthew had stayed home from school. "You had better have a damn good reason for why you did not go to school today," I said, sounding a little more than irritated. There was no answer in reply. "Did you hear me?" I asked, as I turned off the water and reached for my towel. Still no answer, but instead the footsteps moved closer to the shower. "I am not kidding. Answer me," I said, but still no answer, as the footsteps stopped right outside the shower. I could hear heavy breathing. I quickly wrapped the towel around my waist. The only thing separating me from the intruder was the shower curtain that hung in between us. As I watched the curtain in fear, I noticed that it started to morph its shape.

I could have sworn it was coming toward me. Nervously, I backed up against the wall of the shower. Once my eyes adjusted, I noticed what looked like two hands pushing through the vinyl drape.

I remained silent because I knew, at this point, it was not one of my children. Reaching deeper into my comfort zone, the hands pressed on. Suddenly the outline of a face appeared and then I heard a deep inhale of breath. The curtain was sucked into the mouth of this unknown visitor. I reached for the curtain, drawing it back quickly, as I prepared for a fight.

No one was there. The bathroom door, which I had heard open, was closed. I ran for the door and flung it open. I ran down the hall, searching all the rooms, but I was alone. There was no one in the house. It was clear to me, at that moment, that whoever had been in the bathroom with me was not of the living.

I dressed hurriedly and left the house for a place with people around. I felt the need, at that point, to be among the living. And to tell you the truth, that moment had scared the hell out of me. I had to calm myself down. I found myself sitting in the White Rose Café, looking around at all of the people and, once again, I was wishing I was living a life like them, without a supernatural clue. I was resenting feeling the isolation and aloneness I was feeling at the moment.

That evening finally came. October 6, 2006, eight o'clock, Central Standard Time, was when *A Haunting* premiered "Fear House" on the Discovery Channel. Things leading up to that premiere had been a blur. I had been doing upwards of four interviews a day. It was a hard time for me. I found myself reliving the nightmare, over and over again, with every interview. It was harder on me than I thought it was going to be. Nothing could have prepared me for the onslaught of publicity leading up to the show, and the overwhelming response that was to come after. Life for us was changing very quickly. We were still getting the usual calling cards from our stalker. The boys found it funny that every time we turned around, there was a new sex toy with a note to throw away. It was kind of funny when you think about it. This guy must have been spending a fortune on dildos, because we would find at least one a week, all of them wrapped in the usual "coming to get you" note. The absurdity of the whole thing seemed to lessen the fear, but at this point it was just one more dildo to hit the can. I had to wonder what our trash men thought when they would empty our cans. And then, on the other hand, I would not want to think about it at all. Life was changing.

We went to my parents' house to watch the show on the night it premiered. It was a very surreal moment to sit there and watch your life as it played out on the screen with someone pretending to be you. The show had its high points and low points. The low ones I just wanted to forget. I remembered the exact moment when the demonic clown came on the screen for the first time. I looked at Matthew and said to him, "Oh boy, you have done it now." I was elbowing him in the ribs and we both laughed. It was good to see him laugh about it. Years later, he would describe the clown as having no eyes. Just eye sockets where the eyes should have been. How do you deal with something so horrible? I often wondered why the specter chose that particular way to play its evil game with him. For years, I found myself uncomfortable talking about the clown. John Zaffis had explained to me that it actually was more common than you would think. To understand this notion, you have to put yourself into the shoes of a child again. Once you do that, it becomes crystal clear why it chose the clown.

The high points left me wondering why they chose that particular moment to portray. The depiction of my dad as an old man, with white hair, got a laugh from the whole family and my mother quickly piped in, "If they decide to show me as some white-haired old lady, I am going to beat you." She was looking directly at me and we all laughed some more, but there was a moment of fear when I had the thought they might just do it. Although it was a joke, there was part of me that felt responsible for how my family was portrayed. I wanted the show to reveal how close we all were. How if one of us had a problem, we all had that problem, until it was solved. I wanted the show to portray how loving my parents were and, at that moment, how young and vibrant they were, as well. But instead, the show characterized my father as an old, white-haired man worried about a fuse box.

Don't get me wrong. I think they did an excellent job of telling the story, in 48 minutes, for a general audience. I had to commend them on how they transformed what was a very R-rated story for a family who was sitting down in their living room for a night of television. But it left me feeling as if our lives had just gotten a whitewash. Much of the story went untold. It left me with mixed feelings.

The kids were excited when the show was over. They had just been on television. For a kid, that was a huge deal. Later, Matthew would tell me he was a superstar at school because of the show and later, when we toured on a national level, it solidified his status. That was a big relief for me, because in the back of my mind I always worried the outcome would be different, causing them to be outcasts among their peers. Michael was never too thrilled with the show. He was not part of it because he was never really comfortable enough to tell his version of events. To this day, I do not discuss Michael and his experiences with anyone because of that reason. What happened to him is his to choose to handle anyway he wants to. The attention and questions that came after the show bothered him a lot. I was told that when he was asked about it, he would tell the questioner to ask his brother or sister. I always felt a little guilty about that. I wish I could have made it go away for him. I wish I could have done so for all of us.

It was fairly late for a school night when we got home. The kids jumped out of the van and ran for the door as soon as I parked. We were laughing and joking around on the way to the front door. Sitting on the porch, waiting for us, was another package that I simply picked up and threw into the trash can, without letting it break into the good night we were having. It was as if it wasn't even there. We went into the house, where we began our nightly routines. Settling into the normal routine that night, after the premiere, took some doing on all of our parts. The kids seemed overly hyper, and Michael had waited until the last minute to tell me he had an English research paper due the next day. In true Michael fashion, he had known about this paper for over a month. Now, pulling a topic out of your ass for a research paper after a long day is not always the easiest thing to do, but when last-minute duty calls, you have no choice but to do just that. I sat on the couch thinking, with Michael constantly questioning me, "Did you come up with something yet?" I was trying my best to come up with some sort of topic that we could write about together quickly, without too much trouble. I looked over at the TV stand and inspiration hit when I saw the DVD case sitting there for Oliver Stone's *JFK*. A perfect topic: "*The Assassination of a President.*"

The research required us to watch all of the "Special Features" on the Special Edition DVD, which also gave me some time to just kick back and relax. Then the writing of the paper started, directly on the computer as we wrote it, editing it in the process. It took us about two hours to get it done and it was extremely late when we finished. "Thanks, Dad, I love you," Michael said, as he proudly walked into his bedroom with his paper in his hands. Disaster had been avoided once more, and life was back on track. The sun would rise tomorrow, and things would go on. Well, when you're a kid and you have a paper due the next morning that you haven't even started, it does seem like Armageddon. And if anyone is going to judge me for helping him write it, then let it be God, because those who would point fingers obviously have never had school-aged children.

I turned out all of the lights and I headed to bed. Just before I was about to close my eyes, I remembered the incident in the shower that morning; now I was awake to face what remained of the night alert and alone.

Chapter 18

Flashback, 1985

It was Christmas Eve, 1985. Cafe Balaban's in the Central West End of St. Louis. I was there with a friend and my current girlfriend at the time. This one I thought I loved, boy - did I think I was in love with her. My first true love. Your first love is always something that you remember, and for some, the one you wish you could forget. Her name was Eve. To me she was a goddess, with jet black hair that she kept cropped short. She was a model from Chicago who looked like she stepped off a Vargas print. Eve, the eternal woman. Eve, dressed in black, with a black, gold-tipped cigarette hanging from her mouth. Her eyes looking over the top of her very expensive Wayfarer sunglasses; everything had to be in place. Everything always matched, and I hate to admit it now, but even I matched. I was no more or less than an accessory. I was just as much an accessory to Eve as she was the trophy on my arm. We made a fucking perfect pair of shallow individuals.

"Excuse me," I said, standing up to head to the restroom.

"Where are you going?" Eve snapped at me, with a look of disdain on her face.

"I was excusing myself to the fucking restroom, without actually saying something unpleasant, if that is okay with you. But now that you have forced me to say it, I might as well go ahead and say I am going to take a piss." This caused Eve's friend Alexis, who was with us, to giggle. Eve shot her an instant glare and she immediately quieted down.

"Well, why not just say so to begin

with? You don't have to make a fucking scene."
It was a no-win situation. I knew if I had gone
the other way, she would have been mortified
as well. An accessory is obviously not
supposed to have bodily functions, at least
ones that are not fun and for pleasure.

I stumbled my way to the bathroom, a
little blurry from the Tanqueray I had already
consumed. Now Balaban's was one of those
classy eighties sort of places that you went to
when you wanted to be seen. The food was
overpriced and so were the drinks. Eve would
not have it any other way. She was a snob
when it came to where we went. She was not
the type of girl you would find in a Golden
Corral on a Saturday night. I stumbled into the
bathroom and stood there looking in the mirror.
I was dressed in an oversized, black tuxedo
jacket from the forties, the coolest baggy pants,
and wing-tip shoes. I had a fresh haircut, with
just enough spike to it. I looked like a million
fucking bucks, but I felt like complete hell. I
was in complete hell. Was this where life was
headed for me, I wondered, as I examined
myself in the mirror? I had to make sure I was
neat and everything was in place. I didn't really
have to take a piss. I just needed to take a
moment to get away from Eve's endless,
narcissistic chatter. "Here Comes Santa
Claus," was quietly playing in the background
as I continued to look into the mirror. It was
Christmas Eve, and I should have been home
with my family. What in the hell was I doing
here? I was miserable.

The door to the bathroom swung open,
and in walked a Santa Claus who stood beside
me in the next mirror. Just the sight of him
reminded me that it was Christmas, and there
was a brief hope that everything was going to
work out. Just the sight of him made me want

to be home with my mom and my dad and my family. It was Christmas in the city and anything could happen, I told myself. I knew I was asking for a miracle, but miracles usually don't come for shallow people.

"Merry Christmas, Santa," I said, looking at the jolly old elf standing next to me.

"Merry Christmas to you, too. Hey, you look like you could use a little gift from old Santa," he said, smiling.

"I don't think much could cheer me up right now, Santa. Woman troubles, you know?" I said to him, smiling because of his gesture.

"I bet I have something to put you right back into the Christmas spirit," he said with a chuckle, putting his hand into a pocket of his velvety-red suit. Santa took a mirror and a razor out of that pocket and began cutting and making lines of coke on the mirror.

"Hey, kid, want to snort a few lines of coke with ole Santa? A little Christmas toot?" Santa asked, laughing beneath his beard. I was shocked. I looked at him with a frown on my face and headed for the door. It was too much to take. "Merry fucking Christmas to you, too," I heard Santa say as the door shut behind me.

I tried to compose myself, but I couldn't. I needed to get out. I needed to get out of there. I had stepped into Christmas hell and it was time to climb my way out of the hole. I went to the table and grabbed my coat. I needed some air. I needed to go. I needed to get some place where people weren't fake— somewhere without a coke-snorting Santa Claus and gold-tipped smokes. I needed to get somewhere that was real. I needed to go home.

"Where do you think you are going?" Eve asked, shocked.

"Anywhere but here," I said as I went out the door, putting my coat on to face the cold. I filled my lungs with the cold night air. It felt good.

"Will you wait one fucking minute!" It was Eve, her voice coming from behind me. We were standing there at an intersection on Euclid Avenue, and we were about to have it out.

"What is your problem, Steven?" she demanded.

"What is my problem, Eve? I don't know who I fucking am anymore. I don't dress like me. I don't talk like me. I don't walk like me. Hell, Eve, I don't even fuck like me anymore. I don't know who I am. I am this man that you have invented and I've got to tell you, I cannot stand myself when I look in the mirror anymore. It is Christmas Eve and we should be with our families, home where people don't care what we look like and what we do, but where are we? We are where you think we should be seen. My God, I just had Santa Claus - Santa-fucking-Claus - ask me if I would snort a few lines of coke with him." I tried to calm myself down, but I took one look at her face, and I knew where this was headed and what I must do. "Eve, I am at rock bottom, and I don't think I'm going to make it back in one piece. I love you, I do, but for the life of me I cannot stand you. And I don't think you even know me."

I thought she was going to try to rip my head off my shoulders by the way she was looking at me. Well, there it was. It was the final straw. That was all that needed to be said. It looked like I would be spending Christmas with my family after all. Eve could not stand the thought of rejection, and what I had just said to her I knew she would consider a rejection, and it was. I loved her, but I needed her out of my life. I needed her to go away.

She walked away from me, leaving me standing alone in that intersection, under a pair of silver bells. It had to look like a scene out of a modern version of It's a Wonderful Life. When I should have been heartbroken and destroyed, I was happy. Santa walked out of the restaurant and looked over at me and waved. I waved back and then I headed to my car, leaving Eve behind. I could hear "O Holy Night" in the distance. It was over, and I was going home.

Thanksgiving 2006

It was a few days before Thanksgiving and things were going well, which was surprisingly nice, considering my track record with past holidays. I had taken a job as a security guard in a local shopping mall, leaving my other job behind. I needed a change of pace, something new. The job required long hours due to the upcoming holiday. It was actually kind of refreshing because I would walk the whole length of the mall, over and over again. It was a mile all the way around, so I knew I was getting some great exercise. But I was tired. It was a daily grind and they would keep track of you electronically, because you were required to "wand in" at different check points. There were times throughout my shift that were dull and boring, and other moments of pure adrenaline.

I usually worked with an ex-cop who was funny, and his stories would occupy those dull moments. We were becoming very good friends. He was a professional kickboxer who received his training from Chuck Norris, the actor. His hands and feet were considered lethal weapons. If he was ever arrested, they would not only cuff his hands but also shackle his feet. On a few occasions, I got to see his skills in action. It was amazing what he could do.

My day off was the Monday before Thanksgiving, and I felt pretty good. My plan was to have a nice, quiet night at home with the kids—maybe rent a few movies and that sort of thing. Lydia came into the house and immediately went into her room. She seemed to be in a mood, but I didn't think much of it.

The phone rang; it was my mother. "Steven, I found a note Lydia wrote. I didn't go looking for it or anything. I found it on the floor. She must have dropped it out of her purse or something like that." I could tell by the sound of her voice something serious was going on.

"A note?" I asked.

"Yes," she replied, with a serious tone.

"What did it say?" I had to know. I never made it a habit of looking through their things, and I know my mom and she wasn't that type, either. But when she found it, she opened it to see what it was and there you go.

"She is planning to marry her boyfriend, Bill." Well, I breathed a sigh of relief. Of course she was. All girls have that fantasy about getting married. "She is planning on marrying him the day after she graduates," my mom said, very worried. Now that was a different story. Lydia was going to college. We had already picked a college for her, about four hours from home.

"What are you talking about? Lydia is going away to college," I replied, now very worried myself.

"They are planning on getting married and she is not going." I heard the crack in my mother's voice and I knew she was near tears.

"Let me get off the phone and see what is going on. I'll call you back." I hung up the phone and took a few minutes to gather my thoughts.

I called Lydia into the living room. She walked in with a look of defiance on her face. She knew what we were going to talk about, and she already had planned her course of action. This was a moment I completely handled the wrong way. I should have just kept my mouth shut and waited it all out, but then again, I couldn't let her give away her future because of a boy.

"I already know what you are going to say and there is nothing you can do about this, so you might as well save your breath," she came at me, defensively, and did not even give me a chance to talk with her first.

"You are way too young and have too bright of a future for this, Lydia," I snapped back at her.

"Well, I am marrying him, Dad, and there is nothing you can do about it, so don't even think you can try," she snapped right back at me.

"I did not raise you to ruin your life this way. This is not like you. What about all of your plans?" This went back and forth for about 15 minutes, and then she turned and headed down the hall, saying, "I am marrying him and you can't stop me."

There. She had said it. A few moments later she came rushing into the living room with her clothes in her hand. She did not say anything. "If you go out that door, you will not come back. I will not live my life constantly worried about you leaving. I just can't do it," I said with my voice trembling. She went out the door and slammed it behind her. I sat there wanting to run after her and remind her that she was my princess. I wanted to tell her how much I loved her and that I didn't want her to grow up so fast. I wanted to stop her, but all I could get out was a whispered, "I love you, princess."

She was gone, running down the street with her clothes in her hand to the waiting boyfriend's car around the corner at the bottom of the hill. My heart instantly broke. I never really understood what that meant, until that moment. I could not breathe. I could not speak. I could not move. She was gone and there was no way to stop her from going. She was gone way too soon. Why did it have to happen so fast? I gave her everything I could. I stood by her in the best way a father could. Where was the helpless, innocent child I held in my arms? This was not the way this was to happen. She was to leave to go to college and come home on holidays. She was to have a great career, and only then would she marry and have a family. Marriage was to be the last thing on the list. She was not to run out my door, at 18, to a waiting boy, with her clothes in her hand. She was making life so hard on herself this way. I wanted to scream. I wanted to die. This was too much for me to handle. I raised her to be strong-willed, and in the end it turned against me.

I sat there for what could have been an hour or more, thinking. Michael came through the door, took one look at me, and asked me what was wrong. I struggled to get the words out, "Your sister is gone. She left this afternoon." Michael had a shocked look on his face as he listened, and asked, "She is not coming back?" That is the moment I completely broke down. It was the worst day of my life.

Thanksgiving came, and I hoped and prayed she would show up at Grandma's, where we always went for holidays. She never came. I walked around in a fog all day long. Every time the door would open, or the phone would ring, I would jump. She never showed up. No word, nothing. One thing we, as a family, always agreed upon was that no matter what we would always be together on holidays. It did not matter where we were or what we were doing. If it was a holiday, we were together. How could she forget our family promise? Looking back, I realized she was scared at the reaction she would get if she did show up. The whole day left me feeling more like a failure as a father.

That night when we got home, there was another can with the usual contents sitting on the porch. I lost it. I started screaming and yelling and I threw the can across the yard, screaming, "If you are watching me, you son of a bitch, come on out and we will handle this now. Me and you, motherfucker!" I screamed and I yelled until I could scream no more. Then I slammed into the house. The phone instantly rang, but when I picked it up, there was nothing but heavy breathing on the other end. I ripped the phone, cord and all, from its connection, and threw it against the wall. Then I stomped down the hallway, leaving the boys with their mouths wide open, as I slammed my bedroom door.

It was a good thing we had another phone, and when I woke up, it was ringing. I answered it to find out I was late for work. "Dammit," I said as I jumped out of the bed, throwing my clothes on as I headed out the door. I drove like a maniac to get there. When I arrived, the mall was packed. I knew it was going to be a horrible day.

About halfway through my shift, my friend the ex-cop and I got a call from a shoe store about a lady who had just stolen something from the store. They saw her take something, but they weren't exactly sure what it was. They just saw her put it into her purse. We got the description of the lady and headed out into the mall to find her. We spotted her about eight stores down.

The ex-cop walked up to her and barely got out the words, "Excuse me," when she took off running. We ran after her. She headed out the front doors into the parking lot. There, the ex-cop took over and caught up to her. He slammed her to the ground, cuffing her behind her back. She was crying as we walked back in and headed to the store. She was saying something about how her baby needed something she could not afford. When we got back, a police officer was already there to meet us. When they emptied her purse there was a pair of tennis shoes in a baby size. You could tell from the size of the shoes we were dealing with a mother of a two-year-old or so. They asked the manager if the store would like to press charges and the manager did not hesitate with the answer, "Yes."

The whole incident did not sit well with me at all. I can understand the importance of having a strict shoplifting policy, but in this case, she was desperate. Why couldn't they see that? It was a desperate act, carried out in desperation. I knew deep down that if I needed something like shoes or food for my kids, I would have done the same. You would be amazed at what you would do for your children. They could have had the insight to see it as well, but instead they walked her away in cuffs. All of a sudden, my job was not exactly the way I imagined it would be. I knew there would be shoplifters, or fights to break up, but witnessing sadness and desperation was not on the list.

She was going to jail for nothing more than a pair of baby's shoes. How senseless and heartbreaking was that? Now, I know you could come up with a lot of reasons for the justification of her arrest, and so could I, but the fact remains she was in trouble and was pushed to a point where she felt she had no other choice. She had never done anything like this before because when they pulled her record, it was clean. It made me sick—and it still does—that I participated in ruining her life, because of her desperation and a pair of baby's shoes.

The world is a tough place to live. The dropping economy was forcing people who would never dream of doing anything wrong to turn into criminals out of sheer desperation. Do you know what it would be like on Christmas morning to have a child and have to tell them you had nothing for them? The social pressure the holiday puts on struggling parents can be immense. Think of how many times we are confronted with the picture of the happy, perfect family during the holiday season? You see them gathered around tables in front of feasts. You see them gathered around Christmas trees, handing out presents. You see the images of children, happy and excited. You don't see the other side of it. You don't see the family that is having a bad time of it, trying to struggle to make things happen out of nothing. I love hearing the phrase "remember the reason for the season." These families cannot even afford the luxury of going to church, because they might not have the clothes to wear or the shoes to put on their child's feet. Now, you tell me how you would react if you saw this type of family walking down the aisle of your church on Christmas morning? Would you greet them? Would you accept them? Be honest with yourself, because facing your own actions is the only way you can change your reactions. What about a bum? A drunken bum who decided to come in and get out of the cold, and it happened to be at your Christmas service? I would like to think I would be open and caring. But do you really know until it happens? There was that phrase a few years back that asked, "What would Jesus do?" I have seen some people wearing those bracelets and exhibiting the most horrible behavior. I saw a young man once in the movies who was loud and obnoxious. He was making fun of people who entered. What did that saying on the bracelet really mean to him? Or was he just wearing it because it was the current thing to do? Compassion and understanding is not a religion. It is a way of life. A way we should all behave, no matter what we believe or what time of the year it is. I learned this from my father, whom I have seen give someone money for food or gas, without question. He did it without hesitation or thought, and he never would talk or brag about it afterward. He did it and it was done. I knew what my parents' reaction was going to be when I told them what had happened at work that day. And I was ashamed when I told them, because I did nothing to stop it from happening. I could have offered to pay for the shoes. Or I could have suggested they let her go with a warning. Instead, I stayed quiet. I did nothing.

December 2006

December 21, 2006, started out as a pretty good day. I got up and got ready for work. The boys were going to stay home that day. The day before, they had put up the

Christmas tree by themselves. It looked God-awful. They thought the last thing you did was put the lights on. So the tree actually had the look that it had been wrapped in barbed wire when the lights were off. This was one of the most horrible, yet memorable, Christmas trees I have ever seen. I looked at it on my way out the door and I laughed to myself. I went to work and when I got there, it wasn't very busy. I was enjoying the walk around the mall, talking to different people I met along the way. It was a good day and for a moment I had forgotten all of my problems. About two hours into my shift, I got a call from the office to call home. I was told that there was an emergency.

I hurried downstairs to the phone and I called home. Michael answered the phone, "There is nothing to worry about, Dad. The fire guys are here now and they just need your insurance information." I listened to what he had said, but all I heard was "fire guys" and "insurance information" and I knew that something serious had just happened.

"I am on my way home," I said. Without even listening to his response, I hung up the phone and headed out the door for home.

When I got there, the firefighters were already gone. Both of the boys met me at the car when I pulled into the driveway. "It really isn't that bad," Matthew was saying, following me as I headed for the door. My kitchen had caught on fire. The cabinets were charred black and the ceiling, where the fire had tried to spread, was a dark, smoky black and the house smelled of burned . . . well, everything.

"What happened?" I asked as I surveyed the damage.

"I was cooking French fries like they do at McDonald's, when some girl I knew came to the door," said Matthew, sheepishly. "I was standing in the door talking to her and then she told me, 'There is a lot of smoke behind you. It looks like you might be burning something.' Well, I turned around and there was smoke everywhere, man. I looked and I could see flames in the kitchen shooting up to the ceiling. So I tried to put some flour on it and it just got worse. Then I started throwing water on it from the sink. While I was doing that, Michael called the fire guys and they were here in no time, but lucky me, I had already put the fire out. They told me what a good job I did and everything," he said, trying to convince me he was a hero in the situation.

I took a deep breath and then I spoke, "Everything is not all right. You could have burned down the house and you could have killed yourself and your brother in the process."

He looked at me with big eyes and replied, "But that didn't happen, Dad. They said if I had not thought to put it out, the house would have been a goner." I could not believe he was going to justify this to me. I could not believe what I was hearing.

I looked at my burned and charred kitchen, and then I turned again to speak with him, "You burned down my fucking kitchen. Do you not see it for yourself? Because if you need me to give you the damn grand tour I will be more than happy to do it, but my suggestion to you right now is to run and I mean run and find a fucking place to hide." He looked at me with shock because I was not getting his point and he obviously was not getting mine, because I had to say once more, "Run and fucking hide. Do you hear me?" He started to head outside and I stopped him, "Not outside. You are grounded for the rest of your damned days. I think going to your room and shutting the door might be a better idea, because that way I do not have to drag your ass back inside." He went to his room and shut the door, and I was left in silence to look at the damage. I just sat down on the couch because at the moment there was not much else I could do.

Saturday night, the night before Christmas Eve, came quickly. My friend Bill and I were booked at a bar in Illinois to do an event for a no-kill animal shelter. The event was going to have a Misfits tribute, as well as pole dancers. We knew the crowd was going to be somewhat Goth even before we got there. We had put together a great presentation, filled with plenty of evidence and footage. It was exciting to do something in front of a young crowd. We were on at about eight in the evening, and it went great. The crowd was full of questions and interest. I have spoken to a lot of crowds in my career, but this was probably one of the best. We got a beer from the bar after we were done and sat down to watch the remaining acts.

Christmas Eve came and there was no stopping it. I had finished my Christmas shopping and I was on my way home. I was not sure if Lydia was coming home for Christmas Eve or not. But when I got home, the boys told me she had called and was coming. I was a little nervous, but I could not wait to see her. It was the longest time we had ever been apart. She came in that night and headed for the kitchen. She laughed when she saw the burned kitchen and commented on how the house still had that charred smell— and it did. I was not sure how long it would take me to get it all cleaned up and to get that smell gone. Most likely longer than it took me to clean the house after Matthew chased his brother and sister through it with a bag full of powdered Ajax swinging in the air. Have you ever cleaned Ajax up off of everything you own? Not an easy thing to do at all. You can't get it wet or it becomes a bigger mess, and this particular kind of Ajax had bleach in it. So, needless to say, if you did get it wet on the carpet, it was going to be ugly. I imagined that cleaning the kitchen was going to be a longer process than the Ajax incident, but at the moment, I had been working so many hours, it was impossible to get to even begin it at that moment. So, Lydia got almost the same impact upon seeing the kitchen as I had.

It was a good night. She stayed for a couple hours and then she was gone again. I found out she lived with her boyfriend's sister, in her basement. I was glad she was someplace safe; however, I was angry with the both of them for harboring her. This was a woman who had children of her own. I wondered what she would do if this was one of her children. Then I thought about it and decided she would be glad her child had someplace to go. I had taken many kids in off the street; I still do. I provide them a place to stay. I would not be in my right mind to let a kid sleep somewhere like the park or in a car. I felt this was God's way of paying me back for all of that, maybe? But I was not going to show it. I was still going to make her think I did not approve; in the hope it would make her come home and do the things she needed to get done to prepare for her life. I know many people had to think I was the biggest asshole to walk the earth, but when it came to the welfare of my child, I didn't care about the opinion of others. That night went by without any arguments. I was just so happy to see her, but when she walked out the door to leave, I felt empty again. I never knew it was going to be so hard to let go. But I wasn't letting go completely until I knew she was going to be safe.

Also, this boyfriend of hers needed to do the right thing by her.

Lydia also came to my parents' house for Christmas. It was okay. Everything was going just fine. She came and she left. My mother was telling me I had to let Lydia go as she walked out the door. I still was ready to fight for her. It is so hard to explain. It's not a feeling I have felt before or since. That feeling that she was in some kind of danger—even though she was safe. The difference was, she was not home, safe under my roof, and I missed her so much. I had never missed someone so much in my life. We were way too close for this. This did not make sense to me. Why would she do this? Did she not love me anymore? Did I do something wrong? The questions just kept churning around and around in my head. Why did this happen? I was being forced to let her go. She did not cut the apron strings. She had ripped them out.

It was a few days after Christmas when I got a message from some lady I had never heard of before, directing me to this blog site. There was something there she wanted me to read. I went to the site and I could not believe what I was reading. There, on the blog, was post after post from my stalker, and he was talking about me and my family.

December 24, 2006

"I was at an event where Steven LaChance was last night. I was so close to him I could have stabbed or shot him in the back and no one would have ever known. He would have been long gone before anyone knew what had happened."

December 26, 2006

"I know where Steven LaChance lives in Union, Missouri, and I know where his kids go to school. I want to get one of the kids and kidnap them. I think the daughter would be best. I would like to capture her and put her through a Forensic Psychological Interrogation to try to break her down. We can discuss this more when we all meet on January 29. Just tell me what to do and I will move forward with it."

I e-mailed the woman and asked her about what they were planning on January 29. That is when she told me they were gathering at some bed and breakfast to discuss how to handle me. Handle me? Who? That is when she started giving names, and at the head of the list was a woman I knew all too well. It was the woman who Helen had asked not to come back to the Screaming House, because she was harassing Kelly and spreading lies about her. But to go this far? This seemed ridiculous to me. It wasn't until I started doing research on the man who had been harassing us. Research revealed to us that the man had worked for the FBI and that he was also in the military at some point, as well. There were also big gaps in his life that could not be fled in by research. Regardless, this guy did have the knowledge and ability to pull off some pretty bad stuff. Then I looked up Forensic Psychological Interrogation. That was the moment I knew I needed some help, and if the police were not going to give it to me, then I was going to have to find it for myself.

Article after article came up with same thing. These articles talked about practices that involved detention and psychological or physical pressures that blurred into torture. The articles also mentioned the CIA and prisoners at Guantanamo Bay. That was enough for me.

I knew at that moment I could not take the chance. I was actually grateful that Lydia was not living at home and that maybe this nut did not know where she was living. I called her immediately and told her that she needed to keep a very low profile. She asked me why and I had to tell her why. I could hear in her voice that she was scared, and I tried to act as calm as I could about it, but the truth is, when someone is threatening your children—I don't care how old they are—the guard goes up and the guns come out.

The first thing I did was make a public announcement about what was happening. I did this for a few reasons. I wanted some type of record out there in case anything happened to any of us. I also wanted the stalker to know I was on to him and that I was ready to turn the tables on him. I talked to a friend of mine, and he collected all the research he needed on this guy—and the process was started. I also got myself a bodyguard to accompany me every time I went out in public. The ex-cop, with the lethal feet and hands, was the perfect choice for a bodyguard. It did not take long to get a description of the stalker from my friend. Someone had made a visit to him, and when he answered the door, they said his full name and added, "We now know where you live." My e-mail friend was able to come up with the location of the bed and breakfast and I immediately put the information out to the paranormal community. It was going to be very hard for them to meet when the paranormal community knew the location, time, and purpose of the gathering. I had covered all bases.

January was a long month. I called in sick one day in January with the flu. All of us had it at the same time. If I had not called in that night, I would have had to handle a call where a woman's leg was cut off when a car hit her in the parking lot. My friend, the ex-cop, answered the call that would have been meant for me. I just couldn't go back there. It was too much to even consider. I could not have made it through something like that, and I understood at that moment that I was in the wrong kind of profession. I left the job and started interviewing for a management position with a convenience store and gas station. I got the job and it paid well. So, I found myself driving back and forth through the snow and the ice, which seemed to continually fall that year.

During that time, my friend Bill and I also met three people who were going to help change my life. The Booth Brothers were twin brothers from England who had made a documentary called Spooked. It was critically acknowledged and received a warm reception on the Syfy Channel. The main plot revolved around Keith Age, who would later star in the film they were getting ready to make called Children of the Grave. The Booth Brothers and Keith Age had seen a photo that one of our team members, Tom Halstead, had taken of the shadow people of Zombie Road. They also heard about the stories of the things we had experienced, down that dark and deserted road. For five miles this road had been closed off to traffic and went down through the thickest of woods you could imagine. It was also very dangerous. They wanted us to take them down to Zombie Road for their new film. Well, of course when someone comes to you and asks you if they could put your work on film, you don't usually say no. It was a way for us to show the world some of the things we had accomplished.

We would have these long phone meetings discussing exactly what we were going to do and how we were going to film it. These meetings were so detailed we even discussed what we would wear. Not one aspect was overlooked in those conversations. Everything was planned out, completely. The only missing item was whether the paranormal activities were going to perform on film or not. That was not something we could plan. In the course of our conversations, one of our team members came up with a haunted building that had been used for many different things during the years. One of those things was an orphanage. The building was called the Pythian Castle and was currently being used for weddings and banquets. It was also put on the list for filming. It was decided we would meet at the haunted hotel in Eureka Springs, Arkansas, where a paranormal convention was being held at the beginning of March 2007.

Chapter 19

February 2007

The last week in February was rough. I had not seen Lydia since Christmas, and for the most part I did not talk to her either. Most of the time when we would talk, we would fight because I was doing everything I could to have her reconsider marriage and go away to college instead. She wasn't having any of it and she started planning a wedding. She was going to get married in June, right after she graduated, right out of the frying pan and into the fire. She would not listen to me. Her response was "You don't like my boyfriend." That was far from the truth. The fact was, I really did not know her boyfriend because she rarely gave me the chance to get to know him. She called me an education snob because all I wanted to do was to discuss her college plans with her. I was not against her having a boyfriend. I even told her they could still see each other while she went to school. There was nothing wrong with a long engagement; it happens all the time. If it was meant to be, it would be meant to be - four years down the road. She would have nothing to do with the idea or even consider it. She was 18, and I had no clue what I was talking about in her mind. She was pushing her independence and in doing so, to her satisfaction, she was pushing me away.

One night, after a huge blow-up with her, I went to stand up and I could hardly walk. My abdomen was swollen, and it hurt like hell. I drove to the emergency room with Matthew in tow. All I knew was that I was hurting. I was not completely sure why. They ran tests and x-rays, the whole routine. The end result was that the Crohn's disease I had when I was younger had come out of remission - due to severe stress. There was so much swelling in my abdomen that it was pressing on my spinal column; I was barely able to walk. I was immediately given pain medication and a strong round of steroids, as well as another medication to force the disease back into remission. I was completely out of service for the next four days. We were only a week away from filming *Children of the Grave*.

The medications worked quickly, and within four days I was up and walking with no problem. The steroids had reduced the swelling, and it was no longer pushing onto my spinal column. I wanted to hide. I did not want to see anyone or talk to anyone. However, I needed to be there for the filming. I had given my word and, in this business, sometimes your word is the only thing that matters. I was very ill. It amazes me how stress will attack the body and shut it down. I had just been through too much, too quickly - and it took its toll on me.

The Saturday before filming started, Matthew and I went out to get our wardrobe for the film. We had all decided to dress in black fatigues and combat boots. Bill and I were going to wear black berets. It was a great idea, because we would need to carry everything, we needed with us. Zombie Road was going to be a very long walk into the middle of nowhere, and we needed to be able to have everything with us for the hike.

In the years that followed, I have often been asked about our clothing choice and I would always reply, "I don't know what you wear in the woods, but we Missouri boys know how to do it right." It amazes me still today what an influence we had on people with our clothing choice. You still see forms of it all of the time with different groups. It was the inspiration for the name change, from Missouri Paranormal Research to the Paranormal Task Force. Even before filming, we had already discussed how and when to change the name. Our target was going to be May for the change, and the opening of new departments in our group. There was actually a lot to do to make this change possible, and we worked very hard to make it a reality. We were the Paranormal Task Force now, and we dressed the part. I had mixed feelings, at first, about the name change. It felt strange to give up the name we had already been working under for three years. Now, when I look back, it was one of the best moves we ever made. And in the end, it would turn out to be my last move with the group before I left.

Chapter 20

March 2007

We started the trek down Zombie Road late in the evening of March 11, 2007, with cameras in tow. There is a psychological impact the road has on you when you start at the top and work your way down, farther and farther into the darkness below. You descend away from civilization, away from anyone who could hear you scream. You are completely on your own, isolated. The bluffs from the Meramec River rise up around you like castle walls. The road breaks apart in spots, and you have to jump across high ravines to make it to the other side. You can't run, because if you do, you are likely to lose the road in front of you or find yourself falling 20 feet down a dark ravine. Help will not come, and the coyotes will be more likely to find you before anyone knows that you are missing.

It had already been a very long day of shooting at the bottom of the road. With more than a few Red Bulls in our systems, we stood at the top of the road and gathered our team to make our way down. We were making sure all of our equipment was working. All of the batteries were charged, and everyone had a flashlight of some sort. You could feel the excitement in the group. Our goal was to film the shadow people. There was this feeling of not knowing if we were actually going to meet that goal or not.

Keith Age and the Booth Brothers had selected us because of the photos of things we had captured on the road in the past. Tom Halstead had more riding on this than anyone because it was his photo of the shadow people that had brought all of us to the road that night. His reputation was riding on this journey. There were months of planning for this one night at this location. It was all riding on capturing film evidence of the shadow people of Zombie Road.

We began our journey from the top of the road and we were not very far in when we heard people screaming at us through the woods. The locals had heard we were there and what we were doing. On the road in front of us was written: DEAD PEOPLE THIS WAY.

There was a large arrow at the end of the phrase, pointing straight down into the darkness. We all were a little nervous. I have heard Christopher Booth talk about this moment on more than one occasion. He always describes this moment as a The Hills Have Eyes moment, and he was exactly right. We knew of the horrible things that had happened on the road in the past. We knew of the satanic worship and sacrifices that had been made on the road before. And here we were, with these faceless voices screaming at us in the darkness, knowing full well we could be in serious danger.

"Bring lots of guns," a police officer had told us earlier in the day. Most people would have stopped at that point, but we didn't. We were not going to let some vigilante group of locals stop us from filming what could be the best evidence of shadow people ever caught on fi lm. Bill took the lead, and I backed up the group at the rear. My feeling was that if we were going to be attacked, they would come from behind and they would have to get through me. Also, I had always been afraid we would lose someone in the darkness of the road. I could not imagine what would happen to the person that simply walked away from the group and got lost on the road at night, by themselves. We were armed with every type of camera you could think of, along with a thermal camera as well. Keith Age was following Bill, and behind him was Phillip Booth with a camera, filming the whole scene. Christopher Booth was in the back of the group with me. We were both filming with handheld cameras. We were two miles down the road when the voices we heard became way off in the distance and eventually disappeared. The bluffs were beginning to rise around us, making it impossible for anyone to attack us from any angle except the rear. But there was no one there. Not a sound.

Keith, who was filming with the thermal camera, instantly halted the group. He saw, in the thermal camera's view panel, the eyes of a pack of coyotes. We were surrounded. You could hear them surrounding us in the woods and above the bluffs. Worst of all, you could see their eyes. "Now, I want everyone to stay tight. We have a group of coyotes surrounding us," Keith warned.

"Coyotes, mate? Is that something we need to be concerned with?" Christopher began quizzing Keith on the coyote situation, immediately.

"Hell yes, we need to be concerned. They usually go for the weakest in the group, and I think the weakest in this group would be the Englishman from LA, so you better stay with the group, Chris," Keith said, half joking and half serious.

Christopher looked at me, and I could not tell if he was frightened or excited. He finally spoke up, nervously, "I would like to see the fucking Ghost Hunters bunch do this one." Then we started to laugh.

Farther down the road we went. The

road in front of us would break apart, and in the space where the road had broken apart was a 20-foot drop - straight down into the ravine below. The first person had to jump across the break, and then we would hold the hands of the others, one by one, and pull them to the other side. I remember one moment when Philip lost his footing and I thought for sure he was headed down the ravine, into the darkness below. But at the last moment, Keith grabbed him and pulled him to the other side. The road began to level off as we worked our way down.

We finally made it to the area where the shadow people had been spotted time and time again. The group was moving very slowly, pausing at moments to see what they were getting on thermal. During one of these pauses, I looked at Christopher and all of a sudden it became very cold. I could see his breath and I could see mine as well.

"Steven, it is getting fucking cold," he said, while filming. We turned around behind us, and there, in both of our cameras, was a huge, rolling, black mass that covered the road. "Do you see it?" Christopher asked. "Yes," I answered. I could see it and it was moving very slowly. We could not have been more than six feet away from it. We both stood there, filming. We were both amazed at what we were capturing. Once it had moved on, we moved to catch up with the group again. Suddenly Keith motioned for us to stop, and that is when it happened.

I have been asked about this moment over and over again through the years. It was very cold and the air around us had a strange feeling to it, almost like something was sucking the air right out of the atmosphere. Then, they started to step out from behind the trees. We had found the shadow people of Zombie Road.

There must have been 15 to 20 of them. They made no move toward us. They just stood there and observed us, as we observed them. Some of us spoke things, in exclamation. Some were just quiet and watched as they slowly faded into nothingness. We had met our objective. We were thrilled, and there were other things to come our way that night, but after that moment, nothing would compare. I can remember walking out of the woods that night, thinking we were all changed by the event. How could you not be? We got a glimpse of the "other side." Not only that, but we had captured it on film. The group was quiet as we walked out of the woods in the early morning. Each and every one of us knew we had seen and filmed something that had never been captured before. We felt accomplished, but at the same time, changed and humbled. No words can describe the feelings we felt that early morning in 2007. We went back to the hotel where Keith and the twins were staying and had a good hard shot of Jack to celebrate our accomplishment.

I look back at the moment years before, when I challenged Bill to disprove the legend of Zombie Road. Had I not made that suggestion, we would have never filmed the shadows we caught that night. It is funny how one simple decision can lead you into something great. My theory is that the shadow children cooperated with us to show the world they existed. And Tom Halstead was on cloud nine, because he had proven to the world the validity of his photo.

I have not been back to Zombie Road since that night. There is no need for me to return there. It was time to move forward and leave Zombie Road and the shadows in the woods behind. We had proven our theories.

Chapter 21

April 2007

I am standing in a crowd of people. I cannot make out what is going on in front of me because the crowd is so large. Everyone is trying to watch something, but I cannot make out what it is. There is loud music playing - something from the Misfits. I feel the crowd push forward and my feet lift off the ground as it surges forward. I can feel the bodies pushing in on me from all sides. It is crushing and I find myself not being able to breathe. I want to just take a big breath of air but the crowd around me keeps pushing. I want to scream, but I have no air to scream and besides, the loud music would just drown me out anyway.

I feel a sharp pain suddenly in my back and I can feel something warm begin to run down it. What was I feeling? I try to raise my arm, but my hand cannot lift due to the surging crowd. I hear someone behind me. A girl begins to scream, and I can feel the crowd separate from me, creating an opening as I fall to the ground. I put my hand to my back and I bring my hand forward to my face. I am bleeding. I am bleeding badly. I try to make it to my feet, but the world seems as if it is closing around me and I fall to my knees. I can hear the screaming of the crowd around me as I collapse. Why am I bleeding? I reach behind me again and I can feel something sticking out from my back. I pull and it comes out into my hand. I bring it forward and I see I am holding a bloody knife. I have been stabbed in the back. I collapse all the way to the floor. I roll over to my back and I can see the faceless figures of the crowd. I know I am dying. I know there is

*no help for me. I lay there watching the
screaming crowd as I start to black out.*

It was the Saturday afternoon before
Easter, and I was lying on the couch taking a
nap. I sat up and I looked around the room.
The boys had made plans with some friends
for the night, and it was just me there, alone. I
could still feel a sharp pain in my back. I
hurriedly reached around and felt where the
pain was coming from and there was nothing
there, nothing more than a muscle spasm. It
was just a remnant of the dream. My phone
rang and I jumped at the sound. It was Bill."
You ready for tonight?" he asked.

"Yeah, I will be there," I said in return.

"Okay then. See you in a little bit." Then
he was gone. We were doing another benefit at
the bar for the no-kill animal shelter, same deal
with the same crowd. I dialed the phone and
my friend the ex-cop picked up on the other
end. "Are we still on for tonight?" I asked.

"We sure are," he responded.

"Okay then, I will see you soon," I said.

Before I could hang up, he added,
"Steven, it's going to be okay. If he shows up,
I'm going to get him. I promise." I was
speechless for a moment. Had it seemed that
apparent to him?

"I sure hope so," I replied, and then I
hung up the phone.

Bill and I had decided to wear our
Children of the Grave fatigues and berets to
the event. It was a great way, we felt, to begin
the process of the name change to the
Paranormal Task Force, instead of Missouri
Paranormal Research. I can remember having
trouble buttoning up the shirt and when I
looked down, I saw my hands were shaking. I
told myself to pull myself together. I was going

with a bodyguard. Not just any bodyguard, but a good one. I knew he would handle any situation that could arise.

The bar was crowded that night. My bodyguard was near me, surveying the crowd as I spoke. He did not seem alarmed and showed no signal that I should be alarmed, either. Things went great. The crowd loved the information and loved the ghost footage we had to show them. There was not enough time to take all of their questions during the presentation. There were simply too many of them. So afterward, I was working the crowd, talking to people and answering the questions I could. Then a loud sound of music drew all of our attention to the stage as the pole dancer came out to dance. The crowd pushed forward as the music grew louder and the show became more intense.

I could see my bodyguard point at me, making a gesture to look behind. He was desperately trying to make his way through the crowd to get to me. I can remember thinking, "Oh my God, the stalker is here." It all went into slow motion, almost like a car wreck. I turned around and saw the faces behind me. "Where is he?" I whispered to myself. And then my gaze fell onto one guy in the crowd, a blond guy. He was smiling at me, and it wasn't a friendly smile. His smile was menacing. It seemed as if the world stopped when I made eye contact with him. I knew the moment I saw him that he was my stalker, and so did my bodyguard, who was forcing his way through the crowd. The stalker immediately tried to leave, but the crowd would not let him get to the door. So, he moved forward past me and headed into the bathroom.

"You stay right here," my bodyguard told me, as he headed into the bathroom. It seemed like hours passed with no one appearing at the bathroom door. I was beginning to worry, and then I saw the blond guy shoot out of the bathroom. He started pushing and shoving people in the crowd to make his way out the door. He looked scared as he pushed, and then I saw my bodyguard walk out of the bathroom door with a smile on his face. He started heading behind the stalker, right out the front door. Later, I found out that he had pinned the stalker to the wall in the bathroom and had a little chat. His words, not mine.

There was another visit made to the stalker's house, and I never knew what took place from there. I knew they had him on the run, judging from his reaction that night in the bar. I never heard from him again. No more little packages and no more threats. He was gone out of my life for good, and in the end that is all that mattered. It was over. When I look back at the whole thing now, I still cannot believe that I could not get any help from the Union police; had I waited for something to happen, I either could be dead or one of my children could have been hurt. It was a huge relief when it was finally over, but it took a long time until I would no longer find myself looking behind my back, looking for him to be there. It changed the person I am today. Sometimes when I am in a crowd of people, I find myself being extremely nervous and more than a little guarded. I have been told before that I seem like a snob or stuck on myself. This is not the case at all. The truth is, I am never quite sure if I can trust the strangers I meet out on the road. It takes a lot for me to go out there to talk and to do the things necessary for an author. I have had some tense moments since then as well. I had this one guy come up to me during a signing and start talking about the executions he did when he was in Vietnam. He got very graphic. Marie was sitting next to me when this happened and then he began to tell me how much he enjoyed it. I thought for sure we were in trouble that day. Eventually he left, and when the signing was over, I made sure we were not being followed. Since then, I have looked at pictures of me in crowds, signing copies of a book. I always look like a deer in the headlights. I am not sure I will ever be comfortable in a crowd setting. When I open a door, I half expect to see a package, or when I am walking through a crowd, I anticipate those steely eyes stalking me from a distance, once more ready to pounce. But if it happens, I will be ready. I am no longer innocent where that is concerned.

May 2007

Lydia's graduation came quickly that year. My princess was graduating from high school. I went, of course, even though things between us were still very tense. I had mixed feelings through it all. As I listened to the scholarship awards, I shook my head knowing that Lydia could have been one of the award winners, if she had not made the decision to get married. I got to talk to her and give her a hug when it was all over, but she seemed so distant from me. I can never remember a time when we were so distant. She was getting married in a month, and the closer it came to the day of the wedding, the more we fought. I just could not bring myself to go. How would I give her away, in front of the eyes of God, when I would be lying that it was okay? I just could not do it. I was against it and I was not going to act any differently. And we were fighting on almost a daily basis.

My dad bought me a pink tie to wear to the wedding with my black suit. I had, for a moment, decided I would go. The day before the wedding Lydia called me, screaming that I was supposed to get a tuxedo, and now they were not going to get a discount on her fiancé's tuxedo because of me. She knew I was wearing my suit, and I even told her about the tie my dad bought for me to wear. I told her then that I was not coming. I explained to her that you can only push a person so far before they snap. I was heartbroken. I threw the tie away because I would not and could never wear it. I did not go to my Lydia's wedding, and, in some way I feel as if that moment in my daughter's life was stolen from me.

A few weeks later, in the middle of the night, I got a phone call from Lydia. "Why did you not come to my wedding?" she asked. I explained to her that she was never going to talk to me the way she had, the day before the wedding, ever again. I told her if she could not show me respect, then I had no room for her in my life. We talked for a long time and when I hung up the phone, I was sure we would be okay. It took almost a year for us to finally be good again. It was the worst year of my life. I could not live without my daughter any longer and I could not argue with her anymore. I felt such a loss when she was not around. It almost killed me. Daddy loves you, princess.

With all of these things going on at once, I decided to write a book. Christopher Booth and I had long talks about me writing a book on the Screaming House, and why I should do it. "*A Haunting* just did not tell the whole story, mate," he would say. He had heard the whole story, and before we filmed Zombie Road, he went with me to the house. It was the first time I had been back since I had left it. Philip and Keith were with us. I was terrified in the car and could not move as we pulled up to the house. Philip immediately jumped out and began filming. I did not get out of the car. I stayed in the car with Christopher and Keith. Christopher saw the emotions hitting me just from being there in front of it. "You need to write the book, mate. If not for any other reason than that it might help you get over this. I know it is affecting you and your life still," he said in the car, on the way back to the hotel. Keith and Philip had fallen asleep in the back. It was just the two of us talking; an instant connection between the two of us was made. There are certain things in life that are better kept a secret. The conversation between Chris and me was consecrated. Some things are sacred. That conversation sparked the idea of writing *The Uninvited*. Without that push, you wouldn't be reading this sequel today.

I can't tell you how difficult it was to write the book. It came out of me so quickly. I wrote the entire first draft in less than a month. The difficult part was facing the emotions that were still left inside me for that horrible place. Activity around my house rose to meet those emotions. There were things flying out of cabinets, banging on the walls, shadow figures; it was almost as if something was trying to keep me from writing it. The more it tried to stop me, the more committed I became to get it done. Morning, noon, and night, I would be writing. The nights were the worst. However, in the end, I had a book. Laura Helbig took the book and did the edit. We then sent it off to four publishers and immediately got a response from Llewellyn Worldwide, which published the book. It was done, and it is true that I left part of me behind on those pages,

and some of myself has been left here on
these pages. I left a lot of things behind.

Chapter 22

June 2007

We got a call about a family that needed help. They were living in a house, which they claimed was haunted, in the woods of Missouri. The wife had been held and beaten in the shower and the door to the oven had been ripped off its hinges by this entity. Bill and I decided we needed to send a team out to investigate. However, Bill was not able to make this one, so I asked Preacher, Rachel, and her boyfriend to assist. At first, when we arrived on the case, things did not seem as violent as the description given to us by the family. It was actually pretty quiet. We began the process of going through the house and taking initial readings, pictures, setting up equipment, and interviewing the family. The master bedroom was located at the end of a long hallway. The family had told us, during the interview process, that most of the activity was coming from there. Footsteps and figures would always lead to that bedroom and at times, it was an impossible room to sleep in. We entered the bedroom and I turned on the light. We looked around and then all of a sudden, everyone in the room began to taste what was described as gunpowder. I have never been a gun enthusiast, so I could only tell you that I tasted something burnt in my mouth. The taste was sort of like when you were a kid and you had those caps you use in a cap gun. Once discharged, they left a smoky residue and if you breathed it in, it tasted horrible. That was the best way I could describe it. It was something like that. We took some EVP samples along with some other things, and then set up equipment to monitor the room. When I turned the light off in the room, I looked back to make sure everything was working, and that is when I saw something glowing underneath a flag on the wall.

I stopped Preacher and Rachel and we went over to check it out. I pulled the flag back and to my surprise there was a note written in glow-in-the-dark ink. The note read something like this:

I write this note to whoever is going to find it and read it. I can no longer handle this anymore. He has taken my heart from me and has destroyed everything that I am. I am no longer a person inside this body. I think he is possessed, and I am afraid that it is now coming after me. I will not become like him. I am ending my life tonight. I have no other choice but to do it. No one can give me any reason why I should not do it. I cannot be hurt anymore by him. I just can't take anymore . . .

The note broke off, just like that. There was something else there, but it was not readable. Below that was a series of claw marks scratched into the wall. They looked like they could have been made by human hands.

Preacher and I immediately began to cleanse the house. We worked from the front to the back, sealing the four corners. When we approached the bedroom, something drastically changed. From the moment we began the blessing in the bedroom, the closet doors began to open and close violently. At one point, a growl filled the room. We continued the blessing until all of the activity had stopped. The house was finally quiet and you could feel that the negativity had been abolished.

Rachel was desperately trying to decode what remained of the apparent suicide note. She sat on the floor with a pen and paper and wrote down every word down along with anything else she could make out. She had a series of words, and for a few weeks afterward was trying to make sense of them. I would get e-mails from her almost daily with some kind of different interpretation. However, that night was the last night I would see her alive.

I was working as a producer for talk radio at the time. I would produce six hours of talk radio during the day, and I had a show of my own as well. I can remember getting ready to go on the air when I heard a news story about a murder-suicide in Sullivan, Missouri. I did not hear the names. I can remember thinking that our little country bubble of safety had been popped once more. There are murders out here, away from the city. They do not happen too often, but when they do, you can bet your bottom dollar they are going to be horrendous.

I wasn't even in my house when I could hear the phone ringing inside. I threw down my keys and darted to pick up the phone. It was Preacher and he began to ramble on so fast that I could barely make out what he was trying to say. "Slow down, Preacher. I am having trouble making out what you are saying," I said. The next words he said were slow and deliberate.

"Rachel is dead. She was shot in the head at close range with a shotgun." I can remember thinking, "Please God, not a shotgun." The case file history of "The Glow-in-the-Dark Case" found that the girl who wrote the suicide note had killed herself with a shotgun. She blew her head off.

Preacher relayed all of the details.

Apparently, Rachel's soon-to-be ex showed up with a box of gifts for the children. He used this as an excuse to get inside of the house. When he opened the box to show Rachel the gifts, he pulled out a shotgun, shooting her in the face at close range.

Then he turned the gun on her boyfriend, just missing him by a hair. Rachel's ex left and went down the street to the local car lot. Someone asked him what he was doing, and he put the gun on the ground for leverage, bent over it, and shot himself in the chest.

I hung up the phone. I couldn't think. I sat there on the couch in complete shock, and then I became violently ill. How do you begin to comprehend something like that? I just kept asking myself over and over, "Why?"

Rachel's viewing was a closed casket, because obviously there was nothing left to observe. Her boyfriend was in complete denial at the moment. You could tell by looking at his face he just simply was not there. I gave him a hug and we talked for a few minutes. While I was talking to him, I noticed the gunpowder burns on his face. It was a very close call for him. Rachel's children were there and it broke my heart to know they would now have to go through this life without parents. The youngest was not much more than a baby, and I just wanted to hold him and tell him it was going to be all right. The funeral service was beautiful and the minister spoke about anger and how you need to let those feelings go, but it is very hard when you are looking at a closed casket of a mother way too young to be in it, and her small children sitting right in front of you. How do you deal with that anger? Those poor babies will never know much about their mother. These children will hear stories, but in the long run that is all they will ever be, stories.

I left the grave site that day and I looked at Preacher and Marie and I told them I was done. I was leaving the group. In my right mind, I could not go on this way. Somehow, I couldn't help but to feel responsible. Could I have brought about the demise of Rachel by simply involving her in the case? The deaths were way too similar. The one thing I did not tell you about Rachel is that she lived on Captain Cromwell's land in Beaufort, Missouri, when she was a little girl. While living there, she was terrorized by something unnatural. Too much had come full circle for me to ever be comfortable investigating again.

"What do you mean, you're leaving the group?" This was the overall reaction from everyone in the group when I told them I was leaving it all behind me. I didn't give any specifics, really. I left quietly. Most of the group assumed it was so I could go be a writer, which was the furthest from the truth. I could no longer take a chance like this with anyone else. I didn't want my curse to become the burden for another innocent soul. I was having a nervous breakdown because I felt responsible for so much. It seemed everything was coming to a head at once. I had the weight of the world on my shoulders, and I was finally falling apart. What if the Screaming House was what really killed Tommy? What if all of the miscarriages that have happened to the females who were close to me were because of the evil that followed me? What if Rachel had died the way she did because of my connection to Cromwell, and I was stupid enough to let her go on that case? It was too much. The train was heading into the station much too fast for me and I felt like I was losing control. I had to walk away. Even today, I know there are those who do not understand why I gave up my group the way I did. But those people need to understand I should have never started the group in the first place. I had no business doing what I did.

In return, with anger as a catalyst, the group tried to wipe me away. They erased my name from EVERYTHING. I was no longer remembered as the group founder; I was nonexistent. They had expunged my name from the website I had built. It was almost like a divorce and the children were taking sides. There should have never been sides to take. They tried to eliminate my presence, when they should have been trying to help me get through it all.

The people who were the closest to me became my enemies overnight. Why couldn't they see what the truth was and what was happening to me? Everybody was worried about Children of the Grave coming out, but at that moment, I felt no one was really worried about me. They just stole what was mine and left me out in the cold, without a second glance. The rational is the irrational when you have been through everything I have survived. Marie, Preacher, and Tom were the only ones who stuck by my side through it all. They may not have completely understood what it was that was happening, but they knew something was wrong.

Looking back now, I can understand why the team felt the way they did. I was always the rock they could count on. Through the worst of times, I was always there, solid and moving forward. They did not know or understand what was going on. Years later, after we put it all behind us, I still don't think they realized what actually had happened and how bad it truly was. I should have listened to Zaffis in those early days when he told me, "You cannot be a case and an investigator at the same time. It's dangerous and it will not work." He was right: it did not work. As a matter of fact, it was disastrous. Instead of turning down the dance, I went right along with the devil's waltz. In the end, it not only almost killed me, but broke me completely down.

In the aftermath, I was treated as an outcast by those who did not understand that all I was trying to do was protect them. They did not understand that the group should have never existed in the first place. It was the wrong thing for me to do. The group was born out of hell, and I had no business leading it into further disaster. All of the feelings came out in an instant. And no one could see I was hurting. No one could understand there was something terribly wrong. The best thing for me to do was to walk away. I did it for them as much as I did it for myself. It was something that had to be done. I do believe it would have destroyed us all had I not.

August 2008

The phone rang one afternoon, about a year later. It was Helen, and I could tell by the sound of her voice she was under, once again. "Steven, I want to tell you something. I just happened to find in Charlie's dresser drawer. A penknife. Now I want you to keep it a secret, because I took it and put it under some magazines next to the bed. Some place where I can easily reach it while he sleeps." The line went dead. I knew instantly, she was going to try to kill him once more. At this point, I was ready to say fuck it, and let her do what she was going to do. I was not willing to ride in at the last act once more and save the day. I had no more hero left within me. If it were not for Marie, I would have done just that.

"Steven, you have to call the police. You cannot let her kill him. If she does and they find out you knew what she was planning, you are going to be just as guilty," Marie pleaded with me. She was trying to talk some sense into me but it was a really hard sell, because at this point, I'd had it with Helen and the monster she held within. Why should I go out of my way to once again save the woman who tried to kill me? She wanted to shoot me in the head and then commit suicide herself, and I stopped her. Why should I do it again? Wasn't God asking too much from me? And then Marie spoke the words that would change my mind, "If you let this happen without trying to stop this, you are playing into the demon's hands. Don't you see that?"

I called the sheriff's department and I told them Helen had a knife and what she was planning to do with it. I explained to them that if they did not get to her before she got to Charlie, she would kill him. They agreed to dispatch someone out. After I hung up with the cops, I picked up the phone and called Helen. I spoke to her calmly and deliberately, like I was speaking to a child. "You need to get the knife and put it in the middle of the kitchen table, do you understand me?" She calmly responded with "yes" to everything I was telling her to do. "Now when the police arrive, they are going to ask you where the knife is. You need to tell them it is in the center of the kitchen table. Do not point to it or move toward it in any way. Let them get the knife without your help., I said to her, afraid if she reached for the knife they might feel it was an aggressive move. "Do you understand me?" I said to her. Once again she calmly responded with a "yes."

The police came and got the knife and then gave her a choice; she could either go to the hospital right then or go to her daughter's house. She chose her daughter's, and they took her there. If you ask her today, she will tell you that she does remember her actions on that night. She will also tell you I called the cops on her, which we both find funny.

Today, Helen and Charlie are divorced. Helen is doing well now, and there have been no more homicidal episodes. In some ways, I think if the demon was still with her, it left when it understood that I no longer cared what it did. I know that attitude sounds cold, and maybe it is, but it ended up saving Helen's life. That was the last incident that I had with her. From that moment on, I understood that I needed to keep a safe distance between Helen and me. There have been times when we see each other, but they are few and far between. Sometimes distance is the best move you can make when the haunted are involved, and from where Helen stood, it was the best thing to do for both of us.

We got together one time a few years ago and went to lunch and did some other things with Marie. That night, Helen was taken away by an ambulance after we left. She thought she was having a heart attack, and when they gave her some medication for an upset stomach, she aspirated on it and quickly developed pneumonia. They had to put her into a medically-induced coma to let her heal. The truth of it was, she almost died. It was a long time until she came around and showed improvement. She had to be on oxygen 24/7 and physical therapy was a must. After several months, she recovered, but now it is easy for her to contract pneumonia and when she does, it is severely life-threatening. She will never be normal again, and it has aged her way beyond her years.

Chapter 23

March 2009

It was late one night when Matthew called me. He had been at work at the local gas station, and he was asking if he could bring someone home with him. He was excited, and I had to ask him to slow down so I could understand him.

"Dad, I have the story. I have the whole story," he kept saying over and over again.

"What story do you have?" I asked him, clearly not understanding where he was coming from.

"I have the whole history of the land the Screaming House was built on, and I have the whole story of the family," he said back to me, even more excited.

"Where did you hear this?" I asked.

"I got it from a Cromwell family member. Dad, they have pictures and everything," he said once again, excitedly. "I am bringing them home to meet you. They want to meet you. They want to tell the whole history to you directly."

1874

It was a stormy summer night. The windows of the large house were rattling with each rumble of thunder. The wind was howling as strange shadows were cast upon the walls. With each flash of light, the flicker of the flames from the oil lamps and candles danced in the darkness. The pounding on the front door sent a very large servant woman scrambling down the stairs to answer it. She had served the captain and his wife, Minerva, for many years, as a slave and servant. It was hard for her to consider herself as anything else, even though all of the slaves at the Cromwell homestead had been freed. Even with their freedom, they all had stayed on to serve the captain and his wife. Screams of agony came from the upstairs bedroom. The mistress was having a baby, and Ivy hurried even faster toward the door to let in Doc, who was waiting outside on the porch in the storm.

"Where is she?" Doc asked as he entered. He handed his coat and hat to Ivy. "This way, Doc," Ivy answered, setting his cane and hat aside. Another scream came shrieking down the steps. Both Doc and Ivy looked upward until the screaming subsided. "She is upstairs. Right this way," Ivy said as she began to lead Doc up the long, grand staircase to the second floor. Doc could make out someone sitting in a chair outside the door, and he assumed it must be the captain, waiting for the birth. His assumptions proved to be correct, and as he moved closer, the captain stood to shake his hand.

"Now, you don't worry about anything. I will take really good care of everything," Doc said as they exchanged handshakes. Ivy opened the bedroom door and another scream escaped out. Doc hurried into the room, with Ivy behind him, as the door was shut firmly, muffling the screams of birth.

The captain sat in his chair outside the door, where he awaited the news about the birth of his new child. He sat there with his head in his hands to partially block out his wife's screams. He assured himself she was in good hands with Doc. He knew the rumors about Doc and the whores from Moselle, but instead of doing abortions, tonight the doctor would be bringing life into the world. He hoped that life would be a son.

All of a sudden, the night was pierced with the first cries of life and the baby was born. The bedroom door opened slowly, and Doc stepped outside, almost blocking the door. "Before you go in there, I think there is something I should tell you," said Doc, looking at him with a seriousness that he had never seen before.

"Everything is all right with the baby?" the captain asked, with a worried look on his face.

"Everything is fine with the baby. There were no complications," Doc said, still trying to block the door and the view behind it.

"Well then, let me in there to see my wife and child." The captain pushed his way past Doc, who was still trying to stop him. Once in the room, he could see the shock on Ivy's face and he knew there was something wrong. He raced over to the bed, where his wife was lying with a bundle in her arms. There was a look of horror upon Minerva's face. This was not the look of a new mother. As he got closer, he saw the baby that she was holding in her arms and he began to scream. He screamed, and then he screamed some more.

These were screams of a broken heart. Minerva was holding a mixed child. The captain knew instantly that the baby did not belong to him, and that was the ultimate betrayal. The baby was a black man's baby. Minerva began to sob violently at his reaction, trying to say she was sorry, but the words would not come out through her tears.

"Ivy, take the baby away," Doc said as he came back into the room. Minerva was crying and trying not to let the baby go, but Ivy got the child away from her and was out of the door.

Doc looked at the captain and said, "Do you want me to clean up this mess?"

The captain did not say a word, but nodded his head yes, and walked out of the room crying - a broken man. Doc, standing next to the bedside looking down at Minerva, immediately put a cloth soaked in chloroform over her face as Minerva tried to fight. She tried to scream for help, but the screams fell on deaf ears, because no white man would care about a woman who had slept with a black man and carried his child. She quickly passed out and Doc went to work. Both of her lungs were pierced with wires inserted into her sides, between her ribs. Her lungs collapsed and immediately began to fill with fluid. Minerva struggled, but she would not make it through the night.

The captain walked into the nursery where Ivy was with the baby. "You know what you need to do, Captain. You need to get rid of this bastard child, this unholy thing. You can't have this running around. Send it back to hell, Captain. Send it back to hell." He pushed Ivy aside to walk over to the bassinet that held the sleeping baby. "What is it?" he asked.

"It's a bastard boy, Captain, and make no mistake, it is unholy. You need to kill it," Ivy said, standing next to him.

"I need to kill it?" the captain asked her, with tears in his eyes.

"You must kill it. You have no choice. You cannot have this bastard ruining your life. Kill it." With this, Ivy put a pistol in his hands. "Just point and pull the trigger. It is as easy as that," she said as the captain pulled back the hammer on the gun. Doc walked into the room and the captain turned to him."It is done. Won't be long now," Doc said, and immediately tears began to roll down the captain's face. He turned to face the bassinet once more.

"Do it," Ivy said, and a loud bang rang out throughout the house. It was done.

"Dress it in its christening gown," said the captain as he left the room, dropping the pistol on the floor at the door.

The baby was hung in a tree near the servants' quarters for all to see. It was hung by its feet, and it was dressed in a white christening gown. The dead baby was hung there as a warning to the servants and anyone who else might see it, to never cross the captain again. All of the male servants were gathered outside the quarters near the tree, lined up, and shot. The farm hands stood aside and watched. One of the servants tried to run and was shot in the back immediately upon trying to escape. On her deathbed, Minerva would not give the name of her lover, and so she sent many innocent men to their deaths. It was a death sentence for all, instead of just one.

Some speculated that the servant who tried to escape was actually the one who deserved to die, but no one ever really knew for sure - no one except for Ivy. Of course she was happy to stand by and watch the sacrifices as they were made. She was a Voodoo high priestess and was gratified to see the land washed in blood. This would make her Djab happy. A Djab is the personal spirit that Ivy had a magical contract with. Her Djab was particularly powerful and aggressive, because it was one of the Loa, or angels. In Ivy's case, her Djab was one of the fallen, one of the angels cast out from heaven along with Lucifer. It would be very happy with the sacrifices that night, especially with the sacrifice of the baby hanging in the tree.

Although pneumonia would be the

official cause of death listed on Minerva's death certificate, the actual cause of death was murder. The problem had been taken care of and the captain's honor would never be tarnished by such debauchery by her ever again.

"There is no God!" the captain screamed to the heavens. He dropped to his knees and frantically started clawing at the dirt. He clearly had gone insane. Behind him, in the darkness, stood a figure, faintly glowing, with something moving wildly in front of it. Again, the captain screamed out in extreme and utter agony, "Why have you deserted me?" Again, something started to move wildly in the darkness as the glowing figure began to slowly move forward. The captain sat up on his knees and began scratching his chest. Blood began to surface, as tears streamed down his expressionless face.

"Because your God does not care," a low, female voice murmured. It came from the glowing figure that waited in the darkness. Her words were deliberate, drawn out, and full of accentuation.

"You have forsaken me," the captain whispered into the air, with tears running down his face and bloody torso. The figure in the darkness began to move closer with something still moving wildly with it.

From behind him, Ivy came into the light of the fire, dressed in all white, from head to toe. Her head was wrapped in white, and in her hand she held a chicken by its feet. The chicken's wings were flapping wildly. In her other hand she held a knife. Holding the squirming chicken over the captain, she took the knife and cut the chicken's throat. As the blood began to pour over the captain, she began to dance, and her eyes rolled back into her head. She was now under possession. The captain began to rub the blood all over his face and body and he began to growl and scream. His eyes turned black. His soul no longer belonged to God. Ivy started to laugh because she knew she had made her Djab proud. With all of the sacrifice and blood, it would stain the land and it would make her more powerful than she ever dreamed of being. Her life would become epic, and the sacrifices of that night would forever leave their mark on generations after, who would no longer worship anything but the fallen who now gave Ivy her strength.

The captain took care of Ivy for the rest of her life. She never wanted for anything. She moved from Missouri to New Orleans, and no trace of her was ever heard of again. A short time before the death of the captain, he made a trip to New Orleans. Family members speculate it was to see Ivy for one last time, but no one ever knew for sure if that was actually the purpose of his trip. Shortly after returning home, the captain died. Some descendants of the captain debate whether he is actually buried in the grave under the small, understated tombstone that marks his grave today. Right next to his grave is Minerva's. Her tombstone is large and ornate. It is the tombstone given to someone out of love. When you stand at the grave, you have this overwhelming sense of sadness and love. She was the love of the captain's life. He loved her more than anything else ever put on this earth. He would not share her, and her betrayal was too much for him to handle. On the night of those tragic events, his heart was broken and he turned cold and distant; a man whose family described him as mean and heartless. It worked as a poison on the generations to follow. The Cromwells were known for being cruel and unforgiving. They also hid their secrets. They hid them well.

The Screaming House was built upon the grounds that used to be the Cromwell slave quarters. It was said, by some family members, that one of the basement walls was actually one of the walls preserved from that original building. If you went into the basement of the Screaming House, you would notice the majority of the walls were built from normal concrete, but one of the walls was built from an older, almost sand-like concrete material. The tree still stands outside where the dead baby was hung for show. The baby is still sometimes seen hanging there, at three in the morning, and you can still hear the captain's screams breaking the silence of the night. His screams of grief, heartache, and despair.

This is the story that was told to me in 2009 by a Cromwell family member. I was sworn to never reveal the source. In a way, it this source will go down in history as the "deep throat" of the supernatural. The Cromwell family member told me someone might kill them, if others knew they had told the story. That was made clear to me, and even though I was given permission to tell the story, I was made to promise to never give away the source. During our conversation, I found the dichotomous worship of Catholicism and Voodoo quite intriguing. I had to wonder if the rituals Ivy once practiced were still practiced by the Cromwells today, imbedded within the families that practiced the ceremonies. Were they raised with the mixture of Catholicism and the worship of the fallen, in the same way I would be a Protestant, or someone might be Jewish? This would make it nearly impossible to break the cycle. The fallen, demons, ghosts, Voodoo, Catholicism . . . the final story was just the same, when you consider it. It was all just a matter of semantics.

I think back to Mr. Winters, the landlord of the Screaming House, and it all makes sense. He is feeding demons, sacrificing families for his twisted beliefs. And more importantly, he is sacrificing children, much in the same way that Ivy orchestrated the sacrifice of the baby, many years before. A spiritual sacrifice. But let's face it, a sacrifice is still a sacrifice, by body or spirit.

Here again I will include the last e-mail contact I had with Mr. Winters. This time I think it will be crystal clear to you what his intentions were and are:

Last e-mail contact with Mr. Winters, landlord of the Screaming House.

November 2005

'The new children are having fun running around upstairs and "screaming" as children do when they're having fun . . . but the parents will stop that soon, when they finish moving in and getting unpacked. When the kids first got there, they immediately ran up the stairs, as little tykes do. They began running in and out of rooms, screaming and laughing with joy . . . It was so nice to hear "little angel screams" . . . I hope their guardian angels will watch over them tonight."

Little angel screams. Those words and the way they were emphasized tell the whole story, now that I know the complete history. They clearly demonstrate the evil intentions of this evil man. It is enough to make your blood run cold.

Chapter 24

Flashback, Autumn 1979

My grandfather was dying. My grandfather was dying of cancer— brain cancer to be exact. There comes a time in a young boy's life when he ceases being a boy and begins to be a man, and this was that moment for me.

Grandpa Joe was everything in the world to me. He was a dapper fellow in his day, with a lanky walk and a fedora perched on his head - a hat I would later make the mistake of filling with water as a practical joke as a boy. This was the only time I ever remember my grandfather getting really mad at me. All in all, he was my buddy. Grandpa Joe was my partner in whatever we did. He was full of old wives' tales, superstitions, and sometimes mischief. Many nights, I can remember him telling me old ghost stories. There were times I actually believed he thought they were true. Now, looking back, I have to wonder if somewhere there was some truth to them. Maybe there was some shard of truth there. Maybe he had actually lived these things.

I know there were times throughout my life when I wished he was there. He used to send me birthday cards, and the age on the card was always a few years older than I actually was. I imagine he did this on purpose, to make me feel much older, more mature. My grandmother used to get so mad at him for that. I can still hear her telling me that he bought the card, and she didn't - because she would have gotten the age just right. I loved those cards.

My grandfather was a permanent fixture

on what was called the "Liars Bench" in Potosi, Missouri. The Liars Bench was where the old men in the town used to gather and try to one-up each other with their stories. Old Frenchmen had a penchant for stories. I often wish I could remember just a portion of them today. I used to sit there and listen to them go on for hours. It is a practice long gone, but I wish the Liars Bench was still there, because I have a story to tell them, and my story is true. I wonder what my grandfather would have thought of all of this. I wonder what kind of advice he would have for me, to get through it. The superstitions of an old Frenchman might come in handy.

I had spent the summer of that year helping my grandmother care for him. I was witness to the loss of dignity that comes with cancer. I had shared with him those moments, when you thought that it was maybe just possible that he could have beat this thing, but in the end, it got the best of him. He lay in a hospital bed, down the hall, dying. I had already gone in to say my last goodbyes. He was there, lying under a mass of wires and tubes. There is that part of you that wants to cry out, "Please, Grandpa, don't leave me." But deep down, the reality is there in your face, the notion that we all must go. This was his end. I suddenly had a fear that my father, who was standing beside me, would pass as well. "Please, Daddy, don't you ever go." Sometimes I think that I want to die before everyone else that I love. The loss would be too much for me to handle. The grief would eat me alive.

I had dealt with the death of my other grandfather at the age of nine. However, we were sheltered from his death because of our ages. I remember going to my grandmother's house after school that day. I remember my mother, in all her wisdom and caring, looking at me as she said one sentence, "Bad day, buddy." There was nothing else more to be said, "Bad day, buddy." I can still see her face. The ugliness of it all had been hidden, but the grief was impossible to hide.

There was no hiding this, and make no mistake, a cancerous death is a dreadful death. The waiting room was cold and dark. It was the middle of the night. I had been coming in and out of sleep, a restless sleep. Every time someone would enter the room, I would wake up. How could anyone actually sleep when a loved one is dying at the end of the hall? I could feel the sorrow building in my chest. I lay there with my eyes closed. I wanted to scream. I wanted to run down that hall and grab him and run. Run as fast as I could and maybe, just maybe, we could escape all of the madness that lay before us, but you can't outrun death. Death will catch up in the end. There was no escaping the inevitable. He was going to die.

That is when I heard it. It was soft at first, a soft sound. "Shhhhhh . . ." I opened my eyes. I was trying to focus through the tears that I had been crying. "Shhhhh . . ." I turned my head to face the couch directly across from where I lay. No one else in the room was moving. Everyone else was asleep. "Shhhhhh . . ." It was my grandfather, sitting there with his one finger to his mouth, an action that I had caught him doing many times in early morning hours, when he thought he would sneak past everyone to sneak out of the house. Of course, I would put him back to bed and we would both giggle as I told him, "You are not going no place, old man." There he sat, as if to tell me that he finally was getting to go. "SHHHHH . . ."

My attention was distracted, and I was completely awakened by the sound of crying coming from down the hall. It was my grandmother. Grandpa Joe had died. He died while I was dreaming about him. I looked back to where I had seen him sitting in my dream and he was gone. "Goodbye, old man, I love you," I whispered.

Autumn 2011

It was near the end of September 2011 when the supernatural activity began to get out of hand around our house once more. Michael had departed for college in St. Louis, and that left Matthew and me as struggling bachelors at home to fend for ourselves. We used to get a kick out of that idea, and the idea of the bachelor pad we were living in. It made us laugh when we would say it, and it really was a good time for both of us. There is that time in your child's life, when your relationship turns into more of a friendship. Your children become your best friends and your relationship dynamic quickly changes. I found that I had finally reached that point in my life with my children. Lydia, who now had two daughters, was quickly gaining a new respect for me as a father. It is funny, but you cannot really understand the sacrifice and the depth of your parents' love until you have children of your own.

I was getting daily phone calls from her now, asking for advice and just simply wanting to talk and share with me. I would often find myself laughing as she told me what kind of trouble one or both of the girls were getting into. Then, there were those times when she would just need some words of encouragement. I could usually tell when that was needed, and I would find myself remembering how difficult those days were when I was raising her and her two brothers. Those memories were strangely triggered by her present problems with my grandchildren. "Everything always comes full circle, baby," I remember my grandmother telling me when she was still alive, and she was right. Everything does come full circle.

Life, for the most part, was good. Matthew and I were traveling the country, going from speaking engagement to speaking engagement, having tremendous adventures along the way. "What was that I just hit?" I asked Matthew in the hills of Pennsylvania, late one night while we were driving. I had hit some type of strange-looking animal in the road while I was talking to Marie on the cell.

"I think it was a mountain lion, Dad," he said, trying to control his laughter. I would have expected to hit a deer, because for miles I had seen the road strewn with their dead carcasses.

"A mountain lion, you're kidding, right?" I asked, hoping he would laugh or something to let me in on the joke.

"Nope, it was a mountain lion. I'm sure of it. Aren't mountain lions an endangered species?" he asked, trying to hold back his laughter while I pulled the car into a gas station on the Pennsylvania turnpike. We had rented a car for the trip, and the only car they had available was a Versa. Not only was I facing the potential death of a mountain lion, I was going to get to explain to the rental company that I had the privilege of killing an endangered species the size of a mountain lion with a Versa. Matthew jumped out of the car to survey the damage. I sat firmly behind the wheel, refusing to get out.

"Come on, Dad, get out and look. It is not that bad." He was trying to coax me out of the car, and I really was afraid I was going to see a horribly smashed-up front end. I got out of the car slowly and walked around to the front. "See, it's not too bad, Dad." And he was right; there were two large dents on the bumper, and for the most part that was it. Then I looked at the license plate. Was that blood on it? I looked closer, and when I bent down to get a better look, a huge chuck of lion meat fell to the parking lot at my feet. Oh boy, I not only hit a mountain lion, I destroyed a mountain lion. The turnpike police were nice about the whole matter and gave me a report number. It was true—we had hit a mountain lion. They found it on the far side of the road, back at mile marker 138. Then they asked us how it was possible for two men way over six feet tall, to fi t into a Versa. They stood and watched, laughing at us, as we got back into the car. When we were on our adventurous road trips, there was always something happening and a story to tell when we got home. We were having the time of our life doing it.

I knew I was sick. I knew it was serious. I had been through enough with my heart over the past few years. It seemed like every six months or so I was getting stents put in, but nothing seemed to be slowing the heart disease down. I felt like a ticking time bomb, just waiting for the moment when the buzzer would sound and all would be over. I was waiting to die.

It was in September 2011. We had been hitting the road hard that year. It seemed as if we would get home, and then it would be time to head out once again. I was so tired and nothing I did could help. Matthew would often have to coax me out of the house, and in the end, he was even packing for us. I no longer had the energy to do much of anything, and I was trying to hide it as best as I could because I knew what the end result was leading to. I was popping nitro like candy. I could actually feel my heart gurgling in my chest, trying so damn hard to push the blood through the hardening and closing arteries. I made my promised appearances and then, when I got home, I would be completely wiped out for a week or more. I knew something was seriously wrong. But how do you tell the people you love that you think you are dying? How do you tell them that you want to live so badly, but your heart just won't let you? How do you lay your head on your pillow at night, terrified you might not wake up the next morning? Even worse, what if someone I loved found me dead? Can you imagine the type of damage that it would do to them?

I wanted to keep it quiet. I did not want to go through what I knew was coming. I wanted to make sure I had everything in order before I even stepped into the doctor's office, because I knew there would be one more catheter done, and I knew, without a doubt this time, it would show I was in big trouble. The activity in the house began to quickly gain in momentum during this time. There was banging on the walls day and night. At night, a shadow figure would be outside the front door and you could see it turning the doorknob, trying to get in. Matthew, at first, did not believe me about the shadow figure. I woke up early one morning and walked into the living room to find him wide awake and frightened. He had seen the shadow figure. He saw the doorknob turn. He saw the figure stand at the front door for two hours and then, when he thought it was gone, it began to knock on the kitchen window, which was in the back of the apartment. When he went to look, there was no one there. The nightmares for both of us were almost on a nightly basis, and we got to the point where neither one of us was sleeping very much. Then the cabinet doors in the kitchen began to open and close on their own. One night, Matthew walked into the kitchen, and I saw him stop; he had the strangest look upon his face. "What's wrong?" I asked him, and he just said it was nothing. I could see he was trying to hide something from me, behind his back. I walked into the kitchen, and every single cabinet door was standing wide open. Then I saw what Matthew was holding in his hand. It was a butcher knife. "What are you doing with that knife in your hand?" I asked.

"I found it lying on the kitchen floor," he said, with a frightened look on his face.

"You found it on the floor?" I asked again, not fully understanding what he was trying to tell me.

"I came in here and I saw everything open and when I looked on the floor the knife was lying neatly there. Pops, I think it was leaving us a present or something. I don't know, maybe a sign or something?"

From that night on, we would walk into the kitchen to find all of the doors open and knives on the floor. Sometimes neatly in a row, and sometimes scattered about. The strangest part of it was you would never hear it happen. I could walk out of the kitchen and turn off the light and go back just a few moments later to find the same scene repeating, doors open and knives on the floor. Shannon Lusk, who is my editor, came to stay one weekend to work on this very book with me, and the activity escalated even more. Electronics began turning off and on without anyone touching them, or even being in the same room. One night, Shannon walked into the bathroom in the middle of the night. When she was finished, she washed her hands and turned off the light. Before she could get the door open, loud pounding traveled down the bathroom walls. She swung the door open in panic and yelled out to Matthew and me. The sound of the banging on the walls was incredible. It was on an inside wall, so I knew it was not one of the neighbors. It happened shortly after three in the morning. Needless to say, no one slept any more that night.

I began to think that maybe I needed to call John Zaffis and tell him what was going on, but there was one thing that kept me from doing it. I knew he would not be happy with me if he found out where I was living. Where was I living? I was living down the street from the Screaming House. For some reason, I thought it was a good idea to put myself where I could keep an eye on it. I felt it had come after me when I lived clear across town, so it was not going to matter if I lived any closer, or not.

There was one more thing. I was also living in the exact apartment where Tommy was injected with the lethal dose of heroin. I understand it was total and absolute defiance on my part. I wanted to show it I was no longer afraid. I wanted to show it that it could no longer touch me or hurt me, because I wasn't going to let it. It was a stupid move. But stupid or not, there was a strange sort of security it gave me, living so close. I don't expect anyone to understand it and I am not going to try to justify my actions. I was living near the house, and that was that. I was living in the apartment where Tommy was given his death sentence, and that was that. Was it an obsession? No. I was no longer obsessed with the house. I just wanted to be safe, and if you think about it, the best way to deal with an enemy is to stay just close enough to observe it. There was no false sense of security. I was living on the frontline, and I knew it.

I completed all of my Christmas shopping the first week of November of that year. Once I had it all done and ready to go, I called the doctor to make an appointment for my heart. My cardiologist wanted to see me right away. The routine was exactly what I expected. The appointment was made for the cardio cath. You know, I can remember walking into the hospital that morning for the test. I can remember thinking, "When I walk out of here, my life will be changed forever." I knew there would be bad news, and I knew where it all was heading. My cardiologist stood over me while I was still on the table. He had this serious look on his face. I can remember looking at him and saying, "I am in trouble, aren't I?" He looked at me and smiled a serious, but comforting smile. "It is time for an operation. There is just nothing more we can do with stents. Your heart is strong, and I'm afraid if we wait much longer, you might have a heart attack that would weaken the muscle, and that is not where we would want to be. You need a bypass."

There. It was said. Finally, they were giving me a bypass. I knew what that meant. They were going to crack open my chest because of where the blockages were in my heart. They were going to have to take my heart completely out of my chest to get to the troubled areas. There were going to be multiple bypasses. I was not shocked at the news, because I already knew it was coming.

The operation was scheduled for the Monday before Thanksgiving. No one had to tell me what the routine was going to be. I had already done enough reading on my own. The night before the operation, I did not sleep at all. Earlier that night I had made a phone call to my good friend and brother, Keith Age. We talked for a while, and I knew I could reach out to him, because I knew if anyone out there was going to understand, he would. He knew the score. He knew exactly where I was headed. "Would you take care of Matthew if something happens to me?" I asked him.

"Nothing is going to happen to you. You are too stubborn for that shit," he said, trying to get me to lighten up.

"I know, but if something goes wrong, will you make sure Matthew is okay?" I asked again, a little more seriously.

"You know I would, but nothing is going to happen. You are going to be all right," he said again, with a little more confidence in his voice. I was making a mental checklist of everything I needed to do and everyone I needed to talk to.

I think out of all my friends, Dakota Lawrence took the news the worst. Dakota had always been like an adopted son to me. "You are going to be all right, Dad. Aren't you?" he asked, and I could hear the fear in his voice and the fact he was trying to fight back tears.

"Of course I'm going to be all right. You know me. Of all the things I have been through, this is not going to take me out. Trust me, I will be fine," I said, and I held my breath because I felt like I might be lying to him. The truth was, I didn't know if I was going to be all right, but the thing is, I was being given the time to say my goodbyes, and time to put things straight. If I was going to die, I was going to be ready for it. The one person who knew everything would be fine was Ms. Pittman. Ms. Pittman was the person who was always there for me, whenever I needed words of wisdom. She was very psychic, and she was also Dakota's grandmother. "Everything is going to be just fine. Don't you worry about this. It is going to be all right," she said to me on the phone while silently holding a fist up to let Dakota and his mother know they had better pull their shit together. Ms. Pittman could, at times, be a woman of very few words, but you always knew to listen closely when she spoke because she was trying to tell you something important. Her wisdom was always there, whenever I needed guidance or a kind word, and on this day I needed both.

The morning of the surgery came. The hardest part of the whole thing was having to tell my family goodbye before being taken away.

How do you appear to be strong in the face of it all? How do you look in their eyes and say goodbye, knowing that it could be the last time? I forced myself to keep smiling when all I wanted was to tell them not to go. It was too early to go. We had not said everything or done everything. But I knew, if this was our last moment, I did not want them to see me crying. I did not want to leave that picture for them to remember. So when it came time, I smiled and told them I loved them.

I was dead for a total of 38 seconds on the table. There is that point in the surgery when they remove the life support and basically restart your heart. At that point, for all intents and purposes, you are dead. Now, I know you want me to tell you that there was a white light that came down from the heavens. You want me to tell you that I saw my sister and all of those I have loved who have passed. I saw none of that. The only thing I can remember is this sharp pain shooting throughout my entire body. A feeling like my whole body was being slammed down upon a hard surface, and I had the instantaneous thought, "I know why babies cry when they are born. It hurts."

I then opened my eyes and I was in the ICU with Matthew looking down at me. When Lydia came to see me, I asked her to come closer to talk to her. "I didn't see her. I didn't see my sister," I said to her, with tears in my eyes. Secretly, I was hoping that if anyone was going to be there, it would be my sister. I felt like I had missed my chance to see her, talk to her, tell her how much I missed her, and I missed the chance to tell her I loved her. It just didn't happen. I was not given the chance.I was in the hospital for nine days due to complications. My right lung had collapsed during the surgery and I was not able to go home until it was better. On Thanksgiving morning, they put in a pump for my lung by inserting a tube into my right side. My older brother watched from the hall, and I can remember keeping my eyes locked on his while it was going on. I tried to keep it all out of my mind by watching him. The truth is, though, I felt like I was falling apart. I had never fully understood what it was like to have your body completely give out on you, until that moment. When you cannot breathe—that changes the game completely. There is a panic that is biological, telling you that something is terribly wrong. But I got through it. I came home. I had survived something else in my life, and when I got home, the supernatural activity had completely halted. No more banging, open cabinets, or knives. For the first time in years, I could say my life was normal. It felt like all the supernatural activity was over.

I cannot explain it to you any clearer than that. All of the activity was gone, and for the first time in a very long time, I felt normal. I felt like I had before we moved into that damned house. I felt alive again, very much alive. I felt like a storm had passed and the skies seemed clearer, and the atmosphere was lighter around me. And for the first time in many years, I could sleep once again. No more nightmares, no more fear, only good, sound, and peaceful sleep was ahead in my future.

It took about six months for me to understand the message I was given when I came back into my body from what I assume was death. "I know why babies cry when they are born. It hurts." My whole adult life, I had run around complaining about someone did this to me or this horrible thing happened to me. I was never strong when dealing with my life. As a matter of fact, in some ways I was behaving like a big, old, whiny wimp. The message was given to me in order to understand that I was going to get to live more life, but with the understanding life is gonna hurt sometimes. Sometimes, it is going to hurt so bad that pain is going to resonate throughout your whole body and take your breath away. Life is not good or even easy all of the time, but it is within those hard times and pain when the work on the soul is really done. It is supposed to hurt. Without the pain of life, the lessons would not be learned. I needed to accept and even embrace the pain as much as I did the happier times. Life hurts, and guess what, my mother was right when she told me she never promised me a rose garden. In complete contrast, Ms. Pittman was also right when she told me to stop and smell those roses. This is the contradiction of life, and within those contradictions, a soul can and will become whole again.

Chapter 25

August 2012

I look back throughout the years, and I see how everything seems to have come full circle. I remember Zoe and the Tower card. I have a clear understanding now of the message it was trying to give me. All I was ever willing to see was the destruction that the card depicted. I would not allow myself to see the full picture, the cycle of demise and resurgence. There is a rebuilding. I completely overlooked the idea that sometimes things have to be destroyed in order for them to rise from the ashes, wiser and stronger than before.

Sure, I had seen my share of damage. Let's face it, I had encountered total and absolute obliteration at times, but that is not the end of my story. My story is not going to end with me, a sad, demolished person, because I have been given the gift of rebirth. I have been given a chance to start fresh. I have had mediums come forward and tell me that my vision during my surgery - about the pain of coming into this world - was actually signifying my rebirth. The reason the supernatural had stopped within my life was that it could no longer touch me, because the bond or hold it had on my soul was broken at the moment I died.

Everything that has happened to me was responsible for my rebirth and making me the person I am today. There are always going to be haunted houses. There are always going to be those who want to hurt others for their own selfish or evil ends. There are always going to be people who choose to serve something other than a kind, loving, and impartial God. People you love are going to die and move on. You are going to die and move on, but while you are here, it is your responsibility to live your life to the fullest. To live fully means to have pain, as well. Bad things will happen to you.

There are people who are going to try to hurt you and destroy you. But just remember that out of the rubble you will build again and live again. Life hurts and through that pain is how we grow. The tower in the end can be rebuilt. I have been asked before if I would like to go back and change the horrible things that have happened to me. I can honestly, without hesitation, answer "no." I am the person I am because of every single thing that has happened to me during this life, and because of those things I am stronger.

So, in the end, there is not much more to say. Bless those who hated me and hurt me. Bless those who lied to me and beat me down. Bless those who deserted me and forgot about me when I needed them most. And may God's blessing come down upon the demon that tried to destroy me completely, because in the end even the wicked need to be blessed and forgiven. BLESSED ARE THE WICKED.

"When Jesus therefore had received the vinegar, he said, It is finished: and he bowed his head, and gave up the ghost."
- *John 19:30*

Epilogue

March 6, 2013

I left Union, Missouri, on August 10, 2012. I think "left" is the wrong word, and "moved" just doesn't fit what my intention actually was. I ran away from Union. I ran away from all of the pain, the heartache, and the memories that haunted me day in and day out every time I would walk down a street or pass by one of the places that played its part in that whole old nightmare. I ran away from my family and my friends. I needed to decompress. I needed to learn how to live once again, without having to look around every corner or being afraid to enter every dark room.

I can remember the sense of relief I felt as I drove away from the Union city limits. I felt free for the first time in years. Free to once again feel my life was on some sort of normal track. Maybe I cannot find the right words to explain those feelings, but they were there and they were real. The first time I had really allowed myself to feel in a long, long time. I had a tear in my eye as I saw I was finally leaving it all behind me. The wicked hold it had on me was finally letting go and I was free.

I drove 15 hours straight to get to my new home in Myrtle Beach, South Carolina. I drove as fast as I could, almost as if some unseen hand was going to come up from somewhere and rip me back. I ran. I ran as fast as I could. I did not give myself time to think about what I was doing. I was leaving behind two of my grown children, my mother, father and my grandchildren. Don't you see it was something I had to do? The other option was to stay there and die. The place was killing me.

That I knew. I knew if I stayed there it was going to get the best of me, so I went as far east as I could. I did not stop until I made it to the water.

For six months I stayed there at the beach. And every day when I woke up, I felt a sense of security I had lost a long time ago. I was healing. I was putting it all behind me, and I was beginning to heal the wounds, which by staying in Union had just ripped further and deeper into my soul. I was becoming whole again, and as I began to feel again, I understood I had made a serious mistake by running so far. With healing comes understanding. I understood I had left every single person I loved behind.

The day before Thanksgiving, I was in my kitchen getting things ready for the next day's feast, when a knock came on the door. The FedEx man was there, handing me a package when I opened the door. I was taken aback a little by its arrival, because I had not expected anything. I opened it and saw it was mail sent to me by my publisher, Llewellyn. They had received this and had sent it on to me. It was a 156-page book, and on the cover it said, *The Roman Catholic Church: An Analysis of the Steven LaChance Haunting*. It was written by a demonologist for the church. I took it out onto my patio, in the sun where I felt safe, and for the rest of the day I read.

It started off with an explanation of the choirs of angels who fell with Lucifer. It explained about the cherubim. All the things that I had uncovered myself or suspected were finally being explained to me by someone else. The strangest part was that a lot of the information in it were things that this priest could not have possibly known. These were things I had not shared with anyone publicly until I had written this book. This book was already written and was in the process of being edited at that point.

This priest knew so many things about myself and my life that he could not have possibly known. I had always thought the haunting had started with my ex-wife, but I was never quite sure exactly how they were connected. He explained to me that the haunting had started before my first child was born. He knew my ex-wife had been doing something she should not have done. I had always suspected this. He talked about her emotional demeanor when she had thrown Michael to the ground so many years ago. I had always told people that she was not the same person I had married. I knew there was something wrong with her, but I could never put it into words. The priest made it crystal clear. She was possessed at the moment she did something no mother would ever do. I sat there reading, and at times I was crying because he was right. How could I have been so stupid? I knew all of this and yet I needed this complete stranger to come along and make sense of it for me. Had it been one of my cases, I would have picked it out right away. Why did I not see it for myself?

I continued reading as he went step by step and point by point, explaining to me things that in my heart I knew to be true. My haunting started with her. My haunting began way before she left me, and I had not seen the clues about where we were headed. The priest named a major demon in his report, Belial, whom the church believed was very much part of this haunting and the possessions.

According to Wikipedia, "Belial is a term occurring in the Hebrew Bible which later became personified as a demon in Jewish and

Christian texts." In one of the Dead Sea Scrolls, Belial is the leader of the Sons of Darkness:

"But for corruption thou hast made Belial, an angel of hostility. All his dominions are in darkness, and his purpose is to bring about wickedness and guilt. All the spirits that are associated with him are but angels of destruction." – The War of the Sons of Light Against the Sons of Darkness

What does this mean? The easiest way I can explain it to you is that Belial is one of Satan's commanders in the war against God, or anything holy, for that matter. He falls at the top of the hierarchy of the fallen, at the right hand of Lucifer. A cold chill ran through my body. I shut the report for a moment and walked away to clear my head. That was the first time I heard the name, and this will be the last time I ever speak or write about it again.

I thought back to a dream I had a few years ago. Those of you who had read my book *Crazy* might remember this dream, from the last section of the book. I told very few people that this was actually my nightmare. Here it is again, because it is very important to my case and my life.

I was in an old farmhouse. The floors were wood, and I could hear them creak and moan beneath my feet.

I was following my grandmother. We were moving almost as if in slow motion, and she would turn occasionally, motioning and whispering to me, "Follow me, child."

The house was very old. There were no modern amenities that I could see as we passed from room to room. It must have been rather large because it seemed to take us forever to reach the back door. My grandmother stepped outside, saying, "Follow me, child."

The land outside was flat and dry. There was a windmill in the distance. Nothing fancy, just one of those scaffolding types made from wood. There were storm clouds bubbling up in the distance and the wind was blowing.

Somehow, I had lost sight of my grandmother and I started to panic, thinking that I had lost her. I looked around, not seeing her until I heard her voice.

"Over here, child."

There she was, sitting in a rocking chair with her back to me. Relieved, I went over to where she was sitting.

"Kneel down here, boy," she said, motioning for me to kneel next to her chair. Of course, I did as she asked. We sat there with her rocking; the clouds were bubbling up closer and closer over our heads. We said nothing. We sat there quietly. The wind blowing. Quietly.

Then she spoke, "Listen to me carefully. It is in the bloodline." Instantly my grandmother cracked into several ravens, which began to fly into the angry clouds above.

I thought about this dream as I read something the priest had included in the report. He spoke about the possibility of generational things being at play with the haunting as well. Oftentimes, priests' families will be plagued with demonic activity. The activity is actually an attack against the priest - by causing harm and distress to his family. My family are descendants of the Order of St. Michael. This is a French order of knighthood that was granted to nobility. It was named after St.

Michael, the archangel who led the armies of angels against Satan and the fallen, defeating them. Billions of angels fell from the heavens at St. Michael's hands. It makes sense when you put Belial in the context of the haunting and relate that to the historical significance of St. Michael and his "relation" to my family. I think about my grandmother's words, and I now fully understand what she meant when she said, "Listen to me carefully. It is in the bloodline."

The report continued, and for many reasons, I am not going to tell you everything included in it. One of the major reasons is that it dealt with very personal details of the case that were not only mine, but also everyone else's who had been affected by the haunting. The report concluded with a final finding, which was that the Roman Catholic Church found that the haunting was a classic case of demonic infestation, oppression, obsession and possession. In the end, that is all that really matters.

I closed the report with a greater understanding of the haunting that changed my life. It had answered the questions I had spent years trying to find answers for. What struck me even more was that I had the answers the whole time. I may not have had a specific name or religious understanding, I just needed to trust my own heart and my own thoughts, because the answers were there right in front of me. Maybe it was because some of it was so hard for me to handle, or I was not ready to admit understanding, so I had blocked it out or did not want to really accept the truth. In fact, I felt, after reading the report, that I might have been performing this strange masquerade for a truth I really did not want to know. Whether I accept it now or not, it is what it is. I can no longer run from it under the guise of seeking it.

A strange contradiction in thought, but at the same time I can see it was the way I protected myself from it and the truth.

When I finished reading that day, I could feel the final steps of healing and understanding had begun. With each passing day afterward, I became more and more homesick for my family and my friends. I wanted to go home. I wanted to be back with those who mattered most to me. This was not home. This was a self-inflicted sanctuary that I no longer needed, and with that understanding all events and circumstance began to pull me back to where I belonged. Back to home.

On December 7, 2012, I packed up and headed back home - home to where I grew up. This was my childhood home in Washington, Missouri. I drove straight through the night, and I could not get there fast enough. I arrived early the next morning at my father's and mother's house once more. The last time I had stayed there was when we had first fled the Union house. Now I found myself there by choice. I felt safe and protected. Later that morning, my granddaughter Caroline came through the front door. She had no idea I was there, and when she saw me, she ran to me and put her arms around my neck with the biggest hug.

Those days are behind me now. I found a place to live in the town of Washington. This was my homecoming. Things fell into place quickly, and before I knew it, life was back to a normal pace. The beach seemed like a long time ago, and I could not imagine what I was thinking when I moved there. I moved halfway across the country to end up coming home again, but I guess that is part of the learning journey, isn't it?

I settled into my new home and started my journey once more, only to receive some disturbing news shortly afterward. The phone rang. I could hear Bill on the other end of the line. He sounded worried and not like himself at all. "Steven, it's Tom. He is in the hospital. He had some sort of stroke last night. He has not awakened yet. Steven, it is serious." I listened quietly. How could he be talking about Tom? I was getting ready to spend time with him very soon. As a matter of fact, I needed to tell him I saw one of his ghost pictures in a movie I had watched a few nights before. He couldn't be talking about Tom?

Unfortunately, he was. Tom Halstead died at 7:10 a.m. on Valentine's Day. It took our breath away. For days, all of us walked around feeling like we could not breathe. We walked around with this tremendous sadness, which would not go away. All of the things that had separated all of us, years ago, seemed so insignificant. We were a family once again and we had been so distant from each other for way too long. Within the shadow of death, we came together again. We came together to remember, and we came together to grieve.

On a snow-covered Sunday afternoon we once again gathered at Zombie Road. We gathered to say our final goodbyes to Tom, who had meant so much to each and every one of us. We stood there on the clearest blue day, in the snow. We shared thoughts of Tom and we prayed together. James played "Amazing Grace" on his bagpipes, which Tom loved to listen to so much. A wreath was put on the edge of the Meramec River. The last thing we did was release balloons. As we watched the balloons sail into the sky, there was a moment that I will never forget. The balloons formed into a perfect heart in the sky. At that moment, you could feel a sense of peace. I have no other words for it. It was a moment that literally took our breath away, and I have to tell you it felt like Tom was with us for that singular moment, and he was happy. We stood there in the snow and that was the instant we said goodbye to Tom. Together.

December 10, 2013

Helen is dead. There is no other way to say it other than just to spit it out. The words seem strange to me now, even as I write them. She died on an ice-covered, snowy Friday—just a few days ago. She went out to clean the ice and snow from her car and when she returned inside, she collapsed from a major heart attack and was gone in an instant.

Gone in an instant? What the fuck does that mean? After all we had been through. After all we had survived, she goes out outside to take care of the most mundane of tasks - and dies? It just doesn't make sense. She was stronger than that. She wasn't supposed to die on me. She was not supposed to die alone. I should have been there. I should have been there to hold her hand. She was like a big sister to me and, in many ways, she had replaced my own sister who had died. Out of all the nightmares and craziness, I was given back something I had lost. Helen was the only one who really understood and knew what we went through during the haunting. I feel so alone. I want to get mad and I want to scream, "This is not fair!" She was only 66 years old. We should have had plenty of time left. Instead, I am left here alone with "gone in an instant."

My phone rang at 10:35 p.m. that Friday night. I answered it, anticipating Helen's voice on the other end of the line. "Steven, it's Patty. Mom's dead," Helen's daughter said, very quickly. I could tell by the way she said "Steven" that there was something terribly wrong. I think I screamed or yelled into the phone. I am not sure. It is all a blur now. The shock overtook me instantly. The fog has not totally lifted from me yet, and I dread the moment it does. The moment when the realization fully hits me that Helen will never be there again when I need her. Helen will never be there again, with a cup of coffee or a piece of cake, to make me feel better when life has taken an unexpected turn. Helen will never be there again with that unspoken understanding of what we went through during those dark days. Helen will simply no longer be there.

I spent the whole day with her last Tuesday, Christmas shopping. We had the best day. We laughed so much all day long. It was like old times, and Helen was like the old Helen. She was clear and lucid the entire day. We talked about things we had never discussed before, and things we had not discussed in a long time. We talked about our families and how much we loved them. We talked about our exes, about how good it felt to finally move on by forgiving them and putting away all of the things they put us through. Helen told me she was in a very good place. The best place she had been in a long time. And then on Sunday, not even a week later, we were in a church saying our goodbyes. It just does not seem possible or even real. I pick up the phone and expect her to be there, and I get angry when she is not there. The veil of grief comes washing over me again.

I always thought people might be afraid of Helen when they met her, but that was never the case. People loved her. When we would go to give a talk or open a movie, people would surround her with questions. Not only did they have questions, but people wanted to touch her. This never bothered her. I would see her surrounded by people, giving them hugs one after the other, answering anything they had to ask her. People gravitated to her light. I can only guess that the same thing is going on in heaven now. You know, she used to say to me, "That old Mr. Winters had better hope I do not die before him, or I will haunt the hell out of him." No one has heard from or received even the slightest sign from Helen yet. I imagine she has her hands full with old Mr. Winters. I would like to think she is busy haunting him, instead of being haunted by him and his wicked ways. I would like to think she is busy and now he is the one running, for once. I hope his guardian angels are watching over him, because he now has a heavy load to carry.

Yesterday I was looking at pictures of Helen from over the years. I could not help but notice the drain the haunted years had upon her. I never really noticed it before, until I was looking at the photographic evidence of what these years had done to her. She had aged way before her time. It was obvious, the toll it had taken on her body. I had to remind myself it was only the outward appearance I was viewing. Inside, Helen demonstrated the strength of giants and the greatness of the saints. I remember sitting in that church listening to the priest years ago, and how Helen began to cry when he told us that the good are the ones the demonic will attack. Helen never knew how good she was. Helen never understood how special she was. The things she did in this life, she did without thought. She lived her life from her heart, and that is why the demonic attacked her. She reflected everything God could ever want from us. The demonic had tried to extinguish her light but failed over and over again. The light that drew people to her, the same light that people desired to touch and be close to, now is the light that shines like a star from heaven.

A Final Word

The years have passed quickly and all of the trauma and the hurt of those years seems so long ago now. I am now a married man to my husband Rick. Yes, I am in a gay marriage and before you begin to try to construe things into something they are not, let me explain it to you in the same way I explained it to my daughter Lydia. "Sexuality is neither black nor white. Most people's sexuality can be found somewhere in the grey areas." That was the case for me. It is more about loving a person for me than their sex. It is still true when I first got married all those many years ago to Krista, I planned on staying married for the rest of my life. Obviously, as you all know, it didn't work or turn out that way. I am married to an amazing person now and I plan on staying married to Rick for the rest of my life. He is a good man with a big heart and a huge capacity for love which in return makes up for a lot my insecurities. I have given him a million reasons, but he remains.

In 2017, we began the process of building our house in Playa Del Carmen, Mexico. It took over two years to be completed. Our home is very much a reflection of who we are. It is very modern, but with touches of the old and spirituality. The spiritual especially in the bedroom where we sleep. The nightmares do not plague me anymore. I am not saying I do not have them, but they have come less and less through the years. I spiritually cleanse the home monthly, smudging with sage and palo santo. I will not tell you there is no paranormal activity in the home because there is at times, Mainly, small things like lights and things coming on and going off on their own. Nothing frightening at all, and I actually miss it when it doesn't happen for a long time. Something tells me it is those who protect me making it known they are watching.

My father passed away suddenly this past October. My parents have always been my best friends in this life. I have been told I made a huge difference in their lives as well. From what I have heard, "There was life before Steven and then there was life after Steven." I have never been completely sure what that means fully, but I do know my birth was an important moment in my parents' lives. Of course, the birth of a child is important in any parents' lives.

Our children are our legacy we leave behind and we give to this world.

I miss my dad. I talked to him every single day and sometimes multiple times a day. I still talk to my mom just as much. They have always been my touch stone in this life, and all of this has changed me in ways I never imagined. You know they say you don't fully mature until you lose a parent. I believe that is very true. I understand that now.

I look in the mirror now and I see my dad looking back at me. He didn't always agree with me, but he always respected me enough to know I was honest with my words and my feelings. Sometimes it freaked him out that I had no filter. I would always tell him exactly what was on my mind. There is a lot to be said about being straight forward and to the point with people. I know my dad respected me for that even though at times we would clearly disagree.

This has changed me in ways I never saw coming. It has made stronger and wiser in ways I never thought was possible. I am willing to deal with things more head on now even the uncomfortable things. It's hard to explain the symbiotic relationship between a father and his son. It's carried in the genes and is imprinted deeply in our DNA. I haven't lost him as much as I gained an even stronger relationship with him. I talk to him constantly in my mind and in my heart. That is difficult to explain. The communication is still there but it has just changed its form.

My father was a very loving and accepting man. I saw him grow and evolve through the years in his beliefs and what he believed his truth was. When I came out to him when I was 29, he told me he loved me no matter what and nothing was going to change that. And it never did. In fact, I watched him change his ideas about so many things throughout the years of his life that followed. He became accepting of LGBTQ ministers. At one point he wanted to hang a gay pride flag at his church. This church was in rural Missouri, and it took a lot of talking to convince him that he could love and accept me without putting himself and church in danger of repercussions. Other kids had gay support groups and PFLAG. I had my mother and father who were always there to support me no matter what. When I was 32, I broke up with my then live-in boyfriend. My Mom was the first person I called for advice. She was the ear I needed to listen because at that moment in my life I felt like I was never going to find someone to love and to love me in return. She put my mind at ease and told when the time and person was right, I would know it. These were words which turned out to be prophetically wise.

My parents were always there for me when I needed them. I realize now that my siblings had no idea how close I was to my parents and just how much my parents knew about my life. My relationship and experience with my parents was, and is, very different than theirs in many ways. It's as if being the gay son had somehow brought me closer to them and my ability to communicate with them was much easier for me than it was for my brothers. There was and is no unfinished business between us ever. We talked everything out completely even during these later years when it has become much more difficult.

The one thing I can tell you without question is that when Rick stepped into the picture, they accepted him completely. They quickly grew to love him as their own son. On our one-year wedding anniversary my mother told me that she thought my marriage was the best decision I made with my life. She loved seeing me so happy. She didn't say it but I am sure there was a part of what she was saying that was referencing the conversation we had about finding love those many years before.

I have been very lucky to have my mom and dad in my life. They are and will always be my heroes. That will never be lessened or tarnished by anyone or anything. The more I have learned about all aspects of my parent's lives, it has always brought to me a clearer understanding of who they were and what they were about. There are people in this world who hold resentments and misunderstandings of who their parents were and why they made the decisions they did because they never take the time to put themselves in their shoes and understand the motivations for what, how and why they made the choices they made. That is not the way it was and is for me at all. The more I have learned about my parents lives the more respect I have gained for them and their decisions in this life. I can honestly say I can see them for how very human they are and for the sacrifices they made for me in this life to make it better. Their unwavering love throughout the good and even not so good times in my life has been a solid, stable driving force which has helped me become an adult they could and are proud to call their son. I am lucky and blessed to have had them.

I think out of everything my dad did in his life he would want to be remembered as one of the best fathers and grandfathers there was. Our family was very lucky that we had him. I am not just saying this. There are very few men who could walk in my father's footsteps. He was the best man I knew, and he was the best father and grandfather to my children I could have asked for. I lost a huge piece of my life when he passed away. He was not only my dad, but he was also my best friend. I know in the coming months and years that piece will never be filled or replaced in my life.

I talked to my dad almost every single day. Even living in Mexico I still talked with him at least once a day if not more. I am missing that right now as I do every single say since he left us. What was our last conversation about? Strangely enough we talked about ghosts. My father's last words to me were his last words to me he said every single time we hung up the phone. His last words to me were, "I love you." My Dad came to visit me the morning before his funeral. It was very early in the morning. About 5:30am. I woke up and he was standing in the corner watching me. He was dressed in his suit. The suit he was going to be buried in the next day. He was only there for a moment and then he was gone. It was the most reassuring thing he could have done. It was his way of reminding me he was still there. Of all the mornings he could have visited that morning was the perfect moment because that was the morning, I needed the strength of my father the most.

Life is moving forward as it always does. We take its pain and challenges and we put it to work for us in various ways. Rick and I are getting ready to move from Playa Del Carmen. We find ourselves once again building a house. This time more so in the mountains than near the shore. We missed the seasons, and this new move will give us more of the seasonal changes and cooler weather. I am still the same guy in many ways that I have always been but in happier times I have found myself growing in various ways. I still find time to thank the universe for all of the blessings it has bestowed on me throughout my life, and I also always try to remember to bless the wicked. It is not the good times when you learn from the most. The real learning comes in those times of challenge. I think that's really the difference in everything for me. My demons hate a good mindset and cannot bear the idea of a grateful well lived life. I wish I had known this decades ago, but life is a journey. I hope by sharing my challenges and journey I have been able to help someone else in theirs.

A Professional Evaluation of
The Steven LaChance Case

Some Things to Consider

First, what you are about to read is something which came to me unsolicited and without my participation in its creation. It is the analysis, thoughts and ideas from a Roman Catholic Priest and Demonologist. You will find out he was trained by some of the Churches leading Exorcists. I know where he is located, and I have seen photos of him as well. I have on two separate occasions spoken with his office. I am going to withhold his identity because I want to protect him and his congregation from any unsolicited contact. Living in the whirlwind of this haunting I understand the lengths people might go to gain access to him. So, yes, in a sense, I am protecting him. As you will read in the report, he has given me clear permission to do with its contents as I see best. I acknowledge the words of the Church and have accepted the apology from the Church for not getting to us soon enough to help. This is also something you will read in the report.

I am grateful the amount of time this member of the Demonology Clergy took to offer their thoughts and analysis of what happened during the haunting. The education they offer is welcomed and I am grateful for their thoughts and input. However, with many other things in life, I don't completely agree with everything that is written and I can assure that very few of you out there will either. This doesn't make it not valuable because a lot of it I found value in and do agree with. I also want you to keep in mind that it was written in 2012 and the Churches stance on many things has changed. The report has been edited not changed. It went through some punctation edits and there have been a few passages deleted which could be considered hurtful and misconstrued by some. Those passages were very limited and pertained to the Church's standing on certain issues and not the actual case itself. Even with this the report is very personal in nature.

Second, there are some conclusions in the report I do not fully agree with. My ex-wife Krista gets a whole lot of the blame laid at her doorstep. Though she does deserve some of that blame for certain things, life is a two-way street, and it does take two to tango. What I am saying is that she is not responsible for everything that happened to us. I played a part in my own life and haunting as well. I think it is unfair to classify her as completely demon possessed in her actions. I am sure that if this report were rewritten today, the fact that I am a gay man in a gay marriage would find itself in the mix somewhere. That is called a prejudice and is not the case. It wasn't the case for the breakup of my marriage, and it was not the reason for the haunting as well. I think it would be unfair to the LGBTQA+ community if I did not point this out. Even the Church's idea over the past twelve years has changed toward our community as well. But I cannot share this report without saying that being gay has nothing to do with a haunting or the demonic, just in the same way being a heterosexual does. It is sexual behavior that is often the problem which is a very different thing separate from sexuality. The Churches stance on this is clearly pointed out within the analysis. There are many gay Christians in this world and churches who accept a diverse community.

Why is it important to point this out? There was a time not too long ago where exorcism was considered a viable solution to being gay. Of course, it wasn't a solution, and it did serious harm to some who underwent these exorcisms. There are way more people in this world who believe in a loving God than a hateful one today. Please keep the year difference in mind when reading the report because there is a difference between outdated archaic ideas and the realities of spirituality today. In fact, the current Pope made a statement and apology to the LGBTQA+ community just the other day which acknowledged that everyone is welcomed within the Church.

Right after reading the report for the first time, I was shaken by what I had read. I picked up my phone and immediately called my mother who reminded me that this is "just one point of view." She was right. This is just one idea and I think it would be unfair of me to not point out there are many ideas and beliefs in this world surrounding spirituality and the supernatural. This report is just one of those beliefs. I have had many people help me through the years of the haunting. Many of them had different ideas and solutions. It would be unfair to them to say that this report is the only way, or the final say on it. Like with anything I have shared with you I want to ask you to go into the reading of this report with an open mind. Be ready for the parts you disagree with. Let it spark in internal conversation, first within yourself of what you believe, and then second to spark conversations with others. Those two things would make not only me happy, but I am also sure the Church as well. All anyone can ask from anyone when concerning these subjects is to consider the possibilities and then make up your mind about what you believe in the end. In doing that, we will all learn from this exercise in sharing.

This report is not going to be like any other paranormal document you have ever read. It is very important, and it is a one of a kind. It really gives us a glimpse into the workings of Catholic Demonology and the handling of these type cases within the Catholic Church. Names in the report and identities within the report, just like in the book, The Uninvited have been changed to protect those involved. In some cases, even the genders were changed. The names and identities will correspond with what you find in the book and are the same as you will read in the report. This was done not to conceal anything from the public but as a way of protecting others from the attention that can surround a case like the Screaming House. For those of you who have a copy of The Uninvited you might want to grab it because during the report you will see it is used as a point of reference throughout. In a sense, The Uninvited has just become a Demonology textbook. One word of caution. The Priest has given me permission to share this with anyone and in any way I see needed. However, there is a warning to take into consideration. This report is not meant for children. He was very clear with this instruction. With all of this in mind, here is the Roman Catholic Church's evaluation and analysis of the Steven LaChance Case.

THE ROMAN CATHOLIC CHURCH

A Professional Evaluation of The Steven LaChance Case

10/29/2012

This is a professional evaluation on the Steven LaChance case by a Catholic Priest and Demonologist.

Dear Steven LaChance,

I am a validly ordained Catholic Priest. I have been ordained since 2002 and living FAITHFULLY in religious life since 1995 under four vows of poverty, chastity, obedience, and our fourth vow of redemption.

I am also a Demonologist - and I am not kidding or exaggerating. I have been involved in this work for the past twelve years. I have been very successful through Our Lord in removing demons out many individual homes and out of their lives. I also have the battle scars to prove it. I was not appointed to becoming a Demonologist; I was given this gift by Our Lord which is why I have been so successful in removing demons out of people's lives.

I was trained by some to the top Exorcists in the Catholic Church. As all Exorcists will tell you in the Catholic Church, this is not easy work and can be very dangerous. This is not an exaggeration. When a demon is removed, they don't forget who removed them. Demons have been known to come back later to cause problems in an Exorcist's life. In addition, all Catholic Priest who are good Exorcists will tell you, after each case is completed, the Exorcist loses some of his humanity.

I am writing concerning your book entitled "The Uninvited" or, more specifically, your case I would like to offer you a professional evaluation, based on my thorough knowledge and experience in the field.

Before I begin, I want to first apologize on behalf of the Catholic Church. The priest who blessed the house you were living in was obviously afraid and basically did not know what to do or how to do it. Many priests are basically afraid or do not want to get involved in this type of work. There are many reasons for it. Some just don't believe or want to believe demons exist based on the liberal theology they learn. One specific reason is the commitment involved with this type of work. All Catholic priests who are Exorcists will tell you that once you step over the line and enter this fight there is no turning back. You either fight the demonic and continue to fight them the rest of your life or they will conquer you. That might sound odd, but the demonic will attack a priest worse than any other individual. Just look at the priesthood scandals involving priests abusing children. Though each priest who did such a horrible thing to a child is responsible for his actions, what most people do not realize is that there is a powerful demon (demons) in charge of and instigating such sexual abuse. This has been confirmed by Our Lord, that there is a major demon that specializes in causing the falls of individuals who have some type of authority (priests, teachers, and coaches) through sexual abuse. Again, I repeat, as you will soon learn, all these individuals are still RESPONSIBLE for their actions and behaviors. No one can ever blame a demon for their behavior. A demon cannot force your free will unless you invite the demon to do so. More on this later.

This powerful demon does not just go after priests, he has helped cause the downfall of coaches - such as the football coach at Penn State - and many teachers in the public schools, as demonstrated in the national and local media.

All Exorcists including myself will tell you, once you step over this line and take on the demonic, there is an overwhelming attack on the priest's sexuality. The demonic has been known to go after the priest's family and even kill off their family - especially parents. These are some of the reasons priests do not want to get involved with cases dealing with the demonic. Most of all, you need to be called to this type of work. The calling does not come from a bishop, priests, or themselves. This special calling comes from Our Lord Jesus who therefore provides you with the protection you need to withstand the attacks against the demonic forces. The bottom line, the priest's faithfulness and relationship with Our Lord is crucial to doing battle with the demonic. In addition, the Canon Law of the Catholic Church states that permission must be granted by the bishop in order to do an exorcism on a particular person.

Before I get into your case, I am assuming that the people in the book are all real and that their names are changed to protect their identity. Steve, I do believe your case is real and not a fantasy. I also believe if you would have known me, I could have stopped much of what has happened in your life. There are many things in your case you are writing about that a trained Demonologist / Exorcist can pick up that are very significant. In addition, as we proceed through your case and go through the highlights, I will be educating you along the way on the reality of the Angelic world and the Catholic Faith. With that, let us start from the beginning of your book *The Uninvited*. We are going to ignore the preface and the prologue. Starting in chapter 1 page 3, you are living in Union, Missouri. You then proceed through the birth of the children. Then you come to page 6 where there is a big red flag you probably do not see - your wife and the mother of these children decided to divorce you. Why? First off, this has nothing to do with vou or anything you did or did not do. You wrote that your wife says she never wanted to be a mother, but she did this for you. That is a lie! No mother who gives birth to three innocent children picks up and leaves you and them for this lame excuse unless something is DRIVING her to do this. This was a big red flag right from the start. Your wife was in something demonic and did not know how to get out of it or handle it. The first clue something was demonic going on was the birth of Lydia. You wrote: "Lydia, as if sensing the events that would one day shake our family to its foundation, poked her tiny head into the world and immediately returned to her mother's womb. (Page 5)" How you describe these events unfolding in the delivery room is not normal. Even though I am no medical doctor and perhaps this could be explained medically, it can also be explained spiritually. In infancy, babies have little awareness or consciousness. The point is that though babies are not fully aware of their surroundings like an adult would, they still have some sense that something is wrong or that evil is around, even from their mother's womb. The birth of Lydia was the first red flag that you or perhaps wife was into something demonic. More on this later!

We need to proceed to chapter two, page ten. With the loss of your sister Janice, you describe an argument with her about not liking your wife and she was not happy with the direction of your life. Here is another major red flag. This argument took place on Easter. This is the Holy Season in the Catholic Church when a lot of demonic activity happens. The demonic angels hate Easter. They start overwhelming attacks that most people do not see. The demonic angels are involved in extraordinary activities during the seasons of Halloween, Christmas, Easter and, especially, Divine Mercy Sunday. In addition, there is a phenomenon going on with this event that parallels with the birth of your daughter Lydia that you are missing.

Steve, when God created humanity, He did so with immense intelligence and foresight. Without getting into all the theology of our creation, there is a certain aspect that needs to be brought to your attention. As each person is created by God, the Divine Majesty (God) built into the human nature a natural reaction to know when it is around evil. We all have this condition in our nature. For instance, when someone is around evil, they get cold chills or the room goes very cold, or hair stands up on end. Now I am not saying this is the case all the time. Some of it can be just fear or something else. However, I am saying that, when evil is around, this phenomenon occurs. Often time people will say they feel like they are being watched. This is the built-in tendency for all humans to beware that evil is around. Now, getting back to your case, your sister had these warning signs go off inside her when she was around your wife, just like your daughter did in the delivery room. This is one of the reasons Janice did not like your wife. In the case of your daughter, Lydia, she senses this evil from her mother's womb. Since your wife was involved (or had been involved) in doing something demonic, Lydia could sense this from the womb because of the built-in reaction to evil that God placed in each one of us, beginning at conception.

At this point, I need to go through another reality with the demonic. When the Angels were created by God, they were given very elite intelligence in their nature. They did not earn this intelligence; it was given to them freely by God. In the study of Angels (Angelology) this is called Innate Knowledge. Each angel was given their specific intelligence that God wanted them to have. This is much different with humanity. Human beings have to earn their intelligence by education, experience, etc. However, God does provide many souls with what is called Divine Enlightenment or Divine Illumination. Mystics in the Church have this gift from God.

Returning back to the Angels, there were nine choirs of Angels created by God. Each Angel had to earn their way into Heaven by some Divine Test that the Church has never defined nor do we know how long this "testing" period took. We do know they were tested before they entered into Heaven. Some failed the test and started a rebellion. The Angel who started this rebellion was given the name Lucifer from the Creator. Lucifer means: "light bearer" The following are the nine choirs of Angels according to their rank from the top down:

First choir: the Seraphim. Saint Michael the archangel is a Seraphim.

Second choir: The Cherubim Lucifer was the archangel for the Cherubim.

Third choir: The Thrones: they make up the last of the choirs of the Heavenly court.

Fourth choir: Domination.

Fifth choir: Virtues.

Sixth choir: Powers.

Seventh choir: Principalitie.

Eighth choir: Archangels.

Ninth choir: Guardian Angels.

Do not confuse the Archangel choir with the archangel title. The archangel choir themselves are a distinct choir. However, Archangel also means "Chief" or ruling angel in Latin. So, each choir has a chief or Archangel of that particular choir In each one of these choirs there is ranking. The highest rank in each choir is given the title "Archangel" which is the ruling angel of that choir.

Back to Lucifer - Lucifer was the chief or Archangel of the Cherubim choir when he was created. Lucifer rebelled and lost this position among the good angels after a big fight or rebellion in Heaven. (A side note: most people do not realize that this was a huge and vicious fight in the Heavenly realms). When Lucifer rebelled and began this fight, he convinced a third of all these Angels to go with him. Michael from the Seraphim class got the rest of the good angels which, was two thirds of them, and fought against Lucifer and his angels. Saint Michael and his angels won and threw Lucifer, along with all the angels with him, into a place we now call Hell. The estimates of theses angels (who are now called demons) that fell into hell were in the billions. This is not an exaggeration. According to one of the Doctors of the Catholic Church, the angels who became demons came from the Cherubim choir, Virtue choi, the Powers choir, the Principalities choir, Archangels choir and the

Angels choir. There are no angels in hell from the Seraphim, Thrones or the Dominations choirs This is a vital piece of information you need to know about the demonic angels. The higher the Angel is in these choirs the more intelligence and thus power they have for example, Saint Michael the Archangel from the Seraphim class has the most intelligence, and thus the most power. Saint Michael is a head of all the angels,
including the demons. With the demonic, Lucifer whose name was changed to Satan after the fall, is ahead of all the evil angels There is a lot more I could say about this, but for the sake of time we need to move on.

All demons enter someone's life by way of invitation no demon ever came into someone's life without first being invited by the individual themself or they become victims because someone else invited them. Now how are they invited? They are invited through various ways: the most popular and the most dangerous are individuals using Ounja boards, those who participate in Satanic masses or Satanic cults, those who participate in voodoo, and those who participate in the Nigenan cults or the Santena cults, the occult, etc. In my experiences these are the most dangerous because often the demons from a higher choir come through these means. When these demons come through, they usually bring with them other demons who are assigned to them from the lower choirs of demons They can also be invited by witchcraft, sorcery, using tarot cards, going to psychics, going to palm readers, being cursed or trying to curse someone else, etc. In addition, more and more cases are coming to us because there are many individuals who get involved in this kind of work (such as paranormal investigators who do not know what they are doing) who are either possessed by a demon/demons or are having bad experiences beyond the normal in their life. They go to explore hauntings or various cases with paranormal activity and the demon or demons causing this activity latches onto them.

Now, finally, back to your wife. In blunt English your wife either knew, or did not know, she invited a demon into your MARRIAGE by something she was involved in. This took place way before she divorced you, Steve. Demons also like to attack those who do not practice any form of religion. In other words, demons like sinners who do not repent. Sinners who do not change their lives are prime meat for the demonic angels. The demonic angels especially enjoy going after those individuals who are narcissistic. (A narcissist is a person who looks in the mirror and sees themselves as god - selfish and self-centered.) As all Exorcists will tell you, those in mortal sin can easily become agents of the demonic. It is also important to take note here Steve. Because of the marriage you were in with your wife, they will attack you because they were invited into the marriage. Your wife knew deep in her heart that she did something wrong; invited this demon or demons into both your lives through one of the various diabolical methods mentioned above, did not know how to handle the activity or havoc the demon or demons were causing in her life, became afraid and did not want any of this activity to infect you, or worse yet, the children. She probably thought she was going insane with all this demonic activity now in her life. As a result, she divorced you to get away from the children, thinking she was going to protect you and the children. Unfortunately, this doesn't work, nor will it ever work. Now Steve, even though you did not know this was going on in her life, the demons will start to affect your life because of the marriage It is not a coincidence that you rented these apartments and houses and had all these phenomena happen to you. The demons who were affecting your wife GUIDED YOU, after the divorce, to these apartments and houses you are about to rent. You did not select these places on your own. They were cleverly placed in front of you cleverly by these demons because these demons knew full well that these apartments and house you are about to rent have what is called demonic infestation, especially the three-bedroom house for rent in Union (page 23). The demons in this house are by far worse than the demons who were invited into your life by your wife. I will prove more about all of this as we proceed through your book.

On page 11, you write about your sister's death. I find it odd that this happened. Many red flags go up simply because of the signs happening in your life that you are not aware of nor can you understand. However, I will say this, I am not sure the demonic is completely innocent in the death of your sister. The demonic could have instigated her death, but I am not sure. There are too many questions that need to be answered. First, your sister who you love very much is removed out of your life (page 9), your wife, who you obviously loved, is removed out of your life and according to page 12 you are very angry and even hate God. All these signs are pointing to the demonic paranormal activity now in your life. You can be sure of this Steve, this type of hatred you describe on page is inspired by the demonic. Then you turned into an agnostic on page 13. Perfect, now the demonic has a clear opening in your life. I am almost sure there was probably other demonic activities going on in your life that are not mentioned in this book. This includes the time frame before your sister Janice died, especially around the pregnancy with Lydia, your first born, and after your sister died. The entrance points to the demon or demons entering into your marriage is either during the pregnancy with Lydia (but before she was born) or before Lydia was conceived. Thus, somewhere along this timeframe, your wife invited the demons into her life and then eventually into your life. One final word about entrance of the demonic into your life. The demons enter your life very slowly. Rarely, do they rush in to cause trouble quickly. Demons often make some type of entrance into someone's life, and then LEAVE for a while, getting their victims to think whatever was occurring in their life is now over. However, demon or demons are in the background watching and planning their attacks.

Going back to the book, notice on page 13 something out of the ordinary is described by Lydia, your first-born child. You write on page 13, "Early one morning, about a year after Janice's death, Lydia told me she has seen Aunt Jan. She was in my closet last night wearing a pretty yellow dress". No, she wasn't. What Lydia saw was a demon imitating Janice's soul. That is exactly what Lydia saw. If Janice was a good soul, she would not be appearing in Lydia's closet Janice would appear to Lydia, very gentle and asking for prayers or something good. No good soul would be in a closet to scare someone.

At this point, I need to continue to educate you. When a demon enters your life by way of invitation, (your wife) the very first victims of their assault are always the children.

This is true of all demons in all the cases I have studied by Exorcists who have more experience than me, and all that I personally been involved with. Why? Because the demons know full well that a child does not recognize that they are demonic and thus the demons attempt to make themselves "friendly" with the child because they are naive. If you speak to the child, they will eventually tell you something odd about what they see. For instance, did Lydia see Janice and was she completely normal looking or was something out of place, like her eyes missing or she looks normal until you look at her feet and see something that belongs to an an animal? When you are dealing with the demonic, they have the ability to imitate anyone or animal they choose. However, here is the problem the demons have; no demon can ever perfectly imitate someone or something, not even Satan with all his power. The problem is that children do not see this as odd, but as something normal. They still have child-like innocence and are very naïve. In addition, all Exorcists will tell you the main reason the demonic go right after the child is because the demons know that this is the best way to terrorize and mentally torture the parents. The demonic angels are very successful in this endeavor.

What most people do not consider is that the human soul in each of us can be seen. We take the soul for granted. The human soul can also be seen by others. Each of our souls, independent from the body, can see, hear, talk, touch, feel, think, speak, etc. Everything I am explaining here is all recorded in the Sacred Scriptures. For example, the Transfiguration scene shows us that Jesus took Peter, James and John up the mountain and is Transfigured before these three apostles. Elijah and Moses both show up at the scene and speak with Jesus (Luke 9:28-36) However, in the book of Deuteronomy, Moses died, and his body is buried (Deut. 34), yet he shows up in this scene. Moses does not have his glorified body because Jesus did not die on the cross nor did Jesus rise from the dead yet, nor has the Resurrection of the Body happened for humanity. Thus, the evidence of the reality of the human soul is shown here. This is only one of the many examples in the Sacred Scriptures that describes the concrete reality, though in spirit, of the human soul.

Notice how you write on page 13 that Lydia was sure she saw Janice in her closet. Only demons would do this to a child, and they usually get away with it because most parents, including you Steve, pass it off as the child's overly active imagination. I am not denying that this is a reality with children, however, in your case, as we will soon see, and you admit on page 13, this was not her imagination. If this was a good spirit, such as a good angel or even Janice's human soul, they would not be in a closet. Why this is all important facts is because I am showing you all the demonic activity in your life before you even move into this three-bedroom house you rented. One philosophical point we need to make clear here, the demonic world (this includes demons and human beings who are bent to do evil) are never satisfied. Evil (demons) always get worse, never better, until they are fought against by the Divine and humanity. More on this later.

On page 15, this is not true. The landlords were not renting to you because of the demonic. I am not saying that some landlords would not rent because of two boys; however, they could be sued for discrimination.

The demonic was guiding you to the appropriate house they wanted you to have to cause more harm. Thus, it would not take much for a demon to influence a potential landlord by causing them to say 'no' simply by having their presence near, causing ill feelings in the potential landlord's body (as mentioned previously) or by just whispering to them, "NO". Thus, you are being rejected not by the landlord but by the instigation of the demon.

In Chapter 3, on page 16, you write about the first two-bedroom apartment. Your first acknowledgement of paranormal activity was when every cabinet door in the kitchen was standing open while you were the only one home. You wrote that the kids were off with your parents, and you just came out of the shower. This is first time you acknowledge demonic activity in the book. However, this is not the first-time demonic activity has happened in your life. Again, more evidence that a demon (or demons) is now part of your wife. I could be wrong, but this demon was invited into your life from your wife, unless you omitted from this book something you might of done that caused you to invite this demon into your life. Again, I can only go with what is written here in the book.

I would like to go off the record here for a moment. Do not take this the wrong way Steve, and I do not want to sound like I am a male Chauvinist because I am a conservative Catholic Priest, however, women do have a greater tendency to invite demons into their life. They have a curiosity factor that sometime gets the best of them. Most men operate through the use of reason, where women operate through their heart or through their feelings. I am not saying they do not have reason, because all women have the use of reason. and can be very intelligent. But, if you go back to the Garden of Eden in Genesis, the serpent did trick Eve into taking the apple simply by getting her curious. The serpent did not tempt Adam because of reason, and Adam would have been more alarmed that the serpent was speaking since he was the creature put in charge of naming all the animals and creatures God created. Similarly, women want to know about relationships, their future, gossip etc., and this almost becomes an obsession with them. Thus, they become obsessed with wanting to know whatever is on their mind. They will tend to go to extremes to find out whatever it is they want to know where men normally do not become so obsessed with such matters. Because of this obsession and the drive that they must know something, they will resort to mediums, psychics, or participate in a séance, etc. (as mentioned above). Hence, in comes the trouble with the demonic. Most of these mediums, psychics, tarot card readers, etc., get their business from women. These are just the facts, and the results can be quite damaging. I am not saying that men don't have their problems, we sure do. I am only relating to you what might be relevant information that might be needed to understand what happened as written in your book. You must remember one very important fact about any type of medium that tries to communicate with the other side. They can never guarantee that what they are communicating with is a good spirit. Nor can any of these individuals who practice such nonsense ever claim it is all white magic. There is no such thing as white magic, it is all black. Often what they are communicating with are demons under very clever disguises.

Back to the book on page 16, you said that a woman was dead in this house for four days and then wondered if you were in a haunted house? The answer is no. Many people die in their homes or are found dead in their homes and no demonic activity occurs. Again, the demons must be invited by someone. This demon is attached to you by something evil your wife did.

I would love to discuss the rain that came down and the significance to this city, but we do not have that time to discuss this here because of the details that would be needed to explain it.

Moving on to chapter 5, with this three-bedroom house for rent in Union with Mr. Winters you found advertised in the newspaper with a rental price of $600, it probably did raise a red flag in your mind but for the wrong reasons. This is very low rent for a decent house of this size. Was it a shack you asked? Obviously not, however, it was obviously this low in price because no one wanted to rent it.

You finally met Mr. Winters on page 25. This man is evil and a pathological liar. Unfortunately, you did not pick this up, however, Lydia did. You wrote about his wig. Most men do not wear wigs unless they are insecure and are trying to hide something. This wig also seems to come off his head a lot which Mr. Winters keeps on putting back. At his age, does he really need to be that insecure about his looks? Or again, is he hiding something under that wig? His complexion as you describe 1t was pale white. Now his pale white skin can be cause by a bad heart which is possible with an elderly man. It can also be caused from great anxiety and fear because of the knowledge Mr. Winters has of this house.

Mr. Winters knew full well this place was haunted. By even allowing any innocent children into this house with all the harm that can occur to them is evil I suspect he had something to do with this house being haunted in the first place. I also suspect he or his family had also lived in this house when all this evil activity started. What infuriates me about this evil man is his advertisement. His advertisement was appealing for an innocent family with children with the knowledge that this house was dangerous. Then after vou finally move out of this house, he does the same thing again to the next family.

Then Mr. Winters takes you on his pathetic tour. Mr. Winters shows you the kitchen and starts to brag about it. Then on page 26 he says: "Now, this house was built in the 1930s. The mudroom attached to the kitchen was there for the menfolk who came home from work all dirty. They would clean up there before entering the houses that their wives had spent all day cleaning". Now, what person would keep a mudroom attached to a house? Any moisture in this room would thus create mud and be tracked all over the house So why keep it? I am a former building contractor that specialized in renovation of old houses before I became a Catholic Priest. I know houses like the back of my hand No normal person or contractor would keep this as a mudroom. They would have built either a bedroom out of it or turned it into some spare room for recreation or whatever, but not keep it as a mudroom. He kept this room, as it is, for an odd reason.

Then Mr. Winters takes you down into the basement. This infuriates me even more because in this basement is where most of the evil is. He first tells you that he is in the process of replacing this wallpaper. This is a lie! No, he is not in the process of replacing this wallpaper or it would have been done by now. This wallpaper is very old with bare spots which tells me it has been up for a long time and might even been the original or next to the original since 1930.

Then at the bottom of page 26 and top of page 27 he says, "See here," as he pointing to the ceiling, "that's a butcher shower the men used to clean themselves after they had slaughtered the hogs. Obviously, they couldn't use the mudroom for that dirty job." OH Really! Here is how sick this man is. So, you keep a shower in your house that was used to wash off blood from an animal while there is no concern for any germs, bacteria, or whatever possible disease that was left behind What about the drainage from the water in this butcher shower used to wash off the animal's blood? Where did that go? On the floor or down a drain that had no plumbing in the 1930's to drain into a public sewer system? Thus, this water and blood was drained first onto the floor (which could seep into any crack in the floor) and then it went under the house, and not into a septic tank! They had no septic tanks or indoor plumbing in the 1930's.

Oh, then he shows you the fruit cellar. How sick. This is no fruit cellar; this is another lie!

He just said they used this shower to slaughter the hogs. Where did they slaughter these hogs, outside? I doubt it. They slaughter them in this room he calls a fruit cellar after the hogs were led down through those slanted doors you described on page 27. Or why has the shower outside this so called "fruit cellar" room to wash off the blood from the hogs? And where did all the blood from the hogs they slaughter go, down another drain or onto the floor? Why this concrete ledge in this room?

Can goods whether fruit or cured meat can be stored on wooden shelves. This is a bit odd that there is an concrete slab in this room which takes a lot more time to build. Concrete is used to hold heavy items or used in holding structure, or pavements etc. not for shelving. This slab is where they placed the hogs they slaughtered. They would need something this strong if the hogs were very fat and heavy. This slab was also used for something evil. I also doubt that there are any electric lights for this room. (This whole basement probably has very little lighting.) This fruit cellar is very significant, and we will return to it later.

After you handed Mr. Winters the application on page 27, you left, and you write that he was off to begin his next historical tour with others.

Moving onto chapter 6 on page 29, you mention that evil had set its sights on your family. Yes, you are right about this, but it started because of your wife. That demon or demons led you to this house because a more powerful and vicious demons are waiting.

Now on to Matthew, your youngest son. He has an experience described on page 30. This was not a dream but a demon coming to torment him. Matthew describes this creature as a man. but he is not a man, but a demon. It is possible that this demon came from the old white house because Matthew has similar experiences later as written in your book. Or it could have been the demon as discussed above. Regardless of which one it is, this demon has evil plans. However, notice the demon went right after your youngest son. This is very common with demonic infestations with houses. Now, why did Matthew see him and not Michael who is sleeping in the top bunk? The goal of the demonic angels was to go after the youngest to torture you, Steve. Matthew did not have a bad dream; he was purposely awakened by something the demon did and then stood in the corner as Matthew described. Again, the key here Steve is that he is your youngest and the last one born. which would cause you the greatest harm if lost. The loss or harm to any child would cause you great distress, but the other two do not have the title of being the baby of the family, where Matthew does. Notice the demon did not bother the other two children.

Then on page 31, you wrote that you saw the shadow of a man. This was not a shadow of a man, but the actual demon going by. The demon did this on purpose, to achieve exactly what you said: "Thus little guy has really gotten to me." In other words, you started to question your sanity.

At this point we need to discuss demons very briefly. Can you see a demon even though they are created into a pure spirit? Yes, you can see a demon or even a good angel. However, your eyes need to be trained for this. In our pathetic culture with our so-called sciences (such as the psychological profession) we want to see thing made of material. There is very little room in these sciences to see spiritual beings. Yet, the demonic loves the psychological profession because these so-called professionals will deny that the demonic exist. Thus, often time people see things or hear voices and tell one of these professionals, they end up being diagnosed with some mental disease when this might not be the case at all. This allows the demons to continue working on these individuals who are now considered mentally sick. The reason for this is that they go undetected. A demon never wants to be detected, unless they are very powerful demons from the Cherubim choir or even the Powers choir. These demons from these choirs laugh at these professionals.

Remember this, the goal of a demon is to get their victim or victims to despair and lose their place in Heaven, and thus, drag them down to Hell. No demons ever want to go back to Hell as a failure. Demons want the destruction of humanity because of their VICIOUS HATE FOR THE DIVINE, of which Jesus died on the cross for our salvation. They do not want us in Heaven to enjoy the blessedness of God's glory which they freely gave up. This is why demons come viciously after the priest because of the sacrifice of the Mass and the presence of Our Lord in the Holy Eucharist, thus, the priesthood scandals in the Catholic Church.

Again, can you see a demon? The answer is yes. They will travel about by way of orbs that can be capture by a camera; often you will see a big black mass with red or green eyes; or they will camouflage themselves into a form of a human soul that previously existed and possible condemned to hell; they will even take on the form of a human body, a human soul or an animal. These are just some of the ways the demonic angels will manifest themselves.

Let's return to the book. Next, you claim you had a nightmare. No, this was not a nightmare, and you were not hearing things. This was the demon terrorizing you. The demon was getting you to question your sanity to lead you to despair.

We have to stop for a moment and discuss this phenomenon which happens again and again in your book. I hope you remember, but in the Gospel of Matthew, the apostle talks about the birth of Jesus much different than Luke does. The birth narrative in this Gospel has to do with Joseph. Now I do not want to go deep into this theology, but basically Joseph finds Mary pregnant and knows full well that this child is not his because he never had sexual relations with Mary, even though they were betrothed (which is like our engagement.) So, Joseph decided to divorce Mary, who is pregnant with Jesus, quietly, so he would not cause her any sorrow or pain. However, that night an Angel was sent by the Eternal Father who tells Joseph in a dream, not to fear but to take Mary as his wife that She will give birth to the Eternal Father's Son (Mt. 1:18-2). Without going further here into theology, the point I am making is the communication of the Angel by a dream. More specifically, Angels have the ability to go into what people consider as "dreams" to communicate with the individual. These are not exactly dreams as you will see.

What the good angel did for Joseph, evil angels do the same in the opposite direction. This is exactly what the demon did to you. Though the demon is evil, the demon is still an angel with this ability. This is called a diabolical obsession, which are demonic temptations through very intense absurd thoughts that the victim cannot free themselves from. The victim is tormented by a fixation that dominates their thoughts. These thoughts make the victims think they are going insane. This is compounded by the feeling of sadness and depression. Under the diabolical obsession these thoughts or impulses can turn into the urges to hurt someone. The victim sometimes wants to make a pack with the demon which they think will get them out of this trouble. In addition, the thoughts of profaning the Holy Eucharist in the Catholic Church and the thoughts of suicide are also common. The victims of diabolical obsession also have bad daydreams and nightmares.

That demon your son Matthew saw is causing these phenomena called diabolical obsession through what you call a nightmare. This is actually not a normal nightmare, but the demon going into your mind and showing you whatever the demon wants through various evil images along with an evil voice. This can happen while you are asleep or even wide awake. For example, under a diabolical obsession, a victim of the demon will be wide awake, and all of a sudden see blood run down a wall, or see a demon's ugly face, or be shown some very scary or ugly image. This is part of diabolical obsession. The victim is not dreaming or seeing things but have images displayed before them instigated by the demon. The demon is controlling this phenomenon. Now, these images are often coming from past true events which the demons are using to terrorize a person. This phenomenon can also include a person speaking a language they never learned. This is NOT a diabolical possession. This is only one of the steps toward a diabolical possession.

What is the difference between a dream or a nightmare versus this phenomenon just described that fall under the category of diabolical obsession? Here is the difference. Dreams and/or a typical nightmare, comes from within the persons own faculties such as the imagination and consciousness. With this kind of diabolical obsession, when this phenomenon occurs, it is coming from the outside or exterior part of the person instigated by the demonic. (The good angels do the same thing for God's greater glory such as the good angel who communicated to Joseph to take Mary as his wife.) The victim can see these images and even hear what is going on in the image because of the influence from the demonic. Plain and simple, get rid of the demon or demons, these phenomena will stop.

The next category is diabolical oppression, which is much different from diabolical obsession. This is the next step toward a diabolical possession. Under the diabolical oppression there are exterior forces from the demonic angels influencing the victim or victims' property and material things. As you will see on the bottom of page 31, after you had this experience/nightmare what happened next? You felt a pressure on your chest. You experienced a leaning or a pushing down into the bed and pinning you to it. This is another form of diabolical oppression.

The following are some of the forms that fall under diabolical oppression. The demons can also scratch, bite, claw, choke, trip someone, push someone down the steps, slap, punch, sexually molest or assault the victim both male and female, spit at you, cry loudly, sing, cry like a baby, growl like any of the animals, bang, turn water faucet on, turn on and off lights, open cabinet doors, open any door in the house and then slam it, prevent doors from opening, walk loudly across the floor above the room you are standing in or walk loudly in the attic or roof, stamp loudly up the steps especially at night when you are in bed sound asleep, turn a warm room very cold or hot, have a room smell like sewage or rotten flesh, shake the whole house, use four letter words, throw books off of a bookshelf, smash sacred items, do physical harm to pets include killing them, cause fires, play games with you while you are in the shower (especially with women), move toys or items around the room or have the toys or other objects float in mid-air, cause static on electronics such as the TV or Radio, or telephone, cause an infestation of insects such as bees or roaches in your home or just one room, rearrange the furniture in a room or the whole house, affect your health, etc.

These are commonly held errors or beliefs in this field usually held by "Paranormal Investigators":

1) There no such thing as a negative energy - they are demons; there is no such thing as a ghost taking or living off your energy - they have their own energy and do not need yours.

2) There is no negotiation with these spirits such as saying to the ghost in your house "You can live here just leave my family alone." This is a major error, the spirit whether it is demonic or occasionally a human spirit needs to leave or be forced out of the house or building;

3) There is no such thing as a good human spirit coming back to settle their affairs.

4) There is no such thing as doing work on a house, such as construction, and a human spirit (who is now deceased) gets angry and causing trouble because you are working on your house, that might have formerly been theirs.

5) There is no such thing as making a demon angrier, they are always angry.

6) There is no such thing as white

magic, it is all black.

7) There is no such thing as a psychic, medium, or sensitive giving any guarantees that who they are communicating with are good spirits, they are usually evil spirits.

8) Spiritual orbs are not the only way a spiritual entity can travel.

9) Those in this line of work do not necessarily need the history of the building or the house, (or the item if it is cursed) it may help, but it is not necessary.

10) Electronic equipment is not needed in solving any demonically infested house or building, it may help, but it is not necessary. In addition, the electronic equipment cannot be totally trusted when investigating demonic angels, they will manipulate /deceive what you are seeing on the film or equipment.

The demon was there, but you did not see it because you were not looking for a demon. Fear takes over a person when they experience this type of diabolical oppression and thus you are more worried to survive this painful and shocking experience than to look for a demon created from pure spirit. In addition, all demons can travel very quickly; they get in, do whatever, and get out. However, one thing the demonic likes to do, get their victims afraid. The more fear they can instigate in you, the more you will become isolated, depressed or despair. Never, ever fear a demon. This is what they want, fear that can eventually lead to mental illness and despair.

On page 32 a conversation with the demon begins. The demon says: "You know you want to look at me. Look at me for I am glorious." See how pompous and arrogant they are. You wrote about a foul stench, well that is what is smells like in Hell. Steve, you then say: "Please God" and the demon responds: "God isn't here. God doesn't exist. You've said so yourself, haven't you." From the demonic perspective, only this part is true because they were in the background listening according to what you were thinking and doing on page 12-13, especially where you wrote: "With time my anger at God lessened, and over time I became at best agnostic, and at worst an atheist." As I mentioned above, this was a clear opening for them. Now, do not torture your mind with this because this was not all your fault as I have been explaining. First, based on what was going on, God knows you did not mean this. Second, you have given me no evidence in this book, at all, to demonstrate that you had invited demons into your life. Third, I made it clear to you that your wife did invite them into your marriage. Fourth, and most of all, how can anyone hold you responsible for such things that you have no idea at the time were happening?

At this point, I do have to bring in another subject before we return to this book. From my perspective as a Catholic Priest and Demonologist, it causes me great sorrow to walk into someone's house and see nothing and I mean nothing that represents God. No pictures, crosses, images, statues, bibles, or anything that is Holy. Even Holy Protestants have Bibles on their tables, or perhaps the famous picture of Jesus knocking at the door, or a picture of His face. This is so sad, especially among Catholics who should have holy items around. Why? These items are held

sacred and the demonic despises them. From
the lower choirs of demons, most are afraid of
such items because of their sanctity. A blessed
item by a faithful, holy priest, can keep off
demons from the lower classes from entering
the person's home. If you ever studied any
cases where a Catholic is having similar
experiences like you had Steve, the first thing
they go after are these images. Why? They
can't stand them, and it poisons their eyes to
look at them. Thus, they make attempts to
remove them or break them. Now this is
unfortunate, however, it is a clear sign to the
victim that there is a demon involved. What I
find in many homes are things that have no
power to ward off any demonic spirit. Pictures,
trinkets, even things that represent the
demonic such as a statue of Satan or a demon.
This is so sad because it doesn't have to be. In
the Catholic tradition, all rooms are supposed
to have a Blessed Crucifix or image of the God
or the Blessed Mother. Many Catholics do not
follow this tradition and it is sad. Do you really
think a demon wants to look at these items?
However, do not misunderstand; there are
more demons from the lower choirs of angels
than there are from the higher choirs of angels.
For example, a demon from the cherubim or
power choir can get past these sacred items.
These demons from the higher choirs are very
powerful. These demons will usually destroy
these items or remove them. The demon in Mr.
Winter's three-bedroom house is a powerful
demon from the Cherubim, power choirs or
both. More on this later.

Let's return to this conversation you had
with this demon on page 32, the words "God
isn't here. God doesn't exist. You've said so
yourself, haven't you." This is what is called a

half-truth. Half-truths are lies from God's perspective. The demon continued to push you down into the bed with increased pressure. Finally, you could see the demon's white eyes glowing in the dark along with its ghostly hands coming to choke you. The demon says: "God isn't here. It's just..." It paused and revealed its face to me; the face of Christ possessed; Christ gone mad."

This was no dream or nightmare Steve; it was happening to you by a demonic force. This part of the conversation with the demon reveals just how strong and powerful it is. This was done by the demon to scare you, to place doubt into your mind that God really doesn't exist, show you how strong it is, and get you to doubt your sanity. If you told this to a shrink, he is able to put you on some heavy medication. At this point, I need to make you perfectly clear, the Demonic all fear the Divine - Father, Son and Holy Spirit. Most demons are terrified of God with the possible except of one choir, the demons from the Cherubim choir. They will be arrogant enough to fight at times (such as the battle in heaven with Michael and the good angels (Rev. 12: 7-9) or try to negotiate with the Father (as in the book of Job 1:6-12) or with Jesus (as in the Gospels (such as the Demoniac at Gardarene, Mark 5:1-20). But they are afraid of the Divine. More than likely, God did hear your cry and sent a powerful good angel to get rid of this demon. As you describe in this experience, it seems to me, someone forced it off you because of the way it ended. I am not totally sure. Before we even get to Mr. Winter's house, look at all the occasions of diabolical activity in your life before you move into the Union House.

A few more final words for this section.

This is not, I repeat this is not a diabolical possession. However, it is one of the steps toward diabolical possession. This is the normal sequence that happens after someone first invites the demon or demons into their life, which is then followed by demonic infestation, followed by diabolical obsession, diabolical oppression, and finally onto a diabolical possession. There is a phenomenon in this field also called Perfect Possession. A perfect possession is someone who wants to be possessed and there is nothing anyone can do about it.

I will say this, regarding Mr. Winters, when he goes before God for his judgment, it will not go well. I am not judging him, just stating the facts from Sacred Scripture where in many places Our Lord warns those who lead His little ones astray. This man is very evil, and we will continue to discuss Mr. Winters later.

Finally, this maintenance guy named Ben is not completely innocent. This man also knows full well that there are problems in this house that are not normal. Anyone who goes into that basement knows there is something wrong. Ben was surely doing work in the basement to know that something is wrong here. Yet, he went along with all of this for the cheap payment Mr. Winters gave him for doing maintenance.

Let us move on to chapter 7 on page 34. You finally get the call from Mr. Winters that he selected you from among many candidates who looked at the house. This is a lie. Yes, many individuals looked at the house, but not to rent it.

Then Mr. Winters makes all these excuses that he cannot meet you at the house to sign the lease. He wants to meet you at a restaurant. Well, the first time he was late, (the open house). I could maybe excuse this, but this is the second time he is late. Then he gets out of the car and frantically arranges his wig while getting the paperwork all ready. This is unacceptable and shows how evil his character is. He has no regard for your time but comes up with all these excuses for his time. Then he rudely eats in front of you. These are all signs that there is something very wrong with this man. Then a major red flag comes when you could not meet him until 2:00 PM because of work but could meet him at 6:00 PM. Then Mr. Winters gets noticeable fidgety with your proposal. You mentioned above that he had on a wool jacket that was unsuitable for a hot Missouri day. Was this in the summer? Sounds like it to me, so there should not have been a problem with meeting you at 6:00 since the sun does not go down until later, which could be around 9:00 PM. Why was he fidgety? Not because he is afraid to drive in the dark because that wouldn't be an issue. Or was he fidgety because the demonic become more active at night and he knows it.

Chapter 8, on page 37, he is late again. You begin the second tour and how ironic, on page 38 he asked: "You don't believe in ghosts, do you, Mr. LaChance?" This is completely unacceptable to ask. Then he lies right to your face with this statement: "Well, I haven't heard any such nonsense about this house having ghosts; however, not everyone can live in an old house such as this." And why not? Is it really the old house or the demons that reside there? It is impossible for anyone to be scared by the old house. What people fear are the demons in the house. There is no way this evil man does not know that this house is haunted with demons by that comment about ghosts. Then Mr. Winters jumps frantically after the ice maker completes its cycle on page 39. "What was that?" he asked, trying to catch his breath. He would only have this reaction, if he already had many experiences with other demonic phenomena in the house. For Mr. Winters to jump like this only means he was on edge from these experiences.

And for him to allow you, Steve, to bring in your young children into this house to live is outrageous. However, from his perspective, the money from the rent is more important than the safety of your kids and you. On page 39, then Mr. Winters leaves, and so do you, but the lights in the house were coming on, one by one. Notice, this happens at night, when lights come on and off because you would not see this demonic activity during the day. Was this what Mr. Winters was afraid was going to start happening while he was there?

Chapter 9, on page 41, you are commenting on the stress that was suppressed over six years since your wife abandoned you and now crashed down on you. Steve, you have held up very remarkable under all these circumstances, but you are only human. However, you were encountering evil angels and had no way of fighting them, much less understand what was going on in your life, you are lucky you did not have a nervous breakdown. Nor is there anything wrong with pushing these feeling out of your mind. Suffering like this can only be endured, and dancing with the pain will only cause the pain to get worse. One of the things I hope this evaluation and this letter accomplishes is to put some more closure on what happened to you.

It is not a coincidence that God had me read your book and then respond to you in this letter. The Divine Lord never forgot you and as we proceed, I will show you where He did help. You must keep in mind with the demonic, they can do nothing, and I mean nothing, without God's approval. There is a reason why all this happened in your life.

Let us return briefly to speak about your wife again since you write about her on pages 41-42. You mention that you were falling into a depression, which would be considered normal under what you were going through. However, you do not need, and I repeat, you do NOT need therapy. You would have wasted a lot of money, and not gotten anywhere. (One side note, with all this stress that was in your life, only God could have kept you from losing your sanity. You wrote: "I had to keep it together for the sake of my children." You were only able to keep it together because God helped you — more on this later.) What you do need is first, an understanding on what is happening here. Men deal with the use of reasoning and understanding, and then we can handle the situation confronting us much better. The psychological profession could not help you with this at all. Why can I say this? Because the problem is not you Steve, it is the demonic who were invited into your life. Why go to therapy or take needless medication which would only prolong this problem or make it worse? No help from the psychological profession would have done anything to stop the exterior forces of the demonic.

Let us get to your wife now. You had known your wife since you were twelve years old, and you were best friends. According to page 5, you married your wife at the age of twenty-three. This is a very long time for you to get to know her. However, there is a major problem here, you obviously knew your wife for a longtime, and more than likely, your wife had a good character. A good enough character to become best friends and want to marry her and have children. Now it can be true that sometimes we do not want to see things in a potential spouse, however, I do not think this is the case.

You then write the following on page 42: "It had become so bad for Lydia at home that she had been happy to see her mother leave. And Matthew, the child that his mother had always resented, went looking for a mother figure everywhere, especially at school." These statements are very serious to write and provide a clue on what is happening. But then you wrote the following statements: "The day his mother left, he (Michael) ran to her and held on to her legs. "Mommy, please don't go," he begged. She pulled his arms away from her and threw him to the ground. He began to scream." When I first read this statement, everything became much clearer. Now Steve, put your feelings aside and look at these statements again because you are missing something very important.

There is a major character change in your wife! She went from a good character (for you to become best friends and then marry her) to a bad character. The statement you wrote with Michael proves my point. The action of an innocent child running up to his mother and begging her to stay and all she did was throw him to the ground is coming from a vice called hatred. This is an action of diabolical hatred. If you reread these statements, this was building inside of her.

This kind of hatred only comes from the

driving force of the demonic that was invited into her life. No one has this type of character shift in their personality - from a good character to a bad character - without the help of some exterior evil force. This is why I have been saying all along, somewhere either before the pregnancy of Lydia or during her pregnancy with Lydia, she invited the demonic into her life. It is also a possible sign that she is currently demonically possessed! However, I cannot be totally sure that she is demonically possessed without interviewing her. I do know this, first your wife most likely does not know what she is doing or realize what is happening to her, and second, I am very certain that what I discussed with you above via the phenomena of diabolical obsession and diabolical oppression - is also happening to her which is the next step to a diabolical possession. I would even risk saying this about your wife - if you found out where your wife presently is, right now, one of the following would be true:

1) Your wife is under the care of the psychological profession and on medication.

2) Your wife is diabolically possessed and living an evil and destructive life.

3) Your wife found a minister or priest who was able to help her, first get rid of the evil and then bring about some healing and forgiveness in her life by allowing God into it.

4) A combination of all the above.

I am willing to risk saying this because of one absolute truth, demonic hatred like your wife displayed with Michael and even Lydia, always gets worse. This hatred never gets better unless a radical change occurs to stop it. I wonder if your wife was ever baptized. I am guessing you were baptized because you wrote on page 4; you were born into devout "Lutheran Parents."

Let's return to the book on page 43, the dream you had here was most likely not from the demonic. However, there is a demonic influence in it with your wife. In dream you mention a pounding on the door, not a knock. Most people knock on the door unless they are very angry. When you answered it, your ex-wife was standing there holding something. Then you mention something odd, the weather radically changed from bright and sunny, to storm clouds raging in the sky with crackling lightning and thunder crashing. This is the same type of weather in the description of God in the Old Testament when Moses was up on the mountain receiving the Ten Commandments (Exodus 19:18). The author describes the weather first, to demonstrate the presence of God along with His power. Then, in the dream, your wife first shoves the bundle into your hands and says: "I told you before, I can't be a mother" and runs away before you realize what happened. Steve only you can answer this question… did your wife ever speak to you about not having children before the conception of Lydia? For example, when you to were best friends, where there any conversations with her about not wanting children? If the answer is yes, this dream came from the depth of your conscience where those conversations with her are recorded.

I do have a problem with this. Every woman knows that having a sexual relationship can lead to a pregnancy. Yet, your wife not only cooperated with the sexual act, but she also carried them to term without aborting them. What woman who does not want to have children takes a risk of getting pregnant? All women know when they are fertile and can get pregnant. You see, this is a lie about her not wanting to have children. Even without the demonic involvement in your life, if she did not want to have children, then why have sex? Why carry them to full term? Why not be on some form of birth control? (Even though the Catholic Church condemns this practice, except for natural family planning, birth control was still available.) After having Lydia, why have two more children? You see, there are too many decisions she is making (or not making), by her own free choice, to have children. Even if you wanted kids and she did not, there are still ways of preventing pregnancy without you knowing. I do not believe your wife did not want to have children. Nor do I buy this lame excuse she gave you that she did this for you because you wanted to be a father.

Returning back to page 6 of your book for a moment, you describe this event after four years from Matthew's birth, you came home, and your wife was sullen and depressed and the next words: "I am leaving you." I disagree, the woman you married left before Lydia's birth. Then she says: "It's not that I want to divorce you, I want to divorce the children." She stood to cross the room. "Dammit, (how ironic she uses this word) Steven, I never wanted to be a mother. I did that for you. You always knew you wanted to be a father. It was, and is, just not for me. I can't do it. I try and I try, but I just can't seem to do it. This is the right thing. This is the most right thing that I can do for them and for you. It's me. It isn't you and it isn't them. This is about me." This is all under the vice of Pride. If she could not be a mother, could she not go to therapy and learn how to be a mother? These are all lame excuses. Here is the real issue. When she says: "You have until Friday for you and the kids to find someplace to live. I haven't paid the rent in six months. Tomorrow they are turning off the electricity." Now we both know that she was stealing the money, did you ever find out for what? To behave like this with innocent children is an intrinsic evil. Here is the first of seeing a good character shifted to a bad character. However. there can be many questions asked and perhaps even answered. But there is one question, that is so crucial to all these conversations and question is this: Who stole the love out of her heart? Could it be she was having an affair? That surely is possible — but if she was having an affair, then the person she is involved with is also serving the demonic angels. This scenario is extremely dangerous for her as well as it was for you. My final word on this Steve, no matter what the scenario is, one thing is for certain, the demon angels are directly involved in your wife leaving you and the children.

To finish up this chapter, at the very bottom of 43, after you wrote about this dream, you wrote something very unusual: "I've heard people refer to the hours between midnight and 6:00 AM as the lonely hours, the suicide hours." I must admit, this is the first I have heard of this spoken. For not knowing too much about the demonic, the hours of midnight and 3:00 AM are known as the witching hours for the demonic. You see, with the demonic, everything they do is always in direct mockery to the Divine. Jesus hung on the cross from twelve noon until three in the afternoon, the demonic mock or do the direct opposite. They like to do most of their damage between twelve and 3:00 AM. This is why most taverns in this country are closing their doors at two a.m. This is one of the things I meant above that this dream you wrote about on page 43 had demonic influence on it. Another indication that the demonic is very much involved in your wife's life.

Next is chapter ten, where you are moving into Mr. Winter's three-bedroom house. The incident with your neighbor making a claim that your father hit his vehicle was fraudulent. Who do you think inspired this scam? However, on page 47, a car drives by, slows down and the passenger says, "Hope you get along okay here." This was also a warning from God because the passenger said it in a very kind way, beginning with the word "Hope". Here is the first proof that many people in the public know about the haunted house you are about to move into. It is also proof that Mr. Winters knows this house is dangerous.

Next, comes chapter 11, where you mention something very odd, those doors on each of the interior doors had an old-fashion hook and eye latch on the outside of the doors, which Mr. Winters would know and did nothing to correct it. It seems to me that Mr. Winters is very cheap.

Then on page 49 the picture of the two Angels which you try to hang in the living room with the cherub wallpaper border. The picture falls four times. The demons in the house are knocking it down including tossing it at you as you walk away. Here is another proof that God was trying to warn you concerning this house. Note something is very important here. The picture of the two Angels is knocked off the wall four times but the cherub wallpaper border

stays on the wall. Why? One reason, the
demon that oversees this house is from the
cherubim choir and he is very strong and not
alone. This cherub has other demons under his
command infesting this house. The picture of
the two angels you have are probably from the
Seraphim choir, who threw the cherubim and
all the other evil angels who side with Lucifer
out of heaven. Basically, these demons do not
want to look at this picture. It is also possible
that these demons recognize that the picture
was blessed at one time. Regardless, they do
not want this picture up because it poisons
their eyes.

On page 51 you discuss with your
daughter that people do not like walking In
front of this house. This should have been a
very big warning sign to you, especially the old
man. This is another sign from God. Why don't
they like walking in front of the house?
Because the house is full of demons, and they
harass people who walk on this property as
you will begin to experience. Here is also solid
proof that if all these people knew about this
house being haunted with demons, then Mr.
Winters also knew about it. Haunted stories
like this in a small town get around quickly.
What is important here, is that this seems to be
public knowledge, and this is the reason why I
stated that those who were there for the
opening house were not there to rent this
house but to explore it to see if this was really
haunted. I also find it ironic that no one in this
town told you or even tried to warn you of this
before you move into the house. However,
their action of crossing the street to avoid
walking on this property and then walking on
the other side is a clear warning.

After this you discuss that the house
was very cold, this was not the air conditioning.

This is a sign that the demonic is removing the warmth out of the atmosphere. One of the many reasons this is done because demons want to mock the Father, Son and Holy Spirit. One of the symbols of God is fire, so they mock it with coldness. This is not always done by the demonic though; it is one of their signs that they are present.

On page 52, Lydia comes downstairs somewhere between midnight and eight in the morning; because the closet door kept opening and boxes were moving around her room. Notice the demons go after the children first, on a Sunday morning which began at midnight, the beginning of the witching hours.

In chapter 12, page 53 you speak about Sunday morning and going to Church. You wrote: "Did I go to Church? No, between my marriage breaking up and Janice's death, I was completely turned off to the whole idea of organized religion." This was a big mistake. because that is what the demonic wanted of you. The demonic want us to stay away from God, especially Jesus Christ, so they can attack. 'Then you wrote, how could I possibly know that my negative attitude toward faith was a clear invitation to dance?' Unless you were exposed to a priest or minister who speaks on the demonic angels you would not know this could happen. Steve I am not judging you. Had I been in your position I am not so sure if I could have done a better job. This is one of those experiences in life that ultimately God must answer. However, I hope this letter puts some more closure on these events. and that you are a better person for it.

Page 55 is crucial for understanding what is going on in this house. You sent Matthew and Michael into the house to get a garden hose. Your sons go down to this basement, which is going to be crucial to all these events. Michael comes out to you, and Matthew, —Your youngest— is still in the house. You hear Matthew scream and you run into the house. You see Matthew shaking and pointing. Matthew says: "Monster." this is no monster he saw this was one of the demons or the Cherubim demon in this house. Notice, again, that the demon always appears to your youngest son. I caution you here, this is a different demon than the one Matthew saw in his bedroom at the apartment. The demon that was making your life miserable back in the other apartments is different than this one That demon was invited by your wife this demon is here for an entirely different reason. Remember one of the reasons the demons do this is to get at your sanity, Steve. This is a common occurrence in houses infested with the demonic. They always go after the children, especially the youngest, to get at the parents.

At the bottom of page 56, the demons turn on all the lights and start to play games with the frigid temperature in the house.

Page 57, Matthew goes to the bathroom and starts to scream. The demon reappears to him the second time, yet no one believes Matthew because he does not have the vocabulary to say, there is a demon in the basement. There is a demon in the bathroom. Had he said this, this might of change your reaction a bit. All Matthew can say is that there is a monster in the basement and bathroom. Then, after your conversation with him, he says at the bottom of the page, "A clown, a monster clown came after me." Notice, the demon had a clown outfit on to mock what a child usually enjoys seeing at a circus: clowns. Observe how cruel these demons are to your children.

On page 58, you saw, at the doorway that led into the living room, an old man wearing a red flannel shirt. This old man had something to do with what is happening in this house. (Is this the same man you saw in your "dreams" through a diabolical obsession on page 81?) In addition, Steve, you were not seeing things, you saw the soul of this old man who is now in hell. How do I know this man is in hell? Because there is only Heaven, and in our Catholic Faith we also believe in souls in purgatory who are still going through a final purification, but they are saved. God would not let these souls come down here and terrorize you and your children. In addition, Heaven is a very beautiful place, why would any good soul (who finally made it into Heaven) want to leave it in the first place? There are rules that the demonic must follow, when they step over these rules, the Divine steps in immediately. One of these rules is they cannot come up to you and outright Kill you. If they could, there would be no humanity left. Nor can any demon force you to do something against your will.

Moving onto chapter 13, page 60, the demons are doing their typical annoying activity with turning on and off the lights. Now on the top of 61, you wrote that you walked into the living room and felt a shock run through your body. It was like an electrical shock, which started deep inside your body and worked its way out. "Every hair on my arms and neck stood up." This is what I was trying to explain to you. God placed, in all human beings, a phenomenon to alert them when the person is around this type of evil. This was not electricity. if it was it would have killed you or seriously hurt you. I wired many houses that I renovated, and I know enough about electricity that you most likely were not touching anything that was a conductor for it. The wooden floors cannot carry electricity and you did not mention that you turned on any lights. However, the old electric called knob-and-tube (and even the new 12-2 wiring) can be interesting to work with when someone is attempting wiring and they do not know what they are doing. I have taken many walls down in renovation jobs and was shocked to see the electric behind the wall, and question why the house never burns down. Electric wires were run in walls that made no sense and it becomes clear to me that the person who did the work (often the former homeowner) did not know what they were doing. This is the main reason when I start any renovation job, I cut the electric power to the whole house and segregate it to one or two live lines from the basement.

Back to the book, what you experience here was a demon that passed through you. It could be considered a temporary possession, where they go into someone without being invited, cause trouble, and then leave their victim quickly. Only powerful demons from the higher choirs can do this type of activity. This at times can, be a step toward a demonic possession which would have happened to you Steve, or one of the children, had you not moved out of this house or gotten these demons out the house.

In philosophy we use a term called nature. For instance, we say human beings have a human nature. So, without getting too philosophical, the activity the "person" can do will determine the nature of the being. For example, human being cannot create. Only God can create out of nothing, therefore God has a Divine Nature. Or look at it another way: Give one example of what a Divine Nature can do? Answer: A Divine Nature can create out of nothing such as a human soul for a human being. So, a human nature can pro-create where an angel does not have this ability. Angels cannot produce children; only human beings can produce children. Likewise with the angels, the activity that is being done can determine what choir the angel came from, which at times can be very difficult, however. When you have God on your side, the discernment on which choir the demon or demons comes from can be done rather quickly. One way to do this is to study authentic Exorcists and learn from their expertise and experience.

On page 62, you come home, and the lights are on again. You go through your house in panic looking for someone but find no one. However, the demons in the house see they are getting to you by this panic. Then you call Mr. Winters to see if he was in the house. After telling him all the lights have been on you could hear him clear his throat. Another clear sign that he knows what is going on in this house. And then he tells you another lie: "Well, you know these old houses, Mr. LaChance. You can never tell." Oh yes you can, Mr. Winters knows this house is haunted with demons. If this was an electric problem, why would Mr. Winters risk a fire in the house, when the electric can burn down the house and he would lose money? Money is the only thing he is interested in with this house.

Your father comes over to look at the circuit box and finds no problem. However, there an electric code violation with no door on this circuit box. All circuit boxes have to have a cover on it in the basement due to humidity, moisture, and basically safety, especially when children are around. It seems to me, that Mr.

Winters was very tight with money.

Interestingly, on page 63, after your father inspects the electric, he turns and looking at the wall where a showerhead hung down. "That's a butcher shower, Steven." You asked him what he meant and he said, "That's where the farmers used to clean up after slaughtering, before going upstairs to their wives. Don't see many of those anymore." No, you don't, because most normal people would remove all of this because of germs, disease, and for sanitation reasons. The water that drained out of this shower went onto the floor and probably drained under the house. All kinds of mildew and mold could be under this house.

On page 64, after the box fell (caused by the demons) and your father was holding out his arms, you saw tears in his eyes. He was experiencing the same thing you did and did not think this was electric. I think your father knew, at this point, what was going on in this house, but was afraid to tell you. Then he got up and left.

Chapter 14, page 66 your father finally asked the question: "You don't think you rented a haunted house, do you?" After that question and your answer, I think at this point you began to at least wonder if the house was haunted, though you did not want to tell your dad. Let's proceed to page 69; after you saw someone up at the window when you came home, then you had seen this quick movement out of the comer of your eye. For some reason, though many in the field have guessed, the first time we saw a potential demon is out of the corner of our eyes. I do not have an explanation for this phenomenon; however, this is a regular occurrence. Many people, who are having experiences with the demonic, first see them out of the corner of their eyes.

In the fourth paragraph on page 69, you are describing a typical demonic apparition. These are very common apparitions, although new to your experience Steve. You wrote: "He was solid in form, except his form seemed to be made up of moving churning dark gray and black smoke or mist.... His form was still a churning mass of blackness. I couldn't see his face, but I could see his eyes watching me, staring directly at me, challenging me." What you are describing is the spiritual make-up of a demon from the higher choirs. This is probably the head demon from the cherubim choir in charge of the demonic infestation occurring in this house. In order to get rid of a demonic infestation, especially one involving many demons, you have to go after the ringleader, the head demon. All the cherubim demons are leaders. They can have thousands of other demons from the lower choirs under their command. The rest of the demons will follow the head demon because many of the demons from the lower choirs are often forced to do the work for the leader. These demons from the lower choirs can be very cowardly: they do not have very much power. However, these demons from the lower choirs can be extremely annoying. They can sit for hours and all they will do is howl and get on your nerves. This occurred on page 70 when you were locking the front door to leave when a loud, painful, tortured, agonized scream came pouring out of the house. This was a demon (or demons) from the lower choirs: they usually are many demons though and could be in harmony with one voice. Regardless, whether it was one demon or many demons, they accomplished their goal, to frighten you and the children. After you get the car started. Matthew sees a demon (basement monster) standing in the upstairs window. This is mostly likely the same demon Matthew saw in the basement.

As you are driving away, you are thinking what is most typical; What was the smoky apparition? What was the awful wail? What was the thing in the window? What you did witness was some of the demons in the house. When you get to your parents' house you finally admit that the house is haunted.

Chapter 15, page 73, you are lying in bed thinking and feeling guilty about letting Matthew down about the basement monster. Well, most people would not have done any better. You cannot blame yourself for not having the knowledge and then the understanding of what is going on in your life. God often does this to people, by having them experience the situation instead of reading and learning about it out of some book or in some classroom.

After breakfast, your parents, the kids and you head over to the house. You wrote on page 74, that the house seemed perfectly normal like all the houses on the block. The demonic will give that impression to human beings so they can lure them inside and cause them trouble.

Finally on page 76, you called Mr. Winters and finally see he is nothing but a pathological liar. After explaining to him what happened the night before, Mr. Winters says: "Now, I, myself have never seen a ghost (which is another lie), but I do imagine it would be a frightening thing to see. (Just like the episode on the final tour with you and the ice maker dropped ice into the container from the refrigerator and Mr. Winters jumped, page 39) I do recall being told once that ghosts are always around us. Perhaps you just tuned in to them, if just for a moment?" Steve, this is a rehearsed answer he gives to all the families who called him about these events going on in his house. And then one of his insane lies - the drug dealer who left everything behind because he was running from the police. Would not the police confiscate his belongings then or notify next of kin if he was arrested. If the drug dealer really was arrested by the police, why hold on to his possessions? Most landlords throw drug dealers possessions out in the trash unless the landlord wants to hold on to them for all the years he is in prison. This scenario does not make sense. Mr. Winters is only telling you these lies because he does not want to lose the rent money. At least you see right through these lies. The fact is this woman and man (the so called "drug dealer") are too scared to come back to the house for their belongings. Then the third phone call comes with Mr. Winters, offering advice about a priest blessing the house, or getting one of the priests to do an exorcism. If he was a Charismatic Catholic (another lie) why not have the exorcism done before anyone rents the house. These phone calls show just how guilty Mr. Winters is about this house.

Then Mr. Winters says something rather strange about some people who practiced witchcraft and burned a lot of candles. Rather strange he knows about these candles and witchcraft bringing evil spirits into the house. Or does Mr. Winters have experience with some form of witchcraft from his younger days? All the more reason to have this house thoroughly blessed, after all is he not a Charismatic Catholic who knows about such things? This is so sad and pathetic.

Moving onto chapter 16, page 79, where you wrote, "the odds of someone moving into a haunted house were about the same as dying in a plane crash," except there is a small problem here. The odds are getting greater to move into a haunted house because so many individuals are turning away from Our Lord and going after things that invite the demonic into their lives such as Satanism, witchcraft, the occult, all these sources of mediums, the popularity of Ouija boards (even among the Masons), over doing it at Halloween, etc. These are all invitations to the demonic to enter into our life. As God goes out of our life, in comes humanism, secularism and superstition.

On page 81, you had this dream. The dream is the key to what happened in this house. As I explained earlier, this no ordinary dream, but diabolical obsession. Let us look deeper into this dream, which is more like a vision or trance. You begin by writing: "Worn, flowered neon-print wallpaper is peeling off the walls of the stairway." On the bottom of page 26, you wrote: "I am in the process of replacing this wallpaper," Mr. Winters said. The wallpaper he indicated lined the walls heading down to the basement. It was neon bright with large flowers. Where it had peeled away, it left large, bare patches. Obviously, this is the basement of Mr. Winters' house.

The vision/nightmare you had continues: "It's barely visible in the moonlight cast through the basement window below. I grasp the handrail and steady myself; calming my nerves, I begin my slow descent into the moonlit darkness below. The stairs seem to go on forever. With each step I hear a familiar creak that announces my progress." This dream is now taking you back to a particular time in this house where there is no electricity. The occurrence of this event is at night (probably midnight) where the moonlight is providing light for the basement. You're grasping the handrail and steadying yourself, and calming your nerves is a description of the fear of what you are about to see. You know in this "dream" you do not want to be here, but in spite of your fear you proceed down the steps and into the basement. Most people would run but you continue down here. Because of one reason, you want to know what happened in this basement. The demonic are leading you through this dream which is actually a diabolical obsession because of their evil intent. The stairs going on forever is a means to explain that this event, though it took place a long time ago, is coming out of eternity (specifically from hell) for an evil intention. You continue to step down into the basement in fear and caution. The vision/nightmare you had continues: "I hear water running, and I'm going to investigate its origin. A few steps more and I see a candle burning." These are some of the details associated with this evil act. You mention you see a candle burning, and then a candle that was lit unattended. The candles and moonlight must be here because the individual involve needed to see in the basement at night along with you. There is probably no electricity in this house at that time. There is probably a third candle, or maybe more candles. You did notsee these candles because they are in the "fruit cellar" and that door is closed. Is this a dream; yes, according to normal standards, but it is actually a diabolical obsession. The vision/nightmare you had continues: "Dismissing the candle from my mind, my attention turns to the sound of the rushing water, and along with the water I can hear breathing. It's the labored breathing of a man; he is excited, perhaps even sexually excited. I turn back to the candlelight. The old butcher shower is running. A man stands beneath it showering by candlelight in the darkness of the I basement. You dismissed the candle from your mind because the demonic is drawing your intention to rushing water along with the breathing. Thus, the demonic mocking of God by rushing water, mocking the Sacrament of Baptism, and the breathing mocking Our Lord who breathed on the Apostles and said, "Receive the Holy Spirit, what sins you forgive they are forgiven they are forgiven in Heaven, what sins are held bond, they are held bond in Heaven." The labored breathing is a combination of guilt, fear, or anxiety, and the demonic. I don't think the sexually excitement has anything to do with the dream although it could be related to his sins (such as raping his victim). You see the old butcher shower running water on a man underneath it. This man is evil, either he is diabolically possessed or there is a diabolically obsession associated with him. Based on this man's eyes. He was diabolically possessed.

"Throughout the basement, the man doesn't see me. I watch as he tries to cleanse himself, purify himself of a dark substance, scrubbing his already raw skin. His face is hidden by the shadows. His labored breathing becomes panic as does the pace of his scrubbing. He can't get clean." The water and breathing echo throughout the basement because it echoes through eternity by way of mockery. The man does not see you yet, because he is not allowed to see you. His vision of you is being blocked. You are allowed to see that he is trying to cleanse himself, and the key word here is purify himself by scrubbing his already raw skin, but he cannot do it. His face is hidden by shadows. These are not shadows they are demons who are blocking his vision from see you. His labored breathing becomes panicked as does the pace of his scrubbing. He can't get clean because this is impossible to clean off the man's soul. "It's blood, he is washing off blood. Is he looking at me? I can't tell in the dim light. but I sense his evil eyes on me as he continues washing."

First off, the man you are seeing is already dead. This man you also see is Catholic. The man turns and you see his frontal torso in the light. You then see blood that he was trying to wash off. What you are seeing is a human soul who has been condemned to hell. This man is evil and at one time demonically possessed. This man was trying to wash off the stain of sin off his soul which he cannot do. To wash the soul clean is a divine action primarily through the sacraments. The blood on his soul is the result of the sins he committed. It is permanently on his soul, and he will never be able to wash it off because he never repented from these sins. These unrepented sins caused him to be condemned to Hell for all eternity The blood he is trying to wash off is human.

However, the following is only speculation: This man either killed his victim or victims or seriously hurt someone a long time ago. I suspect some of the victims were female, and he raped them. Because of the candles, there is no electricity in the basement. Electricity was just beginning to go into houses around the 1950°s. So, these possible crimes probably happened before the 1950s which is well over 62 years ago. I also suspect he killed his victim or victims in the fruit cellar room on the concrete slab that was used for a shelf. It is possible that he slaughtered the person or persons with the same instrument used on the hogs in those days. (It's also possible that the old man you saw in the living room looking at you and the children was a victim of these crimes OR the same man in this vision / trance you saw Steve, who did these horrible crimes.) The slaughter victims of this man might have been offered as a sacrifice to please the demons that possessed him. This evil man might have dis-member his victim or victims and buried them in the mudroom. If you took notice, the concrete floor was probably never disturbed in the basement, because back in those days' they did not have jackhammers and to swing a large sledgehammer in a basement is very difficult. It would be easier to bury the victims in the mudroom. The mudroom would provide cover for someone digging at night without any suspicion from the neighbors. (I could be wrong about all this, and more evidence would be needed before going to the police, like digging up that mudroom to look for human bones.) I can be 100 percent certain on this, the man you saw in this vision or trance Mr. Winters knows. This man is evil, he was diabolically possessed, and is condemned to hell for his crimes and sins he had committed in this house. Remember, Mr. Winters is Catholic (and not practicing) and this vision / trance has the mockery of the Catholic sacraments (Baptism, Confession, the Sacrifice of the Mass) all over it.

It is also highly possible that Mr. Winters knows about these crimes this man committed in this house. The vision/nightmare you had continued: "The room begins to spin. The sound of his desperation matches the tempo of the rushing water. Still the room spins, spins, spins I can still feel his eyes on me. I can't breathe. Oh my God, I can't breathe." The spinning in this vision / trance is to confuse you. The sound of his desperation matches the tempo of the rushing water. Here is also a sign that the man who done whatever is very guilty, of which he can no longer repent. This Catholic man knows right from wrong which is why the details in this experience are shown to you. Only a Catholic knows full well how deep and serious this guilt can be, as described by the panic on washing off his soul which cannot be done in hell. The words the room spins, spins, spins is a description of someone falling from the judgment seat of God into Hell. You can only feel his eyes on you, but he cannot see you because more than likely Steve, you probably were not even born when all this happened much less be in this vision. In addition, you are probably not the only one who saw this vision or experience. There are many clues or divine warnings here given such as the victims were raped (the sexual arousal) and killed (the human blood on this man's souls) which serves as a divine warning on what the diabolical angels have been able to accomplish in this house.

This is closer to a vision or a trance then a dream provided by the demonic. Why would the demonic show you this vision? One reason, all the demons are full of pride. The higher the choir the demon is from the more vicious is the pride and part of that pride is the ability to brag. The demons love to brag of their accomplishments, and even mock using their successes as a form of mocking Christianity and God. The demon you saw in the kitchen is the same demon Matthew saw who possessed this man. Notice the evil pattern, you had this vision or trance that obviously occurred in the basement, Matthew your youngest son saw the monster who is a demon associated with the basement. This demon is strong and very powerful (but not more powerful than the our Divine Lord God or the good angels). This same demon you saw in this vision was inside this man. Again, this man you saw in this vision is dead; he is a Catholic; this man is demonically possessed in this vision/trance; this man invited these demons into his life; he is trying to wash the sins off his soul off like baptism does; these sins are now a permanent part of him forever; this man never repented so he did not use the Sacrament of confession before he died thus the guilt in this vision; this man is condemned to hell forever; this man probably sacrificed his victims to these demons which is a mockery of the Sacrifice of the Mass; and most of all, these same demons are now looking for other victims in this house. These demons missed their goals with your family because there was Divine protection (more on this later); they will not miss their goals with the next family who rents this house. This head demon is a Cherubim because of the activities going on in this experience. Anytime you have someone who is brutally murdered the cherubim (or power) demons are involved. The demons from the power choir also have the ability to instigate someone being killed, but more than likely it is given to the Cherubim. (For example, Satan, formerly known as Lucifer, head of the cherubim choir is responsible for all abortions. Molech (Lv. 18:21; Ez. 16:20), another cherubim demon in the Old Testament was responsible for all the Israelites who sacrificed their innocent sons and daughters to him.)

You mention you sense his evil eyes. The eyes are one of the main signs given to an Exorcist that the person is possessed by a demon. Demons hide in someone who is possessed, however, if they are discovered they become outraged. The demons' number one place of entry into someone they are possessing is through the eyes. Entering through the eyes is the most popular entry for diabolical possession. Entering through the eyes is very important because of us seeing the Glory of God, the Beatific Vision. {Blessed are the pure of heart for they will see God. (Mt. 5:8)} Notice the mockery here by the diabolical angels. This is one of the many clues the Divine gives the Exorcist that the person is possessed. The demons that possess someone have a hard time stopping their effects on their victim's eyes. This is why Exorcists are trained to pay attention to the eyes of the person who is possible possessed, it is the point of entry by the demons. In addition, the eyes will never lie. However, this form is the most popular but not the only way a demon can enter a person. Diabolical possessions can enter someone by any of these methods:

Through any of the senses: eyes; ear; nose; mouth; they can penetrate through the body like electricity can do to a human body through the natural sense of touch: getting a diabolical tattoo anywhere on the person's body especially around the genitals; getting body piercing especially around the genitals; sexual rape, which is common among women including sodomy; and by eating something cursed. etc.

Again, the man you saw in this vision is

either related to, or is known by, Mr. Winters. I suspect he is part of his family. I also suspect that Mr. Winters' family built this house, which is why he does not sell it in his old age. Mr. Winters is very greedy for money. But he is smart enough to offer very cheap rent to keep someone occupying this haunted house by signing a lease (page 89). In chapter 17, page 84, the demonic activities continue with the rattling of the door handles, which gets harder and harder. The rattling grows louder, and they steal the warm temperature in the room. A bolt of electricity shot through your body and a horrible stench filled the room. Then the screaming began, soft and then very loud. These are demons from the lower choirs causing this activity. Then the doors slam to the kid's bedroom which sends you into a panic, the desire effect the demons want. Your poor mother is listening to all this, another desired effect by the demons, as you cry out to her to come and get all of you. Then the house shakes with all kinds of crashes, (more than likely from some of your belongings.) and then Lydia screams. "Daddy! Daddy, what is happening?" In order to cause this much chaos in the house along with the house shaking there has to be a lot of demons cooperating with each other to achieve this effect. This is one of the many proofs that this is a demonic infestation which is going to the next step of diabolical oppressions. When you ran up stair to get to your kids, the doors would not open because the demons are holding them shut. Finally, you plead to God, "God please! Please help me!" I prayed loudly, and just that quickly the doors fell open. Why did this happen after you prayed? These demons heard this prayer and let go of the doors because they were afraid of what God would do. God always hears these prayers of desperation, and all the demons know it. That is why they let go of the doors. You grabbed all the kids and finally got out of the house. When you got to the car the diabolical oppression was still happening in the house. You drove to the top of the hill to waited for your parents and noticed that you could see the blackness move from room to room. At this point, the demons already knew where you are, they saw you leave; thus, they were not searching for you. They accomplished what they wanted, to terrorize you and the family. In addition, they wanted to drive you insane and almost accomplished this goal if it wasn't for your father.

Chapter 18, page 87, your parents, your brother, and you return to the house. It was very wise of your father to bring your mom and brother. Of course, everything started quickly, and it also stopped quickly, to achieve their goal of driving you into insanity and despair. The demons stop to make it look like nothing happened. They also stopped because your parents are faithful Lutherans, but this will not stop them. The demons keep up their ruthless assault on your family, the electric feeling your mom feels, the whispering voices, the putrid smell, the breathing between Rita and you, the rustling of the trees, and then you finally leave. You get to your parent's house and settle down and decide to call Mr. Winters in the morning to get out of the lease. Thus, a demon did follow you because the dream or vision you had previously, repeated itself again. This is the second time you had the dream. This is important as you will see later. However, I have to mention, after this dream you describes various symptoms that are closely related to a heart attack. The sweating, the breathing, the heart pounding. are all signs that could have led to physical sickness (of course mental sickness) which has happened in many cases with diabolical obsessions.

In Chapter 19, pages 91-92, you set up another meeting with Mr. Winters at 1:00PM. He comes with a very large woman who is oddly wearing a flowered muumuu that almost perfectly matches the wallpaper on the stairway to the basement. Does this flowered muumuu also match the wallpaper in the Vision or nightmare you had on written about on pages 81 and 89? Starting to see a pattern with all these flowers that are similar on the wallpaper going down to the basement, in the visions on 81 and 89, and now the flowered muumuu. This is not a coincidence. Mr. Winters introduces his friend named Lillian. Is this really a friend or a relative? How is it that the neon flowering wallpaper going down the basement (which is very old because it is peeling off the wall with large bare patches) and now this Lillian shows up with similar flowering pattern on her muumuu? Was this "style" of wallpaper purchased and installed many years ago, when Lillian bought this muumuu? Did she have this wallpaper installed because she owned this house at one time? Very odd! You mention, on page 92, you wrote something curious, Mr. Winter's says: "We don't have long to stay, you know. I must return Lillian to the home very soon." He made a little loopy gesture with his hand, leading me to believe he was referring to a nut house. And how did she become mentally ill, by owning this house? By living in this house? Or is she involved in some evil intent with this house? She would not be here with Mr. Winters unless she knows something about this house. Is

Lillian related to this man you saw in the visions/trance from the basement? Then on page 93, Mr. Winters says: "I have never heard anything about this house being haunted (which is a lie). And I, myself, don't really believe in ghosts and such, (if this was true - why jump when the icemaker dropped the next batch of ice and fearfully ask: What was that?), but I do notice, Mr. LaChance that you seem to burn a lot of candles, which has led me to wonder: do you practice witchcraft her in my house, stirring things up and such?" You see how evil this man is, now accusing you of witchcraft? And how does he seem to know about candles and stirring things up with witchcraft? By asking these questions shows he had been involved in some type of witchcraft. The Catholic Church burns a lot of candles, does that mean we are involved in witchcraft?

After Lillian chimes in with her Indian chief haunting this land, which is a lie, then Mr. Winters babbles: "I hardly think any of those old wives' tales have anything to do with this house. I've been sitting here for many moments now, and I've felt nothing odd." And why should he, the demons already have his soul. The lying, the greed, the pompous pride, etc. demonstrates where his soul is.

Then this conversation gets more pathetic, Lillian says: "That charged feeling you sometimes get when you move around the house?" Lillan laughed. "Well, that's your ghost, honey. I felt it as soon as I walked in the front door." Oh really, that's your ghost Steve. According to Lillian, we are to believe that your soul can come out of your body at any time and then your body will feel an electric charge when your soulless body runs into your soul. Are you kidding me? Is this woman mentally sick? If this happens you are dead. What she is saying here comes from the distorted New Age movement.

So, at the bottom of page 93, Mr. Winters does not want to let you out of the lease unless someone else leases it, and perhaps that will be his cousin. On page 94, suddenly, he seems to be concerned about children being in the house. He wasn't too concerned about your kids, nor will he be concerned about any kids. It is ironic he calls the children "Little Angels".

Moving on to Chapter 20, page 95, this was a smart move on your part to get out of this house. but NOT having your children help with the move. On page 96 you finally begin to fight back. However, never say to demon that they won; they won nothing. In the end they will always lose. There is an old saying: "Evil has its hour. but God has His day." One day these demons will pay a heavy price for all they put you and every other victim they tortured. But as I said in the opening pages, had I known about this case, they would not have accomplished nearly the amount of destruction they caused.

On page 96 you mention that Mr. Winters shows up to meet the next residents of this house. Then you see a car pull up to the curb. In the car were a man, a woman, and two small children. You became outraged. Again, this proves just how evil Mr. Winter is. Then he says: "Aren't they sweetest little angels." I taught a lot of theology concerning the demonic. One important fact, demons love to go after children. Look what they did to your kids. At this point, it should also be clear to you that Mr. Winters is on the side of the demonic angels in this house. On page 94, Mr. Winters lied right to your face when he said: "Of course not. I certainly wouldn't want any more little angels in this awful situation." And in the car that just pulled up, are more victims, especially the children for the demonic angels in this house. And you witness with your own eyes, (along with your father) just how ruthless Mr. Winters is by bringing in more children into this house to become victims of the demonic. This incident is another reason to believe that Mr. Winters is guilty of bringing these demons into his house. Then your father did something very wise, he said to you: "Let's go son. We're finished here." And so, you left. Had he not done this, you might have done something very wrong. Remember, the demons there would have instigated you to do something extreme which would not be good. It was best for you to leave, only for now.

Finally, you arrive at your new house, Mr. Winters showed up asking for the keys to the house you forgot to hand in and says: "You know some people simply aren't meant to live in an old house and everything that comes with them. I just think you are one of those people." Does that go for all the other victims he rented his house to also? Does that also mean the woman who left her belongs that are in the shed? Does it also mean the man who is the so-called drug dealer on page 76? Do his words 'everything that comes with them' also mean all the demons that have been in the house for a long time?

After moving everything and finally settling in, of course on a Saturday night, you get all the kids to bed. You finally fall asleep, only to have another nightmare or vision. Did a demon latch on and follow you to this house? More than likely, the answer is yes.

On page 102, you are seeing a sleep technician. You wrote you fell into a deep depression, and you were extremely fatigued. Well, this is normal under the circumstances you went through. However, if you had in your hands what I am explaining in this evaluation of your case, it would be a different story. You wrote: "I felt like something was literally sucking away my energy." What you are describing here is how an Exorcist feels after battling the demonic angels. Again, you did not know about all these phenomena. If you look back to the beginning of this evaluation, I stated that when you are in this line of work - exorcisms and demonology - after each case you lose some of your humanity. This is probably what you are feeling because you wrote that the medical tests came back all normal.

On page 103, the sleep doctor mentions that you are suffering from sleep apnea. Then you asked about the nightmares and the doctor says this: "No, Mr. LaChance, with this type of sleep deprivation you should not be dreaming at all. No dreams. No nightmares." And why? Because the demonic is causing all this terror and it is not coming from within your body or mind. Can you recover from all this demonic terror? Yes. One of the ways is to live a Holy and prayerful Life (More on this later).

In chapter 22, and page 105 you wrote that your dream life returned which, is a good sign. Then you wrote that you felt something watching you. This is not your imagination, something is watching you, a demon. Notice on page 106, you describe a typical demonic apparition. The demon first fills you with fear and then approaches your bed. You can make out this creature has blond hair, but the eyes glowed in the dark. The eyes of the creature were white, stark white. No pupils or iris. Steve, if you ever see LIVE film coverage of exorcism, you will see the victim's eyes do the same thing. No pupils, no iris, stark white, which means the demonic are present. Again, you cannot fear this, if fact, in this line of work, you want to see this because as I wrote previously, this is one of the many Divine signs to us that the demons are present in a diabolical possession. In your case now, this falls under Diabolical Obsession. Your daughter then wakes you out of this nightmare.

In chapter 23, page 109, on a Sunday morning, three years after you move out of the Union house, Shelia calls you about Helen March, another victim, with two children, a girl, and a boy. Steve, is Helen March the same family who moved in after you move out on page 96 or is this a different family? I suspect Helen March is a different family which leads me to the next question, what happen to the family on page 96 who moved in after you? Is that family another victim of this house?

In chapter 24, page 111-114, after going through brief history with Helen, Charlie and their kids, Helen finds the same ad in the newspaper about your former house that is available to rent by Mr. Winters.

In chapter 25, on page 116 you write after much debating you finally call Helen. Helen goes through the same scenario you went through with Mr. Winters. Helen, Charlie her husband, her daughter Patty who lived there for only a short time, Charlie's son who died a few months after leaving the house (this is odd), a teenage daughter (I think this daughter is Kelly) and a grandson now live in the house that terrorizes them.

On page 116, Helen describes a typical diabolical oppression with the kitten. She had just gotten a kitten the other day and was upstairs. When Helen went into the bedroom she found the kitten dead on the floor. The kitten's neck and back were both broken. This was done by a demon from the Power choir.

On the next page, page 117, you describe more diabolical oppressions from the demonic. A suicide call to the police; gutters catching fire; the transformer in front of the house blew; whispers and things moving; her grandson pushed down the step and hurt; Charlie doubting all these phenomena; the feeling of someone watching her; lights are on when returning to the home; doors open, and windows opening.

In chapter 26, you go into a rather bizarre event at the library and courthouse, which no one seems to want to help you find information about the house. In fact, they seem to deliberately withhold information. Then on page 120 you mention finding out that the Union house was built by a Sears kit in 1936; the land was owned by a Captain John T. Cromwell; the Union house was standing right were Cromwell's slave quarters was located; the house across the street from the Union house was known as a murder house because a woman murdered her husband and herself in 1971; a big gray house where a man shot himself in front of his son. Demons normally infest houses where they are invited, or a terrible crime occurs inside them. I am not aware of any cases of demons going from someone's house where a terrible crime happens or were invited, and then moving to a new location. They normally stay in the place where the crime happened or where they were invited. I never been to this city, or these places which you are writing about, but if you look, especially with Mr. Winters house where there is a demonic infestation, there is probably a Catholic Church within a block or two of this house. People dying from tuberculosis or another horrific disease in the nursing home at the top of the hill during the Civil War has nothing to do with these events. Even if they were buried on the property with unmarked graves, that still does not matter. The Indian chief or the abortions with the whores of Moselle, if these events are true (even though they are evil), would not cause such demonic. terror.

However, Captain Cromwell's history could invite these demons into this house, especially if his remains are under the house. You mention he was a 33rd degree Mason. So was my own deceased father. I also know that Masons will use Ouija boards in some of their rituals. Ouija boards are famous for inviting demons into the house. Cromwell also headed the town's moral committee, which was responsible for passing judgment on any townsmen who committed transgression. In addition, the slaves were involved in voodoo which is another invitation for the demonic. How does the man in your nightmare or vision get to take a shower in the basement with human blood on him? There might be a better explanation, is the man in the butcher shower Cromwell's son or grandson? If Cromwell sold his soul to the devil, then the demonic was always around him, and easily transferred onto a relative such as his son or grandson to continue the evil behavior. Most of the time the son and grandson do even worse evil than his father or grandfather.

Without going into too many details, in

the Sacred Scriptures beginning with the Second Book of Samuel, King David has one of his sons inherit the Kingship. This was Solomon who in the beginning of his throne Solomon followed the Yahweh (God) very closely (Book of Kings) including building Yahweh the Temple in Jerusalem. However, Solomon became very powerful and began to sin against Yahweh. Solomon began to marry wives of other nations which infiltrated into the Israelites religion with evil pagan practices. One practice was worshipping idols that were known to have demons behind them. He even brought some of these evil practices into the Temple which, Yahweh resent and threaten punishment. As a result, during the reign of Solomon's Son, Rehoboam, (a very evil man), Yahweh lived up to his threat. "Israel has been separated from the House of David until the present." The point I am making here is that a father who does evil in the sight of Our Lord God, enables his son to carry out even more ruthless evil and thus in comes trouble and chaos. This is all very sad because it does not have to be this way. There are many examples in the Scared Scriptures of a father doing evil in the sight of the Lord, and then their sons do the same or even worse. This is very common among the demonic and very well could be the same in Mr. Winters' house.

Just like I explained earlier with your wife, there was already demonic activities going on in your life before you even met or moved into Mr. Winters house. The key to all these activities is in this vision/nightmare you had Steve, and finding out who the man is in the vision/nightmare. If you just had one nightmare, I would not give it much significance. But, since this same vision/nightmare keeps on occurring than it is more than a nightmare. Normal dreams do not keep happening repeatedly to terrify you. The man in the vision/nightmare is partially responsible for all the evil happening in this house. He is the one of the many individuals who invited the demons either by some pagan practice or some horrible crimes. However, it is not crucial you find out who this man is to get these demons out of the house. Finding out who the man in this vision/nightmare you are having will only solve a mystery on how these demons got into the house in the first place.

Moving onto chapter 27 page 124 you start to discuss Kelly and all her problems. Notice the demons go after the children first. Kelly begins to show signs that she is cutting herself, mood swings, and hearing voices, hurt others or kill others (ideas to kill others is from the demons that are in the Cherubim choir). This is serious diabolical obsession.

Though you did not mention it, the grandson was probably having similar experiences. Notice the words: "she cut herself with the hope that her self-sacrifice would appease the voices." You can never negotiate with a demon. Look closely at these words: this is the mockery of Jesus self- sacrifice on the cross with all the cuts. This idea did not come from her but from the demonic and of course they are never satisfied, this always gets worse. These demonic activities come from the evil angels out of the Virtues and Power choirs.

At the bottom of the page, you asked this question: "Do you want me to help you find help for this haunting?" This part of the work is so unfortunate, because in this line of work there are so many frauds and individuals who make things worse, as you will begin to experience.

On page 125, you mentioned something that is very annoying in this city. The mansion that was haunted was built on top of a series of caves and caverns. A radio show host clamored to broadcast from the mansion on Halloween. This is just great, and people wonder why all these demonic activities goes on in their life. Here you write that in the mansion, every member of the family that lived there committed suicide. The dog was even shot. Why would anyone want to challenge the evil in this mansion by staying in it overnight for Halloween? This is a demonic playground, and the demonic laugh at how stupid we humans are. Every person who goes into this mansion is inviting the demonic into their life. Why? For the thrill of being scared. Why is it that so many human beings want to be scared like this? For the challenge? And to have a radio show host promote this sort of thing is pathetic. This is not the only radio show host that promotes such stupidity during the month of October.

Then we come to a psychic named Betty who gives tours in such a place. So pathetic, yet tragic. Here is a person, probably charging you for the tour to make money on this evil, inviting you to: What? Dance with the demons in this mansion? Why would visitors to the mansion want to dance with the demonic? After all, this psychic named Betty was surely guaranteeing all those on these tours she gives that no evil demon or evil human soul would latch onto them Right? (While the mental hospitals keep filling up and the psychological profession/pharmacies/drug manufactures are making money with all the medication they give out because of the demonic angels.) Do not misunderstand Steve, I am not blaming you. You and Helen are desperate to find help. However, I am pointing out to you how easy it is for people to invite the demonic angels into their life. It does not take much for the demons to enter someone's life, especially if the person is not baptized and living in HABITUAL mortal sin. The demons laugh at us because they full well know that Jesus Christ taught us all how to live and this is not what He taught us. It is that simple!

Getting back to the book on page 125, you pick up Helen and drive off to this haunted mansion. Obviously, you both are nervous. You finally get to this place and go into the vestibule to see a small middle-aged woman with red hair. Is her hair naturally red or dyed red? Then you write that this woman had to be the famous Betty whom everyone had told you about. Oh really, and what credentials or REAL experience does this woman have to be so famous? Is she giving people advice about the future? The demons can do that!! Is it because Betty can see spiritual entities? Well so can you and Helen. Both of you saw the demons and human spirits in this house. Both of you have experienced the demonic activities. So, what makes this woman Betty a psychic? This woman is a major red flag.

Then we come to the huge dining room where you are given a liability waiver to sign. And why are liability waivers being signed in a haunted house, where the demonic are infested? Shouldn't this mansion be safe for a tour? (Being a former building contractor, I know for a fact that if the building is structurally unsafe or fire hazard the building inspectors (building codes) and the fire marshal would have the building condemn for demolition.) After all, Betty the famous psychic is here. Betty surely has the ability to stop the demons from doing anyone harm, doesn't she? Or could it be so Betty is not sued after one of these demons latches onto or possesses someone? Before we go any further, this woman is evil. To promote such insanity is wrong. The point, the only reason you and Helen must sign liability waivers is because someone had a demon latched onto or was possessed and got into trouble.

So, Betty's tour begins. Betty begins to talk about the history of the house and its former occupants. Then she makes a couple of attempts to contact the dead on the way up the stairs. Now to show you just how fraudulent this is, can Betty ever guarantee that the "spirit" she is talking to is someone who died? Can she guarantee the spirit is not demonic? No, Betty cannot guarantee this, but I can guarantee that the demons in this mansion are speaking to her. Some of these psychics are so fake and fraudulent. A side note here, I am not saying all these "psychics" are all fake. However, the good ones are not called "psychics", they are called mystics. What is the difference between a psychic and a mystic? One major reason, all mystics are given their gifts for the BENEFIT OF GOD, not themselves. A mystic lives very close to God and always prays daily, including going to Mass on a daily basis. No mystic will ever charge for their gifts.

I am a Spiritual Director to a couple of Mystics. Psychics always charge fees in some way, and they can never guarantee that the spirit they are speaking with is good or real.

Now let's get back to Betty's tour in this haunted mansion. You and Helen finally arrive in the attic, after experiencing nothing throughout the mansion. Here Betty informs everyone on the tour that a boy with Downs Syndrome was locked in the attic. where he lived until his death. If this really happened, then it has nothing to do with the demons being in this house. God has a very special affection for those born with a mental handicap because of their innocence. In addition, how does a Down Syndrome child invite a demon into his life? The answer is they cannot invite demons into their life because they have very little knowledge or the capacity to have the knowledge to invite them in the first place. The evil with this has to do with the parents of such a child. However, there are many children who are badly handicapped that there might not have been much the parents could do with the child or there probably was very little help available. Regardless, this has nothing to do with what is going on in this mansion.

Betty then asked everyone to turn off their flashlights and stay quiet, so she can contact the dead. You wrote that this was some form of a séance. A candle was lit in the center of the room, and Betty began speaking to the spirits. Then the room gets cold, which is typically a demonic activity as discussed before. Then, very close to the floor, about the size of a dog, a white, glowing, foggy light floated into the room. The girl next to you turned on her flashlight, which upset Betty who declared that her concentration had been broken and the tour was over. This is so fake. Are you sure this wasn't staged? How does a famous psychic lose their concentration because of a flashlight? If this white, glowing, foggy light floated into the room, how is it that it seems to just disappear after Betty loses her concentration? If this spirit did exist, they are not subject to Betty's command. After the tour, you talk to Betty and set a date for her to visit the house, then you and Helen drive back home.

In Chapter 28, page 127, the day arrives for the investigation. You return the house, very scared with your heart beating in your chest. It is not easy facing your fears but when you are confronting the demonic, you need to have courage. I have been scared on various cases, however, most cases I have been on I was not scared. It usually depends on what kind of demon or demons are infesting the place.

On page 128, you get to the house and Helen invites you inside. There is Charlie, who greets you and says to both Helen and you: "I must tell you two, you're messing with something here that my mother always told me to leave alone. If you aren't careful, you'll find yourself in something you both can't handle." Well Charlie and his mother are right in a certain sense, do not get yourself involved with any demonic spirits. However, Helen and you are not the ones who invited these demons into this house and your life. Both of your families are now victims of the evil spirits. Charlie saying this statement leads me to believe that he was having some demonic attacks. Charlie does not stay but leaves for work.

Betty brings her male assistant Lee with her at eight o'clock. She says that there was something that does not want them here. Betty can feel the resistance. This is a lie. If the demons are providing some sort of resistance, they would be successful in not allowing her to enter the house. So, then Helen and you give her a tour of the house.

After touring the first floor, you proceed to the second floor, but Betty pauses on the stairs. After going through the boy's former bedroom toward the breezeway at the back of the house, Betty walked ahead of you, then

Helen and you feel the force rush by in a cold burst of energy. Looking at Betty, you see Betty lifted about three inches off the floor and thrown against the wall. Helen and you grasped in horror. Now, one of the powerful Demons who is in the house did this to Betty. They had electromagnetic field meters which screamed at the heightened energies they came across. (A side note, the electronic equipment that is used in this line of work is beneficial because the human eyes and ears are not sensitive enough to see and hear what is going on around the place.) After telling Helen and you to wait downstairs, Betty and Lee proceed quickly through the house, including the basement.

Finally, Betty and Lee bring you their conclusions of the investigation. Betty told both of you they had come across the spirit of a man upstairs. That a lie. This was no human spirit upstairs, but a demon. No human spirit has the strength to lift a person off the floor three inches and throw them against the wall. Very powerful demons do these types of activities. In fact, all the indications from the demonic have directed Helen and you to this house because of the children. On page 129 Betty begins to speak about the basement. Before Betty even went down into the basement, both of you already knew that evil existed down there. Betty says: "There is a vortex in the basement where spirits can freely come and go. Sometimes something very bad can come through these vortices. It is possible that something of this nature may have already come through the vortex. It's a very powerful opening. It isn't my place to tell you to move, but if you continue to live here you need to try to avoid that area as much as possible." Let take a deep look at these statements. I don't know why she is using the word vortex. According to the Webster New Practical School Dictionary A vortex is a mass of liquid in whirling motion, forming in the center a cavity toward which things are drawn, a whirlpool. I am not aware of any Catholic Exorcist or Demonologist who uses this term. I think, (though I could be wrong) she means a portal. A portal is an opening in the spiritual plane where the demonic travel in and out. This is very odd she is using this term. Regardless of whether you call it a vortex or portal, there is an opening in the Spiritual plane that needs to be closed. I do agree with her that the portal is down in the basement. More specifically, the portal is either in the fruit cellar, or near or under the butcher shower It is possible it could be both, but it seems to me it is in the fruit cellar. Here is where the demons (and condemned human spirits) are coming in and out from hell into this house. Betty knows that something very evil has come in and out of this opening.

But Helen and you already knew something was very evil in the basement. It is odd to me that she says: "Sometimes something very bad can come through these vortices." If Betty is a psychic, she should be able to distinguish that this "something" are demons. If she cannot do this, then the demonic has done a great job camouflaging their appearances to her. Betty probably thinks she is speaking to a human spirit or even a good spirit when in fact, the spirit she is communicating with is a demon that is under a disguise. This is a common occurrence among many of the psychics who think they are speaking to a human spirit but are speaking to a demon. Most Catholic Exorcists, who are priests, will tell you that those who belong to the psychic industry can be easy manipulated by such demonic tactics. This phenomenon is nothing new, this industry just has a fancy name called psychics. They are the same individuals who are called mediums, sorcerers, magicians, and necromancers, etc. in the Sacred Scriptures.

Betty also says, "It is possible that something of this nature may have already come through this vortex." This statement seems to imply that Betty is afraid to tell you the full truth at the same time it also seems to imply she does not know what she is doing. The statement "It's a very powerful opening." This part is not true. An opening in the spiritual plane cannot be powerful, it is just an opening. A better description for you to understand that a portal is a passageway opened in the spiritual plane that needs to be close off. Then Betty says: "It isn't my place to tell you to move, but if you continue to live here you need to try to avoid that area as much aspossible." This is an unfair statement because Betty is implying the whole basement, and not a particular area in the basement, or there would be more descriptive words in this statement about a certain area in the basement.

Then you write that this is the full extent of Betty's comments before she and Lee left. Helen and you are left confused and both of you never see them again. This is not right. Here is where I have a big problem with these investigators. They come into a house that has "Paranormal Activity", confirm the victim's suspicion and just leave. That is it? Nothing else, no advice or recommendation on what the victims in the house should do next? What about getting the demonic activity to stop? What about getting the demons out of the house? What about closing off the portal to the house? This why so much of these investigators and psychics are so fake and fraudulent. Helen and you asked her to help you and all Betty did was confirm what you already knew. And not hearing from Betty and Lee again only illustrates how afraid and inexperience she is. She is not the only one in this field who "demonstrates such Incompetence. A side note, I do not mean to imply that all these Paranormal Investigators (some have psychics on their team) are like Betty and Lee. There are many teams out there who honestly try to help victims in your situation and are quite successful in doing so. Some of these successful paranormal investigating teams have Catholic Priests or Protestant Minsters working either on the team or advise them on what to do. The difference is this: Are they offering solutions or providing means (Christian rituals) to remove the problem? And are they successful in removing the demonic spirits?

The final paragraph on page 129 was you returning home to inform your kids. Lydia gave a sigh of relief and says: "Maybe now people will believe us?" Then you wrote: "It was a question that hung in the air then and still hangs in the air today." Well, you can inform Lydia that you have an authentic Demonologist who does believe you and all you have been through. That is why God had me respond to your case. I have been praying over your case and Our Lord has been directing this response to you. There are too many demonic incidents written in this book that could not be made up.

Moving on to Chapter 29, page 131, Kelly calls you on the phone because she has seen a very cruel demonic apparition. Kelly was sitting on the porch talking to one of her friends that night. Kelly than heard a baby crying and when she looked over at the trees there was a baby hanging by its feet, wearing a white dress.

Notice the words "white dress" in this apparition. First, this is so cruel to do to a teenager like Kelly, but it is typical with the demonic going after the children first. The white dress represents the white dress or gown the Catholic Church uses to put on a newly baptized baby. In relationship to this house, the baby was killed sometime after baptism. However, this is not, and I repeat, this is not the baby who was killed. This is the demonic playing games and mocking the baptism of the child. That baby's soul is in Heaven. In addition, the baby was first heard crying. Most of the extreme cases I have been involved with, and even studied, always have a baby crying in it. The baby represents innocence and is a cruel form of terror to the victim because most people would not do this to a baby. This is a demon hanging from the tree disguising itself to terrify Kelly. Usually when this happens in an extreme case, the demonic are stepping up their vicious torment to cause fear. Again, let's go through the steps, first diabolical infestation; second, diabolical obsessions; third diabolical oppression, leading to the final step of diabolical possession. This is one of the goals of the demons.

Helen, her mother, gets on the phone and is convinced Kelly saw this happening. Helen also expresses how this frighten Kelly which, is exactly what the demonic want. You then tell Helen that you will be over as soon as possible.

On page 132, you finally go over to Helen's house and Kelly is obviously very frightened. Then a thunderstorm begins to come into the city, another occasion for the demonic to play games. Helen and you are sitting on the front porch watching this storm, when you see the same demonic apparition Kelly saw. A baby was hanging upside down from the tree. You wrote that the baby was clearly dead. No, it wasn't, that was the demonic just giving you the impression the baby was dead. There is a demon doing this act and he is not dead. Since this is the second time it happened, it should be clear that a baby was killed sometime after the child was baptized by the man you saw in the vision/nightmare. It is possible that the baby's remains are somewhere in the house, perhaps the mudroom.

Helen and you both go inside and express your thoughts and fears. Then you hear a child humming and playing in the rain. This could be the same demon you saw in the tree or a different one. However, violently, viciously, low growl came ripping through the window from outside. You obviously were in terror which is what the demons wanted. Then you wrote on page 133, "Never before had I heard anything like it, and there was no mistake, it was angry." All demons are angry. There is no such thing as making a demon angry or even angrier. They are always angry, because they lost their place in Heaven, and they know it. That is why they keep coming after us, they do not want us to go to Heaven. It was good that you stayed with them, but they do need to get out of this house or get an Exorcist.

In chapter 30, page 135, you express your feeling of not understanding these events in a haunted house. Part of this statement is true, because there is a mystery with all evil, and we may never find out the answers to it. However, there is always a pattern when dealing with the demonic. You just got to know some of these patterns and then be in close contact with God who guides you through it. Steve, whether you realize it or not, so far you wrote nothing at all in this book that I have not seen in other cases including the patterns you are describing. This was very new to you and unfamiliar, but there are cases far worse than this one! For example, the actual case (not the pathetic movie) involving the Amityville horror. That does not mean I am trying to belittle the significance of this case because this is a very bad case and ranks very high on the worse case scenarios. When dealing with the demonic, always remember that they will go to the extreme unless something is put in there way and forced out. In other words, demons need to be expelled out of the person, place or thing they are instigating.

At the bottom of page 135, Helen calls you over because there is something in the house growling at her. Growling like an animal (such as a bear, wolf, dog, hyenas, etc.) is one of the unfortunate realities of demons. These creatures were so beautiful and because of the sin of pride/arrogance, they became hideous and very ugly. They even have taken on the features of animals and reptiles. This is not an exaggeration, many of the demons now have features that you see in ugly animals and reptiles. In other words, if you took a tour of actual Hell, like many mystics have done, this is what you would see in an actual demon. Thus, the further you are from God the more hideous an angel or a human becomes. As Jesus says in the Sacred Scripture, God did not spare the angels (who are now demons) nor will God spare us. As a result, because many demons look like animals and reptiles, they act like them also.

On page 136, you rush over to Helen's house and find out the same pattern of demonic activity you experienced when you rented this house. You first encountered an electric charge, you smelled a foul odor of rotten flesh (often times sewage), you go inside and hear growling and then more growling, and then all of a sudden it just stops. Silence. The demons do this to increase your anger, resentment, fear, anxiety, etc. Thus, they are wearing their victims down mentally. After all this, Helen reveals on her arm a large bite mark that happen in her sleep. More than likely, Helen probably did not feel this in her sleep when it happened. The typical way the demons do this is to bite or scratch their victims, and then later the pain begins to increase which, causes the person to look where the pain is coming from and then they noticed they have been bitten or scratched. This can happen in the daytime or nighttime. On page 137, you wrote that time was running out, and you are right. Helen should find another place to live.

In chapter 31, page 139, it is so unfortunate that you had to deal with such groups who were amateurs, voyeurs, harlequins, harridans. shysters, drunks and worse. And of course they took all kinds of pictures, video recordings, recordings of voices and noises, etc. but no real solutions. In fact, they even gave you the wrong advice, with the comment: "Whatever was in the house was Just trying to scare you." This is wrong and all these people should get out of this business before they really get hurt. I am not kidding, either. Some of these groups are so naive that a demon could very easy follow them from place to place and manipulate whatever they are investigating. Bottom line. they have no power to get rid of human spirits or demons. Jesus only gave those who followed Him the power to cast out demons. I do not want to give the impression that only Catholic Priests can do exorcisms on a human being, or place or thing. This would not be true, in fact there are many Protestant Minsters that are just as effective in this work (or ministry) as a Catholic Priest. However, the Catholic Priest has so much more power and tools in this line of work than any other minster. Unfortunately, (just like in other Churches) too much liberalism has gotten to some of the bishops and look at the chaos that it causes the Church.

At the bottom of page 139, you begin to see the stark reality of all these psychics. If these psychics were all valid, wouldn't they all come up with the same scenario? On page 140, you demonstrate just how manipulative the demons are with these psychics. Especially, the one group where you mention one of the investigators was thrown against the wall by something unseen. This is not a game or something that you want to get film on to show on TV, which is one of the reasons so many of these "Paranormal Investigators" are in this line of work - to get on TV. Here you can see why the Church is so secretive about all this, this is not for Hollywood to exploit. Now with all these documentaries and various cases hitting the big screen, (especially like films entitled "Paranormal Activity" episodes 1, 2, and 3, and now the recent release of #4) this attracts all kinds of people into this line of work. I have no problem of having the public learn about this phenomenon within reason, but not to make money. Unfortunately, today this is becoming big business, especially as we approach the month of October. It is not a coincidence that the demonic become active during October. It is one of the months dedicated by the Catholic Church to the Blessed Mother. The demonic have a severe hatred for the Blessed Mother.

On page 141, you wrote about one group of investigators, twenty people, who brought cases of beer, hard liquor, and marijuana. They used dowsing rods to apparently communicate with the spirits. Here is a primary example of those in this line of work opening themselves up for possession. Helen joked saying that the house must host quite a party every night. Even though Helen is joking, she is stumbling on another profound reality you are missing, that is the demonic are very attractive. Look how many people showed up. It wasn't just you who was asking for help, this house has a clear reputation that it is haunted by evil spirits, even before you moved into it.

I want to demonstrate to you another incident of the demonic communicating to the investigators. On page 141, you mentioned that two investigators ganged up on Kelly and accused her of witchcraft. They tell you it comes from "psychic impression". That wrongful advice came from a demon to an investigator. The next indignity came when an investigator suggested that Helen should institutionalize her daughter. This person even has a preprinted list. Now how does this person show up with a preprinted list? Is someone advising this person to bring it when this person never even met Kelly? Again, this is more wrongful demonic advice given to Helen and you. Demons always lie to psychics because these people are ignorant and arrogant enough to believe what the demons tell them. Notice, Steve that none of the advice from any of these paranormal investigators has pointed you to God for help. Not once, did you write any of these investigators giving advice to go to Catholic Priest or a Minster.

On page 142, Helen has another bite mark on her arm, and the twinkle in her eyes was gone. This second bite mark and her eyes no longer sparkling are signs from the demonic of their intentions. The bite marks the second time are showing that the demonic are marking her as their possession. Is this also a sign that Helen is not very religious. Why wasn't your family Steve, marked by a demon? At the very least, your kids were going to Church learning about God. The problem here is that Divine Grace is missing, thus enabling the demon complete freedom.

In chapter 32, page 143, you wrote that Helen's health was beginning to get worse. Helen's blood pressure would go very high, before a paranormal event occurred. This is anxiety, fear, and stress which not only breaks down the body but the mind as well. With no Spiritual health there to help combat this phenomenon, there is little resistance that can be done. These symptoms will lead to the breakdown of Helen's free will. The desperate attempt to think you can negotiate with these evil angels to stop all this terror never works. Once the free will is broken down, then the entrance way to a diabolical possession can take place. If there is no Divine Grace from God to resist, no free will to fight, no understanding of what is happening, and unfortunately no valid help, then there only one thing left - cooperate with what the demonic want.Then you write that Helen, and you heard noises coming from the upstairs bedroom. You got to the top of the stairs and found a large, black mist apparition hovering over your head. It was huge and engulfing. Its negativity pulsed through you, making you nauseous. Then you stared at the mist as it hovered around you and above you. You had planted yourself in its path by standing your ground and not backing down. After a few moments it began to swirl, and then it dissipated until it was gone. Steve, never do this again. You are so lucky you did not become possessed or seriously hurt. Human beings are never a good match to any demon regardless of what choir they come from. Even I with all my skill and training in this field would never do such a thing. These demonic angels are way too strong for any human being. I do not know why this demon did not possess you or seriously hurt you, with the only exception of God stopping this creature. You never take a demon on like this no matter how frustrated, angry, or strong you might think you are. These demonic angels have been doing this since the beginning of time, don't you think they could have killed you? Possessed you? Physically harmed you, like throwing you down the steps?

This was an invitation to challenge the demon. Do you realize how easy it would have been for this demon to possess you by entering through one of your senses such as your eyes or nose? These demons are pure evil spirits, you could have inhaled that evil spirit right into your lungs. Then how would you have gotten this creature out of you? Through a medical doctor? Then what would of happen to your children? Who would have taken care of them? You do not have the power to do this - no human being does - and not even a Catholic Priest who is an Exorcist with years of experience can do this!!! Do not do this again! This is a wrong move! You are lucky this time, but I promise you this, you will not be so lucky next time. There are ways of combatting these creatures which I will teach you, but you should never take on demons like this.

Let us move on to Mark, the surveillance expert, on page 144. You wrote that one night he was with a small group in the basement. He Just checked the fruit cellar door to make certain it was tightly closed. He couldn't budge it. He turned his back to walk away when he heard the door scrape on the basement floor as it opened behind him. He turned to see a large, black-hooded figure with red glowing eyes enter the basement from the fruit cellar. Mark screamed and went into shock. This is a major significant event, unfortunately at the expense of Mark. The key is what Mark was doing down in the basement - he was on surveillance. His equipment was probably down in the basement, even though you did not write this in the book. The demonic achieve what they wanted which was to scare Mark and even get him out of the house. However, the demons made a huge mistake here. Why produce this sudden fright in Mark, your surveillance expert? One reason, had he put any electronic equipment into that fruit cellar, or if the electronic equipment took any photos or videos of the fruit cellar with the door opened, you might have caught the portal, (or the vortex) the spiritual passageway demons are traveling through. The demons would know this, thus the viciously scaring Mark to keep him from discovering their entrance to the house. As I was suspecting earlier, this was the entrance to the house the demons are using. There is more to this event. Why was the demon inside the fruit cellar in the first place? What is the significance to the demonic angels for being here in this part of the house? One of our major weapons against the demonic angels is to interpret the reasons for what they are doing. The answer must be in the fact that some human being was doing something evil in this fruit cellar. Now what does this mean? The devil (as well as all demons) is known to do what? Tempt the human race to commit sin against God and His laws. (The Law being The Ten Commandments or the Two Greatest Commandments recorded in Sacred Scripture.)

Back to the vision/nightmare you were having, Steve. The man in this vision/nightmare was in this basement doing something evil. By the demonic tempting him to do something evil, they became successful in carrying out this evil and it enabled them to open the plane up on the site the evil was committed. No opening (portals or vortexes whatever you want to call them) in the spiritual plane can be opened without first some evil act occurring there first. Thus, the demon came out of the fruit cellar; Why? Because the opening in the spiritual plane was inside the fruit cellar. Why was the portal opened in the spiritual plane in the first place? Because evil acts tempted by the demonic happened in this place. What was the evil act or acts? The vision/nightmare provides the clues for this evil act. The man in the vision/nightmare has blood on him. he cannot wash it off no matter how well he scrubs. All blood washes off the skin of a human body - why can't he wash it off in the vision/nightmare? Because the blood is on his soul, meaning he committed a horrendous act or acts such as killing a person or many individuals. (This is not blood from animals. It is not a sin to kill an animal, therefore there is no blood of animals on anyone's soul. Abusing animals is another matter I am not going into.) Then why do we only see in the vision/nightmare this man's soul? Because the man is dead and in hell with these demons who helped him (tempted him or even possessed him) to commit these horrendous acts. Then why would God allow such a thing to happen? God never wants any human being to commit such evil acts, He allows it because of giving all human beings a free will to follow Him and His commands or follow the demonic and their commands. Then why is God allowing Helen and you to suffer such terror from the demonic angels? I do not have the mind of God to fully answer this question, however God never left you. I explained earlier that the nightmares you were having falls under diabolical obsessions, which the demonic angels use to terrorize their victims. Then I explain that this nightmare also falls under visions, which comes from God. Thus, the demons are using this actual event to terrorize you, Steve, to achieve their goals. However, God also has goals He wants to achieve, even though this is all evil. What goals would that be?

The truth! Evil never has the last word with God. God always has the last word. By God allowing you to see this vision/nightmare instigated by the demonic angels, He is also allowing you to see the Truth which is seeing the evidence left behind of what happened, and not the actual Evil act or acts themselves. Do the police see all the evil acts committed? Well, sometimes, but mostly they end up seeing the actual evidence left behind. With the demonic, on one hand, they mock God with their accomplishments by this evil man in the vision/nightmare. Thus, when demonic angels are dealing with God, only the truth can be dealt with and never a lie. On the other hand, by allowing the demonic to mock Him with their activities such as diabolical obsessions (visions/nightmares), in the process they also reveal the truth of what happened in these evil acts for it to become known to human race. This is called, in Catholic Theology, a paradox. A paradox is not an either/or but both. For example, Jesus is either human or divine. Jesus is both divine and human, which is a paradox. Likewise, the diabolical obsessions are caused by the demonic angels to achieve their goals, the diabolical obsession is allowed by God to achieve His goals: the truth, which is a paradox. God was always there Steve; you just didn't see Him working.

Now we get to God in the book on page 144, you stated that the events started to take on religious connotations. One day Helen wasn't home when her mother called. Her mother's name, phone number and time were all on caller ID. You continue by writing that Helen's mother called back and had a strange message on her answering machine. Apparently, a woman had answered Helen's phone uttered the Lord's Prayer and hung up. That was no woman Steve, that was a Good Angel from Heaven. It was not the demonic angels in the house because they can't stand even hearing this prayer, yet alone say it.

Then you write that Helen and you were upstairs sitting in the breezeway when something very large moved by both of you and said the word: "Jesus" in a low guttural voice. Steve, this was also a good Angel, and from the little bit of description you wrote, it sounds like one of the Warrior Angels. What is a Warrior Angel? These are very Powerful Good Angels that no one should ever play game with at all. They are in the Sacred Scriptures, which Our Lord sent one of these Warrior Angels down to guide the Israelites out of Egypt (Ex 14:19). Our Lord warned the Israelite, if they do not listen to him (the Warrior Angel) this Angel would not forgive their sins. Warrior Angels come from all the choirs of Angels and given this special mission as Warriors. According to the Church Fathers of the Catholic Church, these are the Angels who will fight the last War, in the Book of Revelation and within twenty-four hours they will defeat Satan and all his angels and followers. I am not exaggerating these Angels are strong and are no match to the most powerful demon in this house or in hell.

Unfortunately, both Helen and you misunderstood what all this meant. The Angel that said the word "Jesus" was trying to get both of you to call out to Our Lord for help. This was not a diabolical angel because they can't stand Our Lord's name "Jesus". Even from the beginning of the demonic Angels condemnation to Hell, they still will not utter the name Jesus. Even Satan does not use the name Jesus. You were missing all the prompting given to you by the Eternal Father as mentioned above to call out to Him. The Father, Son, and Holy Spirit have been trying to get Helen and you to pay attention to them. Our Triune God wanted to help, if all you did is call out, like you did Steve when the house was in chaos and your kids were locked behind these doors and you cried out "God Please Help".

You reached out to all this Pathetic Psychics, and not one of them help, and some of them made it worse. Why didn't you reach out to God for help? However, notice that God allowed you to reach out to all these so-called psychics or paranormal investigators first - to exhaust all these possible human solutions. They never work, nor will they ever work! Only God works.

When we are dealing with this kind of evil from the demonic angels, you cannot fight this kind of evil with more evil or more vicious evil, this will not work. You can only fight this type of diabolical evil with the opposite extreme: Divine Goodness, Divine Holiness, Divine Power and Divine Mercy. At this point Steve, you recognized that this was all diabolical, why did you not start to cry out here with Helen for Help from God? You did it once and it worked but you never wrote that you cried out to God for Help at all. You wrote that Lydia and you were trying to hang-up a picture of two Angels in this house, why did you not cry out to the Good Angels for help? You obviously believed in good angels if you had possession of a picture of them.

Getting back to the book, naturally the demonic angels saw all this taking place, and what did they do - increase their attacks on Helen and you. You wrote on page 144 day after day, hour and after hour, event after event took its toll on Helen. With each passing day, she became more tired, her smile a bit faded. She was slipping away from us, and we didn't know how to hold on to her. Yes, Helen was slipping away from you and more importantly from God, and right into the control of the Diabolical Angels to be possessed. Once the Divine Lord tries to reach out to Helen, and you, in an extraordinary way (a good angel showing up in this house), the demonic angels are going to increase their attacks. This always happens in all cases I studied that have involved with diabolical angels. Now, it is a battle for Helen's soul between God and the demonic angels. Had any authentic Exorcist (Catholic or Protestant) or myself been there, there would have been a huge war in that house. God never loses His wars with anyone, especially with the demonic Angels. A demon might win a battle, they never win the war. Speaking for myself, God (Father, Son and Holy Spirit) has never lost any of the wars he sent me into with any demon or demons. When you fight with God, God always wins.

We move onto the third part of your book "The Possession". In chapter 33, page 149, you get a phone call at 4 a.m. (of course, after the witching hours of 12 a.m. to 3 a.m.) from Helen, crying and upset that she wants to kill her husband. Again, this is a Diabolical Obsession, but it is more vicious after the Divine had reached out. You wrote: "I think I want to kill my husband Charlie, and I'm afraid I could do it. I have this walking cane that was my dad's. I was lying next to Charlie in bed, and I saw it leaning against the wall and I had the most horrible thoughts race through my mind. I saw myself picking up this cane and smashing Charlie in the head with it. It broke his skull open. And I thought to myself, I could really do this. He wouldn't even have time to wake up. I could kill him, and he wouldn't be able to stop me." By writing this the diabolical attacks are getting worse, and her free will is breaking down, and more importantly, Helen has nothing to fight with against these diabolical attacks. First. the idea came from the demonic, then they show her how to do it - via a walking cane - then, Helen sees that she can do this evil act, then Helen is shown the results of it - Charlie's skull broken open. This is just like the vision/nightmare you had in this house. The demons are doing the same thing here with Helen. convincing her to do this evil act (with no Divine Grace to resist it) as they did with that man you saw in the vision/nightmare. It is the same diabolical pattern - kill an innocent victim, different times and methods used, but the same diabolical act the demons are trying to achieve.

The next major concern is Kelly on page 150, where you wrote: "Then last night... I didn't tell you this, but I woke up and Kelly was standing at the foot of our bed. Steven, she didn't look like herself. She was staring at Charlie and me. I swear she looked like she wanted to kill us. And I understand now what Kelly had to be thinking. I understand completely because I wanted to kill him, too. I wanted to split his head open with that cane. And Steven, I'm afraid that sooner or later I'm not going to be able to stop myself." This is unfortunate because Kelly at this point is possessed by a demon or demons. Helen was right. Kelly did not look like herself because the demonic are inside her. There is no legitimate reason a teenage girl, in the middle of the night, (probably after 12 a. m. and before 3 a.m.) would be standing at the edge of Helen's bed staring at both of them unless the teenage girl had some help. Helens comment on Kelly looking like she wanted to kill them, is true. Kelly was standing at the bed wanting to kill both of them, however, Helen woke up, which is an indication that this will happen again. The comment by Helen saying "she is afraid that sooner or later I'm not going to be able to stop myself" is true for both Helen and Kelly.

In chapter 34, page 151, you asked the question: "What did Helen and you do to deserve this?" The answer to this question can only be answered by God. No one can give an answer to this question, including me. By reading this evaluation of your case, Steve, maybe an answer was given without me knowing it. Ultimately, the answer has to come from God because no matter what answer coming from any human being down here on earth could give, it will never be good enough to explain why all this happened. Only God can provide that answer for this question, and when the answer is received, there will be no more questions.

Let's get to Alex on page 152, who claimed he was a psychic. One major warning that something was wrong is you mentioned he worked as a personal assistant by day and sold sex toys at night. Was this wise to have someone who sold sex toys at night in this MPR group dealing with the demonic? Are you sure he is not possessed by now? You wrote Alex was involved in the occult. and had books dealing with black magic. This fact alone should be a good enough reason to get him out of the group, and, especially, this house. The demonic are toying with him. Having Alex in the house also causes the demonic to play more vicious games if he was trying to use any black magic. A side note, in this field there is no such thing as white magic, it is all black. Never buy into this stupidity, because it is all fake or phony by those who claim they use white magic.

Then Alex says that he is only practicing gray magic. How do you get gray magic? You must mix black magic with white magic to come up with gray magic with is bogus. It was good to see that you were able to discern that there is no such thing as gray magic. A very big note of concern here is that Alex is saying he is only practicing, meaning he has tried this before. Alex is open season for the demonic, the sex toys alone and the occult are enough for an invitation for a diabolical possession. Notice that not even the so called 'psychic' in your group can help, which begs the question, what good is a 'psychic' when the demonic are all over this house and these so called 'psychics' should be able to see them?

You finally remove these books out of the house, knowing full well that he was practicing the black arts. Did you also know, Steve, that by having Alex in this house, practicing the black arts, he could of cause (invite) Kelly and Helen to become possessed if he tried any of those spells, incantations, etc. in this house which, is already demonically infested before Alex got here? It was no coincidence that Helen and you found Alex using these books. God obviously revealed this to both of you whether you realized it or not. You should have removed Alex immediately from the house and the group. This is why I tried to warn you earlier that these "Paranormal Investigators and Psychics" can make all this worse and the demonic love it!

Steve, here is more education when dealing with the demonic. Do you have any idea what a Catholic Exorcist (who is a priest) or myself do before we take on a case dealing with demonic entities? Besides fasting, praying, and studying, we go to the Sacrament of Confession. Do you know why? Because the demonic angels can use our sins to their advantage, and more importantly, our effectiveness in assisting Our Lord in the removal of demonic angels is lessened without confession. Holiness is absolutely required in this field, there no exceptions. I have never been on any case so far without first going to the Sacrament of confession. That is how important this is. If a Catholic priest does not get to confession before getting involved with a diabolical entity, they are risking damage to themselves, and even becoming possessed, depending on what mortal sins they committed. It is far better to go into these cases with a guilt-free conscience from mortal sin (and even venial sin). Here are a few more reasons many priests do not want to get involved in this kind of ministry as I wrote earlier.

This is serious business and to have Alex inside this house with a demonic infestation is a grave mistake. I realize Alex was only trying to help, but help with what kind of tools? Tools (black magic) given to the occult by the demonic? By having Alex stay in the house, he is now at risk for being a victim of diabolical possession and risking even more diabolical activities. Can you be absolutely sure that Alex is not practicing black magic (without you hearing what he is saying under his breath) especially if the demonic angels start playing their games and he gets scared? Continuing with Alex, you wrote that he ran through the house like a madman screaming at unseen entities, challenging them. You never humanly challenge demons like this, especially when we know they fell from Heaven, ultimately from the sin of pride. The prideful demonic angels will respond. I studied a case that a Catholic priest who was an Exorcist (a bit inexperienced), challenged a demon like this and the results were horrible. The demons came out and somehow cut open the groin of the priest. This priest lot some of the functions in his groin and was in the hospital. The good news is much later, he was successful on the case. True story.

Returning back to Alex, if he was taking pain medication for kidney and gallbladder problems, normal would not be a problem, but you wrote he washed them down with alcohol that is a problem. I just wanted to be clear that someone on medication can still function in this field, however, it depends on the medication and more specifically the health (physical, mental, and spiritual health) of the person. Taking medication with alcohol is over the line and Alex obviously needed help himself. You wrote that on one of Alex's tirades one night, an unseen force grabbed him and began sexually groping him. Instead of being frightened the way most people would have been, he seemed to enjoy it. This is dangerous. Here you are describing a sexual violation by a demon and Alex seemed to enjoy it. You are right in saying most people would be frightened, but there is something more crucial here. The demonic angels are using the sins of Alex against him (selling sex toys at night) rendering him ineffective. What is so dangerous about this is the open invitation Alex is giving. Alex allowing these demonic angels to sexual grope him, which, he seemed to enjoy, would normally result in a diabolical possession. Steve, I realize by the way you wrote this that you found out after these events happened, but it is important for you to learn that all this is very dangerous to the physical, mental and spiritual health of Alex, Helen, Kelly, the rest of the team and yourself. Unfortunately, Steve, ignorance here is not an excuse because the demonic angels do not care, they only hate us. Thus, you wondered on page 151 who had let loose this Pandora's box of events. Part of your answer to that question is Alex. Again, you cannot fight evil demonic angels with evil tools received by the demonic. That would be like me, a Catholic Priest, coming into this house and performing a black "satanic" mass (Which I would never do), thinking that this would stop or appease any of these diabolical angels. It would not, if I did something this stupid it would only increase their diabolical activities.

Continuing on page 153, Alex made known to all of you that demons were visiting him at night while he tried to sleep. This would be true, because Alex invited the demonic angels into his life by practicing black magic and his involvement with the occult. I can almost guarantee this "black magic" from the occult Alex was practicing led him to believe that he was a psychic with the demonic angels "speaking" to him. This also started way before Alex was involved with this house. Then you wrote that Alex told Helen and you he wanted to perform a ritual in the basement of the house. Alex called it a "bloodletting ceremony". Alex would make a salt pentagram and stand in the center with another boy named Bobby, he would then cut himself and Bobby and bleed in the center of the pentagram. This will enable the demons to come to Alex in which he will bind them to himself and take them away. This bloodletting ceremony has some of its traces back to Elyah in the Old Testament (See 1 Kings18:28). Helen and you are very wise not to have Alex do this ritual in this house, you surely would have more problems. Alex immediately leaves the house angry, upset, and defiant. By now Steve you should realize just as authentic these 'psychics' really are by all these experiences.

Then on page 154, you wrote that the original MPR group broke up. I agree with you Steve, that Sheila, Mary, and Mark leaving the group, and harboring a grudge against you, has really nothing to do with you at all, but with the house, more specifically the demonic angels. A side note, this even happens to some of the groups who are very successful in expelling demons out of people's houses. The demonic angels will do anything to cause havoc in these groups to cause them to fall apart. Then you wrote that Alex was institutionalized because he became homicidal and suicidal. More than likely, Alex became demonically possessed. This is the results when someone involved in the occult, using black magic, selling sex toys and taking medication with alcohol. Like Helen and Kelly there is nothing inside them that can resist or defend themselves against the demonic attacks. Like I mentioned earlier, we are now getting case of these "Paranormal Investigators" becoming diabolically possessed. This is unfortunate because these TV programs such a *"Paranormal Investigators"; "Ghost Stories caught on Camera"; "Celebrities Ghost Stories caught on Camera"; "Curses"* etc., attract many individuals into this line of work and they never mention the risk that is associated with it.

Moving on to Chapter 35, page 155 where you write about Helen having two more bite marks on her arm. Helen continues to complain that she is afraid Kelly wanting to hurt or kill Charlie and herself. This is the second time you have written on this concern with Kelly. I still maintain that Kelly is diabolically possessed from the demons in this house.

Then Helen described her dream about wearing a black dress, with strands of white, perfectly shaped pearls. Helen then realizes that this funeral is her own. Helen is also glad she dead in the dream. This kind of dream is significant in relation to this case. First, many people have dreams like this concerning their death. They see themselves dead in the coffin.

Abraham Lincoln had a few of these dreams. However, in relationship to this case, Helen's dream is a paradox, as I explained earlier. This is part of the diabolical obsession Helen has been going through, but it is also a Divine Warning a paradox which means both meanings are true.

Let us first deal with the diabolical obsession with Helen's dream. You wrote that Helen is standing in her room alone. This is partly because the demonic angels want their victims isolated to bring them to despair. From this perspective, the darkness could be describing her soul, with the white baptismal character, and all the riches Helen owns are represented by the perfectly shaped pearls. Helen thinks this funeral is Charlie's or Kelly's since she has so much concern about Kelly hurting someone. Then Helen realizes she is dressing for her own funeral because she is wearing her burial dress. Then Helen says in the dream she never looked or felt better and was glad to be dead. For this to happen in a dream, two phenomena have to be present - Helen's body and her soul. She first says she is standing in her room alone: Helen's soul; then she realizes she is dead, which means Helen's soul must see the dead body lying somewhere in the dream. The key words here is Helen is glad to be dead, which means the demonic angels are introducing Helen to the idea of being dead; the demonic angels are convincing her that being dead would be better. Being dead would be an escape from her current situation; thus, the seductive temptation - suicide.

Second, a Divine Warning from God is also present in this Dream. This is Helen's soul shown to her by God from her sleep, meaning that the black dress represents her mortal sins:

397

the strand of white represents the baptismal character; and the perfectly shaped pearls is from Our Lords mouth where He tells His disciples "do not throw your pearls to the swine" (Mt 7:6); the swine representing the demonic angels and the perfected shaped pearls represents the Faith in God. Helen is shown in the dream by God that it is her funeral and not Charlie's or Kelly's. Helen realizes that she is dressing for her own funeral by wearing "my" burial dress. This is an indication that Helen had already picked out her burial dress before she died. When Helen says she "never looked better or felt better and yet I'm glad I'm dead" God is warning her to watch what she is doing, and He is not ready for her to die. In other words, by picking out her burial dress before she died, then being glad she is dead, she is pre-meditating her own funeral. While Helen is alive, she wants to die - this is a Divine Warning that suicide or homicide is lurking, and God does not want this to happen.

On page 156, Helen describes to you that when she woke up, she felt something was in the room watching her. This is true because a demonic angel is in the room instigating this dream, which is why the wretched stench lingers in her bedroom. Helen expresses "I am losing my mind and I'm afraid of what I might do without meaning to. I'm afraid I'll hurt Charlie or Kelly or myself." She begins to cry. This is showing how far the demonic angels have succeeded in breaking down Helen's free-will and intellect.

On page 156, you write that Helen was told many times to move out of the house, which she should have done. The excuse of not having enough money is not valid when it comes to Helen, Kelly, and Charlie's safety and health (physical, mental, and spiritual). The obligation to somehow stop this nightmare without putting another family through what they had experienced is not for Helen or anyone else to decide. Suppose Mr. Winters does not want the Demonic angels to leave, and he is the landlord, then what? Besides, this idea did not come from Helen, it came from the demonic angels in the house.

You finally stumble on Ken Sparks a Demonologist who had investigated about ten thousand cases. After calling Ken and finding out what was going on in the house, he told you that there was a demon in the house. Ken suggests you get the house blessed by a good priest. I agree with Ken's solution, however, you needed an Exorcist (who is also a Catholic Priest) in this house, who knows how to do special blessing and rituals to expel these demons. An ordinary blessing from any priest will not be sufficient to remove these demons. A demon from a ordinary priest. These cherubim demons are strong and must be force or expelled out of the house. There is no scaring these demons; there is no negotiating with these demons: there is no polite or even stern invitation to these demons to leave - there must be Divine Force to remove them out of the house. This is the same Divine Force that Saint Michael used to throw Lucifer and all the evil angels out of Heaven after their battle. It will not be easy, but with God all things are possible.

In chapter 36, page 159 you wrote that finding a priest would not be as easy as you thought. Helen wasn't Catholic and was raised in a strict Baptist home. Then you wrote that Helen could feel Jesus's eyes on her at every turn, staring at her from every painting and crucifix on the walls. Instead of Helen finding comfort in Jesus, she found herself scared and slightly sickened at the thought of the crucifixion. Being Baptist has nothing to do with Helen's reaction. This is crucial. Helen is not feeling this at all, the demonic angels are making her feel this way byall they have done to her. A demon might have gone along with you to meet this priest.

If the demonic angels did not follow both of you then this is the beginning of the stages of entrance for the demonic possession, it is also possible she is possessed already. Many Protestants including Baptists have seen crucifixes and painting of Jesus, and never had this reaction. You, Steve, are Lutheran and did not have this reaction.

At the bottom of page 159 top of 160, the repulsion from the crucifixion; the feeling of Helen being on trial; Jesus know my secrets; Jesus knows deep down she wants to kill her husband and daughter; Jesus knows I want to kill them before they kill me; Father, my house is haunted; feelings that she had just made a dreadful mistake; Jesus is still staring at me; Oh God, His face is covered with blood; Jesus knows my secrets; the eyes of Jesus continued to bear down on Helen… Helen's hands begin to fiddle on her lap. All this describes the guilt, the fear and the despair of Divine Judgment given to Helen by the demonic angels. Helen is not thinking this on her own, but the demonic angels are doing this to her from within. Finally, a date was set for a blessing.

On page 160 you write that the day of the blessing finally arrived. The priest took about five minutes and did not bless the whole house. The priest was obviously very nervous. When Helen asked about blessing the basement, the priest sprinkled a few drops of holy water down the steps. The priest then went upstairs and sprinkled a few drops of water, shoved a plaque in Helen's hands, gave both of you a quick blessing and was gone. First of all someone from the Catholic Church owe Helen and you an apology. I am so sorry this happened with this priest. It is obvious that he was scared, inexperienced and even rude to both of you. However. that is not an excuse for not performing the blessing as he should have done. Once again, Steve and Helen, as a Catholic Priest in this Church I am very sorry this happened to you. Speaking for myself, had I been there, this would not have happened. When I first read this, I did not have to go any further in this book to predict exactly what would happen. The sooner the rituals are done in this house, the better for all of you because things will now get worse. This type of behavior is unacceptable, and, of course, the demonic angels will start up again, causing more fear in all of you. Sadly, Helen called Ken who advised you to do the blessing yourself. Your suspicions are correct in realizing that performing a simple blessing on a house is not going to do the job. The demons are too close to Helen and you; however, they are not impossible to remove.

Moving onto Chapter 37, page 164 you mention Kelly's hamster was not in the cage, but the skull was found on the floor and picked clean. Who did this horrible act, Kelly or the demons? The demons did this act, though Kelly could have been put in a trance by the demons, and, not realizing it, killed this creature. Here is an example on what types of activities come from the demons in the Power choir.

You later describe various groups that

came into the house to investigate. Bill and Trudy, a husband-and-wife team came in first; then Maria and Evan, her husband, came in second: and a Christian women's group who Helen and you invited arrive third; you mention that both Trudy and Maria are both "sensitives." Let's begin with Bill and Trudy first, Bill had been doing electronic voice phenomena, or EVP with a small gray box with a red light on it. Bill asked: "I'm holding a small gray box with a red light on it. If you were to try to speak into the box with the light, I might be able to understand some of what you'd like to tell me. What is your name?" You wrote on page 164 that Bill got a small girl saying "The One." This is a dangerous answer that all of you missed. This was not a small girl answering this question. This was the Cherubim demon who answered in a single voice because the demonic angels in this house are many but speak with one voice through the lead demon from the Cherubim choir. Why would a little girl answer by saying "The One? This would make no sense. It only makes sense coming from the demonic angels. This also demonstrates just how close this demon is to all of you to pick this up on this electronic voice. Electronic equipment is good for picking up spiritual responses and getting evidence that the "spirit" exists, especially for later use. However, the interpretation of what is going on is entirely different. Bill continues with his questions: "Is there something you would like to tell Trudy and Me?" With this question a woman's voice responded, "His point of view is distracted." Now, why do you think this was said? This was another demon responding to the other that answered "The One" by letting you know that this demon is not alone. There are many here. The answer "The One" is an answer for distraction. These demons are playing games with your heads, and they are laughing because there is nothing here stopping them from their demonic activities. To be blunt, the demons know this is all useless. And then the answer played back in reversed where the woman could be heard saying: "Why don't you come and find me." Do you know exactly what this means? Besides this being a throw-back to the old small vinyl records, when played back in reverse you heard a demonic message, this was a demonic challenge. This is a haunted house you all know is infested with demons, and the demonic throw that answer into the mix. This answer from the reverse: "Why don't you come and find me" is an invitation for these demons to harm you

Here is the next set of questions. The recorder Bill has in his care with a demonic voice on it who says: "The One" - what is the probability that this demon comes looking for Bill later? What about the rest of the EVP experts from around the country who were becoming interested in the remarkable sessions Bill had in the Union house (page 165)? Do they have copies of this session? What is the probability that the demon who said this comes looking for them after they play it? Or worse yet, what is the probability that any demon currently around these EVP experts goes and gets the demon whose voice is on this recorder?

Let us put down some conservative odd on this paper. Let's say it is a fifty-fifty chance that this demon will coming looking for them. Thus, there is a fifty percent chance the demon will come looking for them and there is a fifty percent chance the demon will not come looking for them. Is it worth the risk? What are the human being's defenses to fight these odds? Are these odds really good for a human being (especially inexperienced) to gamble with the demonic? Are these good odds when these EVP experts are already investigating haunted places where demonic spirits are infested? Last question - is all this a form of inviting the demons into their life?

At this point, Steve, we need to look at the Catholic Church's rituals on exorcism of the possessed and obsessed. There are certain rules and warnings provided by the Catholic Church that must be followed by a Catholic Priest involved with this ministry.

In the old Roman Ritual on Exorcism (translated from the Latin Version) of the Possessed (and Obsessed) rule number 5 states "The minister must be on his guard against the arts of subterfuges (meaning tricks, maneuvers or schemes) which the evil spirits are wanting to use in deceiving the Exorcist. For oftentimes they give deceptive answers and make it difficult to understand them, so that the Exorcist might tire and give up, or so it might appear that the afflicted one (or place) is no longer possessed by the devil."

Number 14, of the same ritual, states "The Exorcist must not digress into senseless prattle nor ask superfluous questions, or such as are prompted by curiosity, particularly if they pertain to future and hidden matters, all of which have nothing to do with his office. Instead, he will bid the unclean spirits keep silence and answer only when asked. Neither ought the Exorcist to give any credence to the devil if the latter maintains that he is the spirit of some saint or of a deceased party, or even claims to be a good angel."

As you can see Steve, the Roman Ritual advises us to be aware of the deceptions by the demonic angels. In addition, superfluous questions should not be asked of the demonic angels. This not my authority, Steve, this is the Authority of the Catholic Church, which is very wise and successful in these matters. From the Catholic Church's rich history and tradition, this ritual was written under the guidance of the Holy Spirit, based on hundreds of years of experience with Exorcists having bigger brains in this area then I have. From my study of this ritual, there is a debate as to how old this really is. Some say it goes back to 1200 AD, some estimates say 800 AD. Regardless, I have complete trust in the Old Roman Ritual practiced by many of my teachers who have advised me on this subject. One final comment with these two rules (there are a total of 21 rules), notice that the Exorcist should give no credit to the demonic angels if they maintain he is a spirit of a deceased person. Returning to the book, Bill, who is taking these EVPs, just fell into this trap, as I pointed out.

Let's get to Bill's wife Trudy who is a sensitive and can communicate with the spirits. You wrote that Trudy grew up with this ability and always fet in her youth that it was a curse. This is a normal reaction by people who have extraordinary gifts. In my spiritual direction of a few mystics, the gifts, often start in youth, but no one is around to explain to them what these gifts are to be used for, thus they think it is a curse. A demonic spirit can even aggravate this situation even more, especially with the vice of "doubt", where the person begins to question and then doubt, they have such a gift.

You mentioned Maria also being a sensitive with her first experience at the Union house when she was pushed up the stairs. Then Maria saw a strange man walk into the bathroom, when she looked for him, no one was there. Again, this is the demonic angels. I am not doubting their gifts. God gives out gifts like this all the time. How do both Trudy and Maria know the difference between a human spirit and a demonic spirit? Maria just saw a strange man walk into the bathroom. This was not a strange man but another demon. How do they know for sure that the spirit they are speaking with is human and not faking it? I am concerned about their knowledge of the Spiritual world, more specifically, the entire Angelic World made up of both good angels and demons versus deceased human spirits. You mentioned that Maria's first experience at the Union house was being pushed up the stairs. Human spirits, for the most part, do not get involved with harming other human beings, this is what demons do. However, there are a couple of exceptions, I mentioned a phenomenon in this line of work called a Perfect Possession. A Perfect Possession is a complete cooperation of the person's free will and knowledge that they want to be possessed to gain some demonic favor or power. This is much different from most diabolical possessions because the person's free will is not necessarily involved, but the demonic angels force or seduce their victim. Most diabolical possessions fall under this category. There are such people in this world who make contracts with Satan and asked to be possessed (through a Satanic Mass sometimes called a Black Mass and other occult rituals). In other words, the human being takes the initiative, and invites the demonic angels, with complete knowledge of what they are doing, and a totally free will (meaning no one is forcing them to do this, not even the demonic angels) asking, and even begging, the demonic angels to possessed them. This is called a Perfect Possession. These cases are extremely rare, and I have not personally been involved in such a case. I am just aware that this is a possibility with human beings. Why is this important? First, most Exorcists have said that no one can expel any demonic angels under a perfect possession. Therefore, when this person dies, his soul could very easily be condemned to hell because the demonic becomes their god (obviously this is based on God's judgment). The point here is this, if such a human soul is condemned to hell, then the demonic angels can sometime use them in their diabolical activities. According to my studies of the Church Father's interpretation of the Book of Revelation, as we get closer and closer to the end times, this phenomenon will be occurring in many individuals who are not going to be classified as victims of the demonic angels but accomplices of the demonic angels. The second exception is those cases that I have studied involving Judas, one of the former Apostles. In the Sacred Scriptures, before Judas goes out to betray Our Lord after the Last Supper, the text tells us that Satan entered Judas (John 13:27) and later he commits suicide.

Judas has been known to show up in a very few diabolical possessions of individuals. One such case happened in Germany to a woman possessed by the demonic angels. One of them was Judas Iscariot. Thus, if they could come out of hell and be involved in a diabolical possession, they also have the ability to be involved in a demonic infestation of a house.

Returning to page 165, you write that you wanted to try and flush out the spirits by stationing people in every room of the house. Maria and Evan were posted upstairs; you stayed down in the basement with Bill and

Trudy; Helen took the main floor with some other people; and the Christian women in the back yard. Thus, the experiment started. You never mention what each of you were doing in these areas (I hope praying) but, nevertheless, the basement begins to get hot. Then Trudy and you felt something evil standing in the basement. Of course, this is a demon who begins to laugh and mock all of you. You mentioned that Trudy and you were both touched by something unseen, but you never mention that Trudy saw the actual creature. Both of you are fortunate enough not to have been hurt by this demon.

Then in the backyard, the Christian women began to feel they were not alone. Thus, they run back to the house, and one snapped a digital photograph. They get in the house and show you a picture. In the picture was an opening that seemed to flare with fire. It appeared that several entities had walked though that portal and gathered at a fire. You mentioned that you saw several faces and one of them was an old voodoo priest. But you never mention how you knew this person was an old voodoo priest. You write that you saw an image of someone being crucified on a cross that was burning in the fire. It is possible that you discovered one of the many reasons for the demonic haunting. The African countries are filled with cases of diabolical possessed individuals from the voodoo ritual. The man you saw in the picture was associated with voodoo. The voodoo ritual he attended was the beginning of his diabolical possession. Our Lord seems to be allowing these experiences to take place so Helen, you and everyone else can understand what has happened here in the past, even though it is demonic in nature.

Moving quickly through chapter 38, you mention that you contacted John Zaffis in June 2005. You wrote that he was a world-famous demonologist and paranormal investigator. This was good to read, because someone with more experience with the demonic than the other groups you had was badly needed. As far as the large dark spots staining the carpet, I have no answer. It is possible that the large dark spots are coming from the demonic angels as a source for marking their territory because their actual appearance has taken on animalistic features. I am not saying this is urine from the demonic angels because that is not possible. I am saying that these demons could get all kinds of foul liquids and use them on this carpet.

In chapter 39, we have returned to more nightmares everyone is having in the Union house. On page 171 you wrote that "none of us could have been prepared for the second coming of Matthew's demonic clown and the many nightmares and problems it caused." Steve, this demon never left the house. It is highly possible this is the lead demon, from the Cherubim choir. Your concerns for thinking that you were crazy over this evil clown can only be with people who do not know any better or have no belief that demons exist. Someone experienced in this field dealing with the evil angels knows full-well how important this demonic clown is.

Then Helen was watching a four-year-old girl in this house. With all that has already happened in this house, why would you bring a four-year-old girl into this house? For that matter, why bring any child into this house? The girl was sitting on Helen's lap when she raised her arm and said "clown". There is no doubt this little girl saw the same clown as Matthew and you. However, I'm not quite sure Helen saw the clown even though she told you the story. Notice, again, who does this demon go after? The innocent children. As we proceed Steve, you need to start paying attention to the many evil patterns with these demonic angels. Next, on page 172, you wrote about Maria, who had a phobia of clowns (this is not true) and that they had frightened her all her life (this is also not true). Before we go any further, why is Maria, a sensitive and an investigator, that frightened of clowns? Then you mention that Maria has been frightened all her life. Steve, you must be careful when you allow someone inexperienced to do this type of work. First, Maria is not afraid of clowns. Secondly, it is not a coincidence that Maria is here in this house in the first place. Who do you think led her here? How did you and your family get led to this house? How did Helen and her family get led to this house? How about Alex and your original paranormal investigators? How about the other victims who still had belongings in the shed - how did they get led to this house, especially the so-called drug dealer? And how about Mr. Winters? How did he become owner of this house? This is not a coincidence Steve. Next rule, you must understand, when dealing with the demonic, there is no such thing as coincidence. Keep this in mind, that when a demon arouses so much fear in a person, they cannot think rationally. Why do you think the demonic angels make everyone afraid? Because they know that by instilling fear in a human being they are conquering the persons intellect, preventing them from thinking rationally. The demonic angels have been very successful in doing this to you Steve. Get your fears under control! This can be done by Divine Grace. Do you think the Father, Son and Holy Spirit, along with all the good Angels are afraid of the demonic angels? N0! In fact, it is the opposite. The demonic angels fear God and His good angels.

Back to the demonic - demons do not deal with coincidence, they deal with the evil destruction of humans, because they hate God! There is no such thing as a coincidence when dealing with demons, the demonic angels have this all planned. Don't forget, demons are all fallen angels and all angels were given a superior intelligence they never earned, which is called innate knowledge. Do you see how clever the demonic angels are? Don't you see by now these demonic angels had this all planned? Do you see the evil pattern? Helen, Maria, Alex, Maria. Your family, all the other victims were all lead to this house. Why? Because all of you are open prey for the demonic angels with little to no divine grace to resist them. Don't you see by now that all this is part of a bigger more destructive plot by these evil spirits? Why do all these people become paranormal investigators? So they can show everyone the evidence they gather that evil Spirits or demonic angels exist? Most people already know that fact. So they can make money, become famous, suit their curiosity? Look how many individuals have been attracted in this house or any other haunted house. And what is causing this attraction? The demonic angels. Are we up to a hundred people by now for this house? Or is it two hundred? And each person who came to this house was led there by the demonic. How? The evil attraction caused by the demonic angels. And look how successful these demons are in destroying people's lives after they enter. And most of them, if not all, are powerless to resist or fight against them! Why? There is little or no Divine Grace. And all these demons sit there and laugh. Now expand this to what I just wrote with all these other haunted houses. Can you see how evil and destructive all this is by the demonic angels? Do you see the bigger picture of how successful these demons are? Like Betty the famous psychic giving tours in haunted houses! Here, sign this liability paper before we begin this tour. Betty is just one, how many other thousands of Bettys are out there? How many thousands of paranormal investigators are suck up into this demonic trap? How many more victims? Or is it true they are victims? Are we that naive to think that each paranormal investigator, including psychics and sensitives, are not in some way harmed by the demonic after each case they investigate? Steve, you have seen this with your own eyes! What good is an investigation when these paranormal investigators have no idea how to fight or expel a demonic spirit? It is true, with their electronic equipment, they can identify that an evil spirit, human or angelic, is present, and that is good? But what then? Can they get rid of it? I am not trying to place blame on anyone (except for Mr. Winters, who is evil), that is not my intention. However, as we proceed through your book I am educating you on what is going on in this house; who the demonic angels are; what is happening with the demonic angels; how these demonic angels plotted all these events; where the mistakes are being made; where the deceptions from the demonic are; reasons why this is happening; what to look for or what to watch out for; how many people in this line of work have no clue on what they are doing; and so forth.

Back to Maria, we need to be clear here, Maria is not afraid of clowns! What Maria is afraid of, are Demonic Angels that use the disguise of clowns when they appear to her! Do you think it is a coincidence that Maria is a special target in this case? Just like your son Matthew and this four- year-old little girl saw; Maria experienced a demon disguised as an evil clown sometime during her youth. None of this is a coincidence, this is all planned. This demon, under the disguise of a clown, had to appear to her more than once. You have given me enough evidence in this book, (whether realize it or not) there are enough demons in this town to go around in addition to all the invitations for the demonic to enter someone's life. This is not a phobia for clowns, this type of fear (a more accurate word is terror) is caused by exterior forces called the demonic angels. Here is another example of many in the psychological profession having absolutely no clue on what is really going on with this type of victim. Medication does not stop this fear because it is not something caused from within a person but outside the person, via the demons. Medication can suppress the symptoms in the intellect or the body, but medication never deals with the evil spirits. Diabolical possessions are another category that the psychological profession misdiagnoses, and the demonic angels just stand by and laugh. Which brings up the next question - how did Maria discover she was a so-called "Sensitive"? Remember those questions I asked earlier about Trudy and Maria being sensitives and whether they both can distinguish between a human spirit (or soul), an evil human spirit (or soul), a good angel and a demonic angel. These are four distinct realities that participate in this world.

(Another fact the psychological profession is clueless about.) They are now relevant questions. What criteria does Maria and Trudy use to distinguish all four spirits? The same questions also apply to all those who claim to be psychics, they're not exempted in this evaluation. Again, I am not necessarily doubting their gifts, however, the training on how to use these gifts needs to be clarified. This also includes the authentic psychics, which I prefer to call mystics. Before we go any further, here is one final question Steve. Are you sure Maria did not have demons periodically following her in her life before she got involved with this house?

Continuing with page 172, I like to address some of these questions you wrote here - Clowns? Who would have guessed? But we were about to find out just how evil this demon clown could be, and it chose Maria to demonstrate its power and ability to frighten us, even torture us. Part of this is not true at all. Let's begin with what is true. It is true that the demonic clown chose Maria to do something horrible - and we will address that soon. What is not true is the fact that Maria had no prior experiences with the demonic angels before entering this house. This demonic clown from the house was not the first time she had these experiences with evil angels. Who do you think pushed her up the steps? It was not a coincidence that Maria was physically touched but you never mention Bill, Evan or Trudy ever being physically touched. In addition, you are also assuming that this is the same demon from this house that did this horrible act coming up on page 173 with Maria's daughter. But for the sake of education, let us say this evil spirit is the same clown demon the four-year old little girl, Matthew and you saw. You continue to write on how hard this is for you and your responsibilities with it. I can understand how you feel because any normal person would feel the same. But let us also put this into context and perspective. We are dealing with Satan and his demonic angels who always seem to be in everyone's life, tempting us or causing more trouble for others, even from birth via Original Sin and the need for baptism. The perspective is how this fact is related to the events going on in the Union house and how to these upcoming evil patterns.

On page 172, you write that one evening in the Union house Maria tells all of you her nineteen-year-old daughter is expecting a baby. Steve, do you see any warning signs in this statement? There are several warning signs you might have missed because of the agony you have concern about coming later. First, Maria, a sensitive, is inside a house with demonic angels, tells all of you about her daughter; second, Maria tells all of you her daughter, who is nineteen years old, is pregnant; third, there is no mentioning of marriage or any commitment for this new child to be born; fourth, no mentioning of the father of this child and his current status with her pregnancy. Let's go to the next statement you wrote "We were all quiet until she assured us that it was okay, and that Maria and Evan were actually excited to be blessed with their first grandchild." Any warning signs in this statement? How about this warning signs - you were all quiet. Why? Did you all really realize what just happened? Did you all realize that a nineteen-year-old girl, who is still a child herself, is having a baby? How many demons tempted her to become sexually active? At what immature age did she start becoming sexually active? Maria's daughter did not just start having sex when she was nineteen, this is the age she became pregnant. Did Maria and Evan know that their daughter was this sexually active when she was younger than nineteen? And if Maria and Evan, her parents, did know, are they alright that their nineteen-year-old daughter was sexually active even before she became pregnant? With all of this, where is their responsibility with their daughter? The odds that Maria's daughter was fertile the very first time she had sex, then become pregnant, is very slim. You first wrote that Maria was happily telling you all about this event. Did not Our Lord say in the book of Genesis that a man leaves his father and mother and clings to his wife and the two become one flesh. (Genesis 2:24) Most Christians, especially Catholics, do not know what this means. To clarify, Our Lord wants one man for one woman in marriage and to become one flesh. to form a union like the union of the Holy Trinity, before procreation. Children are God's gift to the parents; therefore, the parents are responsible for them until they become a mature adult. Since you are responsible for your children, you are given the authority over them. This authority over children comes from God, not society or some government, that is why we call it procreation because all three of you - God, the mother and the father- are participating in the creation of a child.

Sexual temptations are one of the most successful temptations the demonic have accomplished in this world which is against God's plan. Remember, I am not trying to judge anyone here - that is not my intention. I am educating you on what is happening with the demonic angels in everybody's lives. The point is that this house is not the only house having demonic activities in it.

Continuing on page 171, same paragraph, you wrote "With this, we began to heartily congratulate them. Within the coming week Marie's daughter would have her first appointment with the doctor." Steve, do you see any warning signs in these two statements? These two statements mentioned here are the most dangerous. Why? You are all in a house infested with demonic angels; all of you know it by what you have experienced. After Maria tells you that her nineteen-year-old daughter is pregnant (obviously out of wedlock) instigated by sexual temptation from the demonic. Therefore, from God's perspective, it is considered a sin by the Catholic Church, the Jewish faith, most Protestant faiths and Muslim faiths. All the demonic angels, especially Satan, know all these rules are from God, and all of you celebrate this by "heartily congratulating them".

Bluntly, you are all celebrating the weakness, or more specifically, the results of sinful behavior which is where the danger lies. The major problem here is that the demonic angels in this house are there listening and enjoying their success from all this human failure and most of all no repentance to God for breaking His law. You don't see a problem with all this Steve? Who are we cooperating with, God or Satan and his evil angels? What do you expect God to do, stop these demonic angels from causing further harm when we are cooperating with these demons instead of God in the choices we make? When we celebrate the human weakness or sinfulness of someone else are we not agreeing with the demonic angels who help cause it?

At this point Steve, I must inform you that there is a very big risk I am taking here telling you of all this information. Any of this information I wrote here can easily be misunderstood. I am not saying that the demonic are going to cause trouble to all weak teenage girls or boys (including adults) who have a child out of wedlock. God knows, and so do I, that we are all weak creatures, including myself. This is not the point. The point is that it is dangerous to rejoice at the sinfulness of others in front of the demonic angels! This falls under the sin of Pride, which caused the condemnation of all demonic angels. God knows we are all weak, but God also expect us to ask Him for His help and repent as soon as possible when we sin. Was any of this done? Why is it that we forget about God and what He wants? Now, after all this information I have explained, is it really fair for you to take all the blame for what happens next? Did you start this conversation with Maria?

After this statement there is a mention of the first doctor's appointment within the coming week. Do you think the demons heard this statement? You can never assume that Steve, because there is no extraordinary evil activities going on at this particular time this conversation took place that the demonic angels are not present, watching and listening. The demons heard all of this - and what do you think they are plotting to do? With all this evil, it is our cooperation with the demonic angels (by abusing our gift of sexuality) which is reserved for matrimony as God intended it to be. Do you not see that everything outside of marriage dealing with our human sexuality is condemned in the Sacred Scriptures, which the demonic know better than we do? Point being, human sexuality is exalted in matrimony in the Sacred Scriptures, everything else is condemned. If you go against this rule, which you have the free will to do, then you can say hello to the demonic. Has all this human sexual freedom, beginning in the 1960's, gotten us anywhere?

Returning to back to page 172, where Maria, the night before the appointment with the doctor, wakes up in the middle of the night screaming. The middle of the night is probably the witching hours between twelve and three in the morning. Did you notice, as you wrote this book, how much demonic activity took place during these hours? You wrote about her nightmare "I was standing in the side yard of the Union house. There were all of these people there and they were just standing and staring up at the house." Maria's dream here is significant. First off this involved a diabolical obsession with Maria, just like Helen and you had. (This is not Maria's first diabolical obsession.) In the dream, Maria sees herself standing in the side yard of the Union house. This is probably the same side of the house those Christian women were on when they ran into the house and took a digital picture which you all analyzed in the house. The words: "There were all these people there" represents all the people who came to the house to investigate the demonic haunting. The words: "They were just standing and staring up at the house," represent the ineffectiveness these people had on the house. The key words are "standing and staring" representing them being rendered powerless, and even shocked, by the demonic angels in the Union house. You wrote that in Maria's nightmare "I remember joining them to see what they were looking at when I heard a giggle from behind me." In the nightmare, "Maria joins them to see what they were looking at" represents her joining all those previous ineffective "paranormal investigators and psychics" that left the case. Then after joining all of them, "she hears this giggle from behind her." The giggle from behind her is important. Obviously, this is a demonic angel who is giggling. However, why is this demonic angel giggling? This type of evil demonic giggling usually means that whatever this demonic angel wanted done. was already done. In other words, the giggling can represent an "after the fact" which means the fact took place first and the giggling started afterwards. demonic clown with red glowing eyes behind me. He was holding a baby by its feet, and he was laughing. He had razor-sharp teeth that glowed in the moonlight. He laughed as he held the baby by its ankles and slammed it on the ground repeatedly like it was a sack of potatoes. The description of this demon is he has a deep and low evil giggle. The demonic clown had red glowing eyes behind me. He was holding a baby by its feet and laughing. He had razor-sharp teeth that glowed in the moonlight. The laughing of the demon as he holds the baby by the ankles and slammed it on the ground repeatedly. Up to this point Steve, do you see any warning signs on what was written above? (Now remember, keep your feelings out of it.) How about these warning signs - first, Maria is just as ineffective in the house as the rest of those people in the nightmare. Second, this demonic clown is the same demonic clown the four-year-old girl, Matthew and you saw However, Maria saw more details in her nightmare with this demonic clown than the four-year-old girl, Matthew, and you saw.

Here are a few more questions for you to consider. Why does this demonic clown appear in this dream? Why not have another

demon who is in the Union house show up in
this nightmare? Why didn't a demon from
another haunted house show up in this
nightmare? The answer -because this is not
the first time Maria has experienced a
diabolical obsession. How does this demonic
clown know he should show up in Maria's
nightmare? This particular demonic clown
knows to show up because either he did this
act before to Maria or he knows other demons
who did this to Maria before this event. Notice,
the pre-existing knowledge this demonic angel
has on Maria. This is not a coincidence. This is
not the first time this happened. The terror
Maria has of clowns is from the demonic
angels who use the disguises of clowns when
they appear to her. Maria has experienced this
phenomenon repeatedly in the past. This
demonic clown Maria saw in the nightmare did
this to her because this demon knows about
the success the other demonic angels had on
her from the past. Let's take notice of a few
details provided in the nightmare by this
demonic clown who is controlling this diabolical
obsession. First, notice the increase of details
to describing this demonic clown activities; as a
result, notice the increase of fright; notice the
increase of evil such as holding a baby by its
feet or taking the baby and slamming it on the
ground over and over again; notice the
manipulation from Maria's maternal
characteristics (giving birth and raising
children) by seeing a baby treated this way to
increase her fear, anxiety and the level of
terror; notice this is happening to a sensitive;
notice the increase in detail on the dramatic
appearance of the demonic clown from the red
glowing eyes (which you saw, Steve) to the
razor sharp teeth; notice the desire effect this
particular demonic angel has achieved with

Maria.

One final thing, how about Maria's memory? Here is another experience added to the already long lists of evil events that is causing damage to Maria's memory. What the demonic purpose? At this point, the demons are breaking down, by anxiety and terror, Maria's intellect which is where the gift is used. No mature human adult, (with a daughter who is nineteen years old) has this type of frightful terror of clowns. This frightful terror of clowns is caused by demons disguised as clowns who appeared to Maria repeatedly in her past. Here is one of the major concerns I have with her gifts. If Maria is a sensitive, and perhaps she has this gift, she should have been trained to know how to deal with demonic spirits once she encounters them. Maria does not know how to fight back. Why? Being a sensitive, why hasn't Maria learned this technique? This will never stop until Maria does learn to fight back! This is cruel, but the demonic angels are taking advantage of Maria with this gift and her weakness in using it. The major point - the demonic angels are using this gift (from God) against her because she was never trained on how to use it. The fear from the demonic angels has taken over it. What is even worse with all this is the fact there is no Divine Grace to enlighten, strengthen, and give guidance to Maria with this gift. And whose fault is that? These types of gifts are given to human beings from God; however, they are contingent or dependent on the fact that God directs the use of them! There are so many people with gifts like this from God, but they never have God direct the use of them. Does the parable of the five talents, two talents and one talent in the Gospels ring a bell here? (MT. 25:14-30) Don't you think the Demonic Angels know this fact?

With Maria the appearances of these demonic clowns are not just showing up in her dreams at night, she is also seeing them in the daytime. How? The effective force from the demonic angels is coming from outside her body and mind. This is not an internal problem, her gift is inside her, the demonic manipulation on this gift is coming from the outside. Until Maria realizes that the influences on her interior gift (that came from God) is coming from the demonic angels and not clowns, these demonic angels will be successful in driving her insane! These demonic angels are manipulating her intellect and the faculties of her imagination. There is no Divine Grace here to resist them or to guide Maria on what to do. This is not a diabolical possession; this is a diabolical obsession that started way before she got to the Union house! Solution - Maria must understand that the gift she has from God is being used against her by the demonic angels. Maria must learn to stop being this terrified and fight back with Divine Grace. In other words, the more Maria fights back against these demonic angels the less fear she will have of them. If she does not, she will lose. In addition, there is no Divine Grace here to strengthen Maria's free will to resist. Plus. there is no Divine Grace here to enlighten and guide her intellect on using this gift. I will prove it to you right now with these questions. Would the demonic angels have this much control over Maria's fears and memory if she had learned to fight back earlier in her life with the strengthen of Divine Grace?

Would the demonic angels have this much control if Divine Grace was there to strengthen her intellect and free will?

Would the demonic angels have this much control if Maria had learned how to properly use her gifts for God's Will?

If Maria had not allowed the demonic angels to operate and do this much damage to her life; if Maria would allow Divine Grace to heal her memory of the demonic angels, would the demonic angels have this much control?

If Maria understood the difference between a good human spirit (or soul), a bad human spirit, a good angel, and most importantly an evil angel or demon, why Maria? Here are three reasons:

First, Maria is a spin-off of the name Mary, the Blessed Mother's name, who the demonic angels despise even more than me.

Second, a Divine Gift (or talent, as written in the Gospels) that was given to Maria is being used against her because Maria never used this gift for God's purposes.

Third, gifts like this that Maria and Trudy have (which I do NOT agree with calling people with these gifts by the name "sensitive" or "psychic" which are secular and humanistic names) are very dangerous toward the demonic angels.

If a demonic angel even suspects that a person who might have these types of gifts, they will pounce hard on them to discourage them, to frighten them and ultimately cause destruction to their gift or them. This is done in order that the gifts a person has are not used against the demonic angels By God. Think logically here, Steve. If the demonic angels knew someone has a Divine gift that can be used against them, doesn't it make sense that the demonic angels will go after that person and destroy the gift or them?

Let us look at another evil pattern Steve, with demonic clown. Who sees these demonic clowns? Notice. Steve, they are appearing to children. First, your son Matthew, next the four-year old little girl. That is two little children, along with you, and perhaps Helen. Where is the third child in this evil pattern? How about Maria? On page 172 you mention that clowns have frightened her all her life, meaning since she was a little child. However, when this first started is not clear. What is clear is that this type of fright and terror began when Maria was a child, by a demonic clown. Point being that your son, Matthew, the four-year old little girl and Maria when she was a little girl all saw a demonic clown. This is an evil pattern here Steve! There is one more person. How about Kelly, Helen's daughter who also saw the demonic clown? You never mention this in your book, Steve. I am not even sure you are aware of it, or if Kelly told you that the demonic clown appeared to her several times. I also know for a fact that everything that happened in the Union house is not written in this book. Kelly seeing the demonic clown is just one of the many examples. I also understand that it is impossible for Helen, and you, to remember everything that happened because you felt they were insignificant. Regardless, there is plenty of information here for me to see what has happened. Returning to what I wrote above, before the side note, this is an evil pattern, and the last point I want to make in this regard is that demonic clowns show up to children all the time. This is not the first time this has happened, nor will it be the last. The advantage the demonic angels have with this is that the parents of these children, including Maria's parents, do not believe their children when they tell them they saw what appears to their eyes as a clown when in fact it is a demon. Of course, the parents have be cautious here because the fact that children do not understand many things, including an imagination, must be considered. Clowns, usually from a circus, are there to entertain and make children laugh. The cruelty of the demonic angels is that they know that. They disguise themselves as clowns to entertain the child and by using this technique they start demonic activities. Again, I must state this important fact with these demonic angels, appearing under the disguise of a clown or any other character. They have been invited into the family's life somehow. The adults (including parents and grandparents) somewhere in the child's life invited the demons and the first victims of this assault are always the children. They will never appear unless invited. In your life Steve, your wife invited them. In Maria's life, some adult in her childhood did the same. And in this four-year-old little girl's life - her mother - who dropped her daughter off with Helen in a haunted house. In Alex's life, the person who introduced him to sex. Thus, he begins selling sex toys and ends up in the Union House.

You continue, "All the while the clown kept laughing and laughing. I screamed for people to turn around and help me get the baby away from him, but no one would. No one would turn. No one would move. It was as if something held them in a trance, staring at something on the roof that I couldn't see. It just kept screaming. Evan finally heard me screaming and woke me up." Here the demonic clown keeps laughing and laughing. What, or who, is this demonic clown laughing at? Maria, because God is not here to help her, because God is not really in Maria's life. The demonic angels are controlling her fear, anxiety and terror. The demonic angels are laughing at all the success they had with Maria. The demonic angels have almost destroyed, severed or damaged Maria's gifts, so these gifts can't be used against them. The demonic laugh is a mocking laugh toward Maria, and ultimately toward God. This demonic laugh also serves as a warning they are coming after Maria's soul. I have seen these events play out before in other people's lives such as the Saints who had the gift of mysticism. What is the difference? Bluntly stated, God helped these Saints deal with these diabolical obsessions and activities because God was in their life, but He is not in Maria's life. God purposely does this using the demonic angels to test the Saint with the gift of mysticism. (Here are a few examples: Saint Padre Pio, Saint Faustina, Saint Catherine of Siena, and Saint Mary de Monfort). You wrote that Maria screamed and screamed, and no one would help her get the baby away from this demonic clown, no one would move. Why would Maria witness this in the nightmare? Because part of this is true in the sense that they are powerless as Maria is powerless in helping her get the baby away from the demonic. These people do not recognize the sinfulness of killing this baby. They choose to ignore it. Did not Maria choose to ignore the sins of her teenage daughter? Do you see how much dependency we place on human wisdom and not Divine Wisdom?

You continue to write that "It was as if something held them in a trance, staring at something on the roof that I couldn't see." Part of this is true in the nightmare because each and everyone in this nightmare represent all those who showed up to the Union House attracted to the evil or demonic spirits. By this attraction, all those individuals in the nightmare (represented by those who came to the Union house) focused in on the demonic angels and all the evil, when the attraction and focus should have been on God, not the demonic. The word "staring" represents the state of shock these people are in because they have no power to get rid of them. The words written about Maria, who just kept screaming, represents the depth of terror and fear the demonic angels have achieved with her.

Then you write this, "We went to the doctor with my daughter this morning. They couldn't find a heartbeat. Steven, the baby is dead." Yes, this is true. The baby is dead. How did the baby die? Not by this nightmare! A demon got to the baby and indirectly killed the child, but this happened before Maria had this nightmare. The demonic angels just don't show up one day and decide to kill someone. This is not how they operate, nor can the demonic angels operate in such a fashion because of the rules imposed on them by God. For this to happen, Maria and her daughter had to experience many incidents of the demonic angels working on them. This is one of the reasons I was asking about the suspicious words, "Within the upcoming week" and the meaning of these words. Was it a week, six days, five days etc.? The point being, the demonic angels could have killed this child anytime between the time Maria announced the pregnancy (including the time frame from conception until this announcement) of her daughter in a demonic infested house and the time of the first doctor's appointment. The nightmare was the demonic clown mocking Maria and her pregnant daughter because they had already killed her baby that was conceived out of wedlock. In addition, they were also mocking the fact that God was not there to help them, nor did Maria or her daughter ask for Him for help. However, I want to be clear, this demonic clown did not do this horrible act. The demons that are most likely responsible for this horrible act to Maria's pregnant daughter are the same demons responsible for Maria's terror of clowns, which was only used as a disguise for the demonic angels. Also, Maria's house could have a demonic infestation of evil angels, independent of the Union House. Plus, somewhere in Maria's life, probably when she was young, there was a clear invitation for these demons to enter Maria's life. The demonic clown in this nightmare was successful in deceiving all of you to think it was him, when it was other demons associated with Maria's terror of clowns. Our Lord Jesus warned us about Satan and the demonic angels in the Gospel of John 11: 14-23 where Jesus is accused of driving out an unnamed demon by the power of Beelzebul (Beelzebul is a demon from the Cherubim choir who is very powerful evil angel). Jesus said, "Every kingdom divided against itself will be laid waste and house will fall against house. And if Satan is divided against himself how will his kingdom stand? (John 11:18)" In other words, Steve, Jesus is teaching all of us that all the demons, with Satan as their leader, work together to accomplish their evil goals. There is unity among the demonic angels. There is only two houses, the House of God or the House of Satan. Put it another way, there are only two kingdoms, the Kingdom of God, or the kingdom of Satan, you are either in one or the other, you cannot be in both or stay in the middle of these kingdoms. There is absolutely no middle road down here, this line of thinking is evil.

A few more things you should know with these events. The demons responsible for help killing this baby did not, and I repeat did not possess Maria's pregnant daughter. They don't have to. Look at the success the demonic angels are having with Maria and that success is happening in the same house her daughter is living in. If the demonic angels were able to successfully tempt Maria's daughter to become sexually active at a younger age, then, successfully tempt her at the age of nineteen to have sex and become pregnant, it would not take much for the demonic angels to successfully tempt her to consume something such as alcoholic beverages or an illegal drug or even take a valid medical prescription, which are dangerous for a pregnant woman, or even appear to Maria's pregnant daughter and terrorize her which stopped the heartbeat of the baby and killed the child. Regardless of whatever method the demonic angels used. they are still responsible for the death of this baby. God will take care of the demons. My interest is taking care of all of you. Which brings us to the following questions. Is Maria's daughter baptized? Has Maria's daughter had any religious education (perhaps from Sunday school)? Does Maria's daughter have a spiritual life? Does Maria's daughter even believe in God? Does Maria have any religious items such as a cross in her house to help ward off some of these evil angels from attacking her? One thing is true in all of this, you cannot blame God, there is way too much cooperation with the demonic angels to blame Him. Again, the truthful answers to all these questions will have an effect on the influences caused by the demonic angels.

Do you see the demonic patterns with Maria, Helen and you? Who do the demonic angels go after first? They go after the innocent, and often helpless, children to terrorize the parents. Let's begin with you, Steve, and proceed to everyone else. Where are some of the first strikes of demonic terror with all the kids? How about the event with your wife's pregnancy with Lydia in the delivery room? This also parallels a demonic attack on Maria's nineteen-year-old daughter (which is either Maria's first born or youngest child in her family) who lost an innocent and helpless baby. How about the demonic terror of Helen's daughter who is now diabolically possessed from the demons in this house? How about the four-year-old little girl sitting on Helen's lap who saw this demonic clown? Next, how about the demonic angel in Lydia's closet who appeared to her like Janice? How about the demonic terror of Matthew, your youngest, when he first saw this clown demon? Are you starting to see a demonic pattern with all these children Steve? To be clear, they go after the children first, then they come after all the adults. As a result, the children are affected first and the parents end up filled with terror because they feel powerless against the demonic angels. When this fear reaches a critical point by what the parent is witnessing with their children, then the demonic angels move on to the parents. The adults are who the demonic angels want in the first place, the children are used only as a steppingstone to the adult parents. Why? Look who suffers more the child or the parents.

Returning to the bottom of page 173, after all this, look what kind of affect the demonic angels had on you, Steve. Let's begin with your questions. Did the house do this to her daughter? No, the Union house did not do this to her daughter. Did these demons in the Union house participate or encourage these events? Yes. Was the nightmare a premonition? Yes. Did Marie's dream occur at the exact moment when the child lost its life in the womb of its mother? No. Are the demonic angels responsible for the death of Marie's daughter's baby? Yes.

Let's move onto chapter 40, page 175. The time the phone was ringing was 4 a. m. Helen is on the other side crying and quite upset. She explains that Charlie and she were very tired and went to bed at 10 p.m. She wakes up to the sound of her own voice. It was her voice speaking, but what was so unusual was there was no emotion. Let's look at this part first. This is not her voice but the demon on her bed. More than likely this is occurring between twelve and three in the morning. This is another form of diabolical obsession; however, it is more hideous. The demon here is imitating her voice in her sleep but this event is closer to a trance. This begins a form of confusion inside her intellect, specifically the faculties of the imagination for diabolical purpose. In this hideous act, the demon manages to imitate Helen's voice from outside her which she hears through her ears. Then the demonic voice proceeds to get into her imagination where Helen's normal voice is used in her dreams. Helen is in a trance and not conscious that a voice from outside, via the demon, is coming inside her. She recognizes that this voice sounds like her voice so there is no alarm. The normal voice of Helen is inside her, which at night, is used in this trance (even dreams) via the imagination where a conversation with this demonic voice imitating Helen's voice can take place. The confusion is with Helen's natural voice and the demon imitating her natural voice, so, the consciousness, independent of critical reasoning, hears the same natural voice as Helen. Since the critical reason is shut down because of a trance or sleep, there is no alarm in Helen that something is wrong here while she is having this conversation in this trance or her sleep. Steve, all you must remember in this form of diabolical obsession is during a trance, or even sleep. the part of our critical reasoning is not in use. Critical reasoning is the ability to evaluate and make good and sound judgments, which is inactive during a trance or while sleeping. This does not mean the whole intellect is shut down. The intellect has various faculties, such as the Imagination and memory which are still active while in a trance or sleep. The best way to think of this is using a metaphor of a six-cylinder car. The engine represents the intellect with all its faculties. Thus, the intellect is not running on all six cylinders (faculties) while in a trance or sleeping. Since this is happening at night when the critical reason of our intellect is not functioning because of sleep, or a diabolical trance placed on the victim, there is no alarm or judgment being made when the demon imitates Helen's natural voice. Plus, this takes place at night, during sleep, or an induced trance, so the intellect cannot necessarily engage in critical reasoning to stop the demon's voice from imitating Helens natural voice and allowing it to enter inside her. Consequently, confusion happens in this form of diabolical obsession via a dream/nightmare/trance, where Helen is not actively engaging the demon with all her faculties. The demon can manipulate Helen to agree to something diabolical that she would not agree to if she were fully awake where her critical reasoning is active, much less speak with this demon on her bed. The demons have managed to break down Helen's free will and intellect enough to get her to agree to something they want, whether in a trance or asleep. In blunt terms, through a trance or her sleep, this demon is seducing her (or using a form of hypnotism) for entrance to a diabolical possession, which is the next step they want to take.   Notice Helen mentions the words, "I was talking with no emotions." This is because the demonic angels can detach any emotion (such as anger or fear) from their voice, even when imitating voice of the victim. Helen continues with this event by saying, "I was agreeing to something. I was saying something like, "I can do that." My eyes were still closed, but when I understood that it was my voice I was hearing, I opened my eyes." Let's look at this section as Helen describes it. Notice she was only agreeing to something, not evaluating it, not judging it, nor making a rational choice. but saying "I can do that." In other words, there is no deliberation from Helen here. The demonic angel has convinced her mind (without the use of critical reason because of sleep or a trance) she could do this act (which the act is not mentioned). This is only accomplished by agreeing with whatever the demonic suggested. This is not accomplished by critically thinking about what the demon suggested and making a rational choice to do this act or not. Do people make any rational choices in their sleep on what specific dream they would like to have? No. They may hope or want a certain dream to occur before they fall asleep but because they hope or want a certain dream to happen during sleep does not necessary mean it will happen.

Similarly, in a trance, can people make any rational choice? No. In other words, there is no rational choices being made while a person is asleep or in a trance, nor are there any rational choices of what dreams we will have while we sleep. Therefore, dreams or a trance or what is agree upon in a dream or a trance while asleep cannot be a mortal sin. As a result, Helen cannot be held accountable for what she agreed to in this state. At the same time, Helen can hear and remember the words "I can do that" but her eyes were still closed. At this point, Helen is also slowly coming out of her sleep or a trance because her critical reasoning is awakened when she says, "But when I understood that it was my voice I was hearing, I opened my eyes." Once someone's intellect can understand what is happening around them, the critical reasoning is active again. Understanding is a word implying that rational thoughts are being evaluated and judged by critical reason in the intellect in order to understand them. By Helen opening her eyes, she is coming fully conscious. Critical reasoning is active in the intellect, and she sees a black-hooded figure sitting on her bed next to her: and she was having a conversation with it. When she comprehended what was happening, she yelled, and it disappeared. Helen is using the word 'comprehension' which means she is fully awake. Her critical reasoning is active, thus, by evaluating quickly what is happening, she yelled, and the demons left. The demon left because Helen is now able to critically think on what is happening and the demon lost his power of manipulation while she was in a trance or asleep. However, there is a small problem. All this is in Helen's memory. Even under both forms of a trance or sleep, the demonic can manipulate what is occurring in each state.

Remember earlier we discussed Saint Joseph's dream about Mary becoming the mother of God via the communication of a good angel sent by God (Matthew's Gospel)? These demonic activities seem to point in the direction of a demon from the Cherubim or Powers choir. Only after this type of demon makes entry into their victim do they go get other demons, including ones more powerful than they are, to enter the victim. Higher class demons from the top choirs possess first, then go get other demons from any choir.

Helen then asks you what you thought the demon and her were talking about and what she agreed to. This easily suggests how confused the demon made Helen and how much she remembers what was going on inside her.

Moving on to chapter 41, page 177, concerning Charlie - who was never in a hurry to admit this was a haunted house. You wrote, "It wasn't that Charlie didn't believe his house was haunted; it is just that he had decided long ago to try to coexist with the haunting. He used to say, "They leave me alone and I leave them alone." He also used to warn us, "If you go messing with this thing, you two are going to come across something that you are going to be sorry you came across."

Now, I understand that this came from his mother. It is also true that many people think like this to coexist. It is also, in this line of work, against the rules. By taking this "coexisting attitude" with the evil spirits (whether human or angelic), you have made a negotiation with them. The problem with this line of thinking is this question, "Do you actually expect an evil human or angelic spirit to follow this agreement?" Let me be clear about something here, a good angel or a good spirit (or soul) will not stay long on this earth. They may be sent by God to accomplish a mission or deliver a message, or ask something from us, or even guide us, but they never do any of these activities described in this book, nor are they found by paranormal investigators through their electronics equipment, nor psychics, mediums or sensitives. When was the last time in any of these episodes on TV or the movies you saw a good angel or good human soul? Rarely would this ever be caught on electronic equipment. Yet, it is a fact that good angels and good human souls come down here for good reasons. How is it that they are not caught on tape? Is it very strange that all those spirits caught on camera, electronic equipment, etc. have been involved with a crime or a sin (a suicide, car crash, murder, electrocution, etc.)? Now it is true, many individuals live or coexist with a good angel. In the Catholic Church, we call them Guardian Angels. But how do they know this angel is good? By the activities these Angels do. Now, what about the demonic angels or demonic human souls/spirits? There is no compromise, no negotiation, no agreements, no contracts that can ever be made between these evil creatures and us and expect that these evil creatures will keep their part of the deal. Can any of us force a demonic angel or a demonic human soul to keep their part of the deal? All this phenomenon caught on electronic equipment should first be considered evil. Now, it is true, that the demonic angels have been known to trap a human victim's soul here on earth, occasionally this happens. The solution is to get rid of the demon or demons which are lurking somewhere around this human soul then the human soul will go back to God, where the human soul first came from. Now why would God allow this to happen? My answer at this point is, I really do not know. someday I hope God will enlighten my mind on this subject.

Let us get back to Charlie, he stated in your book, "My house isn't haunted, but I've heard footsteps come walking down the stairs in the middle of the night, and I really don't care to go into the basement much." Charlie continued: "I don't have the time or the energy for all this ghost stuff. I'm too busying trying to make sure the bills get paid. I don't have time for anyone or anything else, living or dead." I do agree with you, Steve, that it is obvious that Charlie does work hard by what he is saying in these statements. However, I do not agree with his denial or lack of concern for the safety and health of his wife and family. This attitude can cause trouble.

Look at your attitude in the beginning of this book, Steve. You were working hard, which is noble, taking care of the bills and the family as best you could. However, your wife obviously got into something demonic that she could not handle. Because of the marriage, the demon also attached itself to you - and look what happened in your life ever since. The starting point of all this demonic activity in your life is with your wife. It is possible your wife had a demonic curse on her. This would also explain why you have demonic activities in your life. I want to be very clear here, and I mean very clear, if there is a curse it is possible with your wife and not you or your family. If a curse is involved here as the starting point to all the demonic activities in your life, you are only having the effects of it and not the actual curse placed on you. Other than your wife, you have given me nothing in this book to convince me that you or your children are cursed. You might be experiencing the effects of a curse, but you have given me nothing to convince me you have a curse on you. And while I am on this subject, that goes for everyone else (except for possibly your wife, and it is even doubtful that your wife is cursed) based on what you have written in this book. A curse is very hard to perform. The rate is 1 out of 30,000 are affected by a curse. These are not my estimates but are from several leading Exorcists in the Catholic Church who have more experience and bigger brains in this field then I do. They are extremely hard to effectively perform; most people cannot perform a curse; if a curse is attempted by an individual, there is more harm done to them then toward their intended victim. Most of all I especially want to be clear, curses can be broken.

Returning to Charlie on page 178 who woke up and saw the same dark-hooded, shadowy figure at the foot of the bed. Steve, this is the same demon you saw in the kitchen one day, in addition to what Helen saw previously on page 175. This is the lead demon in this house from the cherubim choir who wants entrance to someone for diabolical possession. This is also the same demon who is diabolically obsessing Helen to try to get her to significantly hurt Charlie and Kelly, or even kill them. If this demon becomes successful in taking possession of either Charlie or Helen, serious trouble will result. I want to warn everyone right now, this might be the demon called Belial but I am not sure. What I am sure of is how persistent this demon is with Helen. This demon will get what it wants - he is very powerful. Another warning, no inexperienced person should take this demon on, but a trained and experience Demonologist/ Exorcist should fight this evil angel. If someone inexperienced takes this demon on, they will risk becoming possessed themselves. If I am right about Belial (and again I am not sure) Belial has been known to enter a victim for diabolical purposes, then he surrenders his reign to a higher demon from the Cherubim choir for the diabolical purpose they want done. I do know that Belial is from the Power choir, and he is not the only demon from the Power choir who can do these diabolical activities. Regardless, whether this demon from the Power choir retains his reign upon entry for possession is another matter. This is also the same demon Mark saw in the basement. The dark-hooded shadowy figure is using the dark hood to disguise what this demon looks like. This is not the same demon that appears to the children, Maria and you, under the disguise of a demonic clown. That demonic clown is the lead clown for diabolical possession of Kelly.

Returning to page 178 where Charlie saw this dark-hooded shadowy figure at the foot of the bed and then says this, "It was there. I couldn't believe what I was seeing, but it was there. It was like it was studying Helen and me as we slept, and it scared me. I couldn't speak. I couldn't move..." Now, most people in this field do not understand what Charlie said here, however a trained Demonologist/Exorcist knows full well that the key words here are: "it was studying Helen and me as we slept". This is crucial, because this demon wants a diabolical possession. By studying both Helen and Charlie this demon was determining or plotting how to possess both of them. This is another common evil pattern the demonic angels do before they possess someone. Before we go any further, Steve, always watch the "action" of the demonic angels. Most people are very frightened and terrified of them and give this no consideration. The terror inside a person takes them over and reason goes out of use. When you are involved in this type of work, ask yourself this question. Why is this demon or demons doing this particular action? There is always a reason. Notice this demon was just standing at the foot of the bed. Now why is he doing this action? The demon is not there to scare Helen and Charlie, even though that is a secondary effect. There are reasons the demonic angels are doing this act, and, on this occasion, it was to study both Charlie and Helen not only for diabolical possession but also for other diabolical activities once the demon gains entry into someone. This is another diving warning. Take note that Charlie's so-called attitude of negotiation - to leave them alone and they will leave me alone - did not work. The demons were still coming after him.

Returning to page 178, Helen woke up to find Charlie terrified and speechless. After talking to Charlie a while Helen goes back to sleep. Helen claims she went back to sleep for about an hour when she heard a low, deep growling. Helen opened her eyes and near the bedroom window where she could make out a wolf-like animal. This animal just sat there growling. It opened its eyes, a strange shade of yellow, and a glow appeared. From the other corner of the room, Helen sees another shadowy figure shoot across the foot of the bed. Helen said she could hear it moving and then in a very low, very demonic voice it said, "I'm here." Both figures then disappeared but left a foul odor in the room.

These demons are from the lower choirs
- such as the Archangel choir or the
Principalities choir. They are just there to scare
Helen, Charlie and Kelly. This is not the same
demons as the demonic clown, or the dark-
hooded shadowy figure. What is significant is
that this happened right after the appearance
of the dark-hooded shadowy figure to Charlie.
Here is one of the many occasions to prove
that there is more than one demon in this
house. The low deep growling, the wolf-like
appearance of an animal, the strange shade of
yellow that glowed when it opened its eyes, the
low, very demonic voice that said, "I'm here",
and the foul odor are typically low-level
activities of the demons from the lower choirs.
Ultimately, these are just scare tactics these
demons are using because they do not have
the power that the demons from the higher
choirs have.

You continue with what Helen did
afterwards. Helen got up to use the bathroom
and splash some water on her face. On the
way, Helen saw Kelly standing on the stairs.
She wasn't moving; she just stared at her.
Helen asked what Kelly was doing up and Kelly
said 'nothing' and assured Helen everything
was fine. Helen response was 'okay' and told
Kelly to go back to bed. Helen did not sleep
any more that night. It was 3:15 in the morning.
There are some major problems here. First off,
Helen, who is on her way to the bathroom,
sees Kelly standing on the stairs staring. Kelly
is on the steps staring because she is
diabolically possessed. Notice the times this all
took place - somewhere during the witching
hours - which is between twelve and three in
the morning. This is not normal behavior for a
teenage girl. Helen saw Kelly from a short
distance and more than likely it is dark. Had

Helen got a closer look at Kelly's eyes she would have seen something abnormal.

Again, before we go any further, this is serious. Kelly is being tortured by this demonic clown or another demon. By what you have written so far about Kelly, I cannot tell if there is more than one demon inside her. Nor do I have enough information on how this demon possessed her. Point being, the sooner Kelly gets spiritual help via an Exorcist the better off she will be. I do know that Kelly was possessed first by this demonic clown. Also, I want to repeat what I said earlier, Kelly is being ruthlessly tortured by these demons. You only wrote in your book what Helen knows. There is way too much missing that is very important. Demons do not possess someone instantly without first mentally and physically torturing them. Kelly probably has no spiritual life to put up any kind of resistance, thus, it is very easy for the demons to enter her. And if Kelly is not baptized, this could get really ugly. Nor does her mother and father know what is going on with her. This is very cruel and very sad! All this could have been stopped before a demonic possession took place. Once it happens, the demons do not let go of their prey very easily. In addition, notice that Kelly is also the first to be possessed in the family. Whether this demonic clown relinquished his reign once he possessed her is not clear, but something is clear, Kelly was standing on the steps for a reason. Why did the demon have her stand on the steps? Did Helen surprisingly catch Kelly on the stairs, which the demon inside Kelly was not expecting? Or was Kelly on her way to do something diabolical in Helen and Charlie's bedroom or somewhere else in the house as Helen complained had happened many times before? When Helen asked Kelly what she was doing up, she said "nothing." No, she didn't. Kelly did not say "nothing" nor did she say something to the effect of "everything was fine" to reassure her mother Helen. This was the demon speaking in Kelly's voice. The key words here are Kelly wasn't moving and was just staring at Helen. Better words to describe Kelly on the staircase would be that Kelly was in a diabolical trance. This would be like what Helen experienced in the bedroom when she caught herself having a conversation with a demon. This is a very dangerous situation.

Moving on to chapter 42, page 181 where you write if you believed that these horrible evil events had happened, weren't hallucinations or ugly nightmares, then you had to find a way to reconcile with God. Steve, what you wrote here is called conversion. Looking back on all this, it is easy to say this, but when you are going through something like this, it is not so easy. Are you a better person for what has happened? Most importantly, are you closer to God and remaining close to Him? Not just you, Steve, but everyone else, including all those who try to help in whatever way they could. I could see that there were many decent people here trying to help. One thing for sure, Steve, from my own personal experience, God never lets someone go through all this without some Divine Reason for the future. Was this your training ground that God purposely allowed you to go through for some Divine reason in the future?

Let us get to the Alexian Brothers Hospital in St. Louis on page 182. You wrote that this hospital was the site of a famous exorcism case in the 1940 which inspired a book and a movie "The Exorcist." What a big mistake all this was! The Catholic Church should have never allowed this case to go public! Alexian Brothers should have been place under Absolute Obedience to the Holy Father not to talk about this case at all and either send the file to Rome or place in a very secured place. From what I understand, this case was leaked or stolen out of the files by someone who was not part of this Religious Order. This was a major mistake. This is the case that started Hollywood off and running with all the other demonic garbage. Steve, up until this case was made public, there were thousands of cases all over this country and the world that were place under top security, and not to be discussed in public by the priest or Exorcist. Now look what we got. The movie "The Exorcist" was a joke, it is not even close to what happened. And the film maker of "The Exorcist" used, of all people, a little girl (Linda Blair) instead of a boy as the major actor. In addition, do you know how much trouble Linda Blair got in with the demonic angels because of this movie? She is still having problems along with the film makers and other characters. A big mistake and the demonic angels keep on laughing!!

Now all of this is spiraling out of control, with people doing things they should not be doing. Recent case, on the show entitled "Ghost Adventures" which aired on October 20, 2012, these three paranormal investigators go into some building to communicate with the spirits in there and to see if Frank Sinatra would communicate with them, which he never did. They invited all these pretty women and another famous rock star in there to watch and participate in this adventure. They caught a voice on tape and saw some spiritual orbs. Steve, do you know what is sad about this episode? One of these pretty women was scratched on her back. She did not feel it right away when it happened, the pain occurred later. Then they lifted the back of her shirt, and on her back were three very small scratches. You can barely see the scratches, but they were there. And the sad part about this is not one of them in this feature understood what it meant. Nor could anyone in this episode have stopped it. It is bad enough that these women were not dressed decently, but to go into an area where there were so-called spirits without knowing what kind of spirits they are insane. Do you know what all this means? Do these ghost hunters know what all this means? This is so sad!! First off, demons know we have technology available to us that can pick up what are called spiritual orbs. As I discussed earlier, one of the demonic angels' best weapons is remaining hidden or camouflaged. If the demons know we have this equipment to see them traveling in spiritual orb form, don't you think they would remain hidden from this equipment? Did it ever dawn on any of these paranormal investigators that a spiritual orb is not the only way the demonic angels can travel? Did it ever dawn on these paranormal investigators that where their equipment is set up, is a place that the demonic angels will avoid in order not to reveal themselves? Why is it that every time you see an episode of one of these shows, the equipment is set up in one room, but they always here noise in another room where their equipment is not, or they see something with their own eyes that the equipment does not pick up? And the demonic angels keep on laughing. Now the equipment will pick up only what the demonic angel in that area will allow.

How about this woman who I mentioned was scratched? Do you know what this means,

Steve? The demon in that area (which these paranormal investigators never saw) scratched this woman on the back. What does this mean? The scratches are barely visible on this woman's back, but she complains it hurts really bad. That is because the scratch went all the way into her soul and marked her interiorly. Steve, do you think Our Lord was kidding when He announced to John in the Book of Revelation, that those accepted the marked by the beast (the demonic) will be thrown into hell? (Rev. 19:20) This woman has been marked by a demon. This demon will come looking for her at a later time and there is nothing she or any of these so called 'paranormal investigators' can do. I will tell you exactly when this demon who scratched this woman will come back into her life. This demon will wait a few years. This demon will appear in this woman's life when she has started a family. When the children she has are a few years old then the demon will come back into her life. This demon will begin to cause chaos and her life will spin out of control. And this particular woman will not remember that she was scratch by a demon in the building she was in and aired on TV October 21, 2012 under *Ghost Adventures*.

She will wonder why all these bad and diabolical activities are happening in her life, when she should never been in this building in the first place. When you show up in a place where evil spirits are present you risk inviting them into your life. I guarantee it. This goes for all the rest of these individuals who go into these building to investigate a paranormal activity (a demonic haunting) and get scratched or marked in some other way. I guarantee it. This is just one episode I saw on TV where all these people were trying to investigate some paranormal activity and were marked by demons. These scratches will heal on a person's body, but what is not removed is the mark on a person's soul that demons recognize is still there. By the way,most of these people who are scratched are usually women. And the sad thing is, they do not even know what these scratches mean or that a demon will be coming later into their life. Can all this be stopped? Yes, all this can stop. Don't' be surprised Steve, the demons did this to your life by entering when you were just having kids, beginning with Lydia!!

Remember what I have been trying to teach you here Steve is that all demons come into people's lives by invitation. It is one thing to be dressed indecently, it is another to show up in a haunted building and be scratched by a demon. Let me be perfectly clear here, Steve. Evil human souls (spirits) cannot do this, they no longer have a human body, much less material fingernails to scratch someone. Demons scratch people, and it seems that this is their number one form of marking people. Did you ever notice that there are always three scratches? All these paranormal investigators that are scratched always have three scratches. These scratches can take the form of many little scratches in three rows or three columns, but always in sets of three. Why? This is directly related to mocking the Holy Trinity, after someone has been baptized in the Name of the Father, and of the Son and of the Holy Spirit. There is a Divine Mark placed on the soul which, in the Catholic Church, we call a Character. This form of marking (with three scratches) is also mocking our First Eucharistic Prayer (also called the Roman Canon). The priest can select this prayer during the Holy Sacrifice of the Mass. Briefly, this part of the prayer says, "Remember also Lord, your servant X (a person's name is mentioned here) who has gone before us with the mark (or sign) of faith and rests in the sleep of peace." Remember, I told you that most diabolical possessions take place within a block or two of a Catholic Church. There are many reasons for this. One of them is because the demonic angels viciously hate this First Eucharistic Prayer, especially under our Old Rites.

Getting back to the book on page 182, why is it, Steve, that when you entered the chapel of the Alexian Brothers you felt an overwhelming peace? Later you write that this was a true house of holiness, peace and serenity. Do you know why, Steve? That is because the Blessed Sacrament is stored in all Catholic Churches and Chapels. In the Catholic Church, we believe that a validly ordained Catholic Priest has the ability (in Union with the Church) to consecrate the bread and wine into the Body and Blood of Our Lord Jesus Christ during the Holy Sacrifice of the Mass. The real presence of Jesus Christ is present in the host which becomes the Holy Eucharist during Mass and then is reserved in the tabernacle in every Church. Remove the tabernacle and Our Lord, and there will be no holiness, peace and serenity. The only one who made you feel this Steve was Our Lord, who did in this Chapel where He Is present in the Tabernacle. Steve, this is another Divine Sign and a Divine Warning. We are going to return to all of this later, because this is important and ultimately will be the solution to everyone's problems with the demonic angels.

Returning to page 182, at the bottom where you wrote about the Alexian Brothers Hospital being labeled as a place of evil. It is true that one incident can overshadow years of kindness, tenderness and mercy. Here is another reason why this event should have never become public. the people who label this place as evil really have no idea what they are saying, On page 183 you describe in the quiet meditation of that moment, you understood the beauty of the hospital and the power of the message for those who dared to open themselves up to it. In this moment you felt hope and peace for Helen and you. This is very important Steve. Hope is from God, and it is always good to hold on to it. It is one of the three Theological Virtues received at Baptism along with Faith - Hope and Love. Demons from the Virtues Choir rob you of this Faith, Hope, and Love. Then, you give up Hope that very night. Why? Because what Helen told you is a reason to give up this kind of Hope that was inspired by God. God gave you this gift, and you allowed the demonic angels to take it from you!

Let us get into what happened to Helen in the book. You wrote on page 183 that Helen called to tell you she was raped by an unseen force in the house. She had been asleep and woke up because she felt a tremendous pressure on her chest. She felt as though she couldn't breathe or move. There was something large and heavy on top of her. Helen was horrified when she realized she was being raped by the hooded figure that had been visiting her room night after night. We will stop here for a moment to look closely at what happen to Helen. Firstly, there is no doubt Helen was raped by this very cruel demon. Helen never wanted this, nor did she invite this to happen to her. I want to be clear here, so there is no misunderstanding. Helen did not invite this demon to rape her. Unfortunately, this is a typical occurrence with these demons concerning women. They end up getting raped or sodomized by a demon. However, there is something more hideous here than you realize, it is also a way they can possess their victims. The tremendous pressure on her chest, not being able to breathe, not being able to move, feeling something large and heavy on top of her - are all deliberate actions by the demon to immobilize the victim and enter them. This is a rape, but that is not the goal of the demons when they do this hideous act. It is to possess them. You continue to write that she couldn't scream or breathe. What bothered Helen the most was that it wasn't a totally unpleasant experience. It wasn't pleasant that Helen was held against her will, couldn't breathe, couldn't move, the weight on her chest, but along with all this she was sexually aroused, and this scared her more than anything. Let us first look at the rape again here, Helen could not breathe or move or scream because the demon wanted no one to stop or interfere with this hideous act. By the demon doing this to their victim, they can accomplish their goal, possession through rape. This was what this demon was plotting the other night Charlie saw him. Though you did not write about Charlie, he probably was not in bed or the bedroom when this happened. It was done when the demon was able to isolate the victim from others and complete the task. These demons have been doing this to women since the Adam and Eve sinned against God. The sexual arousal is another purposeful act done by the demon. This is done by a demon for an even more cruel reason, to get their victims attracted to them and even have them enjoy what took place. Remember, when you wrote that Alex was sexually groped by a demon, and it looked like he was enjoying it. The purpose of this was to get the victim to want the act to be done again. So, the demonic sexually assault both women and men. However, there are more cases of women being raped then men. Regardless, the act is cruel, hideous and most of all, done to possess the victim. If anything interfered with this hideous act of raping a woman by a demon, then the demon would lose their edge and advantage to the victim. For instance, Kelly probably was not home, Charlie probably was not home, and Helen was there by herself when this rape occurred. The demon was studying the family routine and planned it when there was no one around. If, for instance, Charlie came home and heard something by Helen, went into the room, and saw this hooded figure raping Helen, then there would have been an attempt by Charlie to get the hooded figure off Helen and stop the act. If this would happen the demon would lose the edge and advantage of surprising the victim that an evil angel has this ability to perform this hideous act. The victim would be severely on guard then, and it would be much more difficult for the demon to do it again, however, not impossible. I could get a lot more graphic on what happened here, but for the sake of decency and respect, let us not go any further into the actual act. Point being, Steve, this was a rape to gain entry for a diabolical possession. It is also possible Steve that this might have happened to Kelly. However, again, I am not sure.

Moving onto chapter 43, page 185, where you write about Helen's rapes. It is common for demons to rape their victims repeatedly. However, I am not so sure it was the same demon. There are not enough details here for that to be determined. As mentioned earlier, the rape of a woman is one of the many ways demons try to possess their victims. It is possible that each rape was a different demon to diabolically possess Helen. Whatever the case may be, Helen is being tortured mentally and physically. She needs desperate help as soon as possible, beginning with a priest. If Helen is diabolically possessed because of the rape, the demon could be having profound impact on her internally by forcing her to avoid the subject.

The next sections on pages 185 and 186 provide warning signs of pending danger. First, you wrote that the next night was Saturday, when many friends came over to make sense of what is going on and to advise and support all of you, making it easier for Helen to forget the rape. However, that was a warning sign because you never mentioned any diabolical activity going on while they were there. Again, if this was a warning, why suddenly did the demonic angels go dormant on a Saturday night? Was this a deception? There is a reason for their going dormant.

Then you wrote on page 186 that earlier in the day, "Helen had told me she thought Charlie was having an affair. She could feel it deep down When Helen found out for sure she was going to kill him." Bingo! That is not her talking, that is the demonic angel inside her talking. Notice the change in character when this issue first arose earlier in the book where Helen was very afraid that she might carry out some type of harm to Charlie or Kelly and kill them. Her character shifted when she thinks Charlie is having an affair and she will kill him - with no mention of fear, no morally active conscience engaged, and no concern for Charlie's safety as before. This has nothing to do with any guilt of the rapes playing out in some strange scenario in her own head. However, the demon inside her has started all these accusations against Charlie. You never mention any evidence Helen had on Charlie to suggest that the affair could be true. This is not a coincidence this is happening. There is a parallel, in the sense that rape and adultery are both mortal sins which can bear a lot of shame and guilt.

You probably know this by now but let us consider (or review) the next paragraph on page 186 that contains the signs of diabolical possession. As mentioned above, first, Helen was raped several times by a demon; now, there is a shift in character (remember I mentioned this earlier with your wife in the beginning of the book - notice the evil pattern) which is a major warning sign. The nasty glint in her eyes (as mentioned earlier, all Exorcists are trained to watch the victim's eyes, they cannot lie); the sudden determination in her voice; her eyes becoming very black (a result of the pupils enlarging, or, if her are eyes are already brown, they turn even darker); a chill went up your back when Helen mention killing her husband (the built-in mechanism in the human body given by Our Divine Lord God to alert the person that evil is around); and the confirmation of your suspicions of a character shift by writing, "It was beyond my comprehension that this sweet. neighborhood mother and grandmother, my Helen, who was always ready with a cup of coffee and a piece of cake, could kill anyone." To be clear, the entrance of Helen's diabolical possession is the first rape.

As mentioned in the beginning with your wife, character shifts like this don't just happen without a reason. A side note, Steve, you never mention in this book any details about your wife's eyes, so I would like to drop these questions - Do you remember the time your wife announced she was leaving you and the time your son grabbed onto her leg before she left? - any sudden changes in your wife's eyes? The sudden determination in your wife's voice? A change in how she walked? Do you remember any events, or out of the ordinary activities going on in the house while your wife was still there with the kids? Do you remember seeing her suddenly wearing anything strange? How about seeing a strange piece of jewelry or amulet? Do you remember if she suddenly got a strange tattoo, strange make-up; strange clothes; anything suddenly done out of character? Your wife could have been diabolically possessed before she left, however, I am not sure, other than as I described earlier, the sudden character shift and the unusual phenomena with Lydia's birth which are diabolic signs. With Lydia's birth suddenly you have diabolical actives going on in your life. These events happened for a reason Steve. There is no such thing as a coincidence, not when you are dealing with the demonic angels or God.

Returning to the book with the Saturday night gathering, where you wrote that the night went quietly, some electromagnetic field spikes, amazing EVP, a few cool pictures, and nothing out of the ordinary. Until 4 a.m. when the whole room lit up bright blue from outside and both of you ran to the front porch.

What you saw was a black wolf - blacker than black. This was no wolf; this was another demon. Helen said: "That's the animal that's been in my room at night." A few things I need to mention here, though Helen is diabolically possessed at this point, notice how the demon or demons allows her to function. When victims are diabolically possessed the demonic angels do not stop the ordinary functions of daily living, which could be confusing. Also, the demonic angels like to deceive their victims into thinking they left the particular house they are in, or even the victim they possessed. The demonic angels will also start to deceive the victim and everyone else around them into thinking that no diabolical possession has occurred. Here this demon, in the form of a black wolf, is a distraction to both Helen and you. When you see this black wolf in the middle of the street, you give chase to it, which, as you wrote in the book, was not wise. The demon, in the form of this black wolf, ducked into the alley, which you followed. The wolf turns and looks at you, growling. The demon here is laying down a challenge to you, Steve, and you are completely unarmed. You cannot pull out a gun, a taser, or pepper spray and attack it. Before you even reached for any weapon, this demon could have attacked, and you would have been powerless to resist. This is not just true for you, Steve, this is also true for any police officer who encountered this same demon. You wrote, "I could feel evil emanating from this creature. Unafraid of me, it stood its ground and growled at me. I fell to the ground as I stumbled away from it. I couldn't believe what I was seeing. Then, with one more growl, it ran away. Helen helped me to my feet, and we walked back to the front porch." Why do you think this demon, who appeared as a very black wolf (a very common appearance for demonic angels), did not attack? Why did this wolf demon, with one more growl, run away? The answer to the first question is this demon was told not to attack. That evil you felt emanating from this creature and that one more growl it gave before it ran away was all communication with another demon.

Where is the other demon? In Helen, the demon who is possessing her is standing right next to you, Steve. That demon in Helen told this demon who is under the appearance of a black wolf to return to the place of its abode. In other words, that demon/wolf came from another house infested with demons in the area. After this event, all the pent-up emotions came out (of course instigated by these demons to get Helen to move out of this house). It just would of have been better if Helen and her whole family had listened to you earlier and moved. Perhaps Kelly would not have been possessed, Helen would not have been raped and possessed, and Charlie and everyone else would of not become involved.
\

Moving on to chapter 44 page 189, the description of being sick is probably a virus, as you suspect. Did you catch this virus because the demonic angels are wearing you out? It is highly possible after some of these encounters with them - such as running after a black wolf which was a demon. Was it cold outside when you did this, and thus got sick? Was this demon outside as part of the plan to get you sick and out of the picture so they could work more on Helen? This is very odd. Sunday, Monday and Tuesday, there is no mention of contact with Helen. and suddenly on Wednesday morning the phone rings, it's Helen. Helen's voice sounded different as she speaks with you. You wrote: "Steven? Steven. I think I'm going crazy. No. wait, I am going crazy. Every night I wake up right around three in the morning and every night the hooded shadow is sitting on the side of my bed. It's always the same. He's sitting there, and we're having a conversation. I don't know what we're talking about. I can't remember. And then I always see the glowing eyes of the wolf. As soon as I see the wolf, they're both gone." Helen begins to cry. A couple of comments here. This is Helen speaking for now, and not the demon. The words expressed here would not come from the demon who is possessing her. This is happening during the witching hours, twelve until three in the morning, with the hooded shadow sitting on the bed. What could be happening here is another diabolical trance via sleep (as discussed before) which is why Helen does not know what is being said. The hooded shadow may or may not be the same demon who first raped her. Regardless, the point of this is that the communication being done by the "hooded shadow" and the demon or demons diabolically possessing Helen. In other words, these demons (the hooded shadow figure and the demons inside Helen) are plotting the next move. One thing is for certain, they are doing this for some reason, this is not to scare Helen, nor is it a coincidence. Diabolical possession has occurred already, this is not a diabolical obsession. We are already past the stage of diabolical obsession, the demons are already in Helen. Next, Helen says, "I'm losing it. I keep having bad thoughts, and I can't sleep without the door locked. When I forget to lock it, I wake up to see Kelly standing at the foot of our bed. She just stares at Charlie and me, and I feel like I need to protect us from her. If I don't, I'm afraid she may try to kill us." This is also Helen speaking because there are moral judgments being made here along with health and safety concerns. The demonic angels would not speak like this. A careful note must be made here regarding Kelly. As I discussed before,

Kelly is diabolically possessed. The key is, when Helen forgets to lock the door, she finds Kelly standing at the foot of her bed, staring. Thus, how does Kelly know that the door is not locked and to come into Helen's bedroom unless the demon diabolically possessing Kelly is controlling this event? Helen always seems very concerned about Kelly trying to kill Charlie and her, normally when most people are this concerned for their life, they do not forget to lock the door. The demons inside Helen are prompting Helen in some way to get to bed immediately without locking the door. It is highly possible that the demons in Kelly and Helen are communicating with each other, because there is no diabolical activity happening. Again, the demons in Kelly are doing this for some reason. Is it to kill Charlie? Helen is crying as she continues: "Steven, I think....I... could... kill... Kelly and Charlie both. I think I could. I'm afraid that if I don't kill them first that they will kill me. I know it's not just me. They're acting very strange too. I think someone is going to get hurt. I think... think... someone might die." Let us look at these statements carefully because they are important just like the rest of them above. Obviously, Helen is crying when she is telling you this, proving there are moral judgments being made here. Why is this all important? Believe or not, there are good signs here. Helen being able to make moral judgments is a good thing for an Exorcist to know. If moral judgements are still being made, then Helen never invited the diabolical possession in the first place. Thus, this is not a perfect possession. In addition, Helen still being able to make moral judgments means she still has some control of her free will which is critical to successfully expel the demons in an exorcism.

Though Kelly does very little speaking in your book, it highly doubtful that she invited the demons to diabolically possess her. However, in either case, the exorcism of both Kelly and Helen will be difficult but not impossible. As a result of all this, you can still have hope for both Helen and Kelly, regardless of what happens later.

Continuing page 190 with Helen and your conversation, after you try to speak to her logically Helen suddenly cuts you off. You noticed an immediate change in Helen's voice. Helen's tone got lower, her speech became deliberate and concise. The voice states that Charlie is has been cheating on her. Obviously, this is the demon speaking in her. What you are hearing is the demon forcing or taking over Helen's voice to say whatever the demon wants expressed. This is another sign Helen is diabolically possessed. The fact that you never heard Helen use this kind of language is another indication of a character shift.

The second paragraph written on page 191, even though has vulgar language, is still important. The words are expressing a demonic anger and filth typical of their language they use. The words also provide us some insight into what the demons know about Charlie, such as the fact that Charlie is working with a blonde woman at his job who occasionally brings him home. These words also are an indication of what the demonic angels plan on doing to Charlie, through the possession of Helen. By raising jealousy inside Helen, their plan could go easily into effect. Jealously is a diabolical vice, thus the demons from the Virtue choir are involved in this diabolical possession. There is at least one demon from the virtue choir diabolically possessing Helen. Helen's normal voice reappears again, crying and saying, "What am I going to do? My whole life is falling apart. Where am I going to go?" You wrote that you both continued to talk until ten in the morning, when suddenly Helen abruptly says, "I have something I have to do. I'll call you later." This is probably not Helen speaking here but the demons possessing her. Why would Helen cut you off this abruptly?

After making breakfast, Helen calls back very calm. Helen says, "Steven, I did something I shouldn't have done. I visited Charlie on his lunch hour." You asked Helen if she hurt Charlie. The wicked voice chuckle and says: "I tried, but the son... got away." This can be very confusing on who is speaking here - Helen or the demon. I think this is the demons doing all the speaking here, even though there could be a moral judgment made here with the words - I did something I shouldn't.

In a panicked voice you asked Helen what she did. On the next page, 192, Helen begins to tell you what she was doing. However, this is Helen under the influence of the demonic angels, which is sort of the same thing that happens when someone is under the influence of alcohol -what is doing the speaking, the alcohol or the person or both? The voice tells you that Helen went looking for a gun but could not find the clip. Then Helen's voice says that Kelly's friends were over and knew that Helen wanted to kill Charlie, so they help her look for the clip. Kelly's friends helped her look for a gun clip to kill Charlie and thought nothing of it! Then, Helen's voice goes through this scenario of using a walking stick to kill Charlie, but then rejects this idea.

The next statements on page 192 are a bit alarming, which says, "What could I use? I tried the kitchen next, and Kelly's friends followed me in there. The little angels were so helpful trying to help me find the best way to kill Charlie." It is possible that the demons in Kelly or Helen have manipulated her friends into helping Helen find a weapon. One thing is certain, Kelly nor any of her friends are stopping Helen from carrying out this evil plan.

The next paragraph is all demonic language and not Helen at all, when a butcher knife which is normally quite large in size, was selected as the next weapon in line to kill Charlie. Then one of the boys handed Helen a serrated knife and said "No, use this one; it will cut easier and cause more damage quicker." At this point, no one has a moral conscience to say this is wrong. Either Kelly's friends are on some illegal drugs, or the demonic angels are manipulating them. It could also be the case that all Kelly's friends commit habitual mortal sins, with no Divine Grace in them, which would enable them to carry out this behavior. When the voice says: "He spoke so calmly and with such assurance, and the rest of the kids agreed with him, so I knew he must be right. But I took both. It was weird the way they wanted to help me. They were acting very strangely. Shouldn't they have been trying to stop me? It was funny, as I walked out the door one of the little angels asked if he could watch me stab Charlie." This is all very odd, because even the voice in Helen was saying this was weird. To say the words "the little angels™ in any of these statements is implying these kids are very good. Notice the evil pattern of the phrase "the little angels" in Helen's conversation was also being used in Mr. Winter's conversations. This is all deceptive and a mockery of the actual good angels. Obviously, a good angel would not cooperate with such an evil plan. Therefore, the actual mockery of the good angels also incriminates the demonic angels inside Helen. As a result, using the words "little angels", implies that these kids are like the good little angels. On the other hand, these kids cooperating with this evil plan, reveals the truth that the kids are not "little good angels", but actual demons or agents of the demonic angels who want this eval plan carried out. Bluntly, these kids are not little angels. Steve, this is an example most Demonologists/Exorcists use in this field. In other words, all Demonologists/Exorcists know that the demonic angels always mock the Holy Trinity, the Blessed Mother, the Good Angel, or anyone or anything Sacred. Therefore, when you are dealing with the demonic angels, whatever they are doing or saying by way of mocking can be used against them for the Demonologist or the Exorcist to know the truth. With experience, this skill can easily be picked up.

Getting back to Kelly's friends, there are so many different scenarios here, it is hard to see what the truth is. However, the demons inside Helen have absolutely convinced Helen to do this horrible act. Once this level of manipulation of a person is accomplished by the demonic angels, they can sort of pull back in Helen and let her carry it out, with their assistance. When Helen finally leaves, and the kids are on the porch looking like zombies or robots waving as she drove off, it becomes clear that there is some delusion or even a demonic trance going on in Helen's mind. Looking like zombies or robots is only in Helen's mind, under the influence of the demonic, and not the reality on the porch.

Before we go any further, though it is confusing, there are some facts that can be drawn from what just happened here.

First, Helen is not the type of person to kill someone.

Second, Helen suddenly lost some of her moral judgments and rational thinking which she clearly had on page 190.

Third, Kelly also has lost her moral judgments and rational thinking to cooperate with such an act.

Fourth, there is a diabolical trance from the demonic angels on Kelly and Helen to carry out this type of behavior.

Fifth, by what was written above, clearly these friends of Kelly are not acting normal, which hints at illegal drugs, habitual and grave mortal sin, or demonic manipulation.

Sixth, the boy who suggested to use the serrated knife is either on illegal drugs or being manipulated by the demon. This manipulation comes easy, because this boy is under mortal sin, as one of my professors in this field said, "Those under mortal sin are agents for the devil."

Seventh, the warning was given above that the demonic were planning all along to have Charlie killed.

Eighth, the vice called jealously is being demonically manipulated (demons from the virtue choir) in Helen without her realizing it.

Ninth, the demons responsible for this act, the intent to kill someone, are from the

Cherubim or Power choir. Demons from the lower choirs do not have this kind of power to do these types of activities.

Tenth, the demons who are possessing Helen and the demons who are possessing Kelly are cooperating to carry out this diabolical plan.

On page 193, you write that Helen finally got on the road and expressed that she feels great about what she was going to do. When Helen arrived, Charlie thought Helen was there to take him to lunch. Charlie gets into the car and Helen says that Charlie suspected something. He looked at her funny and was not even sure this was Helen. Charlie is nervous. Helen parks the car by the lake in the park and speaks softly to Charlie. Helen expressed she has the upper hand; and accused Charlie of having an affair. She clearly thinks this was fun. Charlie denies the affair and even calls her "baby". Helen accused him of lying and attacked him with vulgar language and attempted to stab him. When Charlie got out of the car he ran back to work, but Helen tried to hit him with the car. Though she is conscious of what is happening, part of her free will and part of her intellect is being taken over by the demonic angels. Though Helen can operate and function as a normal human being, the demonic possession does not allow her to use the full faculties of her intellect. Therefore, moral judgments are not being made correctly, because critical reasoning in the intellect is being tampered with by the demonic angels. Henceforth, this criterion is not associated with diabolical obsession or diabolical oppression. Though Helen has some use of her free will, she no longer has total control of it. For example, you saw how easy it was to talk to Helen normally and, suddenly, a low wicked voice takes over, with vulgar language that Helen normally does not use. Thus, the demonic angels are infringing on Helen's faculties of her intellect and free will, which is a diabolical possession.

It was good that Charlie did not come home. Clearly Helen was under demonic attack in the house with the bruises around her neck and bite marks on her back.

There are a few more pieces to the story here concerning diabolical possessions. By now much of this should start to make sense. Remember the dream Helen had on Chapter 35 page 155? I stated the dream was a paradox. In the dream Helen is wearing a black dress, a strand of white, perfectly shaped pearls. In the Sermon on the Mountain in Matthew's Gospel, Jesus says this to His disciples, "Do not give what is holy to the dogs, or throw your pearls before swine, lest they trample them underfoot and turn and tear you to pieces." The Liberal Scripture Scholars have wrongly interpreted this passage in most Bibles which says that the dogs or swine represent the Gentiles. This is dead wrong. The Apostolic and Church Fathers say that the swine or dogs are the demonic angels. This interpretation makes so much more sense than interpreting dogs and swine as Gentiles. Notice that Our Lord uses the words Holy and pearls which means that Baptism (Faith) is a Sacred Sacrament and is as valuable as pearls, which were very expensive back in the days of Our Lord. In other words, a person's Faith (through Baptism) is very valuable (like expensive pearls) and it is given to them by Our Lord and should NOT to be thrown to the demonic angels. Things like using a Ouija board, using witchcraft and black magic or participating in séances, tarot card readings, voodoo, etc. are all throwing your Faith away to the demonic angels. I think you get the point. Without getting off track here with interpreting the Gospels, this passage applies directly to Helen. Regarding Helen's dream and this teaching by Our Lord, Helen is baptized, which is represented by the strand of white, the black dress is her soul, the perfectly shaped pearls represent the Faith, Hope and Love Helen received at baptism. In other words, Helen did exactly what Our Lord warned us not to do in Mt 7:6. She threw her Faith away she received at baptism and the demonic angels (swine, dogs, wolves) are tearing it to pieces. This is one of the many reasons Helen and Kelly are possessed. The black dress was not really a black dress, but a representation of Helen's soul blackened by mortal sin. The white strand is Helen's soul and represents the baptismal character, or the mark from the divine (which is mocked by the marks by the demonic angels, such as scratches and bite marks on their victims) that is permanently placed on Helen's soul and can never be removed. Helen's dream on page 155 was a Divine warning.

Returning to the part that I wrote earlier where I did not want to sound sexist or be a male chauvinist, there is an extreme difference between men and women. Women are very concerned about relationships. Men are concerned about relationships, but not nearly as obsessive as women are. Men do not go into bookstores or places like Sam's Club and buy romance novels, which there always an enormous section dedicated to selling these. Women do this because of this obsession. This is important in relation to the demonic angels.

Notice most of the demons are masculine, women are feminine. Satan, Lucifer, Beliel. Molech, Beelzebub, are all masculine names. This also includes Saint Michael, Saint Gabriel, and Saint Raphael - all masculine names. There are feminine angels, but I am not going into that here. One of the basic laws God created is that women, (feminine) are attractive to men, (masculine). Now you can take men out of this statement and put in angels (masculine) thus, the demonic angels are manipulating the attraction between the feminine and the masculine. This is one of the main reasons why there are more women possessed by demons than men. With men, the demons do the same thing but in a different way, such as with pornography. The demonic only have to play games with the natural sexual tendencies of men and they capture their soul in mortal sin. This is why pornography is so addicting to men. The demonic angels are tempting men, who often fully cooperate. However, the demonic do not normally possess men with the use of pornography, they don't have to. Men usually get possessed by not using the God-given gift of reasoning and get involved in Satanism, Voodoo, Occult practices, becoming a warlock, using Ouija boards, etc. The point being, women are more easily diabolically possessed than men are. Case in point here Steve, (if I read your book correctly) it only took you less than two months to figure out that this house is not safe, and you moved out. That is human reasoning operating, whereas Helen has been in this house for close to a year and a half and look what has happened. In short, God did not want you possessed, nor did He want Helen and Kelly possessed.

Moving on to chapter 45, page 195, where you write that Helen called you and was saying, "It tried to kill me!" She was complaining she had bruises and bite marks all over her body. Then you rushed over to Helen. There is no doubt these demons were harming Helen, but they were not allowed to kill her, if they could, they would have done it already. Usually, the demonic angels try to get their victim to commit suicide or arrange for their death in some way such as "suicide by cop."

On page 196, you rushed over to Helen's house. When you arrive, you see Kelly and two friends sitting on the hood of a car. After waving, none of them moved and they were snarling. This is not clear. If all three of them were doing any growling, we have another two victims diabolically possessed. If they were just complaining loudly or grumbling under their breath, then it is just typical obnoxious teen-age or young adult immaturity. I have already pointed out that Kelly is diabolically possessed, I am not sure the other two are. However, it is rather odd that all three of them do this together and do not move. You then write that you went right into the house without knocking, yelling for Helen, "Helen, we have to get you out of here" as the banging starts upstairs. You grab Helen and head for the front door only to be met by Kelly. After a very brief argument with Kelly, who asks for money from her mother using vulgar language, you finally get Helen in the car and go for help. You wrote in the book that Kelly and her two friends were still snarling and angry when you drove away. Kelly and her two friends need as much help as Helen does. The vulgar language used by Kelly and her friends is obviously demonically motivated. I am not sure if Kelly heard you say to Helen that you needed to get her out of the house, but, if she did hear this, the demonic would have motivated this sort of behavior in Kelly when wanting money. It is good no one gave Kelly any money, it would not have been used for a good purpose.

Moving on to chapter 46, you write that you took Helen to the emergency room at a hospital in St. Louis. They take her into the emergency room and the nurse took the routine exams. Helen's blood pressure was 209 over 198, so the nurse took it again. This part is a bit hard to determine because that demons inside Helen could have been playing games with the nurse's instruments when Helen's pulse was only 40 and dropping by the minute. Regardless, the ER doctors were perplexed. The nurse complimented you by saying, "You understand you saved her life." Be careful here, that might not necessarily be true. As I stated earlier, the demonic angels cannot kill anyone. It is against the Divine Laws of God. Taking Helen to the ER was the right thing to do anytime someone's life is in danger. Kelly should have gone with you but that could have been dangerous with her in the car. Regardless, Kelly needs help before it is too late for her, or worse, too late for someone else. However, indirectly, the nurse is right, because Helen could have done something dangerous to herself or someone else. Remember, one of the rules in this field, 'evil never gets better, it always gets worse'. Helen already demonstrated that with Charlie and Kelly is also demonstrating the evil in her is getting worse.

Let's get back to the ER at the hospital. I have seen cases with the demonic angels, in a private room of the ER, levitate all the instruments in the room. This rarely happens, but these demons inside this house (and now inside Helen and Kelly) should not be taken for granted. This is done by the demonic angels to spook or confuse the medical profession. Remember the goal of these demonic angels is to accomplish whatever plan they have, including getting Helen's soul condemned to Hell. A medical doctor or nurse will not be able to stop them. In addition, any doctor or nurse who examines Helen can be physically assaulted, even if Helen is restrained.

In one case, a doctor was thrown across the room with such force that he hit the wall on the other side of the room. At the same time, demonic angels do not want to call attention to themselves in a medical hospital. Often, they will just pull back and wait to cause more trouble. If you took her to a Catholic Hospital (that is still Catholic and not Catholic in name only), there is a better chance for the demons in Helen to go dormant because the Divine Lord might be in repose in the Blessed Sacrament in the Chapel. If Our Lord is present in this Catholic Hospital, He will intervene with the demonic angels. Again, Steve it all depends on the circumstances. Last point, regardless of what I wrote here for your education, I want to be very clear, never, and mean never be afraid to take someone to the hospital if they are demonically possessed. There are some situations in life where God must intervene. If the demonic angels start playing games in the hospital where life is being threatened, let Our Lord handle it. In Catholicism we teach, God gives us life; God is the one to take life away. Any demon who interferes with His Divine Will regrets it. That includes all of us human beings. We are to do all we reasonably can to preserve life, not interfere directly with it.

Then a doctor Smith came in to ask some appropriate questions about Helen having thoughts of suicide and homicide, of which she agreed to having. This is all true, however, what is not true is that Helen is the source of these thoughts, and the medical profession does not know about it. All in all, Steve you did the right thing. You should have gone immediately back for Kelly though. At this point, if I had it my way, (and of course I don't) I would have had Helen secluded and restrained in a private hospital room, with very little medication, so she does not hurt herself or others, and immediately assign an Exorcist to her until these demons are expelled. The Exorcist should be with her every day performing the rituals, as the hospital monitors the results. Keep in mind Steve, as one of the leading Catholic Exorcist, who is a priest has said, "Each time the Exorcist ritual is performed on a victim possessed by demons, it is like taking a baseball bat and hitting the demon over the head." Bluntly, an exorcism tortures the demonic angels.

Moving onto chapter 47, page 199, it is not easy going through something like this Steve, and God was with you through it all, even though you did not believe it at the time. John Zaffis came on the radio, describing that it rained inside an obviously demonic infested house. By the way, this is just one of the many examples that show us how much the good angels and the evil angels can affect the weather.

Let us get to this incident on page 200 when you are driving back home. Your mind was obviously preoccupied with all the events with Helen and your kids. This pure white truck stopped in front of you. These mid-size trucks can very easily block your view of any signs ahead. It is hard to understand what happen with the white truck in front of you and it suddenly disappearing. One thing is for sure, going down the wrong side of the highway might not be demonically influenced. Again, the demonic angels might have confused you, but there was no indication any demons were in your car. If that were the case, the demons would have succeeded in getting you seriously hurt or killed on the highway. However, God is still with you, and if the demons were playing games here, He protected you. If the demons were planning on killing you, they would have made several attempts when you were inside the Union house. This means you were being Divinely protected.

In chapter 48, page 201, Helen woke up in the hospital at three in the morning, and her room was freezing. The demonic angels woke her, and they are playing games with the temperature in her room. I work in a hospital that is part of the Cleveland Clinic, most psychiatric wards do not have any temperature gauges in the rooms controlling the heat. If they did, the patient could easily start to play with the gauges, thus breaking them and even causing harm to themselves. This is usually done by central air (zoning) and controlled at the front desk by the staff. This is also a dangerous sign that the demonic angels are going to cause trouble. You write that Helen went down to the day room to warm up before going back to bed. As Helen walked down the hall, another patient stepped out of the room holding a Bible in his hand and screamed, "This woman is of the devil. This woman is damned! She is damned! Damned!" This is so unfortunate, because the staff grabbed him and subdued him, taking him back to his room as he continued yelling "damned, damned, damned." Steve, you see how cruel the demonic are with the psychological profession and their patients. This man is obviously there for some mental issue he is having. The demons from Helen's room woke him and sent him out in the hallway to do this to Helen. Normally, these patients are on medication to help them sleep. This is not a coincidence he was sent out there. Helen gets to the day room, she sits down, closes her eyes and then hears another voice of a man right next to her. She then hears this man recite verses from the Bible (Mark 5:15 concerning legion; 1 Timothy 4:1… some shall depart from faith, giving heed to seducing spirits and doctrines of the devil, Revelation 18:2… Babylon the great is fallen…) as this man stroked Helen's hair. Part of this was from God, because it would be rare for this to happen around three in the morning with two individuals.

It is good that a nurse came in because this man should not be touching Helen. In fact, no patient should ever touch another patient. Helen returned to her room and sank into her bed, pulling the covers and pillow over her to muffle the scream that was building inside her. The second man's words were running through her mind. Had she indeed become "a habitation of devils, the hold of every foul spirit, and a cage of every unclean and hateful bird"? If Helen is thinking this, then this is a good sign, because the faster she realizes what is happen to her, the faster these demons can be expelled, and she can return to a normal state of life.

In chapter 49, page 205, what you wrote here is true about diabolical possession, if the person listening to you had no understanding of the case, including the medical profession. However, Helen has an advantage to this. There is evidence she is possessed. Have a priest pray over her without medication, in front of a doctor, and see what happens. Have a trained Exorcist look into Helen's eyes and see the evidence. Have the medical profession take a tour of the Union house at night. Better yet, have the medical profession take a tour with a good Catholic priest, at night in the Union House, and see what happens. I guarantee they will change their minds very quickly. For the record, I believe Helen is diabolically possessed by a lead demon from the Cherubim choir. This lead demon has other demons with him diabolically possessing Helen, one is from the virtue choir. The lead demon is very strong and intelligent and will not give up easily.

Solution: Find the name of the Lead demon in this possession, go through the Roman Ritual of Exorcism, and the demon eventually will lose much of his stronghold. If the lead demon is not identified, the rest of the demons will leave. The key is to get that lead demon's name and the reason for this diabolical possession. Once the lead demon name is mentioned and made known, the departure date can be found out also from the demon. Once this is all known, the Exorcist can work on this lead demon and weaken him, thus expelling him and the rest of the demons assigned to him. Once they are expelled, Helen can recover. This recovery and healing can be done quickly if the medical profession does not interfere too much with medication, rendering Helen unable to respond. This type of diabolical possession will require much fasting and prayers for Helen. The full force of

Divine Grace against this demon and the rest of the diabolical angels must be used in this exorcism. The exorcism should take place in a chapel, where the Blessed Sacrament is reserved, with Holy relics. Some pious but holy men and women should be praying before the Blessed Sacrament in another chapel, independent of the chapel used for the exorcism, while the exorcism is going on. The longer that lead demon stays in Helen, the worse it will become, and the greater the stronghold he will have on Helen. Remember this, nothing is impossible for God. That lead demon and those demons assigned to her can and must be removed and sent back to the Hell they came from, under the direction of Our Lord. One other thing, Saint Michael and his angels need to be involved. If those demons come out of Helen and anyone in mortal sin participating in the exorcism is risking becoming their next victim, including the priest. Holiness will win over this evil.

On page 206, let me try to answer these questions you wrote:

How many people who are considered insane are victims of the paranormal?
It is impossible to know the exact count, but in my experience, there are many.

Where does reality end and Schizophrenia begin?
This one is easier to answer, let us first deal with diabolical possessions then we will get to schizophrenia. When someone is possessed, there will always be many signs of the diabolical possession. For example, a profound hatred for anything that has to do with the Sacred. As you can see with this evaluation

of your case, I went through several visible steps that take place before a diabolical possession can occur. Beginning with someone inviting the demons into their life in all the forms discussed above (Ouija boards, black magic, the occult etc.) or become a victim of a someone who invited them. The next stage is the demon or demons entering the person's life and taking up residence in their home, or with an associated cursed object, which is called diabolical infestation. The next stage after that usually is diabolical obsession, as we discussed above. The next stage is diabolical oppression. Sometimes these last two stages can be in reverse. In everything I explained above, these are evil patterns that can be determined by someone trained in the field. Speaking only for the Catholic Church, these are the three stages most Catholic priests throughout the world, who are Exorcists, agree upon. Someone who has schizophrenia does not go through these stages. They might have some minor similarities, but the key is the hatred for anything Sacred.

Could Helen be honest with her doctors and tell them exactly what was happening with her? Would they believe her? Or would her true confession just buy her more time in lockup?

That depends on who the doctor is. If the doctor is a secularist and has no faith - much less believes that demons exist - the answer is obvious. However, you do have many advantages. That advantage is you, Steve, and everyone else who witness all these diabolical activities. This is one of the reasons you were involved in the first place.

Can a person who has schizophrenia have anyone who can bear credible witness to what they experience?

You see Steve, all of you who were in this house and experienced these diabolical attacks must be proven as pathological liars before a secularist doctor (or doctors) is considered right, regardless of how much education or experience he or she has in the medical field. There are many advantages you have, Steve, along with some of the others, because you witnessed this yourself, you saw the evidence. Therefore, your credibility is much more authentic. On the bright side of things, is this a Catholic hospital you have taken her too, with a Catholic Priest on staff as a chaplain? Even if it was not, you can still request a Catholic doctor. There are many men and women who are good Catholic Doctors who would have some understanding of all this. Or you can refuse the treatment and find a Catholic doctor who does. Even if the Catholic doctor does not believe you, go find a Christian doctor. You have plenty of options with the medical field. There is a small disadvantage here, that cannot be overlooked, Helen had admitted to suicide and homicidal thoughts. That must be taken very seriously when considering Helen's treatment by any medical professional. One thing for sure, Helen is not a schizophrenic, any doctor who tells you that (after all the evidence given to them) is an idiot. In fact, get away from that doctor and go find another Christian doctor, because that particular doctor (or doctors) who say this is schizophrenia will only make matters worse. Keep in mind, Steve, some doctors do not believe in God, but think they are gods. Again, there are many good doctors out in the field who could help Helen.

Returning to page 206 and your conversation with Helen where you asked Helen if she told the doctor about the house. Helen was afraid which is understandable. Helen responds: "Not yet. I'm afraid to, but I know if I don't tell him, I can't expect to get the help I need." Steve, you wrote that this was a good sign that Helen was not crazy, and I agree. Unfortunately, Helen could be in the wrong place for this kind of Help.

On the third day Helen was excited to learn that her doctor would believe her when she told him that her house was haunted. You wrote in your book, that the doctor looked Helen in the eye and said, "Yes." There are two things here, first this is good news for Helen, especially since you wrote the doctor looked her in the eyes when he said yes. The second thing about his response of "Yes" is very alarming.

You wrote that the doctor looked Helen in the eye, which he did for a reason. Obviously and sadly, this doctor has experiences with these situations. Again, looking someone in the eye will help a person tell if the person is possessed. In other words, the doctor replying in this way tells me there are many haunted houses in the area and this doctor knows it. This is very sad, because many people are being tortured by these demonic angels. I thought it was very strange, but now it makes even more sense, when you wrote earlier that you chased that demon wolf into a dark alley. This demon wolf growled and went away. Where did this demon wolf go? Obviously to other demonically infested haunted houses. Sadly, this also means many wicked people are inviting these demonic angels into their houses and are being tortured/possessed by them (or, this is happening to innocent victims in the house). Again, part of this evaluation is to educate you.

Returning to the bottom of page 206, where Helen and you were excited about the doctor believing her. Then Helen's tone changed. Her voice lowered, and, with vulgar language, asked about finding a priest. Though this is very vulgar it is extremely important. First, the demons are responding through whatever medication Helen is, which is a very good sign. Second, look at the language and not the four-letter words. Without going into the four-letter words why did this demon ask if you found a priest? All demons know that the number-one enemy to them is the Catholic priest, which is why they attack us so much. Why did the demon say all of this to you? One reason, God forced it out of him. There is no reason for these statements to come out of any demons voluntarily, when they know the Catholic Priesthood has the power to expel them with permission from the Local Bishop. When the Bishop gives permission for a Roman Catholic Priest to do an exorcism on someone, the whole force of the Catholic Church with all its merits is applied. In other words, it is not just the Priest/Exorcist doing the ritual but also with the power of the bishop who is in Union with the Holy Father or the Pope. By these statements This also suggests that God does not want Helen diabolically possessed.

After hearing all these statements, the phone went dead. As you wrote, Helen ripped the pay phone off the wall. The demons obviously did this. Helen did say something interesting, she said: "I had the strength of four men." Even though Helen was crying, this is very important. First off, the hospital let her call you back again Steve, normally they would have isolated her. This is another indication that this hospital has experiences with these types of conditions.

However, this statement Helen says, "I had the strength of four men" is important, because in the next paragraph you wrote that you found a good priest, Father Paul (how ironic we have the same names) who is probably an Exorcist. By Helen saying this to you, she might have revealed how many demons are in her. These are not four men, but four demons, and one of them is the leader. Why did she pick out the number four if it was not significant?

Carol met with Helen in the hospital and called you to say that she thought you lost Helen. Carol says, "Helen just kept changing from one personality to the next. Her mood changed just as quickly. Her daughter was there, and she told me that she didn't know who that person was, but it wasn't her mother." Let us deal with Carol's statements first, based on what just happened with the demons. Changing from one personality to the next was not Helen, but the demons, each taking over Helen's voice and controlling her. Steve, when this happens in cases, be aware not to misinterpret it; this is a good thing. What is going on is that the demons inside her feel threaten and angry by what was revealed by the demon who asked about a priest. Remember this was forced by God. Plus, Helen said she had the strength of four men which might be the giveaway of how many demons are possessing her. This might be hard to find out, but if there were four bite marks on Helen on different days, you might have the answer on how many demons are in her. Each bite mark could have been given one per day, or, four bite marks given over several days. When diabolical possessions occur, God does not just sit by. He makes the demons give signs for the Exorcist or others to understand what is going on here. There is a reason for the number four being used by Helen. Again, I can't stress this enough. When a diabolical possession occurs in anyone, such as Helen and Kelly, there are signs given to understand what is going on, look for them! Do not ignore these signs. It might not be relevant now, but it will become important later. The more signs given and understood under a diabolical possession, the faster the expelling of the demons can be. Remember again, the demons are doing this for a reason, but what is the reason? Why the number four? This is no coincidence.

Helen is released from the hospital on Tuesday, and you are to meet with Father Paul on Wednesday. Obviously, Father Paul has gifts, (something else ironic, this is no coincidence). You get into the final paragraph on page 207 with Helen not returning to the house, which is very wise, and I fully agree with. Helen went to live with her sister in Gerald, Missouri - something else that is good, but needs to be carefully monitored. This can also be dangerous, one always has to be careful, and most of all, her daughter in Gerald, Missouri needs to know what is going on or she will be a victim. Charlie and Kelly went to the house to pick up the pieces and move into a new place to live. However, I am very concerned about Kelly. What does it mean that she went through spiritual counseling, when I know full well, she is diabolically possessed? If Kelly went just through spiritual counseling, then demon is still hiding in her. This can be very dangerous! Demons can leave or hide in their victims who were possessed and come back later to cause trouble - be careful! If this is the case, this demon could come back with seven other demons more wicked than themselves, and it will be horrible (Luke 11:24-26). There could also be a demonic mark on Kelly's body somewhere, be careful here! You let your guard down with the demonic angels and you will pay a heavy cost! The same goes for Charlie, even though this book never gave any evidence to suspect that he is possessed. Charlie is probably not possessed, but was he marked by a demon while living in this house? Just a word of caution, Helen, Kelly, and Charlie want all this behind them, so make sure there is no reason for any demon to come back looking for them.

Moving onto chapter 50, page 209, where you write about the first appointment with Father Paul. Father Paul's office is in a small house next to the Church. Where the priests live is called a rectory in the Catholic Church. Women of the Church (sisters) live in a convent.

After Father Paul's greeting and introduction. Helen and you sit down and begin to explain the situation. Father Paul is right about the house and the surrounding areas, and that Helen and you were suffering from a Demonic oppression. This is an easy diagnosis in this field until the Catholic priest blesses Helen. Blessing a person is also a way to find out if there is a demonic possession. In this field, a priest wants to hold off labeling anyone demonically possessed for several reasons. If the person is not actually possessed, then the person could lead the rest of their life thinking this was their problem. Second. Fr. Paul is making sure this is a real possession which he probably suspects. In a demonic possession, if a priest makes a blessing over the intended victim, the demonic will have a reaction to it. This is a typical procedure when evaluating the case. You do not write here what you discussed with Fr. Paul in this opening session, but he also must make sure for the record this is not a mental illness. You wrote about schizophrenia. If you bless a victim of schizophrenia, they normally do not have a violent reaction, because there are no demons inside them to cause the reaction. Most, but not all, a diabolical possession will have a reaction to a simple blessing performed by a Catholic Priest in good standings with the Catholic Church.

When you describe the reaction you had to Fr. Paul's blessing, it could be that Divine Grace was flooding your soul. I am not sure on what happened in your case after Fr. Paul laid hands on you and blessed you. You never wrote that Fr. Paul used Holy Water, which is required. I am not sure what kind of blessing he did on you. Nor am I sure what kind of reaction Helen had, however. This is a major sign to me, because the demons are now going to hide. They do not give up on their prey easily. If Demons cause a reaction inside their victim, it is a dead giveaway of a diabolical possession. Demons know this, Steve, and will do everything they can to prevent it from being known they are in there. In addition, besides not mentioning any Holy Water being used with Helen, which is something I question. Even a simple blessing will cause pain to the demonic angels, but they can silently endure the pain. What I suspect Father Paul was doing was laying hands onto both Helen and you and asking the Holy Spirit, or Our Lord, if either of you were diabolically possessed or what is the condition was of both of you. You probably did not hear Fr. Paul say these words, because they are normally prayed in silence.

The next red flag is that you drove home and pulled into her daughter's driveway and Helen began to cry. I am hoping that this is not the same daughter, Kelly, who still might be diabolically possessed.

The next few paragraphs on page 210 and 211 where you visited your mother, shows me just how much Faith your mother has. Your mother and your father could have been praying for you all along Steve to prevent you or your children from becoming diabolically possessed and you did not even know it. You mention several times in this book that your parents both came to pick up the kids to take them to Church. Someone was praying for Divine Grace to prevent diabolical possession or anything else demonic from happening. The problem is that no one was praying for Helen and Kelly. These prayers from your mother and father were protecting you and your children.

In chapter 51, on page 213, you write about Bill, who was a total agnostic. Here is another opening for the demonic angels, who already marked Bill with the voice recorder carrying the voice of a demon, who said, "The One". Why would you be a paranormal investigator if you did not believe in demons? What do you think you are investigating? This makes sense now that you wrote this, because these demons knew this all along and will be coming back someday into Bill and Trudy's life. Steve, do you see how easy the demonic angels have it with so many people? How many other paranormal investigators are agnostic? For Bill to say, "I don't care what you want to call it. If it has 'demon' in it, no one is going to believe it." Really? Is the Catholic Church here for no reason at all other than just a bunch of expensive buildings (churches) with expensive art in it? Are all validly ordained Catholic Priests and Christian Ministers just wasting our time and our life because we have nothing else better to do? The Catholic Church has been in existence for over two thousand years. Was that all a lie too? If God did not exist, how did the Catholic Church survive over two thousand years, with all the enemies of the Church attacking her, including at times her very own? We talk about God being merciful, if the demonic angels and Hell do not exist, why should God be merciful? Mercy from what, ourselves or each other? Bluntly, there is no such thing as an agnostic. That is lie!

On the top of page 214. you wrote that Bill was right about the 'demon' being in any diagnoses with Helen. I disagree, he is dead wrong! It one thing to keep your personal aliments or your suffering to yourselves (family and good friends), it is a another whole story to be afraid to admit to the truth about the demonic world. Helen and Kelly are not the first nor the last who have become diabolically possessed.

Let's get to the MPR Halloween party on Zombie Road, planned a week before Halloween. Zombie road, as the name implies, is haunted. You write a brief description here on page 214 that Zombie Road is five miles long, no longer used as a road (and why is that, are too many people getting hurt on this road?), a two-mile hike at night through the woods, a railroad for children (more opportunity for the demonic angels to go after the children of their parents in this haunted area), a scenic ride on the railroad the last mile of the hike and all clearance given. Then Helen called you to go along and you agreed. Halloween is the number-one holiday for the demonic angels. This all should not have happened, not with Helen or you, not with the twenty people in the MPR, not for anyone associated with running this train to make money in this haunted area.

The event begins, it begins to rain, and you all start to walk. Then you turn to Bill and standing behind him was a white figure of a man wearing overalls, a farmer from distant past. That's no farmer, that is a demon, and look who he is behind - Bill the agnostic listening to what he was saying.

At your next stop, you see a shadow figure, blacker than black, rushing down the hill at you. Bill, the railroad guy and you were standing there in awe, and someone asked in a frighten voice, "What was that?' This is probably the same demon or another demon.

Then you encounter a section of the woods where there were all kinds of whispering - you feel eyes staring at you from the trees and you start seeing things. It is interesting you mention that it felt more like The Blair Witch Project. This was another major disaster involving the demonic angels and three kids who had no clue on what they were doing but had to go out and do paranormal investigating in those woods. The reason those woods are so demonically haunted, is because a group of witches in a coven were out there and invited the demons with their Satanic rituals. Enough said, I do not want to get off the track here. You finally get to the small train and begin a journey. You then ask if Helen was there, she responded: "Yes." The train eventually pulls into the station, and everybody seemed to enjoy themselves. Perhaps, but how many of them are demonically marked? It was not a coincidence that demon was behind Bill. You get to Helen, who starts to have the demonic angels speak for her. Helen begins the conversation with four-letter words and a demonic glare. Wisely, you get Helen to the car, and she reluctantly got in, which could be very dangerous for you, Steve. Bill, who noticed something wrong came over to check. You rolled down the window and Helen said some more four-letter words. Bill backed away from the car, and you wisely left.

The conversation on the way home to Helen's daughter's house is typical of someone diabolically possessed. When you arrived, the dogs greeted you, and suddenly dashed away, whimpering as they went. Animals (cats, dogs, horses, etc.) can see and hear things most human beings cannot, thus they saw and heard the demons in the car. The purpose of these conversations is to confuse, manipulate and scare you. Then, in her daughter's driveway, the vulgar conversation continues with Helen, and you noticed her eyes going pitch black. The demon who was doing this was not very powerful, however, those black shadows who were demons surrounding the car are powerful. You are witnessing how the demons can leave her body and come back as they please. Occasionally all of them do leave temporarily. Usually, the lead demon will keep one of the demons from the lower choirs (which have a lot more demons) inside the victim. Point being, you just witnessed the lead demon and the other demons returning to their victim - Helen. They all got back into Helen before the next reaction. You started the engine and Helen tried to grab the keys, and then proceeded to attack. This happened because the demons that surrounded the car went back into Helen, which is why it never happened at the train station or the way home.

There is always a reason the demons are doing this to you. Helen (or the demons) kept screaming profanity at you, and she finally got out of the car and slammed the door. You finally leave as Helen (or the Demons) continue their diabolical communication. You rushed home, obviously very scared, only to have the phone ringing when you get into the house. It was Bill, who was worried about what he witnessed. Bill finally looked into the eyes of evil, and this is not a pleasant experience.

Chapter 52, page 219, obviously quite tired from the night before, the phone rang late in the afternoon. Matthew, who answered it, comes in and says, "Dad, it's Helen's daughter." Helen was apparently at Church and started to act up, crying and angry. That's because the demons did not want to be in this Holy Church. When Helen and her daughter got home, the demons started screaming and yelling at her daughter. Helen finally leaves and drives out the driveway, which is very dangerous. Here is where everyone else can only pray to God that Helen avoids hurting herself or someone else. Helen finally returns later that night, seemingly normal.

Moving onto chapter 53, page 221, it was Halloween 2005, and all your kids are naturally excited about what they would wear that night. At this point, Steve, Halloween is ok for kids to dress up and go trick or treating, if it is not overdone. Their safety is the most important concern. With adults, it becomes a different matter because it can be overdone rather easily.

You fell asleep on the couch, when a loud bang at the door woke you up. It was Helen, and the demonic angels wanted inside your house, indicated by all the profanity uttered through Helen's mouth. Helen kept banging harder and louder with all the profanity. Your cats came around your feet and began to hiss and arch their back. This was surely a warning from your pets. Helen kept on wanting you to let her in, uttering profanity. You wisely do not let her in and go to your phone to call the police. Instead, you call her daughter, who then tries to reach Helen her cell phone. Her daughter calls you back and tells you Helen has a gun and is sitting at the Union house. Her daughter tells you if you call the Police Helen says she will be dead before they get there.

You picked up the phone to call Helen, and of course she answered because Helen was waiting for you to call. The four-letter words right out of Helen's mouth come over the phone. Helen even says she has a gun up to her head, wanting to pull the trigger. At this point I have stop and remind you that committing suicide will not happen. The demons cannot force Helen to take her life. It is against the Divine Law. If they could, this would have already happened. Then you hear the word, "Okay" A second later you hear the glove compartment in the car shut. "The gun is put away. I wasn't going to use it on myself anyway..." Helen was not going to use it on herself because she can't, however, she could have hurt you or someone else. Again, bear in mind, that if the police did show up and saw the gun pointed at them, they would draw their guns and there could be a shooting in which Helen could die. This is different matter, that also includes you and her tangling with a gun if you had let her in, and the police were there and shot Helen. But, again, will the Divine allow this because the demonic angels have boundaries they are forced to obey? If the demonic angels were allowed this type of freedom, they could arrange all of us to die by such methods, and this would not be allowed by God. There is one exception to some of these scenarios with the demonic angels (which technically is not really an exception). If a person or persons were demonically possessed (The Columbine High School Shooting) or a diabolical obsession (the Virginia Tech Shooting) went into the school and opened fire, killing many innocent human beings, then they can take their own life. What happens in cases like this, once the demonic angels have them carry out their plan, such as shooting and killing innocent people, they can pull back out of the person they possessed or pull off the person because the plan was carried out. By doing this, the person who was possessed (or obsessed) see what they did and commits suicide. There is a major difference here. In Helen's case she did not invite the demons in (which, in most cases of diabolical possession, the person who is possessed did not invite the demons to possess them, they become victims of possession). In the Columbine High School case and the Virginia Tech shooting these individuals invited the demons into their lives. Often, people will go to the demonic angels to seek revenge on someone, or many people, thus, inviting them into their life to help carry out the plan they designed. The evil plan can come from the actual demonic angels, or the person or persons who invited them, but just need the help of these demons to carry it out. Thus, as a final word, the Columbine High School shooters and the Virginia Tech shooter are responsible for the possession and obsession because they invited these demons into their life. With Helen, she never invited the demons to possess her; she is a victim of someone else's invitation where the demons infested the Union House. Therefore, Helen is not responsible to God for this diabolical possession.

However, Helen is responsible for not heeding your requests to move out of the Union house, when you told her several times to do so. The difference here is that Helen never realized, by not listening to you and moving out of the house, she would become diabolically possessed. Following the invitation will determine her responsibility to God, not the responsibility to civil law. I want to be clear here, I am not talking about the responsibility to civil law here, only the responsibility toward God.

Let's get back to Helen here at the bottom of page 223, Helen threatened to hang herself in the basement of the Union house, via the butcher shower. Finally, through the phone, you hear a knocking on the car window of Helen's car - it is her daughter. Helen hissed, and asked, with vulgar language, what her daughter was doing there. Then Helen accuses you of calling her daughter. Then you confused her by saying: "No, Helen, you called her." Helen responds: "What?" You continued, "Yes, you called her, Helen. Don't you remember?" A long howling came over the phone. Through shock and confusion, Helen asked again: "I called her? Wait a minute." Then Helen asked what she is doing here in front of the house. You then asked Helen how long she had had these blackouts. Helen answered, "Since Christmas." Notice, Christmas, another Holy Season when the demonic angels become extra active. This is why so many people commit suicide during the Christmas Holidays. Besides depression and loneliness, there is the instigation of the demonic angels.

Then you asked Helen how often and for how long she had these blackouts. Helen says: "Some weeks are better than others. At first it was just an hour or two here and there. Lately, I've been losing days." Technically these are not blackouts, but demonic trances. Then you hear her daughter calling: "Mom? Mom?" Then you remind Helen of all the pain she is putting her daughter (and you) through, and that she needs help. Her daughter took her back to the hospital.

On page 225, you thanked your cats for saving your life. Who knows what would have happened Steve, if you had opened that door? Later you found out that Helen told you that the demon had come to her and told her that she was going to kill you, Steve, and then hang herself in the basement. Maybe this is true, it is hard to say. However, you are right, God was with you that day and every day.

You discuss, in the next paragraph, Helen's many hours of therapy with Dr. Smith and Father Paul to get Helen back to where she is today. John also helped you heal your wounds from these experiences. As far as Helen's full recovery, that is up to God and her.

In chapter 54, page 227 you took some time away from the paranormal activities. Steve, even Demonologists/Exorcists need time away from this field. You now have a better understanding what it means when you go up against the demonic angels. In the process, you lose some of your humanity. Can you get it back? It really all depends on God and the person.

On page 227, I was glad you to see you have returned to the Church and received communion. In the Catholic Church, most priests will tell you that the best Catholics are those who left the Church and came back. Their faith means so much more to them then someone who has been in the Church all their life without leaving. The person who returns doesn't take their Faith for granted and is no longer there because of some "obligation." So, if you have returned to your Lutheran Faith, you will be a much better person for it.

It is good that Helen and you are still close friends. You have been through a lot together and can understand each other. But, regarding the question, "What do we do now?" There is plenty to do. First, both of you need to lead a Holy Life, this includes Charlie and Kelly. There will be no exception to this rule once you have been this involved with the demonic angels. These demonic angels will return if you let your guard down (Luke 11:24-26). Therefore, you need to attend Church, pray daily, read the Bible or Life of the Saints and stay away from mortal sin. If you slip into sin, ask God for forgiveness as soon as possible, do not wait.

Moving onto page 232, where John did not agree with a full possession. I highly disagree. Based on what you wrote here, Helen should have had the exorcism rituals done on her. Her recovery would have been quicker. As far thinking you can hurt the possessed person more, or even kill them through exorcism, is false. Name me one case where a person died at the hands of an Exorcist? I have been in this field way too long to know whoever said that does not know what they are talking about. Exorcisms have never killed anybody. I have been studying and working in this field to long, and never came across one case by any of the other Exorcist where the person died as a result. In fact, it is the complete opposite, where the person died because there was not an exorcism done on them, or, more importantly, not done properly.

Moving on to the final part of the book, the epilogue, as I discussed in this evaluation of your case, Mr. Winters is a very wicked man. After what Helen's family and your family went through (not to mention all those who were in the house before you and Helen) there is another family who will become additional victims. In the end, Mr. Winters will have to answer for all this before God, and it might not go very well.

Solutions

You mention that John Zaffis said that this line of work is not a path that anyone would choose for themselves. It's a path that is chosen for them. This is one of the secrets in dealing with the Demonic Angels. This path is chosen for you by God, which is why I am in the field. It never dawned on me when I entered Religious Life and became a priest that I would become involved in this work. Yet, close to half my time is now in some way spent on dealing with the demonic angels. I am very low key because I cannot, at this point, travel all over the country helping people. On the other hand, half my priesthood has now been dedicated to this line of work.

In the Catholic Church, the priesthood has many advantages in this line a work. As for myself, being a Catholic Priest is the most important weapon against the demonic angels. This is not just a job or some line of work, you have to dedicate your life to it.

I say the Holy Sacrifice of the Mass daily and frequently go to the Sacrament of Confession at least once a month. This is key and very important to keep my soul as free of sin (mortal and venial) as possible. Thus, I can be close to God (the Father, Son and Holy Spirit). In addition, I am also very close to the Blessed Mother and the Saint of the Religious Order I joined. This has to do with how much I love all of them and how much I am willing to sacrifice myself to accomplish Our Lord's Will. This is not lip service. True love must flow from my heart to them. Of course, they all love me, but that is a given. You must have a loving relationship with all of them first, before you can attempt this line of work. Why? Because the effectiveness and success of any Demonologist/Exorcist has to do with the power of their intercession (more on this later). There more to this but I think you get my point in having a loving relationship with God first.

Returning to God, I say the Holy Sacrifice of the Mass every day and sometimes more than once, such as on Sunday, etc. Approximately three hours a day I am praying to Our Lord Jesus Christ on my own. I am not forced to do this. I do this willingly as part of my Spiritual life. By having this Spiritual Life, the communication with Our Lord and myself is very profound. I am enlightened by the Holy Spirit to what is going on in anything that I am sent to confront.

Therefore, though I have studied many years under the leading Exorcists in the Catholic Church. It is Our Lord who is the Primary Teacher. If the demonic angels are His creatures, should not Our Lord be involved in educating us on how the demonic operate? Not everything is recorded in the Sacred Scriptures. To understand how the demonic work, you need to get to more resources, and the primary one, for me, is the education provided by Our Lord. For example, during the Sacrifice of the Mass, I am holding, in my worthless but consecrated hands, Our Lord Jesus Christ in the Holy Eucharist. This is not just the teaching of the Catholic Church; it is a fact. Thus, during the Holy Sacrifice of the Mass, Our Lord is present, communicating to me, especially after I just received Him into my heart. Directly after communion, when I am purifying the vessels, I am asking Our Lord, "What is going on with this case or that case? What do you want me to do about this situation?" Guess what, I get the answers. How do you think this evaluation is coming to you Steve. I was told to send it. A priest is not married like the laity are. We have the time to do this and we are called to do this; to be in Communion with Our Lord and, in my case, with the Blessed Mother and the Saint of our Religious Order. Thus, becoming a Demonologist is now part of my vocation. I did not select it, Our Lord gave me the gifts. This is not just a job or some line of work, you must dedicate your life to it. If it comes from Our Lord, He expects you to use it. Much will be required of the person entrusted with much and still more will be demanded of the person entrusted with more. (Luke 12:48)

		After going through your case, I'd like to present briefly the way I would have addressed it. There are various stages of rituals to proceed through when dealing with demonic infestations. It is to be understood that these rituals are done with the Help of Our Lord and The Blessed Mother. In addition, I make sure my soul is not guilty of any mortal sins, so I go to confession, fast and pray to Our Lord before I perform these rituals. Normally, I go to

Confession anyway just to make sure I have Sanctifying Grace.

In the Catholic Church, the priesthood has many advantages in this line awork. As for myself, being a Catholic Priest is the most important weapon against the demonic angels. We have the power to bless people, houses, and items. There are various forms of blessing we use in two books entitled: "The Book of Blessings" and "Roman Ritual + The Blessings."

In reference to your case, there are many blessing that I would have used from the vast resources as soon as I got there in the house. This is the first stage of the rituals. The Blessing of the Union house, especially the basement, should have been done with Holy Water that was blessed (f possible) during the Easter Vigil or the various Blessings in the Mass or from the books already mentioned. In addition, I would have used Exorcism salt, that can be blessed in the Holy Sacrifice of the Mass. It is in the front section of the actual Mass, in addition to other Blessings that can be done on Exorcism salt. The demonic angels hate this form of Exorcism salt.Blessed At Mass, it can be scattered throughout the house. Exorcism salt will not evaporate like Holy Water used in Blessings. I would have begun here with these two Holy items.

Building a Spiritual Fence can be done at any of these stages, but it is more preferable in the first or second stages. What you do at this part of the ritual is very simple. Go outside and begin at the corner of the property. Dig a small hole in the ground and drop a Blessed Medal (it must be blessed by a Catholic priest) into the hole and then bless the hole you dug and the Blessed Medal with Holy Water. The medal should be a medal of Saint Benedict or

Saint Michael the Archangel, very powerful Saints against the demonic angels. These medals can be purchased in any Catholic catalog or store that sells Catholic merchandise. Say the special prayer to Saint Michael the Archangel after you bless the hole with Holy Water. I included this prayer later in this section on solutions. Fill up the hole with the dirt that was dug out. Then walk away slowly, while saying the prayer of Saint Michael continuously, one after the other, until you reach the next corner of the property. This is a spiritual fence around the property, so all four corners of the property are to be done. Then repeat what you just did before, dig a hole, drop in a Blessed Metal of Saint Benedict or Saint Michael the Archangel, bless the hole dug with Holy Water with the Blessed medal in it, say the prayer of Saint Michael, then cover the hole up with the Blessed medal being buried. Proceed to the next corner of the property, saying the prayer of Saint Michael the Archangel continuously. Do this procedure until you reach all four corners of the property in a box shape and have four Blessed medals in four holes in the ground.

The next stage, if needed, I would have used incense over the whole house, from the basement to the attic, with blessed incense and charcoal. Again, the Catholic Priests have access to these forms of blessings. The incense should be blessed at Mass, if possible. The demonic angels despise this form of blessing, because, like sulfur, raw sewage, or the stench of rotten flesh is used by them and is repulsive to us, it can be countered by blessed Incense. I mean a lot of blessed incense, not small amounts of smoke incense, but lots of incense. Every closet, doorway, window, crawlspace; everywhere that can a demon can possibly hide must have Holy Water, Exorcism Salt, and Blessed Incense used in these areas. When the demons are in the house, you need to be aggressive and go after them full throttle with all the power available, with no holding back, demanding as you go Blessings throughout the building or house. They will leave immediately. There is no inviting them to leave. You must aggressively command them, in the name of our Lord Jesus Christ, to leave this building or home. I would have smothered the entire basement with Blessed Incensed, Holy Water, and Exorcism Salt, especially the fruit cellar and the butcher shower. By the time I am done with the houses, all you see is Blessed Incense lingering all over the house with Exorcism Salt and Holy Water.

If they do not leave under these blessings, the demonic angels will regret the next levels of the rituals. A word of importance, before any Exorcist performs a ritual, he knows that in all cases dealing with the demonic angels that there will be a sign given by Our Lord that the ritual was a success. This is very important to look for, so that you are sure that the demonic angels are gone. You will know when you see it, because all signs given by Our Lord are different in each case. The Lord wall also make it clear to you that this was the sign given, often forced by the demonic angels to give.

A few side notes about the demonic angels' weaknesses that are important to know. All demons were created with pure spirit. This is like what our human souls are made up of, so you get an idea of what I am writing here. Demons can see, hear, think, feel, smell, and breathe They possess free will and are very intelligent.

These are all good in themselves, but they can become weakness. All demons, regardless of the choir they are from, have these abilities. That does not mean the demonic angels use these faculties as we do, they are different. Remember, they have no human flesh, we do. However, demonic angels do operate a little like us, they just have different "apparatus" in their Angelic nature in whatever the Eternal Father created for them. As I said, all demons must breathe, thus "the Breath of Life". Let's go back for a moment, Steve, in your case, remember when you rushed up stairs and challenged the demonic spirit? The demon was in a black mist, and you went up into it. Now, keep that image in mind, and send Blessed Incense into the black mist. What do you have? The same effects on him as sulfur, sewage, rotten flesh, and even ammonia have on us, Blessed Incense has to all demons, no matter what choir they are from, though the higher demons can get past it. Now, what else does this do? Remember, the demons are pure spirit. What is Blessed Incense? It ends up becoming Blessed Smoke. Blessed Incense, to a diabolical angel, is like us taking pepper spray and placing it all over our bodies. In addition, to the suffering they endure by breathing Blessed Incense, the smell of Blessed Incense when it encounters their demonic spirit, becomes agonizing to them. In addition, the Blessed Incense also irritates their eyes. Imagine what happens when those evil red or yellow glowing eyes have Blessed Incense in them. Because Blessed Incense is smoke and can go all over the house, it dissolves and loses its effect. This is why extra attention must be placed on any known open portals. The demonic angels will return temporarily through those portals so this can have no effect on them. Our Lord must close up the portals, thus the need for and importance of Blessed Exorcism Salt. A side note, Blessed Incense, is by far more effective on the demonic angels then the herb sage that is burned in or outside the house.

So, to recap so far, if I did not read your book, I would have started with a simple Blessing of the House. This is the first level, if this did not work; I go to the second level, Re-Bless the House with Blessed Incense, Exorcism Salt, and Holy Water, using more advance Blessing rituals with Psalms. There should also be blessed Items in each room, such as a Blessed Crucifix, including the bathroom and basement. If the demonic angels even touched one of these items, then I would automatically go to the next level. Why? You first need to know what kinds of demons you are dealing with in each case. In some of the cases, we (Our Lord, the Blessed Mother, and our Saints, including me) got one of the demons out of the house by the using some of the above simple Blessings. This is because the demons from the lower choirs will not occupy a house or a building under these conditions. Demonic angels from the lower choirs cannot get past Exorcism Salt and Blessed Incense nor will they normally touch a blessed item like a Blessed Crucifix or a Blessed Image (for example, a picture Our Lord, the Blessed Mother, or a Canonized Saint). These demons from the lower choirs will run at the sight of a Catholic Priest about to do these blessings. I have seen with my own eyes, before I even started the ritual, demons come flying out of the back rooms, closets, or wherever, and leave immediately. They just get out immediately before these rituals begin because they are so repulsed by them.

At this point a Demonologist should know they have eliminated most of the demons from the lower choirs. However, the demons from the higher choirs can get past them. Demonic angels from the Powers, Virtues and Cherubim choirs can get past Exorcism Salt, Blessed Incense and Holy Water. Additionally, the demons from these choirs (Powers, Virtues, and Cherubim) can touch and even destroy items that are blessed. That is why they are placed around the house. If they are destroyed, moved, or whatever, a Demonologist/Exorcist should know these are more powerful demons and thus, we go to the next level. As I said earlier, all rooms in a house should have at least one Sacred (Blessed) Image or Cross in it.

The next level, if the evidence supports that these demons are from the higher choirs, we get to the use of Consecrated Oils that have been Blessed (Consecrated) by the bishop, usually during the Holy Week of Lent, which is once a year. A priest can bless these oils with permission from the bishop (which I do not recommend, you need the Consecrated Oils directly from the bishop) however, if the priest is accountable, there usually plenty of Consecrated Oil in the containers we call "Oil Stock". Since I am in a Religious Order, we have many Churches, thus it is easier to access these Consecrated Oils. In addition, knowing I am in this field, I make sure there is extra Consecrated Oil around for the next year.

Returning to the Demonically infested house, I choose more Psalms from the Roman Ritual for Exorcisms (just the Psalms) and use them with additional prayers and blessings in the House. I go through the house, which already had Exorcism Salt scattered everywhere, (I mean everywhere, no enclosure where a demon can hide can be overlooked, including crawl spaces). In addition, I also have Blessed Incense, with the Relic of the True Cross, and bless the house again with the Consecrated Oil. I go through each room and space in the house, with the Blessed Incense and mark a Cross with the Consecrated Oil (Chrism) on the wall. The Consecrated Oil remains on the wall, and it is highly suggested to the owners, or renters, that this is where this cross should be placed. Only one per room is sufficient). A candle holder for the wall should be placed over it after the candle holder is blessed by the Catholic Priest. It is recommended. that a Blessed Candle (preferably from the Candle Masses) be placed in the candle holder for the wall, but never burned. Never burn this candle on the wall, that is not the purpose, the purpose is the Consecrated Oil on the wall, and the Blessed candle holder for a wall place on top of Consecrated Oil (in the shape of a cross), which represents Christ as the Light of the World One Blessed Candle holder for each room, basement and bathroom where the Consecrated Oil was placed on one wall in the form of a cross is enough. Blessed Incense is also used throughout this ritual. Of course, the Blessed candle holders, with the Blessed Candle in it, are installed on the wall after the Ritual. Again, you never light these Blessed Candles at all, nor should anyone wash off the Consecrated oil. There are a variety of candle holders for the wall that can be purchased through the many catalogs that sell Catholic Merchandise. They do not have to be very expensive, but the homeowner can determine which ones are selected for each room based upon their taste. They are going to be looking at these candle holders installed on the wall so they should select them. The point is not the expense but that each room has a Consecration to it after the ritual, with a Blessed Candle and a Blessed Candle Holder on the wall. This represents the fullness of the Priesthood, the Light of Christ in each room. Most of the demons from the higher choirs cannot get past this form of Blessing. However, of course, the demons from the Cherubim choir can get past all of this. The Cherubim demons are very powerful angels, and very few blessings can be done to expel them, thus we go to the next level.

Before we go any further, I want to be clear. No Catholic Priest, Exorcist, Demonologist (much less any paranormal investigator, psychic or sensitive) can take on the demonic angels one on one. This is impossible, human beings are too weak for one-on-one combat with these evil angels. If someone is stupid enough to do it, they will lose and get hurt. You need the assistance of Our Lord, the Blessed Mother, the Saints, and the major army, the Good Angels, especially those who have been trained by Our Lord as Warrior Angels. All these Angels are led by Saint Michael the Archangel. Saint Michael is an Angel from the Seraphim choir. He has the title of Archangel because as mentioned before, archangel means chief. Saint Michael has Archangel attached to him because He is Chief of the Seraphim Choir and all the Angels in Heaven. Most people in this field do not know this important fact. Saint Michael would have never been able to throw Lucifer, a Cherubim Angel, out of Heaven if he was from one of the lower choirs of angels. Saint Michael is a Seraphim Angel and the most powerful angel in Heaven. All the Seraphim Angels are very powerful, and lead all the other angels, including those with the special commission of being Warrior angels. Are there Warrior angels from the Seraphim choir? Yes, but I do not want to get off track here. It comes all down to one thing Steve, just one thing. Do you have the power to intercede for the victims. All these rituals are used to intercede for to the Father, Son and Holy Spirit for the victims. It ultimately is up to the Triune God to send the Good Angels down to expel the demonic angels and close any portal in the Spiritual plane. Steve, this is the only way I have been successful. I am not there expelling the demonic angels; I can't do this at all. I cannot pull out any weapons or gun or whatever; I cannot physically fight them. They are too powerful as pure evil spirits. We are all flesh and blood, and demons are pure spirits! It comes down to the power of prayerful intercession to God, the Blessed Mother and our Saints. If they are demonic spirits, then God must remove them by prayer. That is the only way this can happen. It is also the reason why you must have a relationship with God, the Blessed Mother, and the Saint first before you get into this line of work and have any sort of results.

Here is one example; this was a live case. In cooperation with Our Lord, the Blessed Mother, and some very powerful Saints, I was on a case where some strong demons were involved. Basically, without all the details, a few young, pretty sorority women in a Catholic University, were bored and drinking alcohol on a weekend night. They took out a Ouija board. and they all start using it. Some very powerful demons came through causing a lot of chaos, not just that night, but later in their lives. Moving forward to when I became involved, the demonic angels infested one of the girl's houses that had three small children and a faithful husband. They were causing a lot of trouble to her, including suicidal thoughts and self-mutilation. I performed the above rituals in their stages. First stage there was a little effect, but they were clearly still there. I went through the second stage and noticed a crawl space I did not know was in the house, nor the owner! It just so happened (how ironic) that a piece of drywall came detached off the studs in the attic. I went into this crawl space and did a through cleansing of it with the ritual. I knew there was a crawl space on the other side of the back wall. This crawl space was above the garage, which shared the wall with the previous area. Anyway, up the six-foot ladder I went. Since there were no lights up there, I brought a construction light with me. There the demon was, of course with four letter words used against me when I arrived. A very large black figure with a low voice and dark reddish, hateful and evil eyes, as you described in the book. I had missed this part of the house, unknowingly at the first blessing stage. I immediately begun the ritual against him, Holy Water, Exorcism Salt, Blessed Incense, Blessing with the relic of the true cross, filling the entire space with Blessed Smoke. This demon was not moving or leaving. It just stood there and stared at me with those dark reddish, hateful eyes. However, I did notice, it was stunned, as if the ritual had incapacitated the demon. Then, suddenly, the demon disappeared. All could do at this point was call on the Eternal Father. I prayed in this crawl space among all this Incense, Exorcism salt, and Holy Water with the true relic of the Cross. Suddenly, I saw the Eternal Father's Glory, make a motion and Saint Michael came immediately and grabbed the demon. It was clear, this powerful demon was very weak. because Saint Michael grabbed ahold of this demon and drug it through the crawl space toward me and said to me: "Let this be a sign for you that this is over." And with that they were gone, and the diabolical infestation was over. The sign that is given must be prayed for from Our Lord. In every case I have done, some sort of sign was sent that it was over for the demon or demons.

Let us return to the next level of attack on the demonic angels, The Holy Sacrifice of the Mass. If the house has human spirit or souls in it, this stage is used. At this stage, the Sacrifice of the Mass needs to be said in the house with the demonic infestation. I specifically recommend, within reason of course, that the Sacrifice of the Mass be said as close to any open portals as possible. If I was doing the Sacrifice of the Mass, I would arrange for it to be in the basement near or in the fruit cellar or the butcher shower, with plenty of lights, and of course, full rights. What does that mean? The Sacrifice of the Mass must be done for Solemnity, which includes the Blessing, (Asperge) and Holy Incense. Of course, the demonic angels are not going to like this and will begin their attacks, as would be expected, but you must get through it. Now, this next part can be very dangerous for those who are inexperienced. Directly after the Consecration of the Bread and Wine into the Body and Blood of Our Lord, you call these demons out. Demand them to come forward. At the same time, you are calling down the Seraphim Angels from God the Father. When the Eternal Father sends the Seraphim Angels, they will expel these Cherubim demons and all the other demons who remain under this demon. Let me explain, as I discussed above, the demons from the lower choirs will run out by rituals written above. However, if they are under a Cherubim demon, (or sometimes a demon from the Power choir) the Cherubim demon will force all the other demons assigned to him to remain and endure the pain and suffering. If we are at this level, there will be other demons still in the house, but they are not there willingly but by force. This is why, no matter what you do, you must focus on the lead demons. The lead demon will force the demons below him in rank to stay regardless of the price they have to pay. You can never make any judgments onyour effectiveness. That is not important, or the focus. Our Lord and what He wants is the focus. Each one of these rituals can either expel the demons or severely weaken them. The demons who remain under a Cherubim demon are so weak at this stage they will run as soon any of the Seraphim Angels (Saint Michael) come down to get them. If this does not work, there are still a couple more stages to go.

The next stage to removing demonic angels requires more preparation but it can be done. I have never gotten to this stage. So far, I have been Blessed by Our Lord by seeing Him remove the demons before I had to resort to this stage. When I speak about Our Lord, I am including the Father and the Holy Spirit. After consultation with Our Lord, I first would repeat any or all the previous stages again. Remember, Steve, in the case I mentioned above, I missed a section of the house in the attic the first time because neither I nor the homeowner knew it was there, and here is where the demons took refuge. However, this would be the next final stage - a Tridentine Mass. This is a Latin Mass with a Priest, a Deacon, and a Sub-deacon. All three of them are needed. I have studied cases where this was used as one of the last resorts. The Tridentine Mass needs more preparation and it is not always easy to find Deacons and Sub-deacons to function in a demonically infested house. But it is still possible.

A word of Warning; God the Father, Son and Holy Spirit will get these demons out of this house, however, there may be a small problem here, Steve. Why would God remove them, if someone like Mr. Winter will only invite them back and even wants them to stay. It is clear to me that Mr. Winters is one of the sources of this haunting. After all the evidence shown, the pictures in the shed, the so-called drug dealer, your family, Helen's family, then this new family who responded to Mr. Winters ad in December 2005 (page 237). Something is clearly not right with Mr. Winters. That is why it is so difficult to remove demonic angels out of houses when there are people in this world (a lot of people) who will only invite them back. This means the only solution to the victims is move out of the house.

In any case that I am involved in, the people who are affected by the demonic angels go on a list that is placed on my altar where I pray for them and everyone else every day during the Holy Sacrifice of the Mass. This is so important; the last thing I want to have to do is return to a house that was cleansed of the demons. These rituals work and have been designed by many of the leading Exorcists, but keep in mind Steve, all those Involved in a demonic infestation, must want the demons to leave and live a Holy Life afterwards.

Saint Michael the Archangel, defend us in this day of battle, be our safeguard against the wickedness and snares of the devil. And be thou of Heavenly Host. I cast into Hell Satan and all the evil spirits who prowl around the world seeking the ruin of souls. Amen.

Conclusion

There is a lot of information here in this evaluation, I highly recommend you read it twice - and of course, please be patient with me with the grammar and spelling errors. No one proofreads any of my cases because of privacy.

The case here is obviously an authentic demonic infestation that went through the stages of diabolical obsession. diabolical oppression, and diabolical possession. All these demonic angels were invited by several individuals and one of them is Mr. Winters. I hope and pray Helen, Kelly, Charlie, you, and all those involved have recovered and healed from this experience.

I'd like to say that there are many people who have failed you in this case. I hope in some small way this evaluation puts some final closure on your case and does not fail you. You have my written permission, here Steve, to make as many copies of this document as you want. You can give copies of this evaluation to all those who were involved in the case if you think it may help them in their lives. You may also pass it on to any Catholic priest or doctor. I stand by every word here I wrote. A word of caution, please to do not give this evaluation to children. There is too much advance material here they could use for the wrong reasons.

It has been a pleasure to write this evaluation, I pray that it helps.

Dear Reader,

There, you have read the entire report. Please take all the precautions the Priest laid out in the report. This is not something he takes lightly, and neither should any of us. Of course, there are always going to be nefarious forces who might want to take of advantage of this for evil means. However, the reason I feel so strongly about sharing it with you is that the more information we can get out about these types of hauntings the better. We live in a society where the devil was long ago heightened to the level of a superstar in entertainment for some, and of course he simply doesn't exist to others. Regardless of your personal beliefs, this report is a learning tool which contains more information about demonology than you are likely to find anywhere else in one place. I, for one, am extremely grateful to the Church for allowing this to be shared.

I want to take this moment to give a note to the Priest who took the painstaking time to share this. It has been read and reread repeatedly. It has brought a sense of peace and helped in the closure of this horrible period in my life. I live a good life now which is free from attack, and I am ever presently aware any moment it might try to crawl and slither its way back into my life. With the education you have provided, I now have the knowledge of how to help myself before things get too out of hand. We made so many mistakes in those haunting years and it took a while, not to only understand that, but also to own up to how we all participated in the attack. Part of healing is understanding your role in what has happened to you. I want to thank you from the bottom of my heart and thank you from my family who

was able to finally get me back from the grasp
of a literal hell. It is my hope this information
can help someone else in the same way. I
know God is at play here and I know this is the
right time to share this because my God is
leading me to do it. Thank you. I am forever
grateful to you. God bless.

With the sharing of this report, I can
finally say to all of you who have followed the
case and have read the books that it is
finished, and I have nothing else to or can say
about this case that has not already been
shared or written. There is no new material to
share with you. There is no change in what
happened. This has been the entire written
documentation of the Screaming House. It is
over and it is finished. I say a prayer and send
a blessing out to anyone who may be going
through something like this. I am always open
to you if you need me. But for all intent and
purposes, the Screaming House books are
complete.

God Bless,
Steven A. LaChance

About the Author

Steven LaChance has been a featured guest on several radio stations across the US, the UK, Canada, Asia, and in South Africa. Steven is not a stranger to television interviews, either, and has had many interviews published in newspapers and magazines across the US.

In October of 2006, *"Fear House"* premiered on the Discovery Channel, as the first show of *A Haunting's* third season. This show featured Steven and the story of the Union Haunting and went on to be rated one of the more popular episodes of that series. In addition, he has been interviewed and filmed for inclusion in numerous paranormal documentaries - the most recent being 1895 Films', *The Exorcism of Roland Doe* for Discovery+ and the Travel Channel.

Steven is also a published author. His short story was published by Barnes and Noble in 2006, and he is a contributor to magazines dealing with paranormal activity.

In 2008, *The Uninvited* was released by Llewellyn Worldwide as a major project. The book received critical acclaim, finding its way on to many "best of" lists. *The Uninvited* was also released in a French version in 2010.

Steven was also included in the books *Weird Hauntings* and *Weird Missouri*.

His book *Crazy* hit the scene in the fall of 2010 with great reviews, and also found its way on to "best of" lists for that year.

Steven has also completed a documentary for the fifth-season DVD release of Warner Home Video's *Supernatural*, the popular television series about two brothers that hunt demons.

Other Books by Steven LaChance

The Uninvited
Crazy: A Prayer for the Dead
Confrontation with Evil

www.ingramcontent.com/pod-product-compliance
Lightning Source LLC
Chambersburg PA
CBHW071442140726
47997CB00005B/1560